Now those who were scattered went from place to place, proclaiming the word . . . and many . . . who were paralyzed or lame were cured. So there was great joy in the city.

ACTS 8:4, 7-8

Word Made Global

STORIES OF AFRICAN CHRISTIANITY
IN NEW YORK CITY

Mark R. Gornik

WILLIAM B. EERDMANS PUBLISHING COMPANY
GRAND RAPIDS, MICHIGAN / CAMBRIDGE, U.K.

© 2011 Mark R. Gornik
All rights reserved

Published 2011 by
Wm. B. Eerdmans Publishing Co.
2140 Oak Industrial Drive N.E., Grand Rapids, Michigan 49505 /
P.O. Box 163, Cambridge CB3 9PU U.K.

Library of Congress Cataloging-in-Publication Data

Gornik, Mark R.
    Word made global: stories of African Christianity in New York City /
Mark R. Gornik.
       p.   cm.
    Includes bibliographical references.
    ISBN 978-0-8028-6448-2 (pbk.: alk. paper)
    1. Christians, Black — New York (State) — New York. 2. Africans —
New York (State) — New York — Religion. 3. New York (N.Y.) —
Religious life and customs.   I. Title.

BR563.N4G68   2011
277.47′108208996 — dc22

                                        2011002990

www.eerdmans.com

For my mother, Sally Gornik
　in memory of my father, Raymond Gornik
　　and for Rita, Peter, and Daniel

Áldott légy Uram
　Szent neved áldja lelkem

Contents

Foreword, *by Andrew F. Walls*	xii
Map	xiv

I. PROLOGUE

Introduction	3
Not with Paper	3
A Changing and Moving Church	5
Looking Ahead	12
1. Born Again in the City: African Churches and Global New York	18
Faith at a Global Crossroads	18
Faith Across Borders	21
Types and Terms	22
Out of Ethiopia	24
Catholic Communities	26
Protestant Churches	27
African Independent Churches	28
Pentecostal and Charismatic Churches	31
Francophone Churches	35
Liberian Churches on Staten Island	36

Headquarter Operations   37
The One and the Many   38
Global Faith, Global City   40
Conclusion: Born Again in New York City   48

II. FORMATIONS

2. **Pastors at Work: Building Community across Borders**   51
   Introduction: Job Description   51
   Religious Biography and Formation   53
      Rev. Yaw Asiedu   54
      Mother Marie Cooper   56
      Pastor Nimi Wariboko   61
   Routes to Ministry   64
   Imagining Salvation   65
   Domains of Pastoral Practice   70
      Spiritual Directors   71
      Agents of Healing   74
      Institution Builders   80
      Cultural Intermediaries   81
   The Workers Are Many   83
   Conclusion: Building Visions   86

3. **Liturgy and Life: Three Churches in Two Worlds**   87
   Introduction: A Church for Life   87
   Membership Has Its Privileges: The Presbyterian Church of Ghana   89
   A House of Prayer: The Church of the Lord (Aladura)   99
   Do Something New in My Life: The Redeemed Christian Church of God International Chapel, Brooklyn   108
   Globalizing Faith   117
      Globalization Is Multi-Faceted   117

Globalization Is Networks	118
Globalization Is Organizational	120
Conclusion	122

III. ENGAGEMENTS

4. Praying Bodies: God and Everyday Life	127
Introduction: Learning to Pray	127
Praying Communities	129
Strong and Spiritual Prayers	129
Sermons with God	132
Prayer without Ceasing	133
Prayer Through the Night	136
Tarry	137
Night Vigil	139
All-Night Revival	142
Praying in the Spirit	143
Prayer with Fasting	146
Prayer and the Material	150
Conclusion: Power in the City	159
5. Reading in Motion: Scripture and the Performance of Faith	160
Introduction: The Subway Test	160
Living in the World Imagined by Scripture	165
Reading in Community	168
Biblical Texts and Identity	171
Preaching for Life	176
Words with Power	178
Conclusion: The Word Abides	180

CONTENTS

6. Witnesses in the City: Dynamics of a New Missionary Movement	181
Introduction: New Patterns	181
A Global Vision	183
Three Mission Strategies	191
Mission as Member Care	191
Mission as Intercession	194
Mission as Church Planting	195
Mission and the Charismatic Powers of Life	201
Mission as a Way of Life	206
Mission Back to Africa	210
Conclusion: Mission in the Way of Christ	213

IV. DIRECTIONS

7. Moveable Pilgrimages: Relocating Sacred Geographies	219
Introduction	219
"Let Somebody Shout Hallelujah"	222
"Let Us Walk in the Light of the Lord"	232
"We are on Mount Tabborrar"	235
Conclusion: Moving Expectation	242
8. Handing Off: Faith in the Second Generation	243
Introduction	243
It Takes a Church	245
Children of the Lord	250
Sons and Daughters of Pentecost	251
Conclusion: Conversion and Community	256
Conclusion: Giving and Receiving	**257**
Crossing Over	257
Living Faith	259

Catholicity in the City	264
Gifts and Challenges	268
The Word Made Global	277
Epilogue: The Word Keeps Moving	279
Afterword, *by Emmanuel Katongole*	285
Appendix 1. Where the Spirit of God Is: Notes on Ethnography and Theology	289
Appendix 2. Survey Data on African Churches in New York City	303
Sources	307
Interviews	307
Focus Groups	310
Books and Articles	311
Personal Communication	338
Printed Church Materials	338
Newspapers	339
Church Web Sites	339
Acknowledgments	341
Index	347

Foreword

This outstanding book addresses one of the determining factors in the contemporary world, and one of the most influential developments in modern Christianity.

The first of these factors is a great movement of people. The modern world order was established by means of a migration that started around the beginning of the sixteenth century and lasted until the middle of the twentieth, as millions of people moved from Europe to the lands beyond Europe, bringing whole new nations into existence and directing the fate of others. Since the middle of the twentieth century, another great movement of people has gone in the other direction; millions from Africa, Asia, and Latin America have gone to Europe and to the lands peopled from Europe, above all to the United States. This is a book about the religious dimension of that movement, about migrants and their lives in their new home and their links with the old. It is a book about modern cities; for all its careful research and academic rigor, the discerning reader will recognize in it the sights and sounds and scents of the streets and subways of New York City, meeting real people, noting how they live, hearing how they pray. A whole sector of city life is illuminated and a web of relations displayed that links New York with Ghana and Nigeria and Liberia.

But this is not only a book about diasporas, but about Africa and about Christian faith, and about the confluence of the two that is one of the most important developments and most outstanding features of the present age of Christianity. Africa is now one of the Christian heartlands, accounting for a massive proportion of the world's Christians. The churches that we meet in this book all have their roots and prior history in Africa. In terms of polity and ethos, they may be classified as belonging to different strands of the Christian typology; but they share so much in

Foreword

terms of outlook and experience that one realizes how limited in descriptive value are typologies based solely on Western Christian history, and how much we need a new vocabulary for the study of world Christianity.

Dr. Gornik offers us here a deeper understanding of African Christianity, and shrewdly points us to the parallels with the Christianity we meet in the New Testament.

Altogether this is a rich work, a feast of a book, one that expands vision, provokes reflection, opens understanding — and excites gratitude.

ANDREW F. WALLS
*University of Edinburgh and
Liverpool Hope University*

GLOBAL CIRCULATIONS: AFRICAN CHRISTIANITY IN NEW YORK CITY

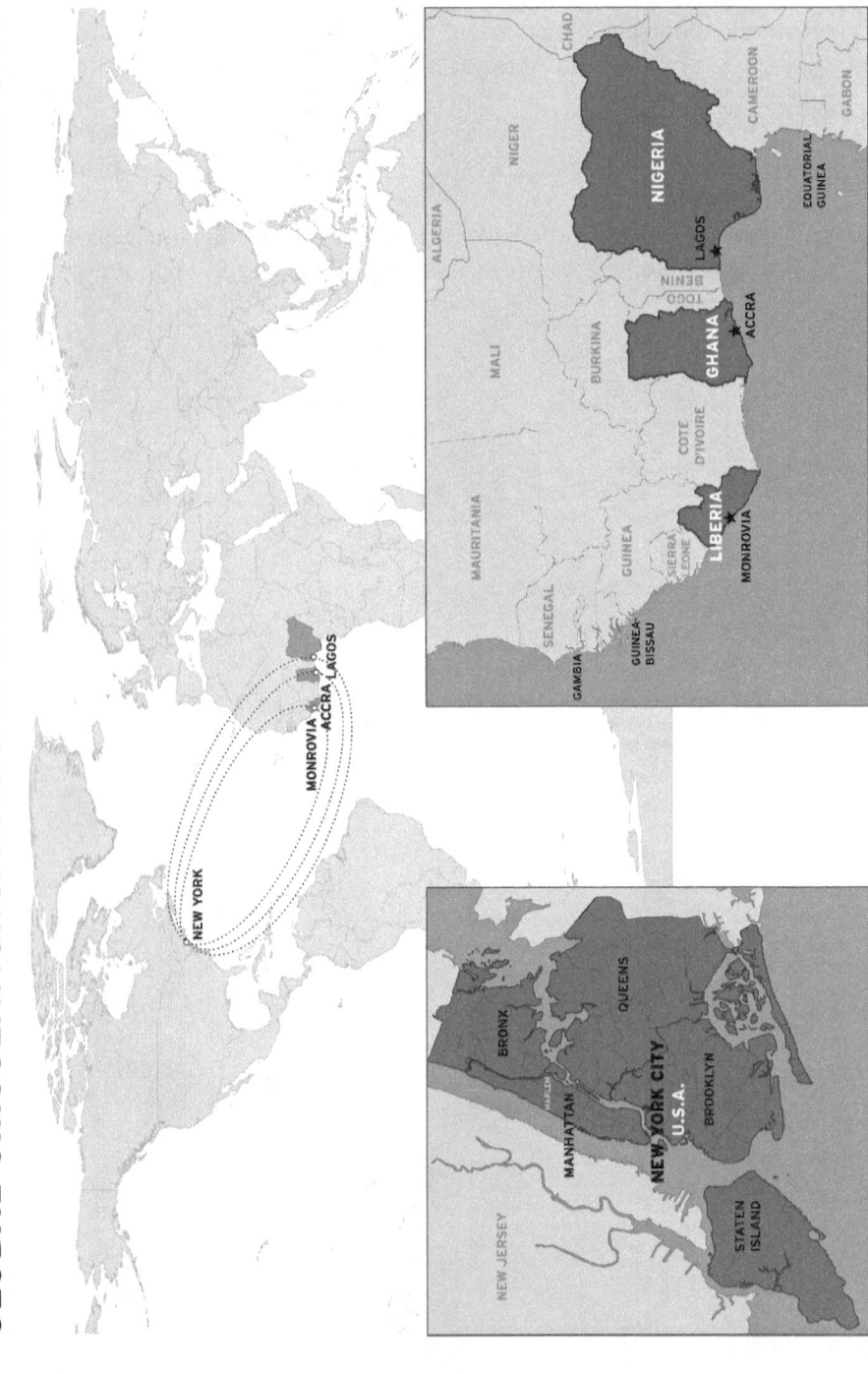

I. PROLOGUE

Introduction

Not with Paper

When Marie Cooper, known to everyone around her as Mother Cooper, arrived from Monrovia, Liberia, at New York's City's John F. Kennedy Airport in 1984, she brought with her two very full suitcases. Among her possessions were white cloth garments, a small wooden cross, and her Bible. With these, Marie Cooper brought across the Atlantic to New York not merely items of personal significance, but spiritual experiences, practices of faith, and religious beliefs. She was bringing with her a church, the Church of the Lord (Aladura), a movement founded in Nigeria that had extended a strong presence to Liberia. She first attended an African American church, but there Mother Cooper felt something missing spiritually. Taking the initiative, this daughter of the Church of the Lord (Aladura) soon began a prayer group. Within a decade, the prayer group became an official branch of the Church of the Lord (Aladura), the first in North America, meeting in a newly formed house of prayer in the Bronx, a community where the storied Yankees play baseball, Spanish is the language heard in the shops, and Merengue music is the rhythm of the streets.

"If you want to know something about Christianity, you must know something about Africa,"[1] writes the historian and mission theologian Andrew Walls. In New York City, you don't have to travel to another country to experience African Christianity; all you need to do is get on the subway. Come Sundays, in venues that span from rented storefronts to retrofitted warehouses, from converted basements to borrowed sanctuaries, New

---

1. Andrew F. Walls, "Of Ivory Towers and Ashrams: Some Reflections on Theological Scholarship in Africa," *Journal of African Christian Thought* 3:1 (2000): 1.

York City is home to some 150 African churches of diverse sizes, styles, types, networks, and languages. It is not just New York; cities such as Atlanta, Washington, D.C., Houston, Dallas, Detroit, Los Angeles, and many others that now have a significant number of African churches. But New York City is a key global hub and appears to have a greater concentration, diversity, and number of operational headquarters. From Times Square to the Bronx, from the far ends of Brooklyn to the edges of Staten Island and the heart of Queens, the churches of Africa are reproduced in New York City, and with them the momentum and energy of a growing and dynamic expression of Christianity. Pentecostal, Independent, Catholic, and historically mission-founded churches — they are all present and thriving in New York City.

African Christianity, most ancient in its expression, is not geographically bound, but circulates through a global and urban world. A grassroots globalization, this is not a movement that receives funding or leadership from the West. In Mother Cooper's story, one that involves overcoming formidable odds, we have a representative vision of the gospel crossing borders through a great dispersion. Like agents of Christian expansion before her, Mother Cooper's transatlantic journey and its end result recalls Irenaeus's observation in the second century that the Christian tradition is most ably transmitted not with words composed on paper, but through human flesh.[2]

The purpose of this book is to explore African Christianity in New York City, how it came to be, its understanding and practice of Christian faith and life, and its involvement in mission. Believing that concrete stories are the key to understanding the church and globalization, I chose three particular ecclesial bodies to anchor this study: the Presbyterian Church of Ghana in Harlem, the Church of the Lord (Aladura) in the Bronx, and the Redeemed Christian Church of God International Chapel, Brooklyn. Each church is unique, and together they provide broader insight into religion and the city in a global world. Throughout, we will be looking at how theological commitments shape a way of being in the city and world.

A recent *New York Times Magazine* featured a cover story titled "Mission from Africa"[3] about African Christians in the United States. The bolded

---

2. Margaret R. Miles, *The Word Made Flesh: A History of Christian Thought* (Malden, MA: Blackwell, 2005), 29, 391.

3. Andrew Rice, "Mission from Africa," *The New York Times Magazine,* April 12, 2009, 30-37, 54, 57, 58.

Introduction

wording on the cover asks, "The Most Profound Change in American Christianity?" How does the West brace itself for something "different," the article asks. To be sure, I too want to argue that the arrival of African churches in the West is indeed a profound development, as the *Times* suggests. But instead of seeing difference, as is often the case, we should realize that African churches, with their independence, zeal and intensity are a gift, part of the one church, not "sects."[4] This is not a term the churches use to describe themselves. They are a popular ecclesial movement rising from the ground up, not imposed from the top down.[5]

A different set of questions will open different perspectives: What do the stories and practices of African Christianity have to teach the West? What do they say about God, life, and family? What signs of hope, critical challenges, and visions of the future do they provide? How might the patterns and commitments of faith in African churches speak to all of us? As theologian Emmanuel Katongole tells us, "it is [in] the life and witness of the Church; in the unstable and multiple histories, in her basic and ordinary witness . . . that the true meaning of baptism . . . is revealed to us."[6]

A Changing and Moving Church

In this new millennium, Christianity is vibrant and growing across the world, especially in Africa.[7] As Andrew Walls has argued with great acuity for over four decades, the Christian "centre of gravity" is moving from the West to the non-Western world.[8] Whereas in 1900 some 80 percent of the world's Christian population came from Europe, America, and Russia, and less than 5 percent from Africa and Asia, at the beginning of the twenty-first century the majority of the world's 2 billion Christians now live in the

---

4. Rice, "Mission from Africa," 32.
5. Jürgen Moltmann, "Preface," in *The Spirit in the World: Emerging Pentecostal Theologies in Global Contexts*, ed. Veli-Matti Kärkkäinen (Grand Rapids: Eerdmans, 2009), ix.
6. My approach and questions in this paragraph owes much to Emmanuel M. Katongole, *A Future for Africa: Critical Essays in Christian Social Imagination* (Scranton: Scranton University Press, 2005), 231-51. The quote is from page 207.
7. Kwame Bediako, "Africa and Christianity on the Threshold of the Third Millennium: The Religious Dimension," *African Affairs* 99:395 (2000): 303-23.
8. Andrew F. Walls, *The Missionary Movement in Christian History* (Maryknoll, N.Y.: Orbis, 1986), and *The Cross-Cultural Process in Christian History* (Maryknoll, N.Y.: Orbis, 2002); Walls, "World Christianity and the Early Church," in Akintunde E. Akinade, ed., *A New Day: Essays on World Christianity in Honor of Lamin Sanneh* (New York: Peter Lang, 2010), 17-30.

"Third World."[9] Consequently, Lamin Sanneh encourages us to think of "world Christianity," faith "boundary-free" among the continents, not a derivative western global product.[10]

Reaching across every segment of these changes in Christianity is Pentecostalism. Allan Anderson's *An Introduction to Pentecostalism: Global Charismatic Christianity* vividly describes this movement in all its global texture.[11] As David Martin in *Pentecostalism: The World Their Parish* and in other writing shows, Pentecostalism is not only theological in meaning, but a social and cultural movement.[12] Jürgen Moltmann recognizes that in worldwide Pentecostalism, "a new formation in Christianity is being heralded."[13] Of course, not all of "world Christianity" is Pentecostal, but much is, and its influence is pervasive across denominations and traditions. In

---

9. For introductions to the changing church, see Donald M. Lewis, *Christianity Reborn: The Global Expansion of Evangelicalism in the Twentieth Century* (Grand Rapids: Eerdmans, 2004); Hugh McLeod, ed., *Cambridge History of Christianity*, Volume 9, *World Christianities c. 1914-2000* (Cambridge: Cambridge University Press, 2006); Dana L. Robert, "Shifting Southward: Global Christianity Since 1945," *International Bulletin of Missionary Research* 24 (April 2000): 50-58, and *Christian Mission: How Christianity Became a World Religion* (Malden: Wiley-Blackwell, 2009); Lamin Sanneh and Joel Carpenter, eds., *The Changing Face of Christianity: Africa, the West, and the World* (Oxford: Oxford University Press, 2005); Sebastian Kim and Kirsteen Kim, *Christianity as a World Religion* (London: Continuum, 2008); Mark A. Noll, *The New Shape of World Christianity: How American Experience Reflects Global Faith* (Downers Grove: InterVarsity Press, 2009); and Philip Jenkins, *The Next Christendom: The Coming of Global Christianity* (Oxford: Oxford University Press, 2002). Jenkins's article "The Next Christianity" in the *Atlantic Monthly* 290:3 (October 2002), 53-55, 58-62, 64-68, also garnered public attention. I will address his approach in chapter 6. From the perspective of the social sciences, see Matthew Engelke and Joel Robbins, eds., "Global Christianity, Global Critique," *The South Atlantic Quarterly* 109:4 (2010).

10. Lamin Sanneh, *Whose Religion Is Christianity? The Gospel Beyond the West* (Grand Rapids: Eerdmans, 2003), 75. For much greater elaboration of his arguments, see Lamin Sanneh, *Disciples of All Nations: Pillars of World Christianity* (New York: Oxford University Press, 2008).

11. Allan Anderson, *An Introduction to Pentecostalism: Global Charismatic Christianity* (Cambridge: Cambridge University Press, 2004); Pew Forum on Religion and Public Life, "Spirit and Power: A 10-Country Survey of Pentecostals," October 2006; Donald E. Miller and Tetsunao Yamamori, *Global Pentecostalism: The New Face of Christian Social Engagement* (Berkeley: University of California Press, 2007); *The Spirit in the World*, ed. Kärkkäinen; David Westerlund, ed., *Global Pentecostalism: Encounters with Other Religious Traditions* (London: I. B. Tauris, 2009); Todd M. Johnson, "The Global Demographics of the Pentecostal and Charismatic Renewal," *Society* 46:6 (2009): 479-83.

12. David Martin, *Pentecostalism: The World Their Parish* (Oxford: Blackwell, 2002); "Have Pentecostalism, Will Travel," *The Times Literary Supplement*, September 17, 2008.

13. Moltmann, "Preface," in *The Spirit in the World*, viii.

Introduction

the twenty-first century, Jesus is the Spirit-anointed Christ, and African Christianity operates under the power and sign of the Spirit.[14]

Naming this development both globally and in the West need not come at the expense of seeing what "American Christians" are doing.[15] Simply citing numbers about Christian adherents or speaking in general terms about a "new paradigm" of "global Christianity" will not tell a nuanced story of changes, connections, convergences, and differences. But the change and shift is real, and thinking through new realities and their implications will require hard work, attending closely to what is taking place on the ground and in theological discourse.

The global resurgence of Christianity begins with a particular body, the body of Jesus. Christianity is diverse because, as Andrew Walls offers, it is grounded in the Word incarnate, and therefore inherently filled with the possibility of new translations. "Christian faith rests on a divine act of translation, summarized in the Gospel of John: 'The Word became flesh, and dwelt among us' (John 1:14)."[16] For Walls this process stands at the heart of Christianity.

> Time is valorized by the incarnation, by the fact that the divine Word took flesh in a datable historical setting. The fact that Christ continues to be formed in local Christian communities whose ways of life are quite different from the one in which the incarnation took place means that for Christians, "sacred time" is not confined to the period of the incarnation, but extends to the whole historical process in which the work of salvation goes on, Christ's presence being demonstrated as he is received by faith.[17]

Following a translation from the thought and idioms of Judaism to Hellenistic culture, Christian history has repeated itself in non-identical stories of successive crossings, translations, and invigorations.[18] While the universal Christian body, speech, and thought unfold in the infinite singularities of human culture, it also crosses and encounters new cultures, and is

---

14. Ogbu Kalu, *African Pentecostalism: An Introduction* (Oxford: Oxford University Press, 2008).

15. Such concerns are raised by Robert Wuthnow, *Boundless Faith: The Global Outreach of American Churches* (Berkeley: University of California Press, 2009), 32-61.

16. Walls, *The Missionary Movement in Christian History*, 26.

17. Walls, *The Cross-Cultural Process in Christian History*, 74. See further Walls, *The Missionary Movement in Christian History*, 26, 47, 51, 85-86, 94, 235, 255, 260.

18. Sanneh, *Disciples of All Nations*.

therefore always open to new commitments, expressions, and visions of Christian faith. There is of course always a vulnerability to this, for it is the Word enacted in the contingencies of human life.

The global expansion of African and world Christianity is part of a particular urban moment. Over half the world's population now lives in cities, and with a population of some 8.5 million people, New York City is America's largest. Yet size only partially gets at New York City's dynamic and its connection to globalization and migration. New York City is not just a "gateway city"; it is a global city, as Saskia Sassen foundationally describes it in *The Global City: New York, London, Tokyo*.[19] Just as New York City serves as a connection point for the global economy, it does the same for African Christianity, distributing a vision of Christian faith by migration and imbrications within a networked time. While we may live in secular age, as the philosopher Charles Taylor describes,[20] the city is a complex space full of spiritual vitality. New York City is a point of convergence, a hub for the spread of Christianity born in Africa (and Asia and Lain America) to move through a world of urban pathways, networks, and circulations. The Word made flesh is still flowing, moving, and travelling, the body impressed as a letter, the Spirit incarnate in physicality and urban space.[21] New York as global city is a place where charismatic joy and witness have come to flourish.

The city in an age of globalization creates a forward space that enables us to see the present and future of the church and world. Through African churches in New York City, we can see the power of religion in our world, the future of ministry in an urban age, and something of the meaning of world Christianity for our moment. When people from Accra, Lagos, or Monrovia move to New York City, they bring their faith and church community with them. Faith travels to New York City not in a disembodied "cloud" of data, but as embodied stories, histories, practices, accounts, and experiences of God, Jesus, and the Holy Spirit.[22] As Peggy Levitt's apt book title puts it, *God Needs No Passport*.[23] But for African

---

19. Saskia Sassen, *The Global City: New York, London, Tokyo*, 2nd ed. (Princeton: Princeton University Press, 2001).

20. Charles Taylor, *A Secular Age* (Cambridge: The Belknap Press of Harvard University, 2007).

21. Karmen Mackendrick, *Word Made Skin: Figuring Language at the Surface of Flesh* (New York: Fordham University Press, 2004), 25-47.

22. Taylor, *A Secular Age*, 553-54.

23. Peggy Levitt, *God Needs No Passport: Immigrants and the Changing American Religious Landscape* (New York: The New Press, 2007).

Introduction

Christians, it is not simply that God is unbounded and their expression of faith follows them on their journey to New York. They are in God, and God is in them. God is already their home wherever they go.

We cannot think of faith and our world or the global economy without thinking about bodies.[24] Within a theological framework, Christian faith moves as the body, in relationship to God, the resurrection, and everyday life. For African Christians, the body is where prayer, fasting, healing, ethical diligence, the Spirit, spiritual conflict, and the work of faith constellate. It is the body that is a point of need and place where God brings flourishing. The body is not only a singular entity; ecclesial bodies are the body of Christ. To be an ecclesial body is to also be a social body. To know God for African Christians is to do so cognitively and experientially, through the body and the senses.

Global networks, African churches included, circulate the body, the Word made global. In a theological framework, this entails a reading of the one Spirit manifested in diverse bodily expressions and experiences in the world. To this end, in my study of African churches I emphasize what Manuel Vásquez summarizes as the "material, embodied, and place-making dimensions of religion"[25] that are part of globally mobile church movements. This entails not only locating and encountering African Christian faith in New York City, but examining how religion is performed and lived in a global world.[26] African churches offer distinctive accounts of human flourishing that are postulated on belief in God, receptive to divine power, and capable of going forward in conditions of great uncertainty. They are stories of "a world in motion."[27]

As noted above, three churches anchor this study: the Presbyterian Church of Ghana in New York based in Harlem, the Church of the Lord (Aladura), and the Redeemed Christian Church of God International

---

24. See Manuel A. Vásquez, *More Than Belief: A Materialist Theory of Religion* (Oxford: Oxford University Press, 2011).

25. Manuel A. Vásquez, "Historicizing and Materializing the Study of Religion: The Contribution of Migration Studies," in *Immigrant Faiths: Transforming Religious Life in America*, ed. Karen I. Leonard, Alex Stepick, Manuel A Vásquez, and Jennifer Holdaway (Lanham, Md.: AltaMira, 2005), 224.

26. Peter Beyer, *Religion in a Global Society* (London: Routledge, 2006), 142-47; Manuel A. Vásquez and Marie Friedmann Marquardt, *Globalizing the Sacred: Religion Across the Americas* (New Brunswick: Rutgers University Press, 2003); Hent de Vries, ed., *Religion: Beyond a Concept* (New York: Fordham University Press, 2008).

27. A. O. Scott, "Stories from a World in Motion," *New York Times*, March 16, 2008, AR-1, 16.

Chapel, Brooklyn. Although I will argue that older typologies of African churches must be replaced by a more fluid model, respectively the three churches in this study represent three founding periods[28] and streams of African Christianity: Protestant denominational or mission-founded, Independent or Indigenous, and Pentecostal or Charismatic. There is, I came to find, a richness of diversity among the three churches, but also, in addition to a common faith in Christ, similarities in conceptions of knowledge, time, and the physicality of faith. By looking at the three alongside one another we gain insight, I believe, into not only the development of African Christianity, but the practice of ministry.

Each of the three focus churches was selected because of their historical periodization, theological emphases in Africa, distribution in three different boroughs of New York City, and diversity of primary country of origin. Michael Burawoy's proposal for global ethnography is suggestive for the present study: "In conducting . . . multi-sited ethnography the purpose is not to contrast perspectives from each site but instead to build a montage that lends greater insight into the whole, into the connections, disconnections, and reconnections."[29] My purpose is to craft a portrait of a heterogeneous African Christianity in New York, lending understanding to the processes of the diffusion of faith, particularly in a context of globalization and the city.

When I first started this research, I was not able to locate a single article or book on the subject of African churches in North America.[30] The situation was far different in Europe. Beginning with Gerrie ter Haar's pioneering work on Ghanaian churches in Amsterdam, *Halfway to Paradise: African Christians in Europe*, African Christianity in Europe has been explored by a number of scholars, including Afe Adogame, Hermione Harris, Kwabena Asamoah-Gyadu, Roswith Gerloff, T. Jack Thompson, and Claudia Währisch-Oblau.[31] Other multi-author studies of Africans in

---

28. For importance of time and periodization, see Ogbu M. Kalu, "A Discursive Interpretation of African Pentecostalism," *Fides et Historia* 41:1 (2009): 77-80.

29. Michael Burawoy, "Manufacturing the Global," *Ethnography* 2:2 (2001): 156.

30. My early research led to a story by Daniel Wakin, "In New York, Gospel Resounds in African Tongues," *New York Times*, April 18, 2004, A-1, 32.

31. Gerrie ter Haar, *Halfway to Paradise: African Christians in Europe* (Cardiff: Cardiff Academic Press, 1998); cf. ter Haar, "Strangers in the Promised Land: African Christians in Europe," *Exchange* 24:1 (1995): 1-33; Afe Adogame, "The Quest for Space in the Global Spiritual Marketplace: African Religions in Europe," *International Review of Mission* 89:354 (2000): 400-409; "To Be or Not to Be? Politics of Belonging and African Christian Commu-

Introduction

non-African settings exist as well,[32] and there have been issues of the *International Review of Mission* and *Journal of Religion in Africa* dedicated to the topic.[33] There is another important body of literature by scholars such as Afe Adogame, Allan Anderson, Kwame Bediako, Ogbu Kalu, Ruth Marshall, David Martin, David Maxwell, and Joel Robbins that describes African Christianity and its connections to Pentecostalism, globalization, and transnational networks.[34]

---

nities in Germany," in Afe Adogame and Cordula Weisskӧppel, eds., *Religion in the Context of African Migration* (Bayreuth: Bayreuth African Studies, 2005), 95-112; "Betwixt Identity and Security: African New Religious Movements and the Politics of Religious Networking in Europe," *Nova Religion: The Journal of Alternative and Emergent Religions* 7:2 (November 2003): 21-41; "Engaging the Rhetoric of Spiritual Warfare: The Public Face of Aladura in Diaspora," *Journal of Religion in Africa* 34:4 (2004): 493-522; "Ranks and Robes: Art Symbolism and Identity in the Celestial Church of Christ in the European Diaspora," *Material Religion* 5:1 (2009): 10-13; Hermione Harris, *Yoruba in Diaspora: An African Church in London* (New York: Palgrave Macmillan, 2006); "Continuity or Change? Aladura and Born Again Yoruba Christianity in London," in *Christianity and Social Change in Africa: Essays in Honor of J. D. Y Peel*, ed. Toyin Falola (Durham: Carolina Academic Press, 2005), 307-34; J. Kwabena Asamoah-Gyadu, "An African Pentecostal on Mission in Eastern Europe: The Church of the 'Embassy of God' in the Ukraine," *Pneuma* 27:2 (2005): 297-321; Roswith Gerloff, "'Africa as Laboratory of the World': The African Christian Diaspora in Europe as Challenge to Mission and Ecumenical Relations," in *Mission Is Crossing Frontiers: Essays in Honour of Bongani A. Mazibuko*, ed. Roswith Gerloff (Pietermaritzburg: Cluster Publications, 2003), 343-81; Roy Kerridge, *The Storm Is Passing Over: A Look at Black Churches in Britain* (London: Thames and Hudson, 1995); T. Jack Thompson, "African Independent Churches in Britain: An Introductory Survey," in *New Religions and the New Europe*, ed. Robert Towler (Aarhus: Aarhus University Press, 1995), 224-31; Claudia Währisch-Oblau, *The Missionary Self-Perception of Pentecostal/Charismatic Church Leaders from the Global South in Europe* (Leiden: Brill, 2009). See also Afe Adogame, Roswith Gerloff, and Klaus Hock, eds., *Christianity in Africa and the African Diaspora: The Appropriation of a Scattered Heritage* (London: Continuum, 2008); Ramon Sarró and Ruy Llera Blanes, "Prophetic Diasporas: Moving Religion Across the Lusophone Atlantic," *African Diaspora* 2 (2009): 52-72.

32. Adogame and Weisskӧppel, *Religion in the Context of African Migration*.

33. Notably, *The International Review of Mission* 89:354 (2000) and *The Journal of Religion in Africa* 34:4 (2004).

34. Allan Anderson, *An Introduction to Pentecostalism*; Bediako, "Africa and Christianity on the Threshold of the Third Millennium," 303-23; André Corten and Ruth Marshall-Fratani, eds., *Between Babel and Pentecost: Transnational Pentecostalism in Africa and Latin America* (Bloomington: Indiana University Press, 2001); Joel Robbins, "The Globalization of Pentecostal and Charismatic Christianity," *Annual Review of Anthropology* 33 (2004): 117-43; Simon Coleman, *The Globalisation of Charismatic Christianity: Spreading the Gospel of Prosperity* (Cambridge: Cambridge University Press, 2000); Martin, *Pentecostalism*; David Maxwell, *African Gifts of the Spirit: Pentecostalism and the Rise of a Zimbabwean*

PROLOGUE

The North America development of African churches is different than in Europe, and only recently has research on both African immigration[35] and churches started to pick up.[36] An exemplar of a globally situated ethnographic study is anthropologist Paul Stoller's *Money Has No Smell: The Africanization of New York City*, an exploration of West African street vendors primarily located in Harlem. Historian Jehu Hanciles has recently provided *Beyond Christendom: Globalization, African Migration, and the Transformation of the West*.[37] Also, in a broader way, the growing diversity of immigrant religious life in America is gaining traction in academic and public forums.[38]

Looking Ahead

Following part one, which includes this introduction and chapter 1, this study is organized into three primary parts: Formations, Engagements,

---

Transnational Religious Movement (Oxford: James Currey, 2006); Ruth Marshall, *Political Spiritualities: The Pentecostal Revolution in Nigeria* (Chicago: University of Chicago Press, 2009); Afe Adogame, ed., *Who is Afraid of the Holy Ghost? Pentecostalism and Globalization in Africa and Beyond* (Trenton: Africa World Press, 2011).

35. A major exception is Paul Stoller, *Money Has No Smell: The Africanization of New York* (Chicago: University of Chicago Press, 2002). See also Jacqueline Copeland-Carson, *Creating Africa in America: Translocal Identity in an Emerging World City* (Philadelphia: University of Pennsylvania Press, 2004), and JoAnn D'Alisera, *An Imagined Geography: Sierra Leonean Muslims in America* (Philadelphia: University of Pennsylvania Press, 2004).

36. Two conferences in the United States have brought together researchers in the field. The first was "African Immigrants, Religion, and Cultural Pluralism in the United States," convened by Jacob Olupona and held at the University of California, Davis, December 2-5, 2004. Much of the proceedings were published in Jacob Olupona and Regina Gemignani, eds., *African Immigrant Religions in America* (New York: New York University Press, 2007). The second was "African Christianity and the Neo-Diaspora," convened by Frieder Ludwig and held at Luther Seminary, Minnesota, March 23-25, 2007. In addition, see Dianna J. Shandy, "Nuer Christians in America," *Journal of Refugee Studies* 15:2 (2002): 213-21.

37. Jehu J. Hanciles, *Beyond Christendom: Globalization, African Migration, and the Transformation of the West* (Maryknoll, N.Y.: Orbis, 2008).

38. Two leading examples are R. Stephen Warner and Judith W. Wittner, eds., *Gatherings in Diaspora: Religious Communities and the New Immigration* (Philadelphia: Temple University Press, 1998), and Diana L. Eck, *A New Religious America: How a "Christian Country" Has Become the World's Most Religiously Diverse Nation* (San Francisco: HarperSanFrancisco, 2001).

Introduction

and Directions. In each part I assemble my arguments based on a close study of the Presbyterian Church of Ghana in Harlem, the Church of the Lord (Aladura) in the Bronx, and the Redeemed Christian Church of God International Chapel, Brooklyn.

The second part is concerned with the formation of African churches in New York City, the stories that tell of beginnings and callings. It is about community building, a work that takes place across borders and is never fully complete. Chapter 2 introduces the three pastors or spiritual leaders of the Church of the Lord (Aladura), the Presbyterian Church of Ghana, and the Redeemed Christian Church of God. It is on their shoulders that so much of the work of building community falls. Chapter 3 then delves into the three churches through their liturgies, histories, and ongoing global relationships.

The third part explores key practices of the three churches as they are in contact with the global city. African congregations in New York are formations of belonging, but they are also ways of encountering a global world. As such, practices, modes of being in the world, point to moments of "friction" where theological conviction and the city meet.[39] Here the clarity of a dynamic religious sensibility emerges. African Christianity is much more than the sum of its ecclesiastical institutions; it is an embodied constellation of concerns, beliefs, practices, and experiences.[40] Prayer, reading Scripture, and mission are each distinctive Christian practices, but at the level of the local church, they are hard to disentangle and are better bundled together as a single expression of Christian life and community.[41] Moreover, worship is not only a practice, but is primarily the setting in which other practices are most profoundly shaped. To formally extricate practices one from another may not be entirely possible, but what each may individually show us will help us to see the whole. In any event, it is the experience of God, the transforming power of the Spirit, that most profoundly shapes communities as they bear the gospel in a global world.

As it did for the early Christians, the experience of salvation stands at the forefront of African Christian belief and practice. They believe God

---

39. For this language, I follow Anna Lowenhaupt Tsing, *Friction: An Ethnography of Global Connection* (Princeton: Princeton University Press, 2005).

40. Derek R. Peterson, Review of *African Christianity: An African Story*, ed. Ogbu U. Kalu, *Journal of Ecclesiastical History* 57:1 (2006): 87-89.

41. Justin J. Meggitt, "The First Churches: Religious Practice," in *The Biblical World*, vol. 2, ed. John Barton (London: Routledge, 2002), 158-59.

has freed them from the spiritual forces, continues to protect and deliver, and leads them to live in Christ-filled ways in every sphere of life. Through the Spirit, they experience signs and wonders, and have authority over all forces that block their way in the city and world.[42] These core convictions guide their church communities and lives.

As we will see, African Christians are forming communities with distinct cultures of faith and practice, carrying within them the potential to shape and influence others.[43] Communities of course change, but they are where people make a home and derive beliefs and practices. In theological circles, "practices" has come generally to refer to something an ecclesial community does with regularity across space and time, grounded in Christian beliefs,[44] thereby creating religious cultures.[45] Ruth Marshall, in her distinctive and important *Political Spiritualities*, following Michel Foucault, writes that "global Pentecostalism . . . is a form of strategic program . . . a specific regime of practices that involves determined prescriptions concerning how institutions should be organized, behavior regulated, narrative structured, and order of knowledge and the rules of its verification determined, authority established, spaces laid and so forth."[46] In this study, I refer to practices as what persons learn to do within ecclesial communities, for the sake of God and human flourishing, and involve a certain bodily competence. Thus practices fit together within the overarching conception of Christian faith found in each church. Chapter 4 discusses prayer and fasting, focusing on how they are key points of interaction with the global city. Chapter 5 explores the practice of reading the Bible. Chapter 6 focuses on the mission of African churches to New York. To this end I examine the aspirations, structures, agents, theology, and dynamics of mission found in the churches.

The fourth part addresses the future direction of African Christianity in New York. Chapter 7 documents how African Christian movements

---

42. See the formative work of Luke Timothy Johnson, *The Writings of the New Testament: An Interpretation*, rev. ed. (Minneapolis: Fortress, 1999), especially pages 99-105. My description parallels his understanding of the claims of Christians.

43. For parallel language, see Wayne A. Meeks, *The Origins of Christian Morality: The First Two Centuries* (New Haven: Yale University Press, 1993), 101.

44. See Miroslav Volf and Dorothy C. Bass, eds., *Practicing Theology: Beliefs and Practices in Christian Life* (Grand Rapids: Eerdmans, 2002).

45. This is featured in the argument of Alasdair MacIntyre, *After Virtue*, 2nd ed. (Notre Dame: University of Notre Dame Press, 1984), 187-88.

46. Ruth Marshall, *Political Spiritualities*, 128; 35-38.

Introduction

are creating reverse pilgrimages, globalized events that enable the leadership and membership to stay closely connected. In chapter 8, I examine how faith is being passed on between generations in New York. These are equally culture- or church-making.

In the conclusion I give an account of the themes, ideas, and conclusions that have been critical to this book. Based on the material developed throughout the course of this project, I then offer an exploration into ecclesiology by bringing the illuminating work of Andrew Walls and Emmanuel Katongole, a Ugandan priest and theologian, into conversation. Taking their lead, I argue for an articulation of catholicity, albeit from below. Finally, having followed the Presbyterian Church of Ghana, the Church of the Lord (Aladura), and the Redeemed Christian Church of God International Chapel, Brooklyn, for some ten years, I end with an afterword that brings their stories up to date.

While throughout I emphasize the particularity and uniqueness of each congregation, the three churches are not "case studies," but a lens through which to view a much wider set of processes, both global and religious.[47] With fewer studies of multiple African churches or movements than there are of single churches, the present study of three churches examined alongside one another may have some significance as well.[48] My hope is that this study not only encourages the African churches in New York City and demonstrates the significance of their development, but also contributes to broader discussions in religious, globalization, cultural, and urban studies; New York City history; and Christian mission, biblical studies, spirituality, and theology.

This project is shaped by ethnographic fieldwork in African churches in New York City that took place primarily between 2003 and 2008, with additional work that continued through 2009. An earlier stretch of fieldwork conducted in 2000 and 2001 provided important background. From 2003-2008, I attended an estimated 250 worship services, Bible studies, prayer meetings, healing services, seminars, community meals, harvest festivals, and other events, recording copious field notes and observations. In addition to focusing on the three churches here, I also surveyed a larger religious field of African churches in New York

---

47. I am making a parallel argument from Arjun Appadurai, *Modernity at Large: Cultural Dimensions of Globalization* (Minneapolis: University of Minnesota Press, 1996), 18.

48. Birgit Meyer, "Christianity in Africa: From African Independent to Pentecostal-Charismatic Churches," *Annual Review of Anthropology* 33 (2004): 451.

City, visiting and worshiping with over thirty-five churches there. This overall process not only provided rich material for ecclesial ethnographies, but also developed a relational network for subsequent interviews.[49] I also collected a wide range of Sunday school manuals, bulletins, newsletters, calendars, tracts, and church booklets.

Over the course of my research, I conducted more than 100 interviews, not including the countless informal conversations I had during a typical week. I interviewed people of different ages and genders, leaders and laity. At various times and events I was able to interview regional, national, and international leadership within each congregation's wider ministry or movement. I was also provided access to a variety of written materials unavailable elsewhere that enabled me to trace the churches' histories.

Because I am speaking of particular congregations, unless otherwise noted I have the permission of the interviewees to use their names. For interviews, I originally envisioned a more structured interview format, but quickly concluded that open-ended conversations about life stories and faith journeys provided far more insightful responses. Not every question was always directly asked, but the answers typically covered the desired range. As my work proceeded, I found myself in agreement with Roger Sanjek, who favors "participant observation over interviews with seated informants, and naturally occurring speech in action over questionnaires or an instrument-mediated quest for culture 'in people's heads.'"[50] This approach is ultimately more productive, I learned.

I have also included photo documentation. Initially I hesitated to do so, concerned about intruding on deeply personal and spiritual moments, objectification, and the further filtering of perspectives. Eventually I came to the conclusion that the benefits of photographs for telling stories were substantial, and they became part of the project. Over the course of my research, I took more than two thousand digital photographs. People, special events, practices of faith, and the material world of African church life in New York City were important interests in my visual selections. As I use them in this book, the goal is for the photographs to share in telling stories of the life of faith in the city. With all of their limitation, I came to believe

---

49. Roger Sanjek, "Keeping Ethnography Alive in an Urbanizing World," *Human Organization* 59:3 (2000): 280-88.

50. Sanjek, "Keeping Ethnography Alive in an Urbanizing World," 281. Roger Sanjek, *The Future of Us All: Race and Neighborhood Politics in New York City* (Ithaca: Cornell University Press, 1998), 9.

Introduction

that they have the potential to tell us very important things about life and performance of faith.⁵¹

A few words about the limits of this study are in order. By African churches I do not have in mind African American or West Indian churches. This focus on African churches does not include other religious beliefs and institutions, such as Islam, that have also traveled to New York City. Finally, unless otherwise noted, by "New York City" I mean the five boroughs, and not simply Manhattan — or the wider metropolitan region.

I began this study in order to understand African Christianity in New York as a global movement, and New York City as a site of the globalization of religion. Along the way I became more deeply engaged in the challenges of African Christianity as a theological movement, its convictions about God, faith, and the world, and its understanding of Christian faith. There is no necessary rivalry between these twin concerns of the global and the theological. One of my conclusions is that the theological and the global are necessary precisely because we cannot understand one without the other. As this story unfolds, I hope what will emerge is some sense of why I became a student afresh of both Christianity and the city.

---

51. In addition to the work of Camilo José Vegara, I found Colleen McDannell, *Picturing Faith: Photography and the Great Depression* (New Haven: Yale University Press, 2004), to be a source of inspiration and insight. T. Jack Thompson is instructive on the complex issues surrounding photography and religion. In this regard, see his *Capturing the Image: African Missionary Photography as Enslavement and Liberation* (New Haven: Yale Divinity School Library, 2007).

1. Born Again in the City: African Churches and Global New York

Faith at a Global Crossroads

Madison Square Garden is sometimes called the "World's Most Famous Arena." Located in the heart of midtown Manhattan, amidst squealing cabs, business deals, hot dog vendors, waves of pedestrians, and the massive Macy's department store, it regularly hosts a who's who of rock stars, sports figures, public life, even the circus. But in June 2005, the arena was filled not with crowds going to a concert or a basketball game, but with thousands of members of the Redeemed Christian Church of God, the largest Pentecostal church in Nigeria and one of the fastest growing churches in the world, meeting for their annual North American Convention, their most important event of the year. Whatever else this event conveyed, it crystallized in the most public of ways that Christianity from Africa had arrived in New York City, the United States, and the West. Part of public culture, high in visibility, and at the center of a global city, African Christianity was representing itself to the world.

In 1998, when I had just arrived in New York City from Baltimore to begin church and community development work in central Harlem, I noticed that the sidewalks surrounding the 125th Street subway station were crowded with groups of African women. Dressed in bright and colorful traditional clothing, they were trying to draw customers to the African hair braiding salons that had sprung up in the surrounding commercial corridor. Just south on 116th Street, the blocks were so filled with Senegalese that it is referred to as Little Dakar or Little Senegal, with shops displaying bright African garb, Youssou N'Dour compact discs, and telephone cards with bargain rates for Africa. Stereo speakers facing the street sent out praise music from West Africa to Harlem. Small businesses ca-tered to the banking and travel needs of Africans. A local mosque frequented by West Africans drew large worshiping communities.

Such experiences of sidewalk life suggested, first, that there was a significant African presence in New York City, and, second, that Harlem was not an isolated inner city, but part of an interconnected global world. It was a community where the connections and changes of a global world revealed themselves.[1] As Jane Jacobs, the urban theorist and activist emphasized, the sidewalks of New York are like a "ballet," a place where "something is always going on."[2]

I knew there had been a religious transformation in Africa of historic character. According to the *World Christian Encyclopedia*, in 1900 there were an estimated nine million Christians in Africa, or 9.2 percent of the population. In 1965, there were an estimated 75 million African Christians. By 2000, the number had grown to over 360 million Christians in Africa, 45.6 percent of the population.[3] If Africa was experiencing historic Christian growth, would it not follow that at least some of the new African immigrants would be Christian? And if the answer was yes, in what churches were they worshiping?

The first African church I learned of was an Ethiopian congregation on East Tremont Avenue in the Bronx. Venturing to the church on a Sunday morning in 2001, I encountered the Ethiopian Evangelical Church, a vibrant Pentecostal church that worshiped in two languages, had parishioners dancing in the aisles, and was making plans for expansion. From this church I learned the name of another African church in the city, and it wasn't long before my short list of African churches in New York City grew much longer. African Christianity — what Ogbu Kalu and others call an "African story" — is also a global story.[4] I didn't need to get on a plane to encounter the richness and diversity of this global story; all I needed was a MetroCard, the local bus and subway fare card.

It turns out that the city is not as disenchanted as is its popular image. With their networks, sounds, prayers, garments, signage, and activities, African churches are helping to make New York a charismatic city, not

---

1. Saskia Sassen, ed., *Deciphering the Global: Its Scales, Spaces, and Subjects* (New York: Routledge, 2007).

2. Jane Jacobs, *The Death and Life of Great American Cities* (New York: Vintage, 1992).

3. David B. Barrett, George T. Kurian, and Todd M. Johnson, *World Christian Encyclopedia*, 2nd ed., vol. 1 (New York: Oxford University Press, 2001), 13.

4. Ogbu U. Kalu, ed., *African Christianity: An African Story* (Trenton: Africa World Press, 2007).

a secular city. New York is not just a "transcendent"[5] urban space, but has a unique energy, a charisma where religion is embodied.[6]

"There is much to be said for concentration on one particular town in order to obtain a detailed and factual study,"[7] Geoffrey Parrinder remarks in the preface to his account of religion in Ibadan, Nigeria.[8] To make such a case requires "grounded" or ethnographic accounts of the city;[9] a "remapping" of the city emerges out of the experience and study of the city from the ground up.[10] "Rather than viewing global cities as central expressions of the global accumulation of capital," Michael Peter Smith finds that "all cities can . . . be viewed in the fullness of their particular linkages with the worlds outside their boundaries."[11] Chantal Saint-Blancat clarifies the research task: "The challenge posed for any analysis of the new modalities of migration — and the cultural and religious consequences they entail — is methodological in nature: how to decode the complexity of relationships interwoven between the global level of the phenomenon and its involvement in the local."[12] African churches become a way of *deciphering*[13] such global linkages and processes.

---

5. This is discussed by Philip Sheldrake, "Placing the Sacred: Transcendence and the City," *Literature and Theology* 21:3 (2007): 243-58. For a similar interest, see Graham Ward, *Cities of God* (London: Routledge, 2000).

6. Thomas Blom Hansen and Oskar Verkaaik, "Introduction — Urban Charisma: On Everyday Mythologies in the City," *Critique of Anthropology* 29:1 (2009): 5-26; Mary Hancock and Smriti Srinvas, "Spaces of Modernity: Religion and the Urban in Africa," *International Journal of Urban and Regional Research* 32:3 (2008): 617-30.

7. Geoffrey Parrinder, *Religion in an African City* (London: Oxford University Press, 1953), 4.

8. Rosalind I. J. Hackett, *Religion in Calabar: The Religious Life and History of a Nigerian Town* (Berlin: Mouton D. Gruyter, 1989), takes Parrinder's words as an epigraph and is also a testimony to the value of single-city studies.

9. On the "anchored" study of globalization, see Manuel Vásquez and Marie Marquardt, *Globalizing the Sacred* (New Brunswick, N.J.: Rutgers University Press, 2003), 3; Peter Beyer and Lori Berman, eds., *Religion, Globalization, and Culture* (Leiden: Brill, 2007).

10. Gyan Prakash and Kevin M. Kruse, eds., *The Spaces of the Modern City: Imaginaries, Politics, and Everyday Life* (Princeton: Princeton University Press, 2008).

11. Michael Peter Smith, *Transnational Urbanism: Locating Globalization* (Malden: Blackwell, 2001), 71.

12. Chantal Saint-Blancat, "Islam in Diaspora: Reterritorialization and Extraterritoriality," *International Journal of Urban and Regional Research* 26:1 (2002): 138; cf. Harri Englund, "Ethnography after Globalism: Migration and Emplacement in Malawi," *American Ethnologist* 29:2 (2002): 261-86.

13. This term and approach to understanding the global city comes from Saskia Sassen, ed., *Deciphering the Global: Its Scales, Spaces, and Subjects*.

Faith Across Borders

With no prior research available on African churches in New York, by necessity my survey depended on footwork and networks to connect with itineraries of faith. There is no overarching association or council of African churches in New York like, for example, those found in Europe, to provide the data. In New York City, African church associations are limited to a particular network, denomination, and on an informal basis country of origin. This is a result of at least four factors: (1) the geographical scale of the five boroughs, (2) the entrepreneurial rather than collaborative dynamic of New York City, (3) the relative newness of African churches in the city, and (4) the sheer diversity of churches. In the United States, census and other related public data do not include religion.

My research was greatly facilitated by the use of local African newspapers such as *African Abroad USA, West African News,* and *Light of the World,* which in addition to advertising money transfer services like Western Union and travel agencies, are filled with paid notices of African churches.[14] A resource that grew considerably in importance over the course of my research was church websites, which have become more sophisticated, comprehensive, and informative. In and of themselves, websites are a new dimension in global representation and reach of African Christianity, especially among Pentecostal churches.[15] At the same time, local church websites, while helpful for basic information such as street location, vary widely. While I made good strides in learning about many of the African church movements in New York City, incompleteness marks this effort. This must be the case, for the city has over 8 million residents, more than 700 miles of subway lines, and approximately 500 neighborhoods. But I found that at this time new churches are being started in every part of the city, especially in the boroughs of the Bronx, Brooklyn, Queens, and Staten Island. Appendix 2 provides a list of African churches in New York City — incomplete, no doubt, but indicative of substantive development. In what follows, I provide a brief overview.

---

14. "Ethnic" newspapers are one of the most important if also most neglected sources of information on new immigrant churches in a city.

15. J. Kwabena Asamoah-Gyadu, "'Get on the Internet!' Says the Lord: Religion, Cyberspace and Christianity in Contemporary Africa," *Studies in World Christianity* 13:3 (2007): 225-42; Rosalind I. J. Hackett, "The New Virtual (Inter)Face of African Pentecostalism," *Society* 46:6 (2009): 496-503.

But before doing so, some brief comments on terminology and types of churches are in order.

Types and Terms

At their best, typologies help organize large amounts of data and make useful generalizations. Within African Christian studies, there is a generally acceptable threefold typology of African churches: mainline/historical, independent, and Pentecostal/charismatic.[16] While such traditional typologies retain salience (and I will describe each accordingly in what follows), especially on historical grounds, they frequently break down as new fluid and hybrid forms of church life emerge. Another weakness is that these typologies minimize the uniqueness of Catholic and Orthodox traditions, both present in New York. One group that might also deserve further consideration, but was not a factor during the period of my research, would be African congregations within the New York diocese of the Episcopal Church (along with the cross-border authority of African bishops in the city). Still, it is possible, I believe, to view churches as historically constructed while finding ways of organizing different ones together without reducing them to an "essence." What I do see is that the growth and diversity of African Christianity indicates ongoing development in ecclesiology.

Even more basic, the terminology of "African" churches in New York City is itself filled with difficulties. Of course there are problems with any facile understandings of "Africa." But the heart of the immediate difficulty is sharply observed in the following ethnographic analysis: "Although the research contains clear indications that many worshippers emphasize a community in Christ without an ethnic suffix, scholars persist in categorizing the worshippers by their ethnicity. The result is a contradictory narrative in which those studied speak of their community

---

16. These categories and others are extensively covered in scholarly accounts. For some of the literature, see Allan H. Anderson, *African Reformation: African Initiated Christianity in the Twentieth Century* (Trenton: Africa World Press, 2001), 3-22. For important discussions, see Paul Kollman, "Classifying African Christianities: Part One: Past, Present, and Future," *Journal of Religion in Africa* 40:1 (2010): 3-32; Kollman, "Classifying African Christianities, Part Two: The Anthropology of Christianity and Generations of African Christians," *Journal of Religion in Africa* 40:2 (2010): 118-48; Matthew Engelke, "Past Pentecostalism: Notes on Rupture, Realignment, and Everyday Life in Pentecostal and African Churches," *Africa: The Journal of the International African Institute* 80:2 (2010): 177-99.

in Christ and 'their identity as primarily Christian,' whereas the researchers characterize the believers as African, Nigerian, Ghanaian, or Salvadorian."[17] Personal interviews and conversations confirmed this. Self-descriptions almost always emphasized "Christian" or "Pentecostal" more than any other appellation.

Gerrie ter Haar underscores similar concerns but with an added emphasis on the international character of African churches.[18] If they are reduced to the "Other," ter Haar believes that Africans will be more easily marginalized in the political sphere.[19] Along these lines, ter Haar identifies a new type of African church — *African International Churches*:[20] "To refer to them this way takes account of their African origin while at the same time recognising the continuity of these churches with the universal Christian tradition."[21] Another description of the most basic kind is perhaps also called for: New York City churches. Working from this perspective, "diaspora" is not automatically descriptive.[22] But in line with the argument I have been proposing concerning the global and local contexts of the churches, the term "global New York churches" is also fitting.

Another challenge is that identifications used in the West to situate Christianity do not always work in the same way within the African context. A key term that is often misused here is "evangelical." Bearers of "good news," African churches are "evangelical" in the root meaning of the word, but they are not American or British evangelical Christianity.[23] It was a mission initiative to Sierra Leone by former slaves who had been relocated to Nova Scotia by the British that played an influential role in

---

17. Nina Glick Schiller, Ayse Caglar, and Thaddeus C. Guldbrandsen, "Beyond the Ethnic Lens: Locality, Globality, and Born-Again Incorporation," *American Ethnologist* 33:4 (2006): 614-15.

18. Gerrie ter Haar, *Halfway to Paradise: African Christians in Europe* (Cardiff: Cardiff Academic Press, 1998), 21-26.

19. ter Haar, *Halfway to Paradise*, 22.

20. ter Haar, *Halfway to Paradise*, 24.

21. ter Haar, *Halfway to Paradise*, 24.

22. For a review of the issues and concerns, see ter Haar, *Halfway to Paradise*, 71-88, and Martin Baumann, "Diaspora: Genealogies of Semantics and Transcultural Comparison," *Numen* 47 (2000): 313-37.

23. For example, Paul Freston, *Evangelicals and Politics in Asia, Africa and Latin America* (Cambridge: Cambridge University Press, 2001). For a varied perspective, see Tite Tiénou, "Evangelical Theology in African Contexts," in *The Cambridge Companion to Evangelical Theology*, ed. Timothy Larsen and Daniel J. Treier (Cambridge: Cambridge University Press, 2007), 213-24.

bringing a message of new birth to Africa, a witness that still today resonates deeply in the experience of so many believers.[24] But "evangelicalism" represents a very specific set of institutions and beliefs located primarily in British and American figures and orbits. David Bebbington's four characteristics of evangelicalism — conversionism, activism, Biblicism, and crucicentrism — do not describe the driving concerns of African churches.[25] For example, there is nothing in Bebbington's definition on the resurrection, the Holy Spirit, or power, central pastoral and theological emphases for African believers. Even as we identify past interactions with the West through the missionary movement and current connections through globalization, African churches have their own histories, emphases, visions, leaders, and institutions independent of the West. So while African Christianity may hold the evangel high, assimilating it as part of the "evangelical" movement is misleading, and ultimately serves to maintain a Western Protestant orientation to Christianity. As James Cox alerts, such a typology may tell more about the West than Africa.[26]

In what now follows, I offer a typology of the African churches as found in New York. There are other ways to organize, such as, for example, by types of music or building. While I will argue for nuance and diversity among all the churches, at the end I will also argue for a unity.

Out of Ethiopia

Christianity has been part of Africa for nearly two thousand years. The Coptic Church of Alexandria tells its story by recounting the journey of the Holy Family as refugees, uprooted from Bethlehem and given shelter in Egypt.[27] There is a tradition of St. Mark's role in the founding of the

---

24. J. D. Y. Peel suggests as much in "Comment" on "Continuity Thinking and Christian Culture," *Current Anthropology* 48:1 (2007): 26-27. On this story and its possibilities, see Lamin Sanneh, *Abolitionists Abroad: American Blacks and the Making of Modern West Africa* (Cambridge: Harvard University Press, 1999).

25. Freston, *Evangelicals and Politics in Asia, Africa and Latin America*, 2. Conversion would be an exception, but I think it is filled with different meaning.

26. James L. Cox, "African Identities as the Projection of Western Alterity," in *Uniquely African? African Christian Identity from Cultural and Historical Perspectives*, ed. James L. Cox and Gerrie ter Haar (Trenton: Africa World Press, 2003), 25-37.

27. Bengt Sundkler and Christopher Steed, *A History of the Church in Africa* (Cam-

Born Again in the City

Fig. 1.1 Ethiopian Orthodox Church Tewahedo Church of Our Savior, Worship, Manhattan, 2006

church in Alexandria. Ethiopia's place in the story of Christianity begins with what Andrew Walls calls a "hint" found in the Acts of the Apostles, with the story of the Ethiopian eunuch, considered by most scholars to be Meroe in modern Sudan.[28] The church of Ethiopia, then the church of Aksum, holds a singular place in the Christian story, both in its continuous history and theological memory.[29]

This tradition is extended to New York City, where a number of Ethiopian Orthodox churches have been established. Since 1984, Ethiopians have been gathering at Ethiopian Orthodox Tewahido Church of Our Sav-

---

bridge: Cambridge University Press, 2000), 7. See also Adrian Hastings, *The Church in Africa, 1450-1950* (Oxford: Oxford University Press, 1994), 1-45.

28. Andrew F. Walls, *The Cross-Cultural Process in Christian History: Studies in the Transmission and Appropriation of Faith* (Maryknoll, N.Y.: Orbis, 2002), 86-87. See Acts 8:27-39.

29. Kwame Bediako, "African and Christian: Recovering an Ancient Story," *The Princeton Seminary Bulletin* 25:2 (2004): 153-61; Walls, *Cross-Cultural Process in Christian History*, 86-91.

ior, worshiping in a chapel tucked away within the famous Riverside Church in Manhattan.[30] There is also an important Orthodox church in the Bronx.

Just as Pentecostal churches are a growing presence in Ethiopia, so also in New York City. The first Ethiopian Pentecostal church in New York is the Emmanuel Worship Center International, originally known as the Ethiopian Evangelical Church. Founded by Pastor Mulugeta Abate in 1989, the church meets in a former nightclub located in the Bronx. Historically, the church leadership has a link with the Mennonites.

Catholic Communities

Statistically, the Catholic Church maintains the largest number of adherents in Africa of any church body,[31] and African Catholics are a thriving part of the Catholic Church in New York City. Because of the Catholic Church's ecclesiology and global organization, they should be considered distinct from Protestant missionary churches. It is also important to tell their story while being attentive to a much longer past that stretches to Augustine and other North African church leaders, the 1995 document *Ecclesia in Africa*, a growth in African vocations, the rise of international priests, and initiatives of both evangelization and inculturation.[32]

Responding to the voices and needs of Catholic African immigrants, New York City's two Roman Catholic dioceses — the Archdiocese of New York that covers the Bronx, Manhattan, and Staten Island, and the Diocese of Brooklyn that incorporates Queens — operate a vibrant network of congregations, communities, or apostolates that serve African Catholics in their language and culture. They are more like congregations within local parishes, defined less by a geographic paradigm than by religious needs. Since the 1990s, a number of Catholic communities have been formed to serve African Catholics throughout the boroughs.[33] In the Bronx, there is

---

30. A. L. Pitchers, "Facing the Reality of the Ethiopian Encounter," in *Study of Religion in Southern Africa*, ed. Johannes A. Smith and P. Pratap Kumar (Leiden: Brill, 2005), 191-203.

31. Bryan T. Froehle and Mary L. Gautier, *Global Catholicism: Portrait of a World Church* (Maryknoll, N.Y.: Orbis, 2003), 45-65.

32. For critical reflections, see Emmanuel Katongole, "Prospects of Ecclesia in Africa in the Twenty-First Century," *Logos* 4:1 (2001): 178-95.

33. Congregational data from the Office of Black Ministries, New York Archdiocese, August 3, 2006.

Born Again in the City

Fig. 1.2 A visit from the Cardinal Turkson, Ghanaian Catholic Community, the Bronx, 2005

the Ghanaian Catholic Community of Christ the King founded in 1995. To celebrate their tenth anniversary, Peter Cardinal Kodwo Appiah Turkson, Archbishop of Cape Coast, Ghana, joined the congregation, along with representatives of the New York Archdiocese. Christ the King parish serves a Latino community, but the Ghanaian Catholic Community also has a home with them to hold services on Sunday.

Protestant Churches

Protestant churches were generally established in Africa in the late eighteenth century and into the second half of the nineteenth century at the impetus of Western churches and mission societies.[34] "Missionary," "mission founded," or "historical" is the terminology used to describe such churches from this period, and it suggests implication in the Western colo-

34. Hastings, *The Church in Africa, 1450-1950*, 242-305.

nial enterprise. However, there has also been interplay between missionary imposition and local agency, with selected appropriation and even resistance. Entering the post-colonial period, it was generally presumed that the historic churches would decline, but instead of fading away in the post-independence period, so-called historical churches grew substantially.[35] Anglican, Presbyterian, Methodist, and Lutheran churches not only held their own, they often expanded.

In New York City, the Protestant churches play an important role for their members, and they appear to be institutionally strong and aiming for increased growth. The historical Protestant churches from Ghana represented in New York City include the Presbyterian Church of Ghana and the Methodist Church of Ghana, with numerous churches in Harlem, the Bronx, and Brooklyn. The Seventh Day Adventist Church has Nigerian and Ghanaian congregations. Vibrant charismatic liturgy, theology, and experience are integral to life in such churches.[36]

African Independent Churches

Known for their white flowing robes are the African Independent Churches or AICs; alternative "I" words that stand in for "independent" include "indigenous," "initiated," and "instituted." By Harold Turner's succinct definition of the AICs, "founded in Africa by Africans primarily for Africans,"[37] cultural intelligibility is an implied goal, indigenous leadership is an explicit factor, and ecclesial particularity is an outcome. Noting a radical commitment to "follow the Word as they hear it" in all of life, Andrew Walls has suggested that they are the Anabaptists of Af-

---

35. David Maxwell, "Post-Colonial Christianity in Africa," in *The Cambridge History of Christianity*, vol. 9, *World Christianities c. 1914-2000*, ed. Hugh McLeod (Cambridge University Press, 2006), 401-3.

36. Elom Dovlo, "African Culture and Emergent Church Forms in Ghana," *Exchange* 33:1 (2004): 28-53; Cephas N. Omenyo, *Pentecost Outside Pentecostalism: A Study of the Development of Charismatic Renewal in the Mainline Churches in Ghana* (Zoetermeer: Uitgeverij Boekencentrum, 2002); "From the Fringes to the Centre: Pentecostalization of the Mainline Churches in Ghana," *Exchange* 34:1 (2005): 39-60.

37. Bengt Sundkler's famous statement of what he then called the "Bantu Independent Churches" in South Africa described what for the West was a view that "in these churches, one would be able to see what the African Christian, *when left to himself*, regarded as important and relevant in Christian faith and in the Christian church." Bengt G. M. Sundkler, *Bantu Prophets in South Africa* (London: Lutterworth Press, 1948), 17.

rica.[38] Stan Nussbaum distinguishes the religious practice and theology of the African Independent Churches from the mainline or missionary model:

> Western missionaries brought a message of some things the God of Israel had done through Jesus many generations ago in a place unimaginably far away and some other things he will do for us in a future world after we die. By contrast, the founders of the AICs announced some good news — that same God of Israel is doing some things right here in Africa. He is sending visions, calling prophets, empowering healers, thundering out to Africans, 'Here I am! Here I am!'[39]

Nussbaum's point is that the African Independent Churches are not inferior to the mission-founded churches, but offer significant and responsive forms of church life and mission. As Inus Daneel maintains, the independent churches are a constructive reinterpretation of Christianity on African terms, not simply a break with the establishment or a protest movement.[40]

There is an extraordinary variety of African Independent Churches in South, West, and East Africa, holding diverse theologies and ecclesiologies.[41] Overall, the African Independent Churches emphasize the experience of the Spirit, healing, testimony, and a rejection of Western modes of worship as imported by the missionaries.[42] Their origins can be traced to leaders, both men and women,[43] with "direct communication with God and/or the saints through revelation, prophecy, possession, and dreams."[44]

---

38. Andrew F. Walls, *The Missionary Movement in Christian History: Studies in the Transmission of Faith* (Maryknoll, NY.: Orbis, 1996), 116.

39. Stan W. Nussbaum, "African Initiated Churches," in *Dictionary of Mission Theology: Evangelical Foundations*, ed. John Corrie (Downers Grove, Ill.: InterVarsity, 2007), 5.

40. M. L. Daneel, *Quest for Belonging: Introduction to a Study of African Independent Churches* (Zimbabwe: Mambo Press, 1987), and "African Initiated Churches in South Africa," in *Christianity Reborn: The Global Expansion of Evangelicalism in the Twentieth Century*, ed. Donald M. Lewis (Grand Rapids: Eerdmans, 2004), 181-218.

41. Hastings, *The Church in Africa, 1450-1950*, 493-539.

42. John S. Pobee and Gabriel Ositelu II, *African Initiatives in Christianity: The Growth, Gifts and Diversities of Indigenous African Churches — A Challenge to the Ecumenical Movement* (Geneva: WCC Publications, 1998), 40-42.

43. Cynthia Hoehler-Fatton, "Christianity: Independent and Charismatic Churches in Africa," in *Africana: The Encyclopedia of the African American Experience*, ed. Kwame Anthony Appiah and Henry Louis Gates, Jr. (New York: Basic Civitas Books, 1999), 428.

44. Hoehler-Fatton, "Christianity: Independent and Charismatic Churches in Africa," 428.

Still, Afe Adogame is certainly correct when he points out that with reference to the Aladura independent churches, "they share many features, the reason for their common typology, but each Aladura has its own religious dynamic. There are also significant differences, especially in specific doctrines and details of ritual acts and performance, the charismatic personality of the founders, their organizational policies and foundation histories."[45]

Nigeria's classically recognized African Independent Churches of the Aladura type are widely distributed in New York.[46] In addition to the Church of the Lord (Aladura), the Cherubim and Seraphim church, founded in 1925 in Nigeria by Moses Orimolade Tunolase, is widely represented in New York City, where their angel-like garments continue to define church members.[47] At least two Cherubim and Seraphim groups operate in New York City.[48] One group is called the Holy Order of Cherubim and Seraphim Movement, and they have five branches in New York City.[49] Also in New York City is the Cherubim and Seraphim Church Organization, based in the Bronx. The Celestial Church of Christ is very active in the five boroughs of New York City. What is called the New York parish was established in 1977, thus making it one of the earliest African immigrant churches in New York.

Christ Apostolic Church is represented in at least three forms in New York. First, there is Christ Apostolic (Agbala-Itura) International Miracle Center in Brooklyn. Second, there is Christ Apostolic Church (First in the Americas) and based in Brooklyn. Third, there is Christ Apostolic of America W.O.S.E.M, associated with Prophet Obadare, based in Brooklyn, with other branches in the city. While typically associated with the independent churches in worship style, the branches and services I visited of Christ Apostolic more closely resembled Pentecostal churches.

---

45. Afe Adogame, "Engaging the Rhetoric of Spiritual Warfare: The Public Face of Aladura in Diaspora," *Journal of Religion in Africa* 34:4 (2004): 494.

46. Hastings, *The Church in Africa, 1450-1950*, 513-18.

47. Matthews Ojo, "Cherubim and Seraphim Movement," in *The Encyclopedia of African and African-American Religion*, ed. Stephen D. Glazier (New York: Routledge, 2001), 82.

48. For further elaboration, see Elisha P. Renne, "Consecrated Garments and Spaces in the Cherubim and Seraphim Church Diaspora," *Material Religion* 5:1 (2009): 70-87.

49. See http://csmovementchurchusa.org/index.htm.

Born Again in the City

Fig. 1.3 Celestial Church of Christ, Brooklyn, 2006

Pentecostal and Charismatic Churches

Over the past three decades, Pentecostal and charismatic churches have strongly come to the fore in Africa.[50] A movement with many strands,[51] African Pentecostalism combines a personal relationship with Christ through the Holy Spirit with the possibility of dramatic transformation, according to Ogbu Kalu.[52] In Matthews Ojo's important analysis, two distinctive themes of Pentecostalism in Nigeria are "piety and power."[53]

---

50. Kalu, *African Pentecostalism: An Introduction* (Oxford: Oxford University Press, 2008); Matthews A. Ojo, "African Charismatics," in *Encyclopedia of African and African-American Religions,* ed. Stephen D. Glazier (New York: Routledge 2001), 2-6; Allan H. Anderson, "The Newer Pentecostal and Charismatic Churches," *Pneuma* 24:2 (2002): 167-84.

51. Kalu, *African Pentecostalism,* 10, 15, 103-22.

52. Ogbu Kalu, "A Discursive Interpretation of African Pentecostalism," *Fides et Historia* 41:1 (2009): 71-90; and *African Pentecostalism.*

53. For elaboration, Matthews A. Ojo, *The End-Time Army: Charismatic Movements in Modern Nigeria* (Trenton: African World Press, 2006), 191-229. See also Sunday Babajide

Kwabena Asamoah-Gyadu emphasizes the prevalence of a holistic spirituality across church life.[54] Newer "neo-Pentecostal" churches designate deliverance and divine blessing as core elements.[55] All the African Pentecostal churches emphasize the importance of the worship of Jesus, celebration, joy, and expectation of blessing.

Pentecostal movements, corresponding to original eighteenth-century Methodist principles, emphasize the Holy Spirit, voluntary association, grassroots readings of the Bible, a heightened sense of personal virtue and discipline, and the reach of a global parish.[56] Thus scholars such as David Martin see Pentecostal/charismatic affinities coalescing to comprise an overall "culture."[57] The ability of Pentecostal churches to adapt across cultures is considerable. In this light, it is interesting to note Rowan Williams's intriguing theological observation about the Spirit and translation: "The Son is manifest in a single, paradigmatic figure, the Spirit is manifest in the 'translatability' of that into the contingent diversity of history."[58] Allan Anderson provides a similar observation: "Pentecostalism with its flexibility (or 'freedom') in the Spirit has an innate ability to make itself at home in almost any context."[59] While there is a stress on the transcultural nature of the gospel, with a flexibility rooted in the Spirit, Pentecostalism can and does take local cultural idioms seriously. This constitutes a dynamic that, along with Williams's and Anderson's points, helps explain why Pentecostalism appears to be so globally adaptable.[60] As a result, as Martin has emphasized, Pentecostalism presents a flexible and strong cultural presence around the world.

Komolafe, "The Changing Face of Christianity: Revisiting African Christianity," *Missiology: An International Review* 32:3 (2004): 217-38.

54. J. Kwabena Asamoah-Gyadu, *African Charismatics: Current Developments within Independent Indigenous Pentecostalism in Ghana* (Leiden: Brill, 2005); see also Emmanuel Kingsley Larbi, *Pentecostalism: The Eddies of Ghanaian Christianity* (Accra: CPCS, 2001).

55. Paul Gifford, *Ghana's New Christianity: Pentecostalism in a Globalizing African Economy* (Bloomington: Indiana University Press, 2004).

56. David Martin, *Pentecostalism: The World Their Parish* (Oxford: Blackwell, 2002).

57. Martin, *Pentecostalism*, 1-27.

58. Rowan Williams, *On Christian Theology* (Oxford: Blackwell, 2000), 125-26.

59. Allan Anderson, *An Introduction to Pentecostalism: Global Charismatic Christianity* (Cambridge: Cambridge University Press, 2004), 282; see also J. D. Y. Peel, "Postsocialism, Postcolonialism, Pentecostalism," in *Conversion After Socialism: Disruptions, Modernisms and Technologies of Faith in the Former Soviet Union*, ed. Mathijs Pelkmans (New York: Berghahn Books, 2009), 183-99.

60. See further Paul Brodwin, "Pentecostalism in Translation: Religion and the Production of Community in the Haitian Diaspora," *American Ethnologist* 30:1 (2003): 85-101.

There are two leading interpretative schools of thought on the origins of Pentecostal churches in Africa, each with implications for understanding their theology and wider social impact. One school of thought, represented by Paul Gifford, sees African Pentecostal churches as a replication or derivative product of western Pentecostalism — more precisely, the sort of Pentecostalism associated with American television evangelists and conservative/fundamentalist Christianity.[61] A related argument is that African Pentecostalism is derived from the American Azusa Street revival of the early twentieth century. A second, more convincing interpretation finds in the African Pentecostal churches a new chapter in the African re-imagination of Christianity, addressing concerns on African terms in a manner similar to the AICs. Along these lines, Ogbu Kalu indicates that the Pentecostal churches are part of a continuing and indigenous effort that follows on the *failure* of the missionary churches.[62] They are not, in this historical evaluation, following in the line of Azusa, but have developed independently, to meet their own requirements.

New York has a wide range of African Pentecostal churches, largely from Ghana and Nigeria, as befits demographic emphases. Ghana's more classical Pentecostal churches and newer charismatic churches are both found in substantial number in New York.[63] The Church of Pentecost, Ghana's largest Pentecostal denomination, has established a major U.S. operation, with branches in the Bronx, Brooklyn, Queens, and Manhattan. The Apostolic Church International has numerous branches in New York, including two in the Bronx, one in Brooklyn, and one on Staten Island. Lighthouse Chapel, founded by Bishop Dag Heward-Mills, is one of the newer Ghanaian churches established in New York, and has some five branches in the city.[64]

Nigerian Pentecostalism is strongly felt in New York.[65] Since the first service in 1995, Redeemed Christian Church of God has expanded rapidly in New York, resulting in more than twenty branches in the city throughout the

---

61. See Paul Gifford, *Ghana's New Christianity: Pentecostalism in a Globalizing African Economy* (Bloomington: Indiana University Press, 2004).

62. Ogbu U. Kalu, "The Third Response: Pentecostalism and the Reconstruction of Christian Experience in Africa, 1970-1995," *Journal of African Christian Thought* 1:2 (1998): 3-16; cf. Kalu, *African Pentecostalism*, 68-71.

63. For extensive studies, see the work of Larbi, Gifford, and Asamoah-Gyadu.

64. According to the Sunday service bulletin, Sunday, June 25, 2006, there are twenty-five branches in the United States, and New York City is the only city with multiple branches.

65. For historical background in Nigeria, the major study here is Ojo, *The End-Time Army*.

PROLOGUE

Fig. 1.4 Apostolic Church, Staten Island, 2009. Note the Ghanaian and American flags on the sign.

five boroughs. Deeper Life Bible Church, founded in Nigeria by W. F. Kumuyi in 1982, occupies a large former industrial building in the Bronx, just across the street from a large African market. Its first branch in New York was founded in the Bronx, and it has one branch in each of the boroughs.

Nigeria's neo-Pentecostal churches are typically set apart by a strong emphasis on deliverance and prosperity. With its heavy emphasis on deliverance, Mountain of Fire and Miracles Ministries can be considered a neo-Pentecostal church. In New York, this Nigerian-based movement has put down roots, evidenced in a finely renovated building in Brooklyn, and with additional branches in the Bronx and Queens. Living Faith Church Worldwide, better known as Winners Chapel, and founded by Bishop David Oyedepo, was started in New York in June 2004.[66] Central Gospel Church began holding services in 2000, and officially opened a branch in a former industrial building on Park Avenue in the Bronx in 2001.[67]

As befits such an effusive movement, not all of New York's African Pentecostal churches are part of an Africa-based ministry or denomination, and have instead been independently started. An important example

66. Olakunle Onaleye, Interview, December 31, 2006.
67. Prince Nyrako, Interview, January 14, 2006.

Born Again in the City

Fig. 1.5 Mountain of Fire and Miracles, Queens, 2006

and perhaps harbinger of future developments is Dayspring Church on Roosevelt Island, started by Pastor Olu Obed, formerly of Redeemed. Dayspring intentionally seeks to move beyond a Nigerian focus. His wife, Eloise or Elsie Obed, founded and directs Lilies International, a radio ministry with offices in New York, Lagos, and River State. To keep in touch with her listeners in New York City, Obed conducts monthly praise and preaching services in venues such as the Hotel Pennsylvania and Waldorf-Astoria, attracting a large and diverse mix of people.[68]

Francophone Churches

A small number of French-speaking African churches are established in New York City. A good example is the French Christian Ministry of New York, started by Daniel Diakanwa in 1994, which ministers to the Congolese community. The church, now named Eglise Evangelique "Amour Du Christ," met at Lexington Avenue United Methodist Church on Manhattan's Upper East Side on Sunday afternoons. When Diakanwa left the church to continue his training in the Salvation Army, it became associated with the Christian and Missionary Alliance.[69] (I am often asked about the Kimbanguists, a signifi-

---

68. See http://www.liliesinternational.org/home.htm.
69. Daniel Diakanwa, Interview, February 15, 2008.

Fig. 1.6 Sign for French African Outreach, Manhattan, 2008

cant independent church movement. They do not have a branch in New York City, but they do operate a small fellowship in the Atlanta area.[70])

Liberian Churches on Staten Island

While most of New York's African congregations gather wherever they can find a place to worship, Staten Island's Liberian Christians are different in their residential cluster. As Liberia collapsed into civil war in the 1990s, a small number of refugees found their way to the United States and resettled in the Stapleton community of Staten Island. Here Bethel Outreach, Christ Assembly Lutheran Church, First United Christian Church, and Trinity Baptist serve Liberian residents on Staten Island. The

---

70. This is confirmed by Daniel Diakanwa.

Born Again in the City

Fig. 1.7 Christ Assembly Lutheran Church — LCMS, Staten Island, 2009

community is also a site for interviews for Liberia's Truth and Reconciliation Commission.

Headquarter Operations

Along with the concentration of African churches in New York, there are also a significant number of overseas operational or administrative headquarters for North Americans operations. No other city in the United States has a similar concentration of international headquarters of African churches. The Church of the Lord (Aladura) in the Bronx is the North American see, and the office of the Presbyterian Church of Ghana Overseas Mission Field (OMF) is located in Harlem.

The Bronx is the headquarters for two Ghanaian Pentecostal churches, the Apostolic Church International on White Plains Road and the nearby Church of Pentecost. Also in the Bronx are the North American headquarters of Deeper Life Bible Church, the Cherubim and Seraphim, Christ Apostolic Church (First in the Americas) and Christ Apostolic (Agbala-Itura). In Queens, Living Faith Church Worldwide (Winners' Chapel USA) has planted its first church and headquarters for North America.

PROLOGUE

Fig. 1.8 Church of Pentecost Branch and Headquarters, the Bronx, 2006. Note the world map and dove symbol on their building.

The One and the Many

Long a part of the Christian story, African Christianity today can be interpreted as a story or series of stories whereby faith seeks understanding on African terms and in response to African questions and needs. In each of these churches we find diverse histories, leaders, and theological emphases, and we must avoid the temptation to flatten out such distinctions. Yet there is also the very real possibility of discerning a shared ethos, understanding of Christ, and spirituality. In my experience, wherever I worshiped — be it Catholic, Pentecostal, Independent, mainline, or Orthodox — I felt like I was experiencing a single story of African Christianity.[71]

Historically, Pentecostal churches see strong distinctions between the independent churches, such as the Aladura type, and themselves. Emphasizing nearly a spare Puritan aesthetic in worship and differences in ap-

---

71. This is something that was suggested by Andrew Walls, *The Missionary Movement in Christian History*, 118.

Born Again in the City

Fig. 1.9 Holy Order of Cherubim and Seraphim Movement Church and Headquarters, Brooklyn, 2006

proach to culture and theology, Pentecostalism is known for stressing the incommensurability of its beliefs and practices with independent churches. Rarely do the leaders mix, or are members encouraged to do so. Historical churches have also struggled with independent movements and Pentecostal churches, again over issues of culture and religion.[72]

On the ground in New York, however, I never heard any public comments by the churches on the differences between them. Instead, in some independent churches, I heard complimentary observations on the Pentecostal churches, and I met some members who moved back and forth between the churches. Generally, members of various churches seem well aware of the overall African church scene in New York, but they are more focused on their own church.

In fact, Rufus Ositelu, Primate of the Church of the Lord (Aladura), finds the label "Pentecostal" to be a "misnomer."[73] It is the independent

72. Dovlo, "African Culture and Emergent Church Forms in Ghana."
73. Rufus Ositelu, Interview, October 8, 2006.

churches, he argues, who first recovered an emphasis on the Spirit in African Christianity, and changed the style of music to a more dynamic and joyful form while also encouraging divine healing.[74] Going in a different direction, Anderson folds the independent churches into the Pentecostal story.[75] If the shift to Pentecostalism that many see is not fully clear, what is unambiguous is that African churches uniformly live and move in the power of the Spirit, and take seriously their cultural context.

Global Faith, Global City

"If you get New York, you are getting the world," asserts Olu Obed, who along with his wife is responsible for establishing the Redeemed Christian Church of God in the New York area.[76] This comment reveals something about how the image of New York inspires people, but more importantly, it shows an understanding of how the city serves as a connection point for the diffusion of the gospel from Africa to New York, and from here to the United States and beyond. Having a church and headquarters for operations in New York City can lend prestige to an African church.[77] But there is more to an African church presence in New York City than profile. Obed is imagining the city as having a strategic role in the spread of the Christian gospel. The language of New York City as stage, platform, node, and strategic site for cross-border movements indicates something of the global city's extraordinary role in the diffusion of African Christianity.

Historical perspective on the global dimension of New York City is important. For more than four decades, African migration to the United States has been on an upward trend.[78] Migration, generally driven by combinations of choice and crisis, is a global phenomenon, bringing people, cultures,

---

74. Rufus Okikiolaolu Olubiyi Ositelu, *African Instituted Churches: Diversities, Growth, Gifts, Spirituality and Ecumenical Understanding of African Initiated Churches* (Münster: LIT Verlag, 2002), 38-39, 192, 201. Rufus Ositelu, Interview, October 8, 2006.

75. Anderson, *An Introduction to Pentecostalism*, 103-6.

76. Olusegun Obed, Interview, February 18, 2004.

77. Opoku Onyinah, "Pentecostalism and the African Diaspora: An Examination of the Missions Activities of the Church of Pentecost," *Pneuma* 26:2 (Fall 2004): 229-30.

78. Yvette M. Alex-Assensoh, "African Immigrants and African-Americans: An Analysis of Voluntary African Immigration and the Evolution of Black Ethnic Politics in America," *African and Asian Studies* 8:1-2 (2009): 89-124.

and beliefs into contact.[79] African migration to New York City, a key site nationally, is central to the expansion of African churches.[80] While less numerous in comparison to New York's other immigrant groups, comprising just three percent of New York's foreign-born population, African immigrants are among the fastest-growing communities in the city,[81] especially over the past fifteen years. According to demographic data from 2000, 92,435 African immigrants call New York home,[82] with the largest influx coming from Ghana and Nigeria.[83] At any given point, the official numerical count is generally considered by experts to be low by 5 to 15 percent, although the number may well be much greater. Among African immigrants to the United States, the West African community is one of the most substantial.[84] They are a growing proportion of the black population of New York City.[85]

Part of the Black Atlantic, Africans have a long-standing history in New York City. A reminder of this was the discovery in 1991 of the "African Burial Ground" in lower Manhattan where the remains of some 400 Africans (out of an estimated 12,000) from the seventeenth and eighteenth centuries were found.[86] It was in 1626 that eight African slaves from Angola arrived in New Amsterdam, possibly the first African slaves in New York. Slavery was legal in New York City until the Abolition Act of 1817, but emancipation itself was not completed until 1827.[87] Brought against their will as part of the slave trade connecting the New World to Africa and the West Indies, African laborers would build the protective wall that came to be known as Wall Street. In the words of historian Leslie

79. Dirk Hoerder, *Cultures in Contact: World Migrations in the Second Millennium* (Durham: Duke University Press, 2002).

80. Sam Roberts, "More Africans Enter U.S. Than in Days of Slavery," *New York Times*, February 21, 2005, A-1, B-4.

81. Arun Peter Lobo and Joseph L. Salvo, *The Newest New Yorkers 2000: Immigrant New York in the New Millennium* (New York City: New York City Department of Planning, 2004), 11.

82. Lobo and Salvo, *The Newest New Yorkers*, 13.

83. Lobo and Salvo, *The Newest New Yorkers*, 36.

84. Marilyn Halter, "Africa: West," in *The New Americans: A Guide to Immigration Since 1965*, ed. Mary C. Waters and Reed Ueda (Boston: Harvard University Press, 2007), 283-94.

85. Yvette M. Alex-Assensoh, "African Immigrants and African-Americans: An Analysis of Voluntary African Immigration and the Evolution of Black Ethnic Politics in America," *African and Asian Studies* 8:1-2 (2009): 89-124.

86. For information on the African Burial Ground in Manhattan, see http://africanburialground.gov/.

87. Produced in conjunction with the New York Historical Society's exhibit "It Happened Here" is Ira Berlin and Leslie M. Harris, ed., *Slavery in New York* (New York: The New Press, 2005).

Harris, "Black New Yorkers built the city, sustained its daily existence, and gave their lives — willingly or not — for its continued prosperity. Subject to physical, cultural, and spiritual violence, black New Yorkers manifested an audacious capacity to survive, to resist repression, and to sustain a diverse community."[88] This history has indelibly shaped American culture and urban life.

As new African immigrants come to New York, they also bring their faith and institutions. Jehu Hanciles, in his *Beyond Christendom: Globalization, African Migration, and the Transformation of the West*, has shown strong links between a historic Christian revival in Africa and migration.[89] Along with other new immigrants to New York City and America, many West African New Yorkers are not just religious, but Christian.[90] The pattern that emerges is clear: as people travel, their faith moves with them.[91]

The history of New York City is crucial for situating the presence of African churches in another, related way. From its days as New Amsterdam, a Dutch West India trading outpost, New York City was built on making money, not ideology.[92] "Its destiny was to be the city of capital," write Edwin Burrows and Mike Wallace in their monumental *Gotham*.[93] When the Calvinist governor Peter Stuyvesant attempted to suppress Quakers, Catholics, and Jews, he would be met in 1657 with the historic Flushing Remonstrance, a declaration of religious liberty from what is now Queens.[94] As a result, observe Kenneth Jackson and David Dunbar, "Although New Yorkers may not be more tolerant than citizens of other cities,

---

88. Leslie M. Harris, *In the Shadow of Slavery: African Americans in New York City, 1626-1863* (Chicago: University of Chicago Press, 2003), 288.

89. Jehu Hanciles, *Beyond Christendom: Globalization, African Migration, and the Transformation of the West* (Maryknoll, N.Y.: Orbis, 2008), and "God's Mission through Migration: African Initiatives in Globalizing Mission," in *Evangelical, Ecumenical, and Anabaptist Missiologies in Conversation: Essays in Honor of Wilbert R. Shenk*, ed. James R. Krabill, Walter Sawatsky, and Charles E. Van Engen (Maryknoll, N.Y.: Orbis, 2006), 58-66.

90. Wendy Cage and Elaine Howard Ecklund cite recent data that suggest that "two-thirds of post-1965 immigrants are Christian" in "Immigration and Religion," *Annual Review of Sociology* 33 (2007): 361.

91. Cage and Ecklund, "Immigration and Religion," 359-79.

92. On background, see Russell Shorto, *The Island at the Center of the World: The Epic Story of Dutch Manhattan and the Forgotten Colony that Shaped America* (New York: Doubleday, 2004).

93. Edwin G. Burrows and Mike Wallace, *Gotham: A History of New York City to 1898* (New York: Oxford University Press, 1999), 306.

94. Kenneth T. Jackson and David S. Dunbar, eds., *Empire City: New York Through the Centuries* (New York: Columbia University Press, 2002).

the tradition in Gotham is of religious freedom."⁹⁵ With its unique history of religious toleration, New York City provides the space for new church movements to thrive.

Immigration is, of course, the quintessential New York story. The title of Frederick M. Binder and David M. Reimers's book about New York, *All the Nations Under Heaven,* communicates this.⁹⁶ People come to New York City for new beginnings, as they always have. But the mix of capitalism and religious pluralism opened — and continues to open — New York City to evangelistic ferment and new religious developments, setting the stage for African Christianity.⁹⁷ Historically, God and Gotham go together, including in Manhattan.⁹⁸ So the quest for a new life, money, religious freedom, and opportunity are built into the historical identity of New York from the very start. African Christianity in New York City should be seen in this light.

Today, New York is what Saskia Sassen calls a "global city": not simply a place or an immigrant "gateway," but a process and a relationship to other cities, constituted not only by physical geography, but cross-border networks, connections, linkages, movements, and relationships.⁹⁹ According to Sassen's multifaceted and groundbreaking analysis in *The Global City,*¹⁰⁰ New York City functions as a command and connection point for decentralized economic activity. As production becomes distributed around the world, global cities are specialized sites of economic activity and supportive services in law, insurance, and architecture. In a global and spatially dispersed economy where speed, access to specialized services, and information matter, Sassen show how cities like New York City are a necessity. To be

---

95. Jackson and Dunbar, *Empire City,* 33. See also Kenneth T. Jackson, "A Colony with a Conscience," *The New York Times,* December 27, 2007, A-29.

96. Frederick M. Binder and David M. Reimers, *All the Nations Under Heaven: An Ethnic and Racial History of New York City* (New York: Columbia University Press, 1995).

97. Burrows and Wallace, *Gotham,* 157, 208-9, 396, 529, 933, 1157, 1170. See also Jon Butler, "Religion in New York City: Faith that Could Not Be," *U.S. Catholic Historian* 22:2 (2002): 51-61. This history is still being unearthed. For an indirect case study, see Burkhard Bilger, "Mystery on Pearl Street," *The New Yorker,* January 7, 2008, 56-65.

98. For a larger discussion, see Jon Butler, "Theory and God in Gotham," *History and Theory* 45 (2006): 47-61.

99. Saskia Sassen, "Introduction: Locating Cities on Global Circuits," in *Global Networks, Linked Cities,* ed. Saskia Sassen (New York: Routledge, 2002), 1-36; Peter J. Taylor, *World City Network: A Global Urban Analysis* (London: Routledge, 2004).

100. Saskia Sassen, *The Global City: New York, London, Tokyo,* 2nd ed. (Princeton: Princeton University Press, 2001)

sure, there is more to a global city than finance. Informal work and new businesses by immigrants create jobs and diversify the economy. And fashion and culture can be equally global in scale.[101] But the global dimension of finance and connectivity are vital to understanding New York.

While not determinedly in contrast to the state,[102] the global city reflects a more "city-centric"[103] view of the world. It is such a world that suggests why New York City may more closely connect to cities at a great distance than to those in its local region.[104] An average New Yorker may relate more closely to Lagos than Albany. In this global world, the importance of the local does not recede, but gains in importance. The "local" is where religion is constructed and lived.[105] African Christian places of worship help us see the intensity of these cross-border relationships.

A global city perspective helps us rethink our understanding of immigration. In 1965, President Lyndon Johnson went to Ellis Island, the famous entry point for immigrants to New York City, and signed into law the Immigration and Nationality Act of 1965. The law is well known for emphasizing non-European diversity and family reunification.[106] As Nancy Foner points out in her excellent study *From Ellis Island to JFK: New York's Two Great Waves of Immigration*, there have been two great periods of immigration in New York. The first wave occurred between 1880 and 1920, during which time "close to a million and a half immigrants arrived and settled in the city — so that by 1910 fully 41 percent of all New Yorkers were foreign born."[107] In this first great wave of immigration, the new arrivals were mostly eastern European Jews and southern Italians.[108]

---

101. Elizabeth Currid, *The Warhol Economy: How Fashion, Art, and Music Drive New York City* (Princeton: Princeton University Press, 2007).

102. Saskia Sassen, *Territory, Authority, Rights: From Medieval to Global Assemblages* (Princeton: Princeton University Press, 2006).

103. Taylor, *World City Network*, 27.

104. Sassen, "Introduction: Locating Cities on Global Circuits," 15.

105. See Kim Knott, "From Locality to Location and Back Again: A Spatial Journey in the Study of Religion," *Religion* 39 (2009): 154-60; Marten van der Meulen, "The Continuing Importance of the Local: African Churches and the Search for Worship Space in Amsterdam," *African Diaspora* 2 (2009): 159-81.

106. Arun Peter Lobo, Joseph L. Salvo, and Vicky Virgin, *The Newest New Yorkers 1990-1994: An Analysis of Immigration to New York City in the Early 1990s* (New York City: New York City Department of Planning, 1996), 33.

107. Nancy Foner, *From Ellis Island to JFK: New York's Two Great Waves of Immigration* (New Haven: Yale University Press and New York: Russell Sage Foundation, 2000), 1.

108. Foner, *From Ellis Island*.

Whereas the first wave involved primarily European immigrants, the second and current wave is characterized by non-European diversity.

Expanding the changes begun in 1965 even further was the 1990 Immigration Act, considered "the biggest change in immigration law since 1965."[109] The 1990 Act "maintained the priority given to family reunification, but placed an increased premium on skills. It also permanently put into place a program to diversify the source countries of immigrants to the United States."[110] Since 1990, over one million new international immigrants have entered New York, and remarkably, today almost sixty percent of New Yorkers are foreign born or children of foreign-born parents.[111]

But while the 1965 Immigration Act, with its revisions in 1990, is generally accepted as the standard explanation for immigration to New York City, Sassen believes that such legislation is not a sufficient explanation for a global city. Instead immigration is located within the operations of globalization and the city and can be one means of evaluating global connectivity.[112] "Global cities," Sassen argues, "are a key site for the incorporation of large numbers of immigrants in activities that service the strategic sector."[113] In her reading of the data, "immigration can be seen as providing labor for the low-wage service and manufacturing jobs that service both the expanding, highly specialized service sector and the high-income lifestyles of those employed in the specialized, expanding service sector."[114] People come to New York City to build a better life — for work.

Following this argument, two types of workers are required for a global city to succeed: high-end professionals and a low-wage labor force. "New York's producer service sector caters to a world market and is heavily internationalized, servicing or making transactions at the axis between a firm and the international market."[115] Low-wage workers are demanded

---

109. Lobo, Salvo and Virgin, *The Newest New Yorkers*, 33.

110. Lobo, Salvo, and Virgin, *The Newest New Yorkers*.

111. Rae D. Rosen, Susan Wieler, and Joseph Pereira, "New York City Immigrants: The 1990s Wave," *Current Issues in Economics and Finance* 11:6 (June 2005): 1-7. Available at http://ssrn.com/abstract=760926.

112. For further elaboration, see Lisa Benton-Short, Marie D. Price, and Samantha Friedman, "Globalization from Below: The Ranking of Global Immigrant Cities," *International Journal of Urban and Regional Research* 29:4 (2005): 945-59, and Michael Samers, "Immigration and the Global City Hypothesis: Towards an Alternative Research Agenda," *International Journal of Urban and Regional Research* 26:2 (2002): 389-402.

113. Sassen, *The Global City*, 322.

114. Sassen, *The Global City*, 332.

115. Sassen, *The Global City*, 155.

for conducting New York's service economy, leading to increased population growth and the generation of cross-border urban zones.[116] As a result, in New York City there has been an "institutionalization of the casual labor market."[117] While a taxi driver or a banker operate on different global circuits, both belong to the same global moment, embedded in and related to the financial dynamics of New York City and the global economy.[118] The global city becomes ordered around a polarization between "corporate capital" and a new low-wage immigrant workforce, a space of contestation for goods and claims.[119]

In spite of the challenges, New York City is still experienced as "a land of opportunity. I've come to explore that opportunity," said Ebenezer Asare of the Presbyterian Church of Ghana.[120] Education and family are also motivating factors in immigration to New York City, but work overwhelmingly predominates. New York City's global image and rough-and-tumble economy meet in the commentary of Justin Emineke, a member of the Redeemed Christian Church of God in Brooklyn: "New York City is glamorous, a wonderland, God's kingdom on earth." Nevertheless, if the imagination of New York City is "God's kingdom on earth," the reality felt on the streets is much different. As Justin bluntly elaborated, the experience of New York includes "working sixteen hour days, exhausted" and as an immigrant in the middle of America's racial politics, "even more degraded . . . looked down on."[121] This experience, common among new immigrants, reveals the ambiguities and contradictions of the global city.[122]

From this description of the global city, I draw three implications for comprehending African Christianity in New York City. *First, the global city is a switching station for the development of African Christianity across borders.* The global city is a new space for new churches and move-

---

116. Sassen, *The Global City* 324.

117. Sassen, *The Global City,* 324.

118. Sassen, *Territory, Authority, Rights,* 385-86.

119. Saskia Sassen, "The Many Scales of the Global: Implications for Theory and for Politics," in *The Postcolonial and the Global,* ed. Revathi Krishnaswamy and John C. Hawley (Minneapolis: University of Minnesota Press, 2008), 86-87.

120. Ebenezer Asare, Interview, August 25, 2005.

121. Justin Eminike, Interview, October 10, 2004.

122. Here films, novels, and short stories provide important description. See Kiran Desai, *The Inheritance of Loss* (London: Hamish Hamilton, 2006); Chimamanda Ngozi Adichie, *The Thing Around Your Neck* (New York: Knopf, 2009); and Stephen Frear's film "Dirty Pretty Things" (2002).

ments. People move to New York City for work and bring their faith, all the while embedded in a wide range of religious circuits. African Christians build community life as a way of responding to and living within the global city. African Christianity becomes a way of understanding our global world.

Second, global New York City serves as a hub for the worldwide operations of African church movements. New York City is a hub for African Christianity not just because it has a large concentration of African immigrants, but also because it is a connection point for a networked world. The global city is a place where distance is closed and resources are concentrated. The agglomeration of networks shows why it is that so many African churches have based their North American operations in the city. Both scale and intensity are concurrent factors in mission and expansion.

Third, African Christianity in New York City illuminates a new cross-border urban geography, one that features African cities.[123] New York City should no longer be viewed in relationship only to economically "important" cities such as Frankfurt, Tokyo, and London, but should also be viewed in an expanded global urban zone that includes Accra, Lagos, and Monrovia. Through the lens of religion, a focus on cities in a global context should include African cities.[124] In fact, Africa should be central, not peripheral, to our understanding of the world. Correspondingly, as Jennifer Robinson urges, seeing such a new urban zone can help to alter Western provincialism in conceptual frameworks for the city.[125]

Taken together, these three features show that, just as New York City is a site for the flow of global capital, so it is for the flow of African Christianity. Global capital and African Christianity are distinct and overlapping circuits. The city is essential to how African Christianity is formed, operates, and expands. Globalization needs the city; the city is facilitator of globalization. Olu Obed, whom I quoted at the beginning of this chapter, has it right: "If you get New York, you are getting the world."

---

123. Explorations in this area can be found in Sassen, ed., *Global Networks, Linked Cities.*

124. On the African city, see Abdou Maliq Simone, *For the City Yet to Come: Changing African Life in Four Cities* (Durham: Duke University Press, 2004).

125. Jennifer Robinson, "Global and World Cities: A View from Off the Map," *International Journal of Urban and Regional Research* 26:3 (2002): 531-54, and *Ordinary Cities: Between Modernity and Development* (Routledge: London, 2006).

PROLOGUE

Conclusion: Born Again in New York City

This chapter has been an exercise in mapping African Christianity in a global urban world. From my survey of African churches, I found that although Pentecostal Christianity is growing, Catholic, historically Protestant, and independent expressions are also very active. The energies of faith and the dynamism of the global city meet in New York, where percolating up from below is a growing population of "born again" Christians, who, like the city itself, are also making a break with the past.[126] Today, by one estimate, nearly one of every ten New Yorkers belongs to a Pentecostal congregation.[127] And New York City itself, a city perpetually breaking with its own past for the new,[128] can be described as a place to be "born again."[129] With this shared, fundamental impulse toward reinvention and renewal, African Christianity meshes its identity with New York while marking itself by the ways it breaks from the city. African Christianity really is a New York story.

---

126. Birgit Meyer, "'Make a Complete Break with the Past': Memory and Post-Colonial Modernity in Ghanaian Pentecostalist Discourse," *Journal of Religion in Africa* 28:3 (1998): 316-46.

127. David Gonzalez, "A Sliver of a Storefront, A Faith on the Rise," *New York Times*, January 14, 2007, A-1, 32-33.

128. Max Page, *The Creative Destruction of New York: 1900-1940* (Chicago: University of Chicago Press, 1999).

129. Cal Snyder, "Reflections on September 11: Lives Lost and Lives Changed," Public Lecture at New York Historical Society, September 26, 2007.

II. FORMATIONS

2. Pastors at Work:
Building Community across Borders

Introduction: Job Description

If the job of being a pastor of an African church in New York was to be advertised, it might look something like:

> Wanted: Spiritual leader who is called by God to build a community of faith across borders that will lead members into a relationship of abundant life with God. She or he must know the worldview and pastoral challenges facing African men, women, and families far from home. Needs to be available at all hours of the day. Expected to help church members with housing, health care, finances, and extended families. Must be able to take ways of thinking and worshiping God in one world and re-fabricate in a new cultural and geographical place. Will be answerable to pastoral oversight in Africa and directly to God. Applications are accepted only from persons who have a transformational relationship with God. Prayer, fasting, and anointing with the Holy Ghost are required. Should be very excited about God's mission, expect to be a vehicle for divine signs and wonders, and adept at recruiting new members. Compensation for the first ten years or longer is limited to the blessing of God and the joy of service; pension strictly eternal. All applicants must have at least one paying job to cover start-up costs for the church.

This description will not often fit a typical North American pastor,[1] but it is a vocation to which scores of African men and women across New York City aspire.

---

1. For the idea of composing a "job description," I am drawing on L. Gregory Jones, "Job Description," *Christian Century,* January 10, 2006, 35. I find a striking contrast between Afri-

Pastors are central to the story that will unfold in this book. I begin here because their vocational identities, spiritual journeys, and leadership styles profoundly set the course for the congregations of the Church of the Lord (Aladura) in the Bronx, the Presbyterian Church of Ghana in New York, and the Redeemed Christian Church of God International Chapel, Brooklyn. This is not an attempt to frame my broad arguments with elite or authoritative positions, but to give appropriate weight to the roles of pastoral leaders in establishing and maintaining communities and religious activities across borders. In many respects, churches are mirrors of their pastors. Each church expresses the concerns, approaches, and commitments of their pastor.

No single appellation captures what church leaders are called — Archdeaconess, Pastor, Branch Pastor, Minister, Apostle, Prophet, and Prophetess are just some of the titles of African church leaders one finds in New York City — so I employ the generic terms of "pastor" or "spiritual leader."[2] Like all pastors, they mediate distinct visions of Christian faith as a way of life.[3] As pastors of African churches in New York they are involved in building communities of faith across borders, helping to shape the outlook and direction of their congregations.[4] Because African pastors lead new immigrant churches, they must typically excel in what Mary McClintock Fulkerson calls "*formation practices*, that is, the practice of starting and defining a new church."[5] Their job is to build communities of spiritual and social belonging where human flourishing can occur. In so doing they are key catalysts in globalizing the gospel.[6] While some aca-

---

can immigrant pastors and what Jones provides as an ideal job description of a typical minister in America. For a study of neo-Pentecostal pastoral formation, see Karen Lauterbach, "Becoming a Pastor: Youth and Social Aspirations in Ghana," *Young: Nordic Journal of Youth Research* 18:3 (2010): 259-78. For questions that help situate pastoral leadership as well as providing additional contrast, see Jackson W. Carroll's *God's Potters: Pastoral Leadership and the Shaping of Congregations* (Grand Rapids: Eerdmans, 2006). In whatever setting they serve, pastors share a conviction that they are called to help guide people into a deeper relationship with God.

2. A ground-up representation of urban church leaders is found in Camilo José Vergara, *How the Other Worships* (New Brunswick: Rutgers University Press, 2005), 123-58.

3. This was the theme of the Faith as a Way of Life Project at Yale Divinity School, organized by Miroslav Volf and directed by Chris Scharen.

4. Michael W. Foley and Dean R. Hoge, *Religion and the New Immigrants: How Faith Communities Form Our Newest Citizens* (Oxford: Oxford University Press, 2007).

5. Mary McClintock Fulkerson, *Places of Redemption: Theology for a Worldly Church* (New York: Oxford University Press, 2007), 52. The italics are in the original.

6. Nayan Chandra, *Bound Together: How Traders, Preachers, Adventurers, and War-*

demic literature attention has been given to the role of non-Christian religious leaders in the diaspora,[7] it is rare to find similar studies of Christian counterparts.[8]

In this chapter, I will first tell the distinctive stories of each pastoral leader: how Mother Cooper came to lead the Church of the Lord (Aladura), Yaw Asiedu the Presbyterian Church of Ghana, and Nimi Wariboko the Redeemed Christian Church of God; what shaped them, and how they learned what they do. Life histories are crucial because they shed light on the path to pastoral ministry and ultimately provide insights into pastoral effectiveness. Second — and this is a theme that will be featured throughout this book — I will describe the paradigm or model of salvation that informs African Christianity and gives distinctive shape to its pastoral work. Third, I describe four domains of pastoral practice: spiritual direction, healing, institutional development, and cultural bridge-building. Finally, I discuss how ministry is distributed among members of the three churches. Throughout, I hope to show how the movement from the development of the practices of ministry to the invocation of church life across borders requires tremendous effort. Such effort makes possible the flourishing of African Christianity in the city.

Religious Biography and Formation

Biographies of religious development among pastors not only record preparation for ministry but also reveal expectations that congregants have for their leaders. The activities of ministry are a piece of an integrated trajectory of ministry that may be described as a pastoral *habitus*, to pick up on

---

riors Shaped Globalization (New Haven: Yale University Press, 2007); see especially chapter four. On the importance of human agency and leadership for the globalization of faith, see Sarah Busse Spencer, "Becoming Global? Evangelism and Transnational Practices in Russian Society," in *Deciphering the Global: Its Scales, Spaces and Subjects*, ed. Saskia Sassen (New York: Routledge, 2007), 79-96.

7. See, for example, Karen McCarthy Brown, *Mama Lola: A Vodou Priestess in Brooklyn* (Berkeley: University of California Press, 2001), and Paul Christopher Johnson, *Black Carib Religion and the Recovery of Africa* (Berkeley: University of California Press, 2007). I adapted the title of this chapter from Johnson. In the next chapter I will define my use of "diaspora."

8. A recent exception is Claudia Währisch-Oblau, *The Missionary Self-Perception of Pentecostal/Charismatic Church Leaders from the Global South in Europe* (Leiden: Brill, 2009), 61-131.

Pierre Bourdieu's terminology.[9] A pastoral *habitus* may be thought of as bodily competence or ability. We might say that pastors *are* their ministries; they do not simply play a role. Body and spirituality meet in the ability to lead, heal, preach, pray, counsel, and develop church life. Traditions, relationships, and networks shape and form the body in such practices. These internalized and durable abilities of knowing, doing, and seeing are appropriated into the systems and persons involved in pastoral ministry. Production and reproduction is involved in pastoral formation; particular disciplines of the self that are associated with Christian life and leadership are structurally passed on to others.

The pastoral lives that I will describe might also be thought of as wisdom, developed through practice over time, which serves the ends of human flourishing.[10] Such wisdom is seen as rooted in the Spirit and a life of prayer, but also in tandem with facing the realities of life. Therefore, to understand and assess the pastoral ministries of Rev. Yaw Asiedu, Mother Marie Cooper, and Pastor Nimi Wariboko, we must first locate them within the stories that shaped them and out of which they continue to operate.[11]

Rev. Yaw Asiedu

A third-generation member of the Presbyterian Church of Ghana and a New Yorker for over thirty years, Yaw Asiedu became the second pastor of the Presbyterian Church of Ghana in Harlem in 2003.[12] For someone growing up in Akropong-Akuwupim, a stronghold for the Basel missionaries that founded the Presbyterian Church of Ghana, few callings were more important than becoming a pastor, and it became Yaw Asiedu's aspiration from an early age. "The call came in secondary school"; it was "to do

---

9. Pierre Bourdieu, *Outline of a Theory of Practice* (Cambridge: Cambridge University Press, 1977), 78-87.

10. For an account of wisdom in relationship to a way of life, see David F. Ford, *Christian Wisdom: Desiring God and Learning in Love* (Cambridge: Cambridge University Press, 2007).

11. The potential of Bourdieu for understanding pastoral formation and my reading of his work comes from Manuel Vásquez. See also Fulkerson, *Places of Redemption*, 48-51, and Manuel Vásquez and Marie Friedmann Marquardt, *Globalizing the Sacred: Religion Across the Americas* (New Brunswick: Rutgers University Press, 2003), 23-24.

12. Yaw Asiedu, Interview, December 6, 2006.

Pastors at Work

Fig. 2.1 Rev. Yaw Asiedu at his ordination service, 2004. Note in the background the first pastor of the church, Rev. Dr. Francis Kumi Dwamena.

God's work." Family and community shaped Rev. Asiedu's "call" to ministry. When it came time to enter the ministry, he reflects, "It's something I wanted to do. I respected working for the Lord."[13]

Moving to New York City in 1975, Asiedu first worked as a bookkeeper and then for over twenty years as a senior planner and production planner for major New York corporations. But over time, the pastoral call became more central. A founding member of the Presbyterian Church of Ghana in New York, Asiedu took on key church responsibilities and roles over the years — Senior Presbyter, Lay Preacher, Bible Study teacher, and Treasurer. He was encouraged in this process by Rev. Dr. Francis Kumi Dwamena, the pastor of the church.

When the position of Minister-in-Charge opened, Asiedu was naturally in place, having acquired skills on the job. But it would take a multiyear sequence of formal services and training in Ghana before Asiedu would formally assume the office. On December 8, 2002, Asiedu

13. Yaw Asiedu, Interview, December 6, 2006.

received his Pastoral Commissioning at Emmanuel Presbyterian Church, Nsawam, Ghana, followed by an induction service in Harlem on June 15, 2003. On September 1, 2003, he officially became the Pastor-in-Charge of the Manhattan congregation. Once Rev. Asiedu's selection as pastor was set, at various times between 2002 and 2004 he travelled to Ghana to take courses in church doctrine and liturgics at Trinity Theological Seminary in Legon and the Ramseyer Training Center in Abetifi. Rev. Asiedu's ordination took place on October 24, 2004, in a service held at the First Ghana Seventh Day Adventist Church in the Bronx, chosen because it offered a much larger venue. Here Asiedu received his ministerial charge from Rev. Dr. Samuel Prempeh, then moderator of the Presbyterian Church of Ghana.

Because Rev. Asiedu's pastorate followed the lengthy term of Rev. Dwamena, who had been ordained to lead the church at its inception in 1988, it began in a period of transition. A dinner and special church service in 2003 attended by denominational leaders from Ghana both honored Dwamena's years of service but also clarified his changing status in the congregation. In Ghana, I was told, Dwamena's retirement would have been regarded much more perfunctorily, but in New York his entrepreneurial efforts required more responsibility and therefore allowed more flexibility in length of service. But the Presbyterian Church of Ghana is keenly interested in order and process, as was demonstrated again here.[14]

Asiedu's style is low-key and soft-spoken. He leads by gentle persuasion and persistence, calling people to "come to Christ" and be "reconciled" to each other. Affectionately and respectfully called "Osofo," which in the Twi language means "pastor," Rev. Asiedu upholds traditions of the Presbyterian Church of Ghana, thereby serving its membership in New York.

Mother Marie Cooper

Mother Cooper describes herself as a missionary with a call to preach the gospel. On the basis of this calling she places herself within the New Testament story. "Two by two" the "Holy Spirit" took the disciples to "different

---

14. Moses Ohene Biney, "Singing the Lord's Song in a Foreign Land: A Socio-Ethical Study of a Ghanaian Immigrant Church in New York" (Ph.D. Diss., Princeton Theological Seminary, 2005), 89-91.

Pastors at Work

Fig. 2.2 Mother Marie Cooper, founder of the Church of the Lord (Aladura) in the Bronx, 2005. Note the cross in her hand and the crucifix on the wall behind her.

places and they started to establish" churches, she explains. Just like the Apostle Paul, who went "place to place," so Mother Cooper interprets her coming to New York City and the establishment of the Church of the Lord (Aladura).[15]

Marie Cooper was born on June 15, 1938, in Monrovia, Liberia.[16] Her ties to the Church of the Lord (Aladura) began in 1953 when she met S. O. Oduwole, a Nigerian missionary sent to establish the church in Liberia. When her mother, who was Pentecostal, died in 1955, the wife of Oduwole, known as Mother Delitia, became her "play mother." This drew her closer to the Church of the Lord (Aladura), and she formally joined the church. As her involvement in its activities and programs grew, she "started to develop in the Spirit." The "Spirit started to use me" and the "love of God filled my heart." But as Mother Cooper emphasizes in telling her story, the "Aladura did not draw me to God. I was just meant to serve God." As part

15. Marie Cooper, Interview, October 17, 2004.
16. Marie Cooper, Interview, March 11, 2005.

of her formation process, in 1965 she lived for three months in Ogere, Nigeria, where the Church of the Lord (Aladura) is based. Here she had contact with the founder of the church, Primate Josiah Ositelu.

Visions and dreams were a part of Mother Cooper's call. In Liberia, a youthful Marie Cooper had a dream that would be important for her calling.[17] "I saw one eye, a single eye, just in the sky, looking down. I saw someone like the Lord, in the sky, and moving toward the east. I said in my dream, that's Jesus, that's Jesus." After she woke up, she felt that it was "incredible the Lord would speak to me." On hearing of the dream, Oduwole assessed, "The eye of the Lord is upon you. He wants to use you."[18] This dream would help establish Mother Cooper on a course for a lifetime of ministry.[19]

Offices and titles are highly structured and regulated in the Church of the Lord (Aladura), with an emphasis in promotion of ministers based not on seniority but on ministerial development.[20] Mother Cooper explains the criteria as a "commitment to the church, the way you serve, and way you carry yourself . . . [being] Christ like." A person is promoted "when people see that in you . . . seeing the Spirit of the Lord in you."[21]

The novice office of the Church of the Lord (Aladura) is crossbearer, which Mother Cooper entered in 1965. A cross-bearer carries a small wooden cross, and the training process in Monrovia involved praying over seven people a day. "You had to do that to develop spiritually," Mother Cooper remembered during a prayer meeting.[22] When you were

17. Dreams have played an important role in ministerial calling in Africa and elsewhere. See Bengt Sundkler, *The Christian Ministry in Africa* (Uppsala: Swedish Institute of Missionary Research, 1960), 26, 30.

18. Marie Cooper, Interview, March 13, 2005.

19. On dreams and the call to ministry in the Church of the Lord (Aladura), see Harold W. Turner, *African Independent Church*, vol. 2: *The Life and Faith of the Church of the Lord (Aladura)* (Oxford: Clarendon Press, 1967), 30. For more background see Sundkler, *The Christian Ministry in Africa*, 5-31. For another view of understanding dreams see David Chidester, "Dreaming in the Contact Zone: Zulu Dreams, Visions, and Religion in Nineteenth-Century South Africa," *Journal of the American Academy of Religion* 76:1 (2008): 27-53.

20. For an earlier review of the process, see Harold W. Turner, *African Independent Church*, vol. 2, 36-41.

21. Mother Cooper, Interview, March 13, 2005. Ritva H. Williams, *Stewards, Prophets, Keepers of the Word: Leadership in the Early Church* (Peabody: Hendrickson, 2006), sees the early church leadership structures evolving out of the work of the Spirit, leading to creative developments. Ecclesiastical roles were rooted in everyday life needs. Something similar may be at work in the Church of the Lord (Aladura).

22. Church of the Lord (Aladura) Service, November 2, 2007.

really formed, that number increased to twenty-one. In 1989 she became a deaconess[23] and then a senior prophetess in 1993, all thus far in the Liberian See. In 2000, she was named an archdeaconess, and this time the ordination was performed in the Bronx by the primate, the head of the Church of the Lord (Aladura). This ordination leaves two primary offices yet to be attained by Mother Cooper, that of reverend mother and reverend mother superior.[24] Pioneering a new branch, as Mother Cooper has done, is one way to advance in the Church of the Lord (Aladura) hierarchy.[25]

Following a number of visits to the United States to see her daughter Joy, who was a student in college, in 1984 Mother Cooper decided to stay, although she continued to go back and forth to Liberia. Residing in New York City, at first she attended two largely African American churches, Epworth United Methodist and then St. Matthew's A.M.E. But feeling that the beliefs and spirituality of the Church of the Lord (Aladura) were missing, within a year Mother Cooper began a prayer group in River Park Towers in the Bronx.[26] The newly formed prayer group met on Wednesday and Friday evenings, and moved around among different apartments. Within a short period of time, Mother Cooper led the prayer group into becoming the first branch of the Church of the Lord (Aladura) in North America. The church receives no financial assistance from the Church of the Lord (Aladura) headquarters or the Liberian See, and as a consequence, Mother Cooper has had to build the church by her own grit and initiative.

In 1993, Mother Cooper was able to purchase a house on Monroe Street in the Mount Eden neighborhood of the Bronx, and it became officially known as a "faith home." In Liberia, a faith home is where ministers live and pray for people; it may include a school and church.[27] Faith homes in Liberia are also sites for midwifery and deliveries. Mother Cooper's daughter Joy was born in one in Liberia. Mother Cooper explains the purpose of the faith home in New York City as a place where "people in need, [the] sick, the unfortunate get help. And also where we do a lot of pray-

---

23. Marie Cooper, Interview, March 13, 2005.

24. Rufus Okikiolaolu Olubiyi Ositelu, *African Instituted Churches: Diversities, Growth, Gifts, Spirituality and Ecumenical Understanding of African Initiated Churches* (Münster: LIT Verlag, 2002), 175.

25. Harold W. Turner, *African Independent Church*, vol. 2, 34.

26. Marie Cooper, Interview, October 17, 2004.

27. For further background on the faith home and its prevalence in Liberia, see Samuel Irving Britt, "The Children of Salvation: Struggle and Cosmology in Liberian Prophet Churches" (Ph.D. diss., University of Virginia, 1992), 172-277.

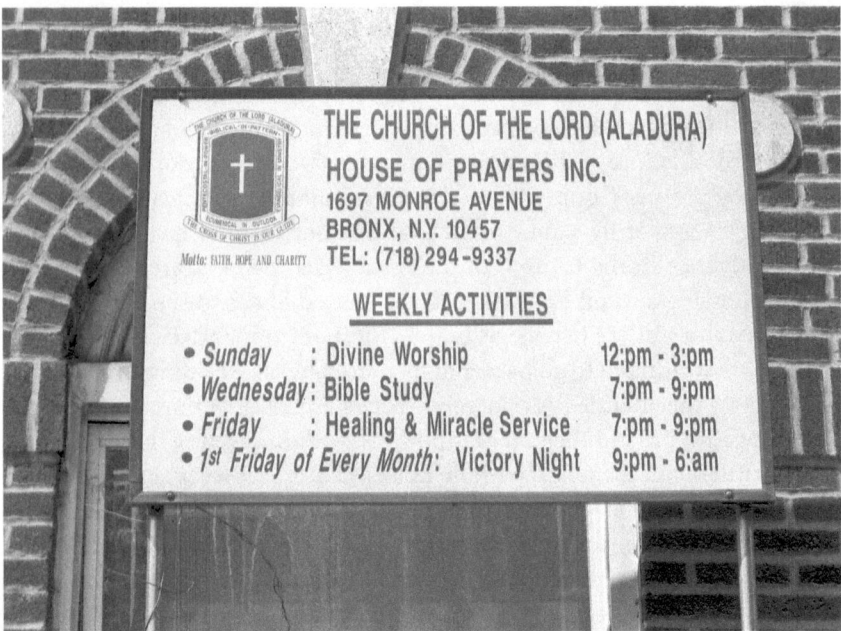

Fig. 2.3. "House of Prayers," 2004

ing."[28] As Samuel Britt explains, the faith home is captured by the images of clinic, refuge, and household.[29] Because the faith home is where prayers are answered, Mother Cooper also refers to it as a House of Prayer.[30]

Mother Cooper's ministerial authority is rooted in her spiritual leadership and prophetic gifts, the use of prophecy and dreams in leading the church. Prophetic authority can become a major factor in conflict over power in the church and how it is used, as is pointed out in Laura Nasrallah's study of early Christian prophecy.[31] However, to my knowledge, this was not a factor in Mother Cooper's leadership during the time of my fieldwork. More relevant are her efforts to form the community, the length of her involvement in the church, and a deep respect for her work of prayer and healing.

28. Marie Cooper, Interview, June 23, 2005.
29. Britt, "The Children of Salvation," 266-77.
30. Marie Cooper, Interview, May 12, 2005.
31. Laura Nasrallah, *An Ecstasy of Folly: Prophecy and Authority in Early Christianity* (Cambridge: Harvard Theological Studies, 2003).

Pastors at Work

Mother Cooper's story indicates the important leadership role women play in the Church of the Lord (Aladura)[32] and are recognized to play in African independent churches.[33] That it is women who share most prominently in the leadership with her may also say something of how women leaders pave the way for women's empowerment in the church.[34]

Pastor Nimi Wariboko

As the cliché goes, if you can make it in New York City, you can make it anywhere. Nimi Wariboko "made it" in New York City.[35] Nimi Wariboko was born on April 4, 1962, in Rivers State, Nigeria, and born again on September 26, 1993, in a Pentecostal Church in Lagos. He was raised and baptized a Lutheran, but it was his born-again experience at one of the parishes of Zoe Ministries Worldwide in Lagos that formed him in the ways of Pentecostal Christianity, especially the practice of reading the Bible, teaching, night vigil, and prayer. At Zoe Ministries Worldwide, Wariboko embarked on an intensive course of Bible study. At his request, the pastor or his assistant would teach him; he would take notes and produce a summary by the next day, repeating the process until he had mastered nearly the entire content of the Bible.[36]

Wariboko first came to New York City in 1990 to start the M.B.A. program in Finance and Accounting at Columbia University.[37] After briefly returning to Nigeria, he moved back to New York and worked as a strategy consultant for investment bankers. Out of concern for his safety following the annulment of the 1993 Nigerian election, one of Wariboko's Columbia professors worked to get him to return to the United States.[38]

---

32. For background and analysis see Deidre Helen Crumbley, "'Power in the Blood': Menstrual Taboos and Women's Power in an African Instituted Church," in *Women and Religion in the African Diaspora: Knowledge, Power, and Performance* (Baltimore: The Johns Hopkins University Press, 2006), 81-97, and "Patriarchies, Prophets, and Procreation: Sources of Gender Practices in Three African Churches," *Africa* 73:4 (2003): 587-88.

33. Philomena N. Mwaura, "Unsung Bearers of Good News: AIC Women and the Transformation of Society in Africa," *Journal of African Christian Thought* 7:1 (2004): 38-44.

34. Bolaj Olukemi Bateye, "Forging Identities: Women as Participants and Leaders in the Church among the Yoruba," *Studies in World Christianity* 13:1 (2007): 1-12.

35. Nimi Wariboko, Interview, November 15, 2006.

36. Nimi Wariboko, Interview, November 15, 2006.

37. Nimi Wariboko, Interview, November 15, 2006.

38. Nimi Wariboko, E-mail Correspondence, June 1, 2007.

FORMATIONS

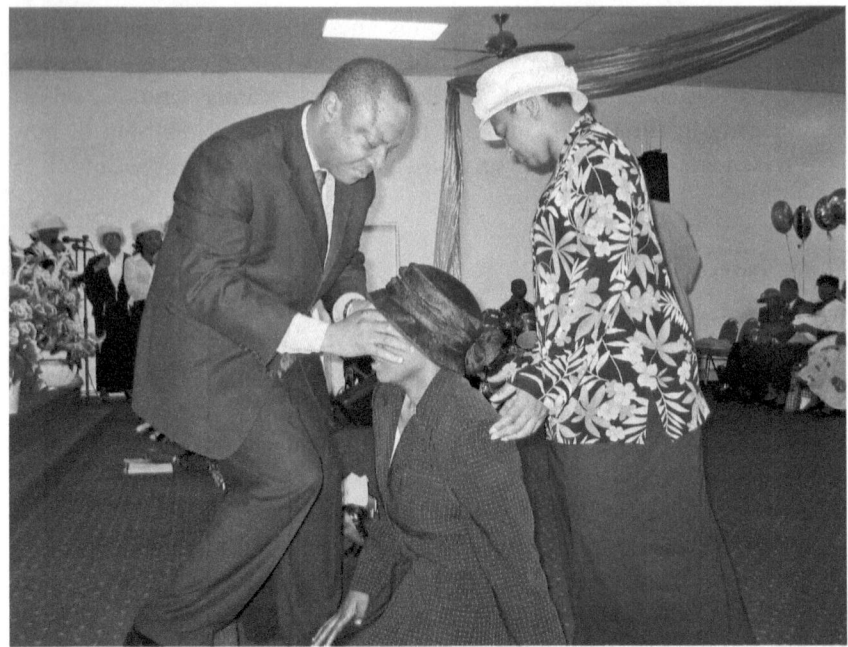

Fig. 2.4 Pastor Nimi Wariboko and Assistant Pastor Wapaemi Wariboko during the consecration of a worker, 2005

Wariboko was able to return to New York City in 1994, when he took up work in corporate finance. This began a career that led to the kind of deals that produce significant compensation and elevated status.

For church life, he attended the Good Shepherd Episcopal Church on Roosevelt Island, serving as treasurer for the vestry. During his search for a church, Wariboko tried Times Square Church in Manhattan, a large and well-known multiethnic charismatic church, but he did not feel at home. In 1995, Wariboko received a telephone call from his cousin in Lagos telling him that there was a Redeemed Christian Church of God congregation on Roosevelt Island. From October 1995 on, he attended the Roosevelt Island branch of Redeemed Christian Church of God "like a visitor." But after completing his final treasury report at Good Shepherd Episcopal in January 1996, Wariboko made a permanent transition to the Redeemed Christian Church of God, led by Olu Obed. At this time, he was re-baptized by immersion, essential for his Pentecostal identity.

Under the influence of Olu and his wife Elsie Obed, Wariboko continued to be formed in ministry, particularly what he calls "the original Redeemed way" and its emphasis on holiness.[39] As Wariboko explains,

> They emphasized the importance of faith, holiness, prayers, and fasting, and sound understanding of biblical teachings. Being right with the Lord at all times is more important than personal fame and glory. I was told a pastor must never put his or her focus on money, fundraising, or gaining personal wealth through the ministry, but should develop industries and talents that will yield income to support the work of God and take care of one's needs. He or she should put emphasis on giving more to God's work and God's people than receiving from the people. The believer must believe that God will always come through.[40]

By March 1998, Wariboko had left the corporate world to begin the first Redeemed Christian Church of God branch in Brooklyn — with over two and half million people, the largest of New York City's five boroughs.

"Nimi does everything as if his life depends on it," his wife, Wapaemi Wariboko, remarks.[41] This was evident in how he built the church: selling his car, spending much of his retirement savings, and working a series of part-time jobs to support his family. This drive was also evident in how quickly Wariboko moved successively through the pastoral offices of the Redeemed Christian Church of God. In the Redeemed Christian Church of God, the offices are worker, minister, deacon/deaconess, assistant pastor, and then finally pastor, the highest position one can attain. Pastor Nimi attained the office of pastor within four years, an achievement that typically requires eight years moving through positions. In addition, while still pastor, Wariboko took on significant academic challenges. He obtained his Master of Divinity degree from Oral Roberts University in 2003 and then a Ph.D. in Social Ethics from Princeton Theological Seminary in 2007 — all this while maintaining a daily spiritual regimen that includes waking at 5:00 a.m. to pray, sing, and devote his mind to the Bible. Wariboko's narrative of success and spiritual discipline is, in many ways, his ministry.

---

39. On this, see Asonzeh Franklin-Kennedy Ukah, "The Redeemed Christian Church of God (RCCG), Nigeria: Local Identities and Global Processes in African Pentecostalism" (Ph.D. diss., Bayreuth, 2003), 130-31.
40. Nimi Wariboko, E-mail Correspondence, June 1, 2007.
41. Wapaemi Wariboko, Interview, May 29, 2005.

Wapaemi Wariboko is assistant pastor of the church, a title that recognizes her ministry in the Redeemed Christian Church of God even as she serves as a public school teacher. She and Nimi have three children. She is not the co-pastor and, as I recall, was never referred to publicly as the "first lady" of the church. In this instance, husband and wife are seen as having their own calls to ministry and distinctive roles. As has been pointed out elsewhere, in Pentecostalism there can be a juxtaposition of egalitarianism and traditional gender roles.[42] As the wife of the pastor in Redeemed, there is a clear expectation that she will be in charge of the children's ministry.[43] However, Sister Wapaemi's work in the church is not limited to this area. Instead, week after week, she can be seen providing pastoral care as she prays with people, preaches, and especially counsels women in the church. Seated on the platform each Sunday are both men and women, in a powerful image of gender equality. Overall, in the Brooklyn church we see what appears to be equality in ministry between men and women at the Brooklyn parish, with no limitations on what women can do in the parish.[44]

Routes to Ministry

These three accounts of pastoral formation indicate that while there is more than a single route for ministerial formation and call, the overall trajectory involves a certain kind of experience and practice being reproduced in each person. For Rev. Asiedu, it is a story that took place over a lifetime, being raised in an institutional tradition and then being further directed in it while in New York. It also required formal training in Ghana. For Mother Cooper, the role of dreams and God's direct involvement in establishing a call to ministry are crucial. Her religious authority is derived from her spiritual connection to God, with visions, dreams, and revelations, but also her singular focus on the disciplines of prayer and nononsense convictions of faith. As a Pentecostal minister, the stress for

---

42. Jane E. Soothill's *Gender, Social Change and Spiritual Power: Charismatic Christianity in Ghana* (Leiden: Brill, 2007) is an important study on the Pentecostal discourse and practice surrounding women in ministry in Ghana that also resonates more widely.

43. Soothill, *Gender, Social Change and Spiritual Power.*

44. For an important account, see Regina Gemignani, "Gender, Identity, and Power in African Immigrant Evangelical Churches," in *African Immigrant Religions in America*, ed. Jacob K. Olupona and Regina Gemignani (New York: New York University Press, 2007), 133-57. This equality appears, however, to stop at the level of the senior hierarchy of the Redeemed Christian Church of God, which seems to be all male.

Wariboko falls on being anointed or filled with the Spirit. He is a "man of God," a common appellative in the Pentecostal tradition for the pastor. Were the pastor a woman, it would be "woman of God."

Although formal seminary training was required of Rev. Asiedu, the internal process of formation, the gifting of the Spirit, and the willingness to do the work are the predominant factors in ministerial development. Once into their vocations, ministers often receive further training. For Mother Cooper and Pastor Wariboko, what is most fundamental is the bodily character of the Spirit, evidenced in dreams, visions, being born again, and an anointing. To be anointed is to be filled completely by the Spirit; in many inflections, this is how actions of the Spirit come to pass. Charismatic gifting for pastoral work is all-defining. For Rev. Asiedu what is at stake in pastoral vocation requires recognition, formation, and approval on an institutional level. In different ways, this is also true for Mother Cooper and Pastor Wariboko. What comes first and has priority differs by tradition.

Imagining Salvation

The starting point of ministry for African pastors in New York is an understanding that salvation is not just for the future, but very real for the present.[45] Each pastor approaches ministry with theological nuance and emphasis, but the task they share is the same: to care for the members of their congregation in a manner that speaks to their spiritual and social realities, help navigate the uncertainties, opportunities, and losses of a globalized world, and most prominently, experience the liberation, power, and healing of salvation.[46] As we will see, the underpinning of a "successful" pasto-

---

45. For a significant argument that emphasizes context in the development of a doctrine of salvation across traditions, see Abraham Akrong, "Salvation in African Christianity," *Legon Journal of the Humanities* 12 (1991-2001): 1-29. For a historical approach that, like Akrong, places salvation at the front of Christian theology, see Mark A. McIntosh, *Divine Teaching: An Introduction to Christian Theology* (Malden, Mass.: Blackwell, 2008), 57-110. For a description of salvation in the early church, see Luke Timothy Johnson, *The Writings of the New Testament: An Interpretation*, rev. ed. (Minneapolis: Fortress, 1999), 99-105. For an additional view, see Girish Daswani, "Transformation and Migration among Members of a Pentecostal Church in Ghana and London," *Journal of Religion in Africa* 40:4 (2010): 442-74.

46. For reflections on salvation that affirm my argument, see Ogbu Kalu, *African Pentecostalism: An Introduction* (New York: Oxford University Press, 2008), 6, 64-83, and Caroline Jeannerat, "Of Lizards, Misfortune and Deliverance: Pentecostal Soteriology in the Life of a Migrant," *African Studies* 68:2 (2009): 251-71.

ral ministry in African churches in New York is this holistic theology or paradigm of salvation that has personal, cosmic, physical, spiritual, and material dimensions.[47] This salvation empowers African immigrants to overcome all obstacles, to bear witness to the gospel, and be transformed in every area of life.

In his book *Imagining Redemption*, David Kelsey provides a careful discussion that begins by asking basic questions about what God's work in Christ means for a pastoral situation.[48] To put "salvation" in the form of a series of questions relevant for the context at hand: What does it mean that Jesus saves? What did Christ's death accomplish? How does the cross deliver? What are the conditions God saves from?[49] African Christians offer decisive and distinct answers that relate to life in New York City. In short, salvation is holistic: through the blood of the cross, God saves body and soul, in the material and cosmic, the immediate and the eternal. That God saves means God delivers in the present reality.

What does salvation mean for the everyday life of African Christians? The life-giving power of salvation is well described by J. Kwabena Asamoah-Gyadu in *African Charismatics: Current Developments within Independent Indigenous Pentecostalism in Ghana*.[50] In summaries that are intended to be descriptive and apply more broadly, Asamoah-Gyadu selects three main themes to describe salvation. First, salvation means transformation and empowerment, linked through a Pentecostal new birth.[51] The horizon within which a new birth is seen is a "salvific process that is conceived primarily in terms of a cosmic battle between God and the forces of evil."[52]

---

47. Waldo César suggests Pentecostalism may represent a new paradigm of salvation in "From Babel to Pentecost: A Socio-Historical-Theological Study of the Growth of Pentecostalism," in André Corten and Ruth Marshall-Fratani, eds., *Between Babel and Pentecost: Transnational Pentecostalism in Africa and Latin America* (Bloomington: University of Indiana Press, 2001), 38. See also Harvey Cox, *Fire from Heaven: The Rise of Pentecostal Spirituality and the Reshaping of Religion in the Twenty-First Century* (Reading: Addison-Wesley, 1995), and Dale Coulter, "'Delivered by the Power of God': Toward a Pentecostal Understanding of Salvation," *International Journal of Systematic Theology* 10:4 (2008): 447-67.

48. David H. Kelsey, *Imagining Redemption* (Louisville: Westminster John Knox Press, 2005).

49. For a statement of such questions, see Gerald O'Collins, *Jesus Our Redeemer: A Christian Approach to Salvation* (Oxford: Oxford University Press, 2007).

50. J. Kwabena Asamoah-Gyadu, *African Charismatics: Current Developments within Independent Indigenous Pentecostalism in Ghana* (Leiden: Brill, 2005), 132-63.

51. Asamoah-Gyadu, *African Charismatics*, 137-41.

52. Asamoah-Gyadu, *African Charismatics*, 142, 143-44.

Pastors at Work

Because Christ has defeated the powers, salvation empowers and can be expressed through "redemptive uplift."[53] Christ's rule also brings anointing and restoration of spiritual gifts. Second, salvation also involves healing and deliverance, a fundamental experience of being born again.[54] This can be also be viewed as an aspect of empowerment and liberation. Third, salvation constructively leads the believer to prosperity and fruitfulness.[55] The totality of salvation is attributed to God, the presence of the Spirit, and the Lordship of Christ.

Salvation also means a new "state" in which people find themselves.[56] To be "born again," the principal idiom of conversion in Pentecostal churches, and increasingly the language of choice in many African church traditions, is to have the Spirit fill the body, thereby affecting every area of life and social encounter. Ruth Marshall speaks of the born-again idiom as identifying a new subjectivity, with attendant political ramifications.[57] As Marshall comments, "The project of conversion involves the elaboration of new modes of government of the self and of others, in which practices of faith are fostered by specific disciplines of the body and the mind, emphasizing purity, rectitude, righteousness and interiority."[58] The theological emphasis of the churches is that we are our bodies, and bodies are part of how believers are saved and live a new life.[59] To be saved is to have a body filled with the Holy Spirit, and live in the power of God's control and direction. Salvation is characteristically described not as a singular past event or future heavenly expectation, but a present and ongoing experience of Christ.

"African maps of the universe" or "cosmologies" require a holistic view of salvation.[60] Here Christian faith is incarnated within a culture,

---

53. Asamoah-Gyadu, *African Charismatics*, 152-54.

54. Asamoah-Gyadu, *African Charismatics*, 164-200.

55. Asamoah-Gyadu, *African Charismatics*, 201-32.

56. Johnson, *The Writings of the New Testament*, 102.

57. Ruth Marshall, *Political Spiritualities: The Pentecostal Revolution in Nigeria* (Chicago: The University of Chicago Press, 2009).

58. Marshall, *Political Spiritualities*, 3.

59. On the importance of the body, see Katrien Pype, "Dancing for God or the Devil: Pentecostal Discourse on Popular Dance in Kinshasa," *Journal of Religion in Africa* 36:3-4 (2006): 296-318; R. Marie Griffith, *Born Again Bodies: Flesh and Spirit in American Christianity* (Berkeley: University of California Press, 2004); Thomas J. Csordas, *Body/Meaning/Healing* (New York: Palgrave Macmillan, 2002).

60. Ogbu U. Kalu, "Preserving a Worldview: Pentecostalism in the African Maps of the Universe," *Pneuma* 24:2 (2002): 110-37. See also Abbebe Kileyesus, "Cosmologies in Col-

turning through salvation all to Christ. Transnational migration has not erased African maps of the universe,[61] and in fact, as Vasudha Narayanan suggests, the maintenance of cosmologies may well be a key feature of religion in a global and mobile age.[62] In New York City, with its new structures and relationships, the encounter with malevolent forces just grows more complex, still requiring that the same spiritual resources be deployed.

Pastoral effectiveness in African churches in New York depends on an approach to ministry grounded in a shared cosmology, epistemology, and doctrine of salvation.[63] Reality is what is seen and unseen; the two are interwoven.[64] Pastors seek to guide their congregants to place their stories and problems in the script of salvation, the living experience of the work of Jesus. The work of the cross is described not by contractual or judicial terms, but with a cosmic and life-giving emphasis. By the "stripes" or blood of Jesus there is redemption from the past, all powers and obstacles can be overcome, and God is continually able to do something new in life. Christ's saving death, the victory of the "blood," continues to overcome generational curses, witchcraft, evil powers, and all obstacles to a life of flourishing.

How do African Christians describe the efficacy of salvation? Testimonies, a staple of worship services and prayer meetings, almost never recount sins or moral failings, or even conversion stories, but offer witness to the present power of God in healing, protection, blessing, and abundance. Christianity in Africa is not driven by the intellectual questions and problems of the West; instead it faces matters of life and death, and must answer these credibly or Christian faith is meaningless. Doubts are not about the existence of God, but concerns regarding how God will save me here and now. The same applies to the African churches in New York City.

Each African church in New York City places their stories within a

---

lision: Pentecostal Conversion and Christian Cults in Asmara," *African Studies Review* 49:1 (2006): 75-92, and Allan Anderson, "Stretching the Definitions? Pneumatology and 'Syncretism' in African Pentecostalism," *Journal of Pentecostal Theology* 10:1 (2001): 98-119.

61. Afe Adogame, "Engaging the Rhetoric of Spiritual Warfare: The Public Face of Aladura in Diaspora," *Journal of Religion in Africa* 34:4 (2004): 493-522.

62. Vasudha Narayanan, "Embodied Cosmologies: Sights of Piety, Sites of Power," *Journal of the American Academy of Religion* 71:3 (2003): 495-520.

63. Britt, "The Children of Salvation," 64-170.

64. See Stephen Ellis and Gerrie ter Haar, *Worlds of Power: Religious Thought and Political Practice in Africa* (New York: Oxford University Press, 2004), 49-69, 97, on the importance of the "spirit world" and its continuing importance in migration.

story of redemption as we have been describing it. For each of the three focus churches, the script of salvation is given slightly different emphases: for Mother Cooper and the Church of the Lord (Aladura), it is the cross that most fully expresses God's saving work and the struggle that exists; for Pastor Wariboko at Redeemed Christian Church of God International Chapel, Brooklyn, it is the victorious and risen Christ that gives abundant life in the Spirit; for Rev. Asiedu of the Presbyterian Church of Ghana in New York, it is simply Jesus who personally saves by faith, plus the embellishments of the charismatic life. But a thread running through each church is salvation as a way of seeing, living, and acting[65] in light of the new freedom and authority in the Spirit. Healing of the body, restoring relationships across generations and borders, protection from all that can go wrong, and the gifts of sustenance are integral. A Spirit-filled passion or pneumatological emphasis stands at the heart of this picture of salvation.

The vocabulary associated with how salvation is described is instructive. Drawing on a range of prominent biblical vocabulary, the terms which are used include "healed," "blessed," transformed," "changed," "born again," and "anointed." Few passages cited by the churches better capture the everyday conception of human flourishing than Psalm 23:6, which reads, "Surely goodness and mercy shall follow me all the days of my life, and I will dwell in the house of the Lord forever." Often used as a communal benediction in Pentecostal and other churches, it affirms God's beneficence in this life. As the noted scholar Robert Alter offers, the concluding phrase, which he translates as "all my days," "does not mean 'forever'; the view of the poem is in the here and now and is no way eschatological. The speaker hopes for a happy fate all his born days, and prays for the good fortune to abide in the Lord's sanctuary — a place of security and harmony with the divine — all, or perhaps at least most, of those days."[66]

Pastors translate this vision of salvation into an effective framework for ministry that can be termed a "pastoral imagination." I adopt the term "pastoral imagination" from Craig Dykstra, a leading expert in ministerial formation and practice. According to Dykstra,

> It is beautiful to see a good pastor at work. Somehow, pastors who really get what the Christian ministry is all about and who do it well are able

---

65. Asamoah-Gyadu, *African Charismatics*, 165.
66. According to Robert Alter, *The Book of Psalms: A Translation with Commentary* (New York: W. W. Norton, 2007), 60.

to enter many diverse situations, whether joyous or full of misery and conflict, and see what is going on there through the eyes of faith. This way of seeing and interpreting shapes what the pastor thinks and does and how he or she responds to people in gestures, words, and actions. It functions as a kind of internal gyroscope, guiding pastors in and through every crevice of pastoral life and work. This way of seeing and interpreting is what I mean by "pastoral imagination."[67]

When a good pastor is at work, the end result, Dykstra reflects, is that the community of faith "comes increasingly to share the knowledge of God and to live a way of abundant life — not only in church but also in the many contexts where they live their daily lives."[68] This provides a wonderful encapsulation of what Rev. Asiedu, Mother Cooper, and Pastor Wariboko do.

It is an African pastoral imagination that guides the ministries of Rev. Asiedu, Mother Cooper, and Pastor Wariboko. In the African Christian context, a pastoral imagination enables pastors to make connections between God, the unseen but real world of spiritual forces, the diaspora journey, and the material and social dimensions of everyday life. It constitutes a particular way of seeing the urgencies of life through the eyes of faith.

Domains of Pastoral Practice

Throughout the course of their regular pastoral duties, Rev. Asiedu, Mother Cooper, and Pastor Wariboko teach the Bible, preach sermons, perform "baby naming" and dedication ceremonies, counsel members, chair meetings, and otherwise lead their congregations. Formed in a way of life and oriented to seeing the world through the eyes of faith, pastors are able to imagine and build communities through four primary and overlapping domains of activity. First, pastors are *spiritual directors*. Second, they are *agents of healing*, directing ministries of healing that lead members into outcomes of liberation and empowerment. Third, pastors are *institution builders*, which means that they must take the idea of a

---

67. Craig Dykstra, "Pastoral and Ecclesial Imagination: What Practical Theology Seeks to Nourish," in *For Life Abundant: Practical Theology, Theological Education, and Christian Ministry*, ed. Dorothy C. Bass and Craig Dykstra (Grand Rapids: Eerdmans, 2008), 41.

68. Dykstra, "Pastoral and Ecclesial Imagination," 57.

church and execute it so it is sustainable. Fourth, pastors are *cultural intermediaries*, helping their members succeed in a new cultural setting. While churches are mediating institutions,[69] pastoral work mediates a way of understanding God, the world, and redemption, not as a simple recipe but a process adapted and calibrated to new settings. The overall effect is a richly woven pastoral ministry.

Spiritual Directors

First, the pastor is a spiritual director or problem solver, a type of ministry that is illustrated by the following story. A Christian woman was experiencing recurring dreams of a "spirit husband." A spirit husband joins a woman in her dreams, and this spirit husband was trying to destroy the woman's life and possibility of a future husband. No Western church or theology in New York was able to appreciate and therefore address this problem — even a prominent American Pentecostal church. But with diagnosis and counseling from an African minister in New York City, the woman traveled back home to attend a prayer camp where she experienced an explanation and deliverance of her problem. Today she enjoys a healthy marriage, and is no longer visited by the spirit husband. In many respects, this is not an unusual sort of story. Pastors are spiritual directors who address spiritual problems through insight gained by prayer, fasting, and Scripture.

In *Patterns of Thought in Africa and the West*[70] Robin Horton considers the role of religion the "world over," but then turns his observations to elements he sees as most salient in Africa. One of the key conclusions for Horton is that religion can provide "explanation, prediction, and control of this-worldly events."[71] Indeed, this is what religion necessarily must do for many people, Horton argues: "On the basis of massive evidence as to the contexts in which religious thought and action are evoked in everyday social life, we can confidently say that the vast majorities of religions, both past and present, are above all else bodies of theory regarding the underly-

---

69. See Margarita A. Mooney, *Faith Makes Us Live: Surviving and Thriving in the Haitian Diaspora* (Berkeley: University of California Press, 2009).

70. Robin Horton, *Patterns of Thought in Africa and the West: Essays on Magic, Religion and Science* (Cambridge: Cambridge University Press, 1993).

71. Horton, *Patterns of Thought in Africa and the West*, 119; cf. 372-73; also, Robin Horton, "African Conversion," *Africa* 41:2 (1971): 85-108.

ing character of the world, from which flow repertoires of action aimed at practical control of the vicissitudes of life."[72] That this is not true of "the religious life of the educated classes in the modern West" is "an exception that proves the rule."[73] Horton observes that, in African church life, religion must effect change or life is lost.[74]

Horton has been criticized for being too rationalistic,[75] but Pastor Nimi Wariboko believes Horton "gets" the essential dynamics of African pastoral ministry.

> For traditional Africans, explanation is based on the use of the idea of unobservable underlying realities of gods to make sense of the contingencies of everyday existence. Failures, sickness, fortunes, and misfortunes are causally linked to a wide range of social conditions via gods. Africans use the interpretive scheme of the spiritual forces to transcend the limited vision of cause and effect relationship provided by common sense. I think this view or definition of religion is correct. [Horton] got it right. Pentecostalism in Africa, or in Nigeria that I know so well, views the import of Christianity or spiritual gifts in this light.... "Explanation, prediction, and control" is now done through the power of the Holy Spirit.[76]

For Wariboko, the features of "explanation, prediction, and control" found in African religion must be addressed by Christian pastors, but in their own ways. This is not a pastoral strategy based on feelings or intuitions, but involves a rigorous intellectual system that responds to the questions and needs of persons and communities.

Pastoral ministry in African Christianity is concerned with life, its fullness and hopes, from birth to death, imbuing each chapter with a sacramental character. It involves the daily work of helping people to see, live, and work ever more deeply in the experience of Christ's salvation. Such work is reflective of the imaginative character of pastoral ministry that Dykstra explicates.[77] It involves a way of thinking and acting drawn from

72. Horton, *Patterns of Thought in Africa and the West*, 119.
73. Horton, *Patterns of Thought in Africa and the West*, 119-20.
74. Horton, *Patterns of Thought in Africa and the West*, 156-57. See further Horton, "African Conversion."
75. Birgit Meyer, "Christianity in Africa: From African Independent to Pentecostal-Charismatic Churches," *Annual Review of Anthropology* 33 (2004): 458.
76. Nimi Wariboko, E-mail Correspondence, July 29, 2004.
77. Dykstra, "Pastoral and Ecclesial Imagination," 41-61.

the scriptural narrative (with its assumption of a complex spiritual world) but also within the African cultural landscape. The Christian *difference* of explanation, prediction, and control is found in Christ and the Holy Spirit, yet internal to culture.[78]

Good ministry in African churches in New York City must therefore have what is sometimes called "cultural intelligence"; pastoral ministry must be able to account faithfully for the frameworks that parishioners bring with them in a new social and cultural context. As bodies exist in global transit, the pastoral imagination must continue to be adaptive to guide in new and complex settings. Malevolent forces can be found in sick bodies, bad dreams, and careers that have ground to a halt. Spiritual direction helps people see the source of their problems and discern how God redeems and directs them into paths of abundant life. Each pastor engages in this sort of problem-solving by way of counseling, applying some level of explanation, prediction, and control.

Mother Cooper provides spiritual direction by identifying the "enemy" as Satan.[79] "We pray every day that the Lord will help us." Satan's angels and messengers are invisible: "Witchcraft [is the] same as Satan's angels. Satan can really possess. . . . Demons are led by Satan." Water is a "cleansing" for "any kind of forces," "protection" from "witches and wizards." Water represents God's creative Spirit that provides protection. "Satan is fighting you to take you away from the Lord," but the "Lord gave us will power." Hence pastoral ministry involves a "struggle"[80] to overcome and live in the protection of Jesus.

Much of Mother Cooper's pastoral ministry takes place outside the church with much larger communities that seek her out. Whenever I visited with Mother Cooper, her telephone would ring with news from Liberia or someone in the New York area seeking pastoral assistance. During one of our conversations at the House of Prayer, she received a telephone call from a woman seeking her counsel.[81] Referencing the Old Testament figure Job, Mother Cooper explained, "God gives us tests, anytime, anywhere." Mother Cooper urged her "to keep going . . . can't give up, no mat-

---

78. For relevant reflections on the gospel and culture, see Miroslav Volf, "When Gospel and Culture Intersect: Notes on the Nature of Christian Difference," in *Pentecostalism in Context: Essays in Honor of William W. Menzies,* ed. Wonsuk Ma and Robert P. Menzies (Sheffield: Sheffield Academic Press, 1997), 223-36.

79. This paragraph draws on Marie Cooper, Interview, February 13, 2005.

80. I came to a similar conclusion here as Britt, "The Children of Salvation."

81. Marie Cooper, Interview, March 15, 2005.

ter how hard it is." Offering a reminder that "you are not living for anyone — you're living for God and yourself," Mother Cooper then quoted from Proverbs: "You know the fear of God is the beginning of wisdom." During the conversation, Mother Cooper was often silent, listening. She asked, "Do you still go to church? Do you still have faith in God?" At the end of the conversation, Mother Cooper said that she intended to "keep" her in prayers, and proceeded to do just that on the telephone. Mother Cooper asked that God would "strengthen her" and "wipe her tears . . . heal her body." She reminded the woman that "at times the doctor gave up," but God did not. Mother Cooper then asked God to "touch her from the crown of her head to the soles of her feet . . . bless her, heal her." The prayer stressed and repeated an interest in the woman as body and soul, and also emphasized God's involvement in her everyday life. This encounter exemplified the centrality of prayer to Mother Cooper's pastoral ministry, and the perception people have of her as a woman of prayer. As the "spiritual leader of the church . . . I do a lot of praying. People bring me their problems and we pray about it."

Agents of Healing

The domain of spiritual direction overlaps with healing. As an integral part of their ministries, Yaw Asiedu, Mother Cooper, and Nimi Wariboko are agents of God's healing power. Healing is not limited to the isolated reversal of illness but addresses all problems, family situations, challenges at work, and a vast array of demonic influences, spiritual beings, and witchcraft.[82] Healing can take place by the touch of hands, prayers, words of knowledge, revelations, water that has been prayed over, visions, and preachments. Pastors are seen as "anointed," that is, completely filled with the Spirit and given over to God, and therefore able to be used by God for things to come to pass. Causation of disease and problems is a complex matter, with spiritual forces seen as a common source.[83] In practice, each church and pastor recognizes a difference between something like "executive possession" (when a whole identity is controlled) and a "pathogenic

---

82. René Devisch, "'Pillaging Jesus': Healing Churches and the Villagisation of Kinshasa," *Africa* 66:4 (1996): 565.

83. David Westerlund, *African Indigenous Religions and Disease Causation: From Spiritual Beings to Living Human Beings* (Leiden: Brill, 2006).

Fig. 2.5 "Local and Global" Healing Team of Rev. Yaw Asiedu, Samuel Asare from Grace Presbyterian Church in Ghana, and Angelina Akiwumi, 2006. Note the open Bible on the desk.

possession" (possessing spirits of illness).[84] This conceptual structure impacts diagnosis and the healing process. A Christian can still face powerful spirits and yet not lose central identity in Christ. It also explains why some situations require continual healing and divine intervention.

While such acts of healing can take place any time and at any liturgical celebration, pastors have especially focused on creating systems of healing in their churches. In the New Testament, James 5:14 provides a description of healing practices within the early church: "Are any among you sick? They should call for the elders of the church and have them pray over them, anointing them with oil in the name of the Lord."[85] In African

---

84. I am adapting the distinctions presented by Emma Cohen, "What Is Spirit Possession? Defining, Comparing, and Explaining Two Possession Forms," *Ethnos* 73:1 (2008): 101-26.

85. NRSV; see further Martin C. Abbl, "'Are Any Among You Sick?' The Health Care System in the Letter of James," *Journal of Biblical Literature* 121:1 (2002): 123-43.

churches in New York City, healing arises out of that same worldview as it pertains to illness, dependence on God, and a frequent lack of access to medical care. It belongs to a story with a number of integral components: God's goodness in creation, salvation that is freedom from spiritual forces, and the Spirit's work in seeing that persons experience the wholeness, joy, and development that is characteristic of God's intentions for them.[86] While the focus is on healing individuals, the mechanisms are communal.[87] Although all members are expected to tithe and make offerings of thanksgiving to their church, there is no fee charged for this ministry.[88]

As a denomination founded by Western missionaries that discounted unseen spiritual realities, powers, and healing, the Presbyterian Church of Ghana has relatively recently moved formally into ministries of healing. But healing and deliverance ministries are now vitally important to the church. The systems of healing at the Presbyterian Church of Ghana in New York City are grounded in transnational networks, linking religious leaders with special skills in healing between Ghana and New York City.[89] Here the key network for healing at the Presbyterian Church of Ghana in New York involves the travelling healing team from Grace Presbyterian Church in Ghana, led by Catechist E. A. Abboah-Offei, who is referred to simply as "the Catechist." Abboah-Offei is regarded as one of the most important leaders of charismatic renewal within the Presbyterian Church in Ghana, and with his travels to North America, his ministry has been extended and has grown in stature. Abboah-Offei and Samuel Asare from Grace Presbyterian Church travel at least yearly to New York, with not less than ninety percent of the church membership regularly cycling through their care.[90] The ministry of

---

86. Here note Wayne A. Meeks, *The Origins of Christian Morality: The First Two Centuries* (New Haven: Yale University Press, 1993), 101, 112-14.

87. See Hansjörg Dilger, "Healing the Wounds of Modernity: Salvation, Community and Care in a Neo-Pentecostal Church in Dar Es Salaam, Tanzania," *Journal of Religion in Africa* 37:1 (2007): 59-83.

88. James Pfeiffer, "Commodity *Fetichismo*, The Holy Spirit, and the Turn to Pentecostal and African Independent Churches in Central Mozambique," *Culture, Medicine and Psychiatry* 29 (2005): 255-83.

89. They are also called "therapy networks." See Kristine Krause, "Transnational Therapy Networks among Ghanaians in London," *Journal of Ethnic and Migration Studies* 34:2 (2008): 235-41.

90. Yaw Asiedu, Interview, November 8, 2005. For a significant account of this development, see Adam Mohr, "'Their Journeys Were Not Without Demonic Confrontation': Healing and Migration in the Presbyterian Church of Ghana" (Ph.D. Diss., University of Pennsylvania, 2008).

the healing team consists of consultations, diagnosis of problems, directives for healing prayers, and preaching for renewal and mission.

I observed more than one of their frequent visits to the church in Harlem.[91] Here is an example. On Monday, the first day that Abboah-Offei and Asare were available for consultations at the church offices during their October Mission 2005 to New York, the room was filled with people waiting for an appointment. Abboah-Offei and Asare came from the Akuapem Presbytery of the Presbyterian Church in Ghana, which at first sent them "as a means of bringing God's blessings" and to help raise funds for the Presbyterian University College Akuapem Campus.[92] The team had been in the United States for seven weeks, holding a retreat as well as services and consultations in a number of churches with only a single day of rest, according to Asare.

A few days later, as people awaited their appointments, an evangelist preached from the pulpit, proclaiming God's love and power to heal. In the back of the room, a group of women sang. Asare described their mission to New York with the acronym "PHD" — Preaching, Healing, Deliverance.[93] All three components marked the team's time with the church, and also in subsequent visits. There was preaching at night vigils, and healing during the night services and in consultations, along with deliverance. The frequency and prominence of the visits, along with the high level of participation, are evidence of the "charismatic spirituality"[94] that marks the life of the Presbyterian Church of Ghana in Harlem.

Consultations for healing were similar to a meeting with a physician or doctor. Before the appointment, individuals filled out a multi-page, confidential questionnaire that asked questions covering everything from their relationship with God to family background to personal life to religious history, probing for anything that might have a spiritual hold on their life.[95] In the counseling (or consultation) session, the team leader "scrutinizes a person's life." Perhaps they need to go to a medical doctor, regularly take their "tablets," or are in need of prayer and deliverance. Dis-

---

91. During the week of October 24, 2005.

92. Correspondence from Rev. C. B. Ahwireng to Rev. Moses Biney, April 13, 2005.

93. Samuel Asare, Interview, October 27, 2005.

94. Cephas N. Omenyo, *Pentecost Outside Pentecostalism: A Study of the Development of Charismatic Renewal in the Mainline Churches in Ghana* (Zoetermeer: Uitgeverij Boekencentrum, 2002), 201.

95. Interview with Samuel Asare, December 13, 2006. See also Adam Mohr, "'Their Journeys Were Not without Demonic Confrontation': Healing and Migration in the Presbyterian Church of Ghana" (Ph.D. thesis, University of Pennsylvania, 2008).

cerning causation was the first step. That is why the one-on-one sessions with Abboah-Offei or Asare were so crucial. To emphasize that medicine can be important, Asare showed me the medicine tablets that he takes.

Church members presented a range of needs or complaints to the team. Mr. Asare leafed through the thick packet of sheets that asked for prayer and healing, requests that included "to grow in Christ," "family needs," "son," "green card," "debt," and "bad habits." The healing team addressed such problems through prayer, reading lines of Scripture, and the repetition of theological beliefs. The different papers, what we could call prescriptions or cures, addressed a range of issues, among them deliverance, demonic foundations, healing, death, and fetishes. Speaking about the team's role, Asare commented, "We don't believe [we're] special people. God will heal him." Still, many people look to the catechist and the team for healing; the healing context is both God and God working through the catechist working through God.

At the Church of the Lord (Aladura) there is a great orientation directed toward healing in the broadest sense. As Mother Cooper describes healing, it is "prayer [that] holds you up and keeps you going . . . brings comfort where [there is] sorrow."[96] Healing is carried out each week at the Church of the Lord (Aladura), animated by prayer and anointed with oil. Near the end of each service, people come forward and kneel for God's anointing. Blessed water may also be offered. For example, if a person is not feeling well, water that is blessed or consecrated may be suggested for use in a "spiritual bath."[97] And as noted above, Mother Cooper began with the development of the faith home, a place of healing.

Healing is integral to the ministry and outlook of the Redeemed Christian Church of God International Chapel, Brooklyn. One of the weekly ministries of the church is the "Expect a Miracle" service held on Wednesday mornings. By definition, people have come because they have a need and require a miracle or divine intervention.

The service I describe here took place in August 2004.[98] Beginning at 10:00 a.m., Sister Catherine Oboh Idusuti, a minister in the church, led the small group of mostly women but also men in song and prayer. This continued for more than one and half hours. Then Pastor Wariboko began to speak in the service, starting with the exclamation, "Let somebody shout

---

96. Mother Cooper, Interview, May 12, 2005.
97. For more background, see Britt, "The Children of Salvation," 600-647.
98. August 25, 2004.

Hallelujah!" "Praise to God — Prince of Peace, El Shaddai, Mighty God, Alpha and Omega . . . may the Holy Ghost come and take control," he prayed. The singing continued, with choruses such as "You are so excellent in my every day" and "He [Jesus] is high and lifted up." Wariboko challenged the church to "be bold and tell him what you need" but then followed quickly with a call to thank God for "saving you." He assured his listeners that "It is not over for you. The Lord Almighty is here," and reminded them that Lazarus was brought back to life. With expectations building, Wariboko then took "prayer points" and "testimonies."

The first prayer point came from a member trying to obtain a "promotion" at work, and a salary increase. Wariboko recalled King Ahasuerus, who "could not sleep until Mordecai was promoted." The pastor said, "We will pray for this sister" and asked everyone present to "begin to raise up your voices and pray" that "God will not allow injustice to reign." The second prayer point came from a woman in need of a visa. Next came a prayer point that the "Lord be manifested" in this building, a recurrent theme, especially in light of the church's vulnerability to the landlord. A fourth person offered a testimony of God's "faithfulness . . . for bringing me here to America . . . the opportunity to study." Wariboko interjected, "God gives grace to study and excel." The fifth prayer point involved a problem with a husband; this was discussed longer than the other issues raised. This woman voiced confidence in God's provision, believing that she should pray and "relax and give everything to God," yet showed emotion as she told of being in a difficult place, of wondering how her husband felt about her. Wariboko responded that by marrying her, the husband had "made a good catch," which drew laughter. Second, he assured her that "no matter how bad it is, God can turn it around." He added, "Keep praying for your spouse . . . maybe [he will] become a great man of God."

Next, a woman in the church told of an unexplainable noise in her apartment, at which point Wariboko declared, "All is well with you. You will not hear any voice but God. . . . The way the lions were silenced to save Daniel, you will not hear any contrary voice." Then a woman recounted a dream in which "someone died. [I was] told to touch him." This was seen as a demonic influence and manipulation, for the dead are not to be embraced. So the group prayed that the "blood of Jesus will surround [this] sister." "A pillar of fire will stand over the house as she sleeps" and "any means of satanic [influence], cut off in the name of Jesus." Pastor Wariboko held her hands and prayed while the congregation lifted their hands in prayer toward her. Finally, one of the participants asked for prayer for her coworker in the hospital. What started at 10:00 a.m. ended at 1:00 p.m., and afterward people returned to work, home, and the streets of Brooklyn.

These examples from three different churches illustrate the importance for ministry of the liturgical setting, the corporate setting, and the everyday setting of dreams, events, and family relationships.[99] The church is an open space for healing and community, a site for the "anointing of the Spirit." In communal settings, not only is the spiritual dimension of healing addressed, but the burdens are shared with a larger group that will pray and be supportive. Systems of healing empower people for an abundant life through spiritual activities such as prayer, deliverance, and communal support.[100]

Institution Builders

African pastors do not just provide spiritual direction and oversight to their congregations; they also comprehensively establish, build, and maintain the institutional life of the church across global borders.[101] Such formation is not a singular event, but ongoing. As leaders of their churches, Rev. Asiedu, Mother Cooper, and Pastor Wariboko maintain contact with leaders of their churches in both local and global contexts. Pastor Wariboko travels in the United States for ministers' meetings, and Rev. Asiedu returns to Ghana for denominational business. Each builds the church, from its weekly programs and activities to its patterns of leadership, on a parenting model.

In interviews and conversations at the Presbyterian Church of Ghana in New York, people sometimes played down the role of the pastor in their spiritual lives. Members turn to Rev. Asiedu for leadership, prayer, and counsel, but they did not join the church because of his pastoring; they are active in the church because it is the Presbyterian Church of Ghana in New York. This is often different in the case of Pentecostal churches, where the leader's charism can be a determinative factor. However, as Pentecostal

---

99. One assessment is Wilhelmina J. Kalu, "Soul Care in Nigeria: Constructing Pentecostal Models of Pastoral Care and Counseling," in *Religion, History, and Politics in Nigeria: Essays in Honor of Ogbu U. Kalu*, ed. Chima J. Korieh and G. Ugo Nwokeji (Lanham: University Press of America, 2005), 202-15.

100. Donald E. Miller and Tetsunao Yamamori draw attention to the importance of communal power in *Global Pentecostalism: The New Face of Christian Social Engagement* (Berkeley: University of California Press, 2007), 146.

101. See Joel Robbins, "Pentecostal Networks and the Spirit of Globalization: On the Social Productivity of Ritual Forms," *Social Analysis* 53:1 (2009): 55-66.

Pastors at Work

movements develop over time, the boundaries between personal calling, authority, and institutional identity may well develop in new ways, and indeed, the reverse trend in historical churches may become evident.

The financial responsibility for the church lies with these pastors. Mother Cooper and Pastor Wariboko founded their churches and birthed them through their hard work, the infusion of their own assets, and constant creativity. To make ends meet, Pastor Wariboko took a series of teaching jobs, while Mother Cooper worked as a seamstress to pay the bills.

Real estate is both a sign of long-term stability and a potential crisis point for most immigrant churches in New York City. Mother Cooper purchased the House of Prayer, where the congregation worships in the basement, and then faced down the bank as it tried to foreclose in a dispute over payments. She eventually won her case in court. Pastor Wariboko had to negotiate with a landlord who sought eviction while he kept raising the rent. After many years of rented space, the Presbyterian Church of Ghana in New York has been able to purchase a building. New York, predicated on flexible capitalism and marked by predatory lending in transitional communities, spawns conflict over real estate and presents multiple challenges for institutional survival, both spiritually and practically. As capital has flooded real estate and neighborhoods throughout New York have begun to change, especially in Harlem and Brooklyn, finding and holding on to space has been a great challenge.[102] Churches may have anchored small-scale revivals, but other forces could seemingly undo their success. Yet God is leading them, working matters out, they believe. Through owning a physical worship space, the churches become increasingly established in the city.

Cultural Intermediaries

The fourth and final feature of pastoral ministry that I highlight is the role pastors play in helping church members bridge the gap between the social and cultural milieu found in Africa and New York City.[103] I invoke the analogy of a bridge builder because it illustrates an important pastoral role

---

102. For one analysis, see Sharon Zukin, *Naked City: The Death and Life of Authentic Urban Places* (New York: Oxford University Press, 2010).

103. A similar suggestion is made by Rijk A. van Dijk, "From Camp to Encompassment: Discourses of Transsubjectivity in the Ghanaian Pentecostal Diaspora," *Journal of Religion in Africa* 27:2 (1997): 149.

in the borderland between two worlds. In his discussion of West African traders in New York, Paul Stoller contends that "variable adaptability" rests on the notion of "cultural competence."[104] This can include a grasp of linguistic and social rules so that people are more socially confident and able to achieve success.[105] Broadly speaking, African pastors perform a role of cultural bridge building, a key activity that can enable their congregants to succeed in a new city. There is a pastoral purpose and strategy involved, an emphasis on enabling parishioners to experience abundant life in Christ.

With his corporate background, Pastor Wariboko models for members the tools required for success in New York. He encourages people to study for exams, work hard for promotions, and take opportunities for advancement at work. He projects confidence and efficiency, stressing time management. In a number of sermons, he urged members to start their own small businesses, and as a result, two members, Segun and Bola Oyesanya, started a financial services group called Spring Forth Associates LLC. A good pastor, parish member Ossai Chegwe believes, is "not about anointing or raising holy hands." Rather, what is important is the manner of spirituality and pastoral interaction. What stands out for him, and so many others that I spoke with, is that Pastor Wariboko is a role model, "a mentor."[106]

Practical advice on family, marriage, and work is very much part of spiritual direction, but for African immigrants in New York it has the additional component of cultural complexity. As pastor of the Presbyterian Church of Ghana in New York, Yaw Asiedu regularly responds to a range of concerns presented to him by parishioners and the larger Ghanaian community in New York. Four are most common, he reports: marriage difficulties, family problems, people needing a place to stay, and financial needs.[107] In addressing such problems, pastors are engaged in an analysis of two — and often more — cultures. Rev. Asiedu, for example, helps parents and children bridge divergent notions of respect and parenting. Marriages can face great strain in a new country; many spouses and families face separation of great length due to travel limitations; family life is conducted in a new culture with different views of parenting; and the financial

---

104. Paul Stoller, *Money Has No Smell: The Africanization of New York City* (Chicago: University of Chicago Press, 2002), 169.
105. Stoller, *Money Has No Smell*, 171.
106. Ossai Chegwe, Interview, May 1, 2005.
107. Yaw Asiedu, Interview, December 6, 2006.

strains of living in New York are omnipresent. These matters can be urgent, and congregation members have access to Rev. Asiedu by telephone or can come by the office. When people come for help, "they don't go [away] empty-handed."[108]

Mother Cooper cites five types of problems she commonly addresses in her ministry in New York: "husband and wife problems," "fiancé problems" for women, "sickness," "job problems," and "childbearing problems." Regarding marital issues, Mother Cooper counsels the husband and wife individually, then brings them together, and "we pray that God should intercede." With sickness, "I fast" and "I tell them to fast too, if they can."[109] Fasting, as I will show in chapter four, is a key spiritual practice. But here it is crucial to underscore how important fasting is seen to be for the work of pastoral ministry.

The Workers Are Many

One of the most distinguishing features of the three churches is the way leadership in the congregation is participatory and shared among a wide group of people. Having seen what the pastors do, we are in a better position to see how they seek to develop a pastoral *habitus* among their leaders, both by involving them in networks and by personal example.

There are no bystanders in the Church of the Lord (Aladura); everyone has a responsibility, whether it is preaching, praying, counting the offering, passing out the Bibles, or anointing with oil. Mother Cooper is not in the regular preaching rotation, with Minister Joy Cooper Chenoweth and Evangelists Eleanor Campbell and Sarah Richards (Kerkulah) typically alternating weeks. The point is that they "get experience," as Mother Cooper puts it; "I have a lot of work to do, [so] I assign people."[110] Hierarchy and titles matter in the Church of the Lord (Aladura), but responding to the Spirit plays an undeniable role in determining who prays, preaches, and leads Bible studies.

The Redeemed Christian Church of God International Chapel, Brooklyn, operates a comprehensive and demanding system of lay pastoral leadership known as "workers." To become a worker, one must be first a

---

108. Yaw Asiedu, Interview, December 6, 2006.
109. Marie Cooper, Interview, January 12, 2006.
110. Marie Cooper, Interview, March 13, 2005.

born-again Christian, a person who has Jesus as their Savior. Once becoming a worker, it is approximately four years before a person is eligible to go to the next level of minister. As noted earlier, this is followed by the positions of deacon/deaconess, assistant pastor, and then pastor. With typically no less than forty workers at any given time in the Brooklyn parish, this works out to be as much as twenty percent of the congregation.[111]

Workers are just what the word suggests: people who work and work hard. Supported by 1 Chronicles 24, which describes "officers of the sanctuary and officers of God" (verse 5) who were appointed for duties, workers are required to do whatever the pastor requires for the operation of the church. It is safe to say Pastor Wariboko asks much of his workers and is strict in his requirements, but this only seems to enhance the workers' respect for his leadership. When called for by the broader Redeemed Christian Church of God leadership, workers can be moved around parishes where needed, although in practice this appears to be based on calling. Meetings are held weekly before church, frequently after church, and a workers night vigil is held monthly.

Pastor Wariboko understands the church to be a dynamic community of the Spirit. At weekly workers' meetings leadership is developed, operations are reviewed, and directions meted out. He may be "first among equals," but his goal is to build a decentralized model of leadership, sharing responsibility and building consensus. Indeed, he would sometimes hear complaints that he devolved too much authority to the ministers, but he deliberately was building leadership that could grow and take on new challenges. More than a leader to the ministers, Pastor Nimi is considered a role model to emulate. His standard is high, and he raises the bar for the leaders not only in their church roles, but also in their professional, educational, and vocational development. Still, this authority is also perceived as the Spirit's endowment and reflective of how the church is structured in the Redeemed movement.

There is a distributional aspect of ministry within Redeemed in Brooklyn and Pentecostalism that Asamoah-Gyadu highlights: "The democratisation of charisma . . . has made the style of ministry in the CMs [charismatic ministries] a task-oriented one. This style of ministry is one

---

111. An argument can be made that in the New Testament, the language of "deacon/deaconess" may be more pastoral than typically recognized. For the discussion, see John N. Collins, "Ordained and Other Ministries: Making a Difference," *Ecclesiology* 3:1 (2006): 11-32. This would be in accord with the functional practice of the Redeemed Church of God.

in which, instead of relying on hierarchies of ministers or on so-called gifts of the Spirit, the laity have been mobilised on the basis of their spiritual gifts and talents to minister in the power of the Spirit in leading worship, personal evangelism, healing, deliverance and others."[112] The association of the Spirit with the individual believer means everyone has a gift, and every *charism* is for the advancement of the ecclesial body. Responsibilities are so carefully distributed that instead of every decision relying on the pastor, the church could "run on auto-pilot,"[113] as one member put it.

A ministers' meeting on October 10, 2004, in the pastor's office begins with a Bible study on 2 Corinthians 3 and Psalm 17:3. Pastor Wariboko identifies the qualities of a worker and minister.[114] First off, they "are to be led by integrity of heart" and "holiness." He stresses that "people read you," and that ministers are "living epistles" and a "living text." Quoting St. Francis, he says that Christians are to "preach, and if necessary use words." Pastor Wariboko adds that being a "Spirit-filled" Pentecostal church does not mean training in holiness and ministry is not required, and because there are limits to human power, workers must "keep praying." This smaller gathering of roughly ten ministers then moves to the adjacent larger "workers' room" as the arriving workers triple the size of the group. Here the workers sing about the "resurrection power of God" and reflect on Matthew 13 and the story of workers in the vineyard of God. The emphasis of the earlier meeting is reinforced: "for every twenty-four hours God gives us, he looks to take an account." After prayer, the meeting is dismissed and the workers and ministers head to their Sunday responsibilities.

The Presbyterian Church of Ghana in New York is organized around a Presbyterian form of church governance whereby congregationally elected women and men lead the church along with the pastor. During my time at the church, a new slate of elders was elected and Rev. Asiedu was installed, replacing the first pastor. The group of elders, known as the "session," meets twice a month and reviews all matters related to the church. From another viewpoint, the Presbyterian Church of Ghana in New York operates through its committees and membership, broadly distributing responsibility to groups throughout the church. Still, in a sermon at the church on July 20, 2007, Catechist Obofa-Offei argued that crucial to the growth of Pentecostal churches in Ghana is their emphasis on lay leader-

---

112. Asamoah-Gyadu, *African Charismatics*, 130.
113. Bola Oyesanya, Interview, June 1, 2007.
114. Redeemed Christian Church of God, Field Notes, October 10, 2004.

ship, an observation likely to have been intended as a challenge to both the church in New York City and the denomination.

In summary, while pastors play a pivotal role in developing and leading congregations, they do not work alone. While the pastor sets the tone or direction of the church, the work of many people is essential to church life.

Conclusion: Building Visions

At the beginning of this chapter, I presented a job description for African pastors in New York City that accords with Donald Miller and Tetsunao Yamamori's observation on global Pentecostalism: "No committee would dream up many of the visions that these pastors proclaim to their congregations; there would be too many naysayers pointing to the difficulties of implementation."[115] The approaches of Rev. Asiedu, Mother Cooper, and Pastor Wariboko are ones of creativity and responsiveness to pastoral opportunities. Their ministries are thriving because of the dedication, vision, and sacrifice they and their families make each day. Yet at heart, they are following a basic pattern of ministry anticipated in Dykstra's analysis: "Pastoral work is first and foremost the work of enabling, teaching, helping, guiding, and encouraging a specific community to practice Christian faith themselves."[116] This is expressed within a holistic conceptualization of salvation. The stories of Rev. Asiedu, Mother Cooper, and Pastor Wariboko show the importance of formation in a pastoral imagination and the place of hard work in ministry.[117] There is a prayerfully formed wisdom to their way of life, and it gives shape to a rich common life.

---

115. Miller and Yamamori, *Global Pentecostalism*, 186.
116. Dykstra, "Pastoral and Ecclesial Imagination," 58.
117. Dykstra, "Pastoral and Ecclesial Imagination," 41-61.

3. Liturgy and Life: Three Churches in Two Worlds

Introduction: A Church for Life

On a Sunday afternoon, in a dimly lit corner of the foyer of the sanctuary where the Presbyterian Church of Ghana in New York worships, I notice a man change from his work clothes to a suit. From the brief glance that I catch, I see that underneath his work uniform are pressed trousers and a dress shirt to which he adds a tie and jacket. He then stuffs the work clothes into a paper bag and steps quickly into the sanctuary to worship God.

As I reflect on this small detail, I am struck by how it communicates something that goes to the heart of African Christianity in New York City. A weekly rest for immigrant workers can be hard to find in a global economy. But this man found something about the worship of God to be so important that he made it a priority above all else, forgoing physical rest and a meal at home after a long day of work and perhaps even an added night shift. Nor did he leave his everyday life outside the doors of the church, but carried it right into the sanctuary with him. Instead of church being an escape or refuge, it is the very place where life happens. At the same time, it is the experience of worship that sends him back out, ready to face the challenges and engage the opportunities of life in a global city.

The most important part of the week for African Christians is Sunday.[1] In their liturgy — another word for praise and worship — there is

---

1. For a powerful account of liturgy as an entry point to African Christianity, see Bennetta Jules-Rosette, *African Apostles: Ritual and Conversion in the Church of John Maranke* (Ithaca: Cornell University Press, 1975). Deidre Helen Crumbley returns over and over again to the theme of life in the midst of worship in her important "Indigenous Institution Building in an Afro-Christian Movement: The Aladura as a Case Study" (Ph.D. Diss.,

a profoundly shaping influence on all of life. People come to the Presbyterian Church of Ghana, the Church of the Lord (Aladura), and the Redeemed Christian Church of God International Chapel, Brooklyn, on Sunday to be transformed, to worship and encounter Jesus. Week after week, something "happens" on Sunday. To miss worship can mean to miss a non-repeatable event — not a lecture, good sermon, or mandated gathering. Worship is where God and human life intersect, where God saves, speaks, heals, provides, moves beyond limits, and controls time.[2] Worship is where people pray, dance, sing, testify, shout, and experience the power of God, the whole person and community engaged with God through the body, the mind, imagination, and desires. Worship is holistic, and therefore transformational.[3] How God is experienced and apprehended in liturgical life is how God is to be experienced and apprehended in everyday life.

A common perception is that as new immigrants, African believers attend church for the social connections and benefits they might receive. There is no doubt that such benefits exist, and it may well factor into initial attendance. As David Ley sums up, immigrant churches can be an "urban service hub,"[4] though this is more organic than structured or planned. Yet the primary reason people participate in church is religious. They come to worship God, the focal point of each week and an expression of the community's most basic experience and beliefs. African Christians begin with

---

Northwestern University, 1989). As background to the importance of worship in analyzing church structures, see Charles E. Farhadian, ed., *Christian Worship Worldwide: Expanding Horizons, Deepening Practices* (Grand Rapids: Eerdmans, 2007). Bernhard Lang in *Sacred Games: A History of Christian Worship* (New Haven: Yale University Press, 1997) argues that the practice of worship across traditions includes six elements: praise, prayer, sermon, sacrifice, sacrament, and spiritual ecstasy. This is a good way of describing what takes place in these three churches.

2. See Simon Coleman and Peter Collins, "The 'Plain' and the 'Positive': Ritual, Experience and Aesthetics in Quakerism and Charismatic Christianity," *Journal of Contemporary Religion* 15:3 (2000): 317-29.

3. On the relationship between "social imaginary" and practices, see James K. A. Smith's important discussions in *Desiring the Kingdom: Worship, Worldview, and Cultural Formation* (Grand Rapids: Baker, 2009), 66-67. See also Richard Eves, "Engendering Gesture: Gender Performativity and Bodily Regimes from New Ireland," *The Asia Pacific Journal of Anthropology* 11:1 (2010): 1-16.

4. David Ley, "The Immigrant Church as an Urban Social Service Hub," *Urban Studies* 45:10 (2008): 2057-74. Nancy Tatom Ammerman describes key sociological aspects of church life in *Pillars of Faith: American Congregations and Their Partners* (Berkeley: University of California Press, 2005).

Liturgy and Life

God and the worship of God.[5] They are communities that believe, confess, and sing that Jesus is alive and still at work.

Worship is much more frequent than once a week in African churches, but Sunday is the focal service. The three services I describe below are accounts from early in my research: August, September, and October 2004. While other services would reveal differences and similarities, these three services represent well each congregation. What I also seek to show is how the liturgical outlook of the three churches is shaped by histories: individual and communal, local and global.[6] In turn, singing, praying, testifying, and hearing the Word helps to shape a world.

Membership Has Its Privileges: The Presbyterian Church of Ghana

Solemnly and slowly the leaders and choir of the Presbyterian Church of Ghana in Harlem process down the aisle.[7] *First in line is the Church Choir, dressed in its pressed white and black uniforms, followed by Rev. Asiedu and a presiding elder. After a selection of hymns and liturgical prayers in Twi from the Presbyterian Church of Ghana — from hymnals that members bring with them — the service dramatically shifts gears. The Church Band has the congregation out of the pews and in the aisles, dancing, marching, and waving white handkerchiefs to the High Life–inflected rhythms and choruses of Ghanaian gospel music with its propelling bass lines, multiple drums and percussive sounds, and cool saxophone notes. Grace Mensah leads the dance song "Trust and Obey" in English, and the second, sung in Twi, is "Ebenezer," which in a summary translation declares, "We thank God, for everything is okay."*

By now the sanctuary has filled with over two hundred worshipers, many in the bright fabrics of Ghana. In their usual corner, dressed in distinc-

---

5. On God as primary point of theology, see David F. Ford, *Theology: A Very Short Introduction* (Oxford: Oxford University Press, 1999), 33-48. In his brief study of theological constants across history and cultures, Andrew Walls lists the "worship of the God of Israel" first. The other three categories that Walls introduces are the ultimate significance of Jesus, a belief that God is active where believers are, and an understanding that the people of God transcend time and space. See Andrew F. Walls, *The Missionary Movement in Christian History: Studies in the Transmission of Faith* (Maryknoll, N.Y.: Orbis, 1996), 23-24.

6. Here I am extending an insight from the philosopher Nicholas Wolterstorff, "Historicizing the Belief-Forming Self," in Thomas M. Crisp, Matthew Davidson, and David Vander Laan, eds, *Knowledge and Reality: Essays in Honor of Alvin Plantinga* (Dordrecht: Springer, 2006), 111-35.

7. Service of September 26, 2004.

FORMATIONS

Fig. 3.1 Members of the Presbyterian Church of Ghana in New York after Sunday worship at Mount Morris Church in Harlem, 2005

tive white and blue uniforms, is the Women's Fellowship. Scripture readings from Old and New Testaments are provided in Twi, Ga, and English, more hymns are sung from the hymnal, and the Apostles' Creed is recited in Twi. Thelma Annan delivers the sermon in English and Twi on the topic of "You Cannot Serve God and Money." Money, she observes, "is the root of all evil." The life of Solomon suggests that it "can lead to temptation," and referring to the life of John D. Rockefeller, she emphasizes that money does not save. Yet money is also "blessed by God."

Immediately following the sermon, the Singing Band performs its selection to time kept by an ododompo, a two-piece, metal finger instrument whose distinctive click jumps out. After visitors are introduced and announcements made, the special offerings that people have made this week are announced to the congregation. These announcements are testimonies to God's provision for safe travel, health, and family safety. Today is also a miniharvest for "Kwame's and Amma's," men and women born on a Saturday. Equal parts cultural celebration, worship, and fund-raiser, the harvest ser-

vice raises over $10,000 for the church. Afternoon has now turned to evening, and the service ends with a recessional hymn, the choir and clergy recessing back up the aisle. As the remaining people leave, spiritually renewed but perhaps also physically expended, they find bottles of water are being distributed in the narthex. Like every other Sunday, this has been a time of seeing friends, hearing the Word, and experiencing enormous joy.

When the always sharply dressed Alfred Kissiedo states he was "born Presbyterian and will die Presbyterian,"[8] he speaks for many in his church. Born in Ghana, Alfred is part of many generations who have been members of the Presbyterian Church of Ghana. A New Yorker for some forty years, Alfred lives in the sprawling Co-Op City in the Bronx. His son is a New York police officer, his daughter a doctoral student in Philadelphia. Kissiedo sits in the same pew in the back each week where he can take everything in, and cheerily greets everyone who walks by him with a handshake and smile, conducting short, knowing conversations. He is a New Yorker, a Ghanaian, and a Presbyterian.

Denominational affiliation is a point of identity and pride for the congregants of the Presbyterian Church of Ghana in New York. With its more than 250 members, the congregation is an active part of the Presbyterian Church of Ghana denomination, which is headquartered in Accra.[9] The New York congregation gathers in Harlem but draws its membership largely from people who reside in the Bronx and even as far away as Connecticut and New Jersey.[10]

Church members are employed in the city as taxi drivers, waiters, healthcare workers, store clerks, and in an array of public and professional positions. A good example is Amma Amponsah, who came to New York from Ghana over twenty years ago and is a social worker for the Depart-

---

8. Alfred Kissiedo, Interview, July 31, 2005.

9. For another study on this congregation, see Moses Ohene Biney, "Singing the Lord's Song in a Foreign Land: A Socio-Ethical Study of a Ghanaian Immigrant Church in New York" (Ph.D. Diss., Princeton Theological Seminary, 2005) and "Singing the Lord's Song in a Foreign Land: Spirituality, Communality, and Identity in a Ghanaian Immigrant Congregation," in *African Immigrant Religions in America*, ed. Jacob K. Olupona and Regina Gemignani (New York: New York University Press, 2007), 259-78.

10. According to Moses Biney, the church membership breaks down as follows: "about 85% are of the Akan linguistic group; about 13% are Ga-speaking and 1% Ewe-speaking." Biney, "Singing the Lord's Song in a Foreign Land," 78-79.

Fig. 3.2 Announcement for General Assembly meeting in Ghana posted in Harlem, 2005

ment of Social Services.[11] High housing costs in New York forced her to extend her quest to purchase a home across the river to New Jersey, but she lives much of her life in New York City. At church she sits in a front pew, the better to dance from and encourage others to join her.

Three influences are important for understanding the life and practice of the Presbyterian Church of Ghana, both in Ghana and now in New York: the Basel Evangelical Missionary Society, the Scottish Presbyterians, and the modern African Charismatic movement.

The first major influence goes back to the European missionary movement in Africa in the nineteenth century, when the pietistic Basel Evangelical Missionary Society began the work that would become the Presbyterian Church of Ghana.[12] For a time they were also joined by Jamaican missionar-

---

11. Amma Amponsah, Interview, August 14, 2005.

12. Noel Smith, *The Presbyterian Church of Ghana, 1835-1960: A Younger Church in a Changing Society* (Accra: Ghana Universities Press, 1966). "History of the Presbyterian Church in Ghana," http://www.pc-ghana.org/detail.htm#beginning (accessed August 28,

Liturgy and Life

Fig. 3.3 Amma Amponsah, Presbyterian Church of Ghana, 2005

ies. A second major historical influence comes from United Free Church of Scotland Presbyterian missionaries, who were "interim" when the mission was expelled in 1917.[13] Reflecting the new role of Presbyterian polity and the need for a new phase in the life of the church upon the return of the Basel Mission in 1926, the mission began to call itself the Presbyterian Church of Gold Coast, later becoming the Presbyterian Church of Ghana at the point of national independence in 1957. A third influence comes from the Presby-

---

2007); Jon Miller, *Missionary Zeal and Institutional Control: Organizational Contradictions in the Basel Mission on the Gold Coast, 1828-1917* (Grand Rapids: Eerdmans, 2003).

13. Smith, *The Presbyterian Church of Ghana,* 161. On the transfer from the Scottish viewpoint, see A. W. Wikie, "An Attempt to Conserve the Work of the Basel Mission to the Gold Coast," *International Review of Mission* (1920): 86-94. Generally on the Scottish role, see Charles Gyang-Duah, "The Scottish Mission Factor in the Development of the Presbyterian Church of Ghana: 1917-1957" (Ph.D. Thesis, University of Edinburgh, 1996).

terian Church of Ghana's encounter with the independent and Pentecostal/charismatic churches in Ghana.[14] During the 1960s, many people were leaving the Presbyterian Church of Ghana for independent and charismatic churches.[15] The Presbyterian Church of Ghana responded by incorporating charismatic elements into its practices, including vibrant music, dancing, deliverance services, and all-night prayer meetings.[16]

Each of these influences — the pietism of the Baselers, the polity of the Scottish Presbyterians, and the new charismatic emphasis — moved to New York City and is potentially evident in any given worship service and in different parts of the church's life.[17] Recalling its pietistic heritage, the church shows a strong emphasis on preaching about the heart and turning to Christ and little in the way of a creedal or doctrinal system; from the Scottish chapter comes the Presbyterian form of polity, pastoral garb, and offices; and there is certainly a charismatic dynamic in much of the music, prayer, and entries into healing and deliverance. These influences show up in any given worship service: exhortations to come to Jesus with all-night prayer services, the solemnity of the hymns alternating with the jubilant Church Band that sends members dancing into the aisles. Each layer of the history and worship of the Presbyterian Church of Ghana seems to find its way into the ongoing life of the church. Indeed, they meld together, providing the church its uniqueness.

The Harlem-based church traces its beginnings to the early 1980s. As the church tells the story, it appeared to many Ghanaian Christians in New York City that they were becoming sick and dying at an alarming rate. The crisis, explained in spiritual terms, could only be resolved or controlled with a response that focused on God. To this end, Margaret "Mama" Ohemeng convened a group of Ghanaian men and women together for

---

14. Cephas N. Omenyo, *Pentecost Outside Pentecostalism: A Study of the Development of Charismatic Renewal in the Mainline Churches in Ghana* (Zoetermeer: Uitgeverij Boekencentrum, 2002), 127-53; "From the Fringes to the Centre: Pentecostalization of the Mainline Churches in Ghana," *Exchange* 34:1 (2005): 39-60.

15. J. Kwabena Asamoah-Gyadu, *African Charismatics: Current Developments within Indigenous Pentecostalism in Ghana* (Leiden: Brill, 2005), 18-32.

16. Livingstone Buama, "The Worship Experience of the Reformed Family in Ghana, West Africa: The Cry and Quest for Liturgical Reform," in *Christian Worship in Reformed Churches Past and Present*, ed. Lukas Vischer (Grand Rapids: Eerdmans, 2003), 216-23.

17. On the connections between pietism and charismatic renewal, see Lamin Sanneh, *Disciples of All Nations: Pillars of World Christianity* (New York: Oxford University Press, 2008), 163-83. David Martin also identifies a broad pattern of lineage between pietism and Pentecostalism in *On Secularization: Towards a Revised General Theory* (Aldershot: Ashgate, 2005), 144.

prayer, to seek "divine intervention."[18] Mama Ohemeng, a Ghanaian who made her home in New York City in the early 1960s along with her husband, set in motion what would eventually lead in 1985 to the formation of the Presbyterian Church of Ghana in New York City.[19] The future pastor, the Rev. Dr. Francis Kumi Dwamena, organized prayer meetings.[20] Eventually the group would be the first Presbyterian Church of Ghana congregation in the United States, even the first outside of Ghana,[21] and appears to be one of the earliest African immigrant churches in New York City.

If an immediate struggle for life led the church into its formation, a longer story of Ghanaian communal life in New York offers the larger context. For more than a decade, Ghanaian immigrants in the metropolitan areas had gathered for "Naming Ceremonies, Birthday Parties, Infant Baptisms, and Funerals. Presbyterians from Ghana who were present at some of these gatherings sang Church Hymns and Songs."[22] When in 1982 Mama Ohemeng put out her call for prayer, she knew whom to call. During the months that followed, prayer meetings continued, and concerns coalesced around a commitment to form a Presbyterian Church of Ghana congregation in New York City.[23] Dwamena became the first pastor, and the new church's first official worship service was held on Sunday, November 24, 1985, at Broadway Presbyterian Church, located near Columbia University. Later they rented Mount Morris Ascension Presbyterian Church (PCUSA), Harlem's "last Romanesque Revival church."[24] In 2001, the Presbyterian Church of Ghana in New York acquired the old Police Athletic League building on 123rd Street, using it for offices and meetings.

As choir member Nana Afwireng explains, "Whatever we do here, we do it this way when we worship at home."[25] Organizational life is based on the *Presbyterian Church of Ghana Constitution*, and the committees and operations follow the *Presbyterian Church of Ghana Manual of Order*. As

---

18. Yaw Asiedu, Interview, March 9, 2004.
19. Yaw Asiedu, Interview, March 9, 2004.
20. Biney, "Singing the Lord's Song in a Foreign Land," 74-75.
21. Yaw Asiedu, Interview, March 9, 2004.
22. *Okristoni (The Christian) Pictorial Journal of Ghana Presbyterian Church, U.S.A Tenth Anniversary Celebration,* 1995.
23. *Okristoni (The Christian) Pictorial Journal of Ghana Presbyterian Church, U.S.A Tenth Anniversary Celebration,* 1995.
24. Michael Henry Adams, *Harlem Lost and Found: An Architectural and Social History, 1765-1915* (New York: The Monacelli, 2002), 192.
25. Nana Afwireng, Interview, August 13, 2006.

noted in the previous chapter, leadership is based in the elders or session, which has a senior presbyter; the pastor is also part of the session. Just as in Ghana, nearly everyone belongs to a committee, group, or choir: the Men's Fellowship, Women's Fellowship, Bible Study and Prayer group, Young People's Guild (Y.P.G), Singing Band, Church Band, and Church Choir.

Each member has a Presbyterian Church of Ghana Certificate of Membership booklet. It looks like a small yellow passport, and is equally indispensable for church members. Wherever they go around the world, this membership book moves with them.[26] On the first page is a place for a photograph, while the next page records personal information such as birth, baptism, confirmation, and marriage. Immediately following then are page after page with two columns — one column is for "Communion" with a place for the date and the pastor's signature, and the other column is for "Payments" with a place for the date, tithe, and signature. Communion Sunday attracts the largest numbers, and members either sign a registry book when they arrive or leave their cards with the clerk. The cards are then kept together in the church office, where Rev. Asiedu signs them after each communion service. Each member therefore has a record of their church activity that is portable to any Presbyterian Church in Ghana congregation, whether in New York or Ghana. Tithes paid in Harlem count as tithes made in Ghana.[27] When a member dies and is sent back home to Ghana, "the [membership] card is referred to the family" so they can receive a church funeral.[28] Perhaps the most important committee of the church in New York City is the Welfare Committee. Established to provide assistance for members in good standing, it produces a written document that spells out in great detail pastoral services and financial commitments regarding births, outdoorings (baby naming ceremonies), children, adults, hospitalization, and funerals.[29] In this way, members share a common spiritual and economic commitment to one another.

Funerals, like that of church member Margaret Amma Debrah, provide a vivid picture of church life in two worlds.[30] When in early July 2006 Margaret passed from this earthly life to the next at the young age of forty-eight, it fell to her church to plan and conduct and pay for her funeral, hold an all-night vigil, raise money from each member to pay for the funeral, and return her body home to Ghana. Rev. Asiedu would be in Ghana to

26. Moses Biney, Interview, June 10, 2005.
27. Moses Biney, Interview, June 10, 2005.
28. Yaw Asiedu, Interview, July 16, 2005.
29. Presbyterian Church of Ghana in New York, "Welfare By-Laws," 2007.
30. Church Services of July 30, 2006 and August 6, 2006.

share in the final burial rites. A committee of fellow "Saturday Borns" — Kwames and Ammas — was formed to make the necessary arrangements, and when the funeral date in New York was finalized, a flyer was produced and distributed inviting church members and Ghanaians in New York. The women in the church purchased a dress for her, and on the day of the funeral prepared her body for viewing.[31]

The Sunday before the funeral rites, the pastor, Rev. Yaw Asiedu, made a short speech to the entire congregation.[32] Margaret was a church member, he reminded them, and the church was her only family in New York City: "This is our problem. Let us all join hands and support ourselves. We would do it for you."

The funeral began on the afternoon of August 11, 2006, with a viewing at Mount Morris Ascension Presbyterian Church. Led by Rev. Asiedu and Rev. Dr. Charles Gyang-Duah, a formal church service is conducted at 7:00 p.m. After a break of several hours, the final funeral rites held in New York moved uptown to Cocoa House in the Bronx, a rental hall next to an all-night laundry and a billiard hall, outside which the lively tempos of Latin music pulsated on the night streets. Inside Cocoa House, the church elders sat at the far end of the room; the chief mourners sat at a slightly raised table on the far side; general mourners filled in the rest of the room. In the corner, a deejay backed by a stack of loudspeakers played music at a volume that made conversation difficult but dancing easy. Women carried around baskets with bottles of water and Snapple drinks. As the night went on, the room filled with church members and fellow Ghanaians. After 3:00 a.m., all the Saturday-Borns gathered in a circle and then faced the video camera, which had been recording two days of mourning. With a framed picture of Margaret Debrah lifted high in the front to commemorate her life and Issac Akrah leading the way, a line danced around the room. With the morning sun soon to rise, people returned home. But this was not the end of the story. A few weeks later in Accra, Ghana, Rev. Asiedu met the family and the body at the airport. There was another funeral and then a burial, presided over by Rev. Asiedu. Margaret Debrah was now home.

A few days after the service, Nana Afwireng conveyed to me the importance of the funeral process: "When somebody dies, everybody contributes . . . we do it for each other so you do not suffer alone." For this reason, the wider Ghanaian community in New York City joins in, including

---

31. Amma Amaponsah, Interview, August 14, 2005.
32. Church Service, August 6, 2006.

Fig. 3.4 Framed picture of Margaret Debrah during final funeral rites, 2006

extended family members and hometown associations.[33] More than congeniality is at work.[34] Jimmy Ado, who is president of the church choir,

---

33. On the importance and role of hometown associations in the diaspora, see Ayse Caglar, "Hometown Associations, the Rescaling of State Spatiality and Migrant Grassroots Transnationalism," *Global Networks* 6:1 (2006): 1-22; Claire Mercer, Ben Page, and Martin Evans, "Unsettling Connections: Development and African Hometown Associations," *Global Networks*, 9:2 (2009): 141-61; Valentina Mazzucato and Mirjam Kabki, "Small Is Beautiful: The Micro-politics of Transnational Relationships Between Ghanaian Hometown Associations and Communities Back Home," *Global Networks* 9:2 (2009): 227-51.

34. Nana Afwireng, Interview, August 13, 2006.

Liturgy and Life

emphasized, "We always associate ourselves with a group so you know a group of people." Otherwise, "you are on your own. . . . We have to help ourselves."[35]

For the members of the Harlem congregation, the Presbyterian Church of Ghana accompanies them on their journey to New York City and "home" again to Ghana. Being "Presby," the shorthand reference that they often use to describe themselves, is part of who they are as New Yorkers, Ghanaians, and Christians. Traditions of Word and sacrament are merged with charismatic forms of Ghanaian Christianity, bringing lives into a focus on God. The faith is expressed in a community that knows how to care for the living and bury the dead.

A House of Prayer: The Church of the Lord (Aladura)

As worshipers arrive at the Church of the Lord (Aladura), they remove their shoes and pile them up in the hallway; women are sure to cover their heads; most men and women will be wearing flowing white robes.[36] *These are signs of entering a holy place. With the ringing of a hand bell that announces the start of worship, Deacon David Rquarm begins the service at noon. The church sings a Thanksgiving hymn, known by its chorus, "For his mercies aye endure, Ever faithful, ever sure," taken from the Church of the Lord (Aladura) hymnal.*[37] *Three white candles burn on the altar. The worshiping community moves into a confession of sin, followed by a recitation of Psalm 51. Thanksgiving is offered to the "God of our founding fathers" including Josiah Ositelu and E. O. A Adejobi.*

Mother Cooper has arrived from upstairs where she lives, and enters the altar area, a sacred space within a sacred space, and she immediately kneels and begins to pray. In the set liturgical pattern, it is time for the Victory Hymns, beginning with "And why should the saints be afraid." Deacon David plays the congas, Mother Cooper swirls the calabash, another member pushes the shakers, and tambourines echo throughout the room. Singing "Oh my comrades! See the signal," the church is expected to stand up for Jesus, and all are doing just that. Then the singing moves into the "Shouts," choruses

35. Jimmy Ado, Interview, August 13, 2006.
36. Service of August 29, 2004.
37. Unless otherwise noted, because the CLA hymns lack titles, I use the first lines for identification purposes, which is the manner used in *The Church of the Lord (Aladura) Worldwide English Hymn Book* (1993 edition). "Eye" is the correct spelling.

sung to rapid percussive movement. There are ten people in the service, but the effect is more like the voices and sounds of a multitude. Bodies sway to choruses that conclude with repetitions of "Thank you, Jehovah God."

After an hour of singing and praying, the service breaks for a lengthy Bible lesson. More prayers and Bible readings follow, along with a vision from Mother Cooper. The sermon, preached by Minister Joy Cooper-Chenoweth, a daughter of Mother Cooper, is titled "The Reason for Salvation," and the lead biblical text is Matthew 7:7-8. "You must be born again," Minister Joy emphasizes in her message of encouragement and challenge. At her closing words, the congregation begins singing, "Who is on the Lord's side/I am on the Lord's side/The Lord is on my side." Prayers are followed by the sung invitation to "Come and pay your tithes," for which white offering envelopes are distributed. "Thank you for your protection. . . . Thank you for your provision. . . . Thank you for our breathing. . . . Thank you for provision," is the sung response. "Children of the Lord shall come," everyone now sings, and the children present come forward to be anointed with oil. Following a closing hymn and benediction, all face the altar, and every voice in the room offers seven "Hallelujahs," seven "Hosannas," seven "Uhrahs," and seven "laughters." Nearly four hours after beginning, the service now ends, visitors are greeted, and members begin to catch up on the week. The candles have burned down to their base.

The Church of the Lord (Aladura) in the Bronx is a branch of the Church of the Lord (Aladura) Worldwide, headquartered in Ogere, Nigeria. "Aladura" refers to "prayer churches,"[38] a term specific to the Church of the Lord but also a more general frame of religious reference for an extended family of Yoruba independent churches in Nigeria.[39] A Yoruba word, "aladura" is variously translated as "people of prayer" and "praying people." In 2007, the church identified 2,124 branches worldwide, with 1,000

38. Robin Horton, "African Conversion," *Africa* 41:2 (1971): 85.

39. For early background as well as additional introduction to Aladura Christianity, see Harold W. Turner, *African Independent Church*, vol. 1: *History of an African Independent Church* (Oxford: Clarendon Press, 1967), 1-34; Rufus Okikiolaolu Olubiyi Ositelu, *African Instituted Churches: Diversities, Growth, Gifts, Spirituality and Ecumenical Understanding of African Initiated Churches* (Munster: LIT Verlag, 2002); J. D. Y. Peel, *Aladura: A Religious Movement Among the Yoruba* (Oxford: Oxford University Press, 1968); Benjamin C. Ray, "Aladura Christianity: A Yoruba Religion," *Journal of Religion in Africa* 23:3 (1993): 266-91; and Horton, "African Conversion."

Liturgy and Life

Fig. 3.5 Exterior of the House of Prayer, Church of the Lord (Aladura) in the Bronx, 2004

branches in Nigeria and 500 in Liberia.[40] Our focus church in the Bronx is the first North American branch of this worldwide movement. The Bronx parish faithfully reproduces broader Church of the Lord (Aladura) patterns of worship, leadership, and spiritual life.[41] Week after week, a complex of twenty-two worship components is performed in the Bronx.[42] But the fixed liturgical range is combined with spontaneity of testimony, healing, prayer, prophecy, and sermon, all ultimately conducted, members believe, under the direction of the Holy Spirit.

The story of the Church of the Lord (Aladura) begins in Nigeria in

---

40. Primate Rufus Ositelu, E-mail Correspondence, May 3, 2007. Within the U.S. there are between three and six branches directly under the Church of the Lord (Aladura), including Philadelphia, Rhode Island, Worcester, and Washington, D.C. (*Church Man's Calendar 2004*, 24th issue, Church of the Lord [Aladura] World-Wide). There is, however, apparently flux with some churches and their relationship to church leadership.

41. For an internal benchmark, see Rufus Ositelu, *African Instituted Churches*.

42. Church of the Lord (Aladura), *The Handbook of Liturgy* (Lagos: The Publication Committee, n.d.).

the 1920s with its founder Josiah Olunowo Ositelu (1902-1966).[43] As Harold Turner recounts in his seminal two-volume study on the church, during the time Josiah Ositelu was in training for the Anglican ministry,[44] he underwent a series of visions and dreams that revealed his life was in conflict with evil forces, but also that God's call and power would surpass them.[45] He turned away from charms to what Turner calls a "simple gospel of faith in God alone, with prayer and fasting." This formula "became the working basis of the church that Oshitelu subsequently founded."[46] Having found spiritual affirmation and authority outside institutional boundaries, Ositelu came into conflict with the Anglican Church. When it led to his dismissal, he joined an emerging group of Aladura Christian prophets and leaders, including Joseph Babalola and Moses Orimolade, who were also creating new religious societies.[47] Continuing with prayer and fasting, and all the while receiving visions, Ositelu formally inaugurated the Church of the Lord (Aladura) in Ogere, Nigeria, in July 1930.[48] At the time, Ositelu was just twenty-eight years old.

In 1947 Ositelu sent Apostle S. O. Odulowe (d. 1965), one of his most trusted apostles in Nigeria, to Liberia to establish the work of the church.[49] The Barclays, a prominent Liberian family, played a logistical role in providing the invitation to Ositelu that would lead to the establishment of the church in Liberia. While they eventually had differences with Oduwole that led to a parting of the ways, the Barclay family saw to the church's beginning.[50] Even when their house was no longer available for worship, the Barclays provided land on which Oduwole could build a new church structure.[51] Through organizing, preaching, and healing, Oduwole built

---

43. Throughout this study, unless quoting a published source, Ositelu will be spelled thus. In both official church literature and secondary sources, the spelling varies between "Oshitelu" and "Ositelu."

44. Turner, *African Independent Church*, vol. 1, 52-53.

45. Turner, *African Independent Church*, vol. 1, 39.

46. Turner, *African Independent Church*, vol. 1, 39.

47. For early background as well as additional introduction to Aladura Christianity, see Turner, *African Independent Church*, vol. 1, 1-34; Ositelu, *African Instituted Churches*; Peel, *Aladura*; Ray, "Aladura Christianity"; and Horton, "African Conversion."

48. Ositelu, *African Instituted Churches*, 127, and Turner, *African Independent Church*, vol. 1, 53, 55, dates the inception at 1931.

49. For an account of the history, see Turner, *African Independent Church*, vol. 1, 133-47.

50. Turner, *African Independent Church*, vol. 1, 136-43.

51. Turner, *African Independent Church*, vol. 1, 143.

Liturgy and Life

the Church of the Lord (Aladura) in Liberia.[52] Samuel Britt assesses that Oduwole's efforts helped to make the Church of the Lord (Aladura) "the most successful new African church in Liberia."[53] Liberian respect for Oduwole's work remains high, and despite his murder in Liberia,[54] the work of the Church of the Lord (Aladura) has flourished.[55]

While the church would continue to grow in Nigeria and expand not only to Liberia but elsewhere in Africa, including Ghana and Sierra Leone, and eventually reach outside of Africa to London in 1964[56] (making it one of the first African Independent Churches in Europe), it was unable to establish a presence in North America until 1984. It was planned for Oduwole to eventually go to the United States, but he was never able to do so.[57] However, a member of his Liberian province, Marie Cooper, eventually went in 1984, and with her came the Church of the Lord (Aladura). The nucleus of what would become the Bronx congregation was present as regular participants in the prayer group, which included David Rquarm, Joy Cooper-Chenoweth, Eleanor Campbell, Sarah Richards, Edwin Flowers, and Esther Mulbah. Mother Cooper and Sarah Kerulah became acquainted with one another in Liberia through the Gates of Heaven, a women's prayer group.[58]

As the prayer group continued meeting in New York, Mother Cooper wrote to the Apostle Thomas, then head of the Liberian see. Responding to the news of the Bronx prayer group, Apostle Thomas encouraged them to move toward becoming a church. During a visit in 1994 to New York by the then Primate Gabriel Ositelu, a son of the founder, the prayer group became a church.[59] For the Apostle Thomas, the founding of the Bronx branch was the fulfillment of the vision that Apostle Oduwole and Liberia would play a role in the church's expansion to North America. Writing to Mother Coo-

---

52. Turner, *African Independent Church*, vol. 1, 137-57.

53. Samuel Irving Britt, "The Children of Salvation: Struggle and Cosmology in Liberian Prophet Churches" (Ph.D. diss., University of Virginia, 1992), 19.

54. His murder by a "deranged" man seeking healing is seen by some as martyrdom. For an account of his death see Britt, "The Children of Salvation," 57-58.

55. Primate Ositelu, E-mail Correspondence, May 3, 2007.

56. Primate Ositelu, E-mail Correspondence, May 3, 2007.

57. Turner, *African Independent Church*, vol. 1, 150. From oral histories, there appear to have been a number of early attempts, including one by the second Primate Adejobi, to establish a branch in the United States.

58. Organized prayer groups are considered a significant form of Christian activity in Liberia and have followed into the Liberian Christian community in New York. They may offer an alternative form of church life, especially for women.

59. Marie Cooper, Interview, May 12, 2005.

Fig. 3.6 Church of the Lord (Aladura) Fortieth-Year Remembrance, 2006

per in 1995, he observed, "For your kindness and concern we will continue to pray for the growth, development and success of your activities in the United States in fulfillment of the desire of the late Apostle S. O. Oduwole which Providence has designated you to perform in his place."[60]

The church in the Bronx may be "a little place, but we have gifts here," Mother Cooper is wont to comment. One of the gifts given by God to the church is listening for the voice of God. God speaks through visions, dreams, and holy words that are shared with the community and world.

60. Correspondence from Cathedral Headquarters in Monrovia to Marie Cooper, December 26, 1995.

Liturgy and Life

"You know people [are] thinking God [is] not speaking anymore... which means God [is] not existing anymore," Mother Cooper asserts.[61] If God is real, if God is living, if God is God, then God must still speak.

Gender can play important roles in the religious experience and practice of Church of the Lord (Aladura), as Deidre Helen Crumbly shows in her important work *Spirit, Structure, and Flesh*.[62] In the Bronx, more than half of the core membership of the Church of the Lord (Aladura) is female, and women provide the primary leadership. What is clear here in the Bronx is the power of women in leadership, both through and with spiritual strength and physical commitment.

The people who attend services are predominately Liberian, a fact that directly connects the church to the early expansion of the Church of the Lord (Aladura) into Liberia. References are regularly made in the Bronx parish to the "Cathedral on Centre Street" or even just "Centre Street," both identifications of the Church of the Lord (Aladura) cathedral located in the capital city, Monrovia. Centre Street is also the location of the provincial headquarters of the church in Liberia. Still, despite the preponderance of connections to Liberia, a broad sense of being part of a much larger church is displayed through the weekly recitation of the Apostles' Creed, perhaps the most universal of Christian statements of faith; prayers for Christians around the city and world and not just for the Church of the Lord (Aladura); and the display of pictures of Christ that reflect Catholic and Protestant portraiture.

And there is also diversity within the congregation, with one member from Ghana, one African American woman, and until recently, a Nigerian. There are no great financial means among the members, and many depend on healing received at church to survive.

Sarah Richards came to New York City from Liberia in 1987, having lived in Houston first for a year. For Sarah, the Church of the Lord (Aladura) has been an enduring part of her life. Born in Liberia, she spent part of her childhood living with the Barclays, the same family who were responsible for

61. Marie Cooper, Interview, August 29, 2004.
62. For a discussion of gender in the Church of the Lord (Aladura), see Deidre Helen Crumbley, *Spirit, Structure, and Flesh: Gendered Experiences in African Instituted Churches among the Yoruba of Nigeria* (Madison: University of Wisconsin Press, 2008); "'Power in the Blood': Menstrual Taboos and Women's Power in an African Instituted Church," in *Women and Religion in the African Diaspora: Knowledge, Power, and Performance*, ed. Ruth Marie Griffith and Barbara Dianne Savage (Baltimore: The Johns Hopkins University Press, 2006), 81-97, and "Patriarchies, Prophets, and Procreation: Sources of Gender Practices in Three African Churches," *Africa* 73:4 (2003): 587-88.

Fig. 3.7 Eleanor Campbell and Edwin Flower, Church of the Lord (Aladura), 2004

introducing the Church of the Lord (Aladura) to Liberia. Upon moving to New York, Sarah came to the Bronx church after learning about Mother Cooper. I "want to go where the Spirit will be free," she offers.[63]

The current primate of the Church of the Lord (Aladura), Rufus Ositelu, maintains personal contact with Mother Cooper by telephone and usually visits the church in New York on a yearly basis. During his New York visits, the primate meets with church leaders and may also conduct installations to church office. Rufus Ositelu is the fourth Church of the Lord (Aladura) primate and third primate from the Ositelu family. Amiable and respected for his pastoral life, he also brings to the role a background in computer science. Perhaps because of this background, Primate Rufus Ositelu is perceived to be developing the church for the challenges of the twenty-first century.

A theology of the cross pervades the Bronx church, visually and in their teaching. Crosses are visible everywhere in the sanctuary and the worship service: a gold processional cross stands next to the pulpit, a cross

---

63. Sarah Richards, Interview, December 12, 2004.

Liturgy and Life

Fig. 3.8 Primate Rufus Ositelu and Mother Cooper, 2006

is built into the wooden pulpit, a picture of Jesus bleeding on the cross is posted over the altar, and a cross is embroidered into the cloth that covers the altar table. Moreover, Mother Cooper and other leaders each grasp in hand a simple brown wooden cross during prayer. Symbolized in these crosses is a life that combats the forces of Satan through the cross of Jesus. For the Church of the Lord (Aladura), the cross fights off the spiritual forces of oppression and creates space for the healing salve of God.

The Church of the Lord (Aladura) in New York City is fulfilling a historic vision of expansion while attending to spiritual needs. When people gather, they do so in the routines that have been established as part of an independent African Christian movement. In worship, they are formed and empowered in the way of the cross.

FORMATIONS

Do Something New in My Life: The Redeemed Christian Church of God International Chapel, Brooklyn

Every Sunday at 10:30 a.m., song leader Omo Obogbaimhe steps to the front of the sanctuary of the Redeemed Christian Church of God International Chapel, Brooklyn.[64] *The choir moves into place behind her, as well as a band comprised of an electronic keyboard player and several drummers. The Sunday school classes that have been meeting in the sanctuary quickly wrap up. The room, once an abandoned warehouse, now carpeted and brightly painted, soon fills with over 200 worshipers who come dressed in an array of western and Nigerian attire; most of the women have their heads covered with wide brimmed hats or wraps. A projector projects the lyrics onto a large screen, and with hands lifted high, the room is soon swaying joyously to the music. The church sings continuous song loops that put Jesus in the fore: "Blessed be the name of the Lord," "Jesus is my firm foundation," "I am here for the Lord," and "Jesus is the Mighty God." A pause to offer a clap offering for the Lord is followed by more songs that offer adoration to Jesus.*

After thirty minutes of singing, Bola Oyesanya, a minister in the church, announces that it is "testimony time, blessing time." Today is the annual "Fruit of the Womb" Sunday, and to frame the occasion, Bola reads Psalm 127:3: "Sons are indeed a heritage from the Lord, the fruit of the womb a reward." All of the parents with children under twelve months are told to gather in the back of the room, thirteen parents in all, and then together dance down the center aisle, singing the chorus "I have a reason to praise the Lord." Next, all expectant women are invited to join them, and three do so as "Come and see what the Lord has done" is sung spontaneously.

Pastor Nimi Wariboko now steps forward and commands the service, calling forward those seeking "fruit of the womb." He recalls the difficulties his Nigerian mother faced in having children, and how after listening to the directives of a Pentecostal minister who commanded her and his father to dance, the result nine months later was his birth. "You can do it for us . . . you did it for my mother . . . you did it for others . . . let the miracle of pregnancy" occur, Pastor Nimi prays. When finished, he shakes hands with the many who had crowded up in the front seeking the "fruit of the womb."

As people return to their seats, Pastor Wariboko begins his sermon, titled "The Power of the Spirit." "When the Spirit of God sets in . . . he will just [make changes] happen." In the "world you live in the world of facts," but God

---

64. Service of October 10, 2004.

can transcend this world of doctors and create a new womb, even overrule a coroner's determination of death. Because of the Spirit, there is a new power inside of you, Wariboko proclaims. "If Paul and Peter can do it, I can do it." As the sermon nears its ending, the pastor calls upon everyone to pray, and the church becomes filled with multiple voices at once, with English and spiritual tongues audible. Speaking over hundreds of people loudly praying to God, Pastor Nimi continually repeats, "He will do it again" and statements such as "Our God is glorious and powerful." He then sings, "Holy Spirit come. . . . Holy Ghost do it again in my life," words that draw in the congregation as they reaffirm the heart of his sermon.

More prayers, announcements, and the offering follow, and then everyone who is celebrating a birthday, a "born-again birthday," or an anniversary is invited to come forward. Person by person, Pastor Nimi asks each individual what they are celebrating, then prays for the group. This Sunday, because of the special "fruit of the womb" occasion, a large array of fruits has been placed in settings in front of the church, and the pastor invites the celebrants to take some. Visitors are now asked to stand, and after being welcomed, are ushered to a room for an evangelistic orientation to the church. As the ministers file off the platform to the pastor's office and workers' room, the congregation shares together in pronouncing the benediction. Everyone is then invited to take home with them pieces of sugar cane, bananas, oranges, and other fruits that fill the bowls. Though it is now early afternoon, few leave. As children play, people are providing counsel on a job search, offering a word of prayer for a problem, and catching up on one another's lives.

Redeemed Christian Church of God International Chapel, Brooklyn, is a branch of the Redeemed Christian Church of God (RCCG), a global ministry founded in Nigeria in 1952.[65] Redeemed refers to itself as a

---

65. The literature on Redeemed is growing. See Asonzeh Franklin-Kennedy Ukah, "The Redeemed Christian Church of God (RCCG), Nigeria: Local Identities and Global Processes in African Pentecostalism" (Ph.D. diss., Bayreuth, 2003), "Mobilities, Migration and Multiplication: The Expansion of the Religious Field of the Redeemed Christian Church of God, Nigeria," in *Religion in the Context of African Migration*, ed. Afe Adogame and Cordula Weissköppel (Bayreuth: Eckhard Breitinger, 2005), 317-41, and *A New Paradigm of Pentecostal Power: A Study of the Redeemed Christian Church of God in Nigeria* (Trenton, N.J.: Africa World Press, 2008); Ruth Marshall, "'God Is Not a Democrat': Pentecostalism and Democratisation in Nigeria," in *The Christian Churches and the Democratisation of Africa*, ed. Paul Gifford (Leiden: Brill, 1995), 254-56; *Political Spiritualities: The Pentecostal Rev-*

FORMATIONS

Fig. 3.9 Sister West in front of the Redeemed Christian Church of God International Chapel, Brooklyn, 2007

"ministry," conveying a more dynamic sensibility than "denomination," a term that is not used by the church. Today the Redeemed Christian Church of God is considered the fastest growing Pentecostal church in Nigeria and Africa, and is comprehensively described in Asonzeh Ukah's *A New Paradigm of Pentecostal Power: A Study of the Redeemed Christian Church of God in Nigeria*.[66] No two answers are the same on the total number of RCCG parishes worldwide, but according to their Web site, there are now "over four million members in about 3,000 parishes all

---

olution in Nigeria (Chicago: University of Chicago Press, 2009); Stephen Hunt and Nicola Lightly, "The British Black Pentecostal 'Revival': Identity and Belief in the 'New' Nigerian Churches," *Ethnic and Racial Studies* 24:1 (2001): 104-24; Stephen Hunt, "'A Church for All Nations': The Redeemed Christian Church of God," *Pneuma* 24:2 (2002): 185-204; Afe Adogame, "Contesting the Ambivalences of Modernity in a Global Context: The Redeemed Christian Church of God, North America," *Studies in World Christianity* 10:1 (2004): 25-48; Olufunke Adeboye, "'Arrowhead' of Nigerian Pentecostalism: The Redeemed Christian Church of God, 1952-2005," *Pneuma* 29 (2007): 24-58.

66. Ukah, *A New Paradigm of Pentecostal Power*.

over the world."⁶⁷ By 2009 there were more than 300 branches in North America and by 2011 nearly 500.⁶⁸

The founder of the Redeemed Christian Church of God is Reverend Josiah ("Papa" or "Pa" in the church's literature) Akindayomi (1909-1980). Baptized by the Church Missionary Society in 1927, Akindayomi joined the Cherubim and Seraphim movement, an Aladura church, in 1931. Discontent with Cherubim and Seraphim and following a "vision" and "call" from God, Papa Akindayomi held the first Redeemed service in Lagos in 1952. At the time of his death in 1980, there were thirty-nine branches in Nigeria, and the church identified itself as an African Independent Church (AIC).⁶⁹

Enoch Adejare Adeboye, a mathematics professor at the time, was Akindayomi's chosen successor to lead the Redeemed Christian Church of God after his death. Adeboye has not merely continued the founder's legacy, but built the Redeemed Christian Church of God into a major force in Nigeria and a global movement.⁷⁰ Referred to by his position as the Redeemed Christian Church of God "General Overseer," Adeboye is also called the G.O. and Daddy G.O; his wife is referred to as Mummy or Mummy G.O. Asonzeh Ukah takes up Max Weber's language to suggest that Adeboye did not simply bring a process of "routinisation" after the passing of the founding charismatic leader, but rather "refounded" the ministry in a manner more like "recharismatisation," represented in the emergence of a new formative figure.⁷¹

In order to attract a new demographic of young Christian converts in the Nigerian universities who would go on to be a future professional class,⁷² the Redeemed Christian Church of God added a new type of parish called the "model parish" to go along with the "classical" parish.⁷³ "Classical" parishes, following the original style of worship that goes back to Akindayomi, employ the Yoruba language for services and are considered very traditional in style within the Redeemed Christian Church of God. Taking a different

---

67. Redeemed Christian Church of God Web site, http://www.rccg.org/.
68. Redeemed Christian Church of God Web site, http://www.rccgna.org/.
69. Ukah, "The Redeemed Christian Church of God," 1.
70. Ukah, "The Redeemed Christian Church of God," 1. See also Ruth Marshall-Fratani, "Mediating the Global and Local in Nigerian Pentecostalism," *Journal of Religion in Africa* 28:3 (1998): 278-315.
71. Ukah, "The Redeemed Christian Church of God," 104-7.
72. Matthews A. Ojo, "The Charismatic Movement in Nigeria Today," *International Bulletin of Missionary Research* 19:3 (1995): 114-18.
73. For a description, see Ukah, "The Redeemed Christian Church of God," 129-37.

tack, the "model" parish, which got its start in the 1980s, embraces English and has adopted more contemporary music and worship practices that appeal to a younger, more formally educated, and aspiring population.

Redeemed Christian Church of God in New York City began in 1995 when Olu Obed held the first service in a rented conference room of the Pennsylvania Hotel, across the street from Madison Square Garden. Believing that God had called him and his wife Eloise (also known as Elsie) to start a Redeemed Church in New York City, Obed carried the sound system on the subway to the first service. Because Eloise had not yet moved to New York, when he began to pray, sing, and worship God, he did so in a room where he was the only person present. Egbefun Adizede was the only other person to join in the service[74] and became the founding member of Redeemed in New York City. In the years to come, she would become a leader at the Redeemed Christian Church of God International Chapel, Brooklyn.

The first service of the Redeemed Christian Church of God International Chapel, Brooklyn, took place in March 1998 in a rented space on Flatbush and Avenue D, with thirteen people in attendance. Later the same year they relocated to another location on Flatbush, this one between Avenues I and J.[75] Flatbush Avenue is a major thoroughfare of social and commercial life for the densely populated African American, West Indian, and African community of Flatbush and the surrounding section of Brooklyn. Beginning in 2000, the church began renting an abandoned warehouse at 672 Parkside Avenue, between Rogers and Nostrand Avenues, and soon the congregation grew to some 200 people. The first time I visited the church, it was winter, and kerosene heaters were placed throughout the room. Renovations to the building came over time, and the presence of the church visibly contributed to the physical and economic redevelopment of the immediate neighborhood.[76]

A strong holiness or moral order, which means modest dress, an eschewal of wedding bands, and strict ethical and moral conduct anchor the church's identity.[77] So also does a sense of destiny or calling. The

---

74. Olu Obed, Interview, February 18, 2004; Egbefun Adieze, Interview, July 16, 2005.

75. Wapaemi Wariboko, Interview, May 29, 2005.

76. Here I reach a potentially different conclusion on the economic role of churches in inner-city neighborhoods than Omar M. McRoberts's important study *Streets of Glory: Church and Community in a Black Urban Neighborhood* (Chicago: University of Chicago Press, 2003).

77. As noted by Matthews Ojo, this holiness theme is prominent in Nigerian Pentecostalism. See Matthews Ojo, "African Charismatics," in *Encyclopedia of African and*

Liturgy and Life

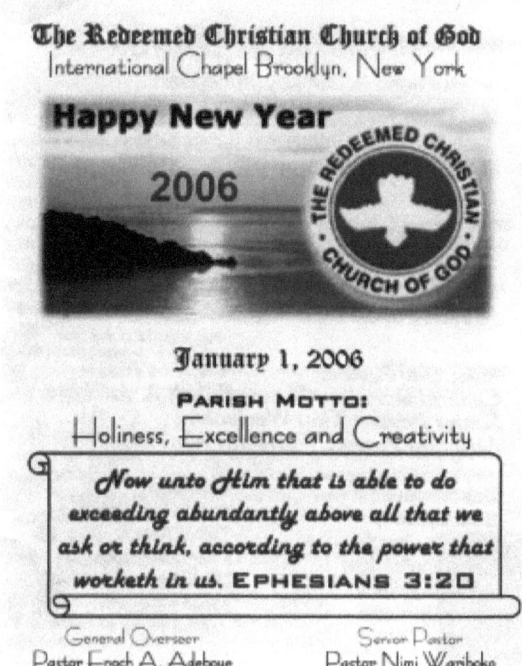

Fig. 3.10 Church bulletin, Redeemed Christian Church of God International Chapel, Brooklyn, 2006

church's motto is "Holiness, Excellence and Creativity," and the thematic biblical text for the church is Ephesians 3:20: "Now unto Him that is able to do exceeding abundantly above all that we ask or think, according to the power that worketh in us." The Ephesians text and motto are printed on the cover of each week's Sunday bulletin, and they lay out Pastor's Nimi's conviction that the church is there to "enable people to step into their God-given destiny."[78] In New York City, where people have for ages come from around the world to succeed, this vision places God at the center of that quest.

African-American Religion, ed. Stephen Glazier (New York: Routledge, 2001), 2-6. At the same time, holiness is considered by Ukah to be distinctive of the classical parish. Within the Brooklyn parish, there is the influence of more than one stream of Redeemed. Marshall, in *Political Spiritualities*, 180, argues that Redeemed is perceived to have maintained its holiness tradition along with the addition of an emphasis on the miraculous.

78. Redeemed Christian Church of God International Chapel, Brooklyn, Field Notes, June 1, 2007.

Fig 3.11 Mother's Day, Redeemed Christian Church of God International, 2009

The Brooklyn parish is given flexibility in operations and decision-making while also lining up with the structures and commitments of Redeemed churches everywhere. There are weekly Bible studies called Digging Deep, numerous monthly all-night vigils, and once a month the Sunday worship is a special anointing service in which God is expected to do particular wonders. Various church departments include the children's ministry, deliverance ministry, building committee, and hospitality. During the week, there are prayer vigils, home fellowship groups, Bible studies, and "Expect a Miracle," all components of the Redeemed Christian Church of God that originated in Nigeria. The workers' program remains the backbone of the church.

Attendance at Sunday worship averages between 200 and 250, a number that declines periodically when members are sent to start a new congregation. But driven by a constant influx of new members and a core group that holds steady, the church always feels as if it is growing and not declining. It is often observed that women numerically outnumber men in African churches, but in the case of the Brooklyn parish, the gender mix is evenly split. The church community generally appears to be young in age, but generational diversity is also apparent.

Church members are almost exclusively Nigerian and predominately Yoruba, but there are also Hausa and Igbo members. Pastor Wariboko is Ijaw. The word "international" at the end of the church's name and a collection of international flags posted at the front of the sanctuary reflect a desire to reach beyond Nigerians to the rest of New York City, as well as the immediate geographical community in Brooklyn, which is largely African American and West Indian. Hospitality and welcome are part of the ethos of the church.

Many of the reasons people give for coming to the Brooklyn parish are expressed by Emmanuel and Omo Obogbaimhe, who have been living in New York City for seven years.[79] Emmanuel can be found each week in the back of the sanctuary operating the sound system, and when she is not working, Omo sings in the choir and serves as leader. Emmanuel works in the corporate world, and in a public testimony, rare for his quiet nature, shares how his knowledge of German was a key in getting a major job. The church claps in response to his good news. When asked why he comes to the church, Emmanuel replies, "I know the power of God is here." At first, Omo attended Times Square Church, a well-known charismatic church in Midtown Manhattan. But "looking for family, home away from home," she made her way to the Redeemed Christian Church of God International Chapel, Brooklyn. Here she worships God and church members help her and Emmanuel raise their children.

Whether at the monthly anointing service or at any gathering, a sense of impossibility always on the cusp of possibility suffuses the Redeemed Christian Church of God International Chapel, Brooklyn. This is due to a belief that Jesus' resurrection is powerfully operative in all areas of life, a result that comes from being "born again." Church members see themselves enfolded into the story of Pentecost. It is perhaps for this reason that the end times do not function as an all-encompassing construct; for the Redeemed, this is resurrection time. The Redeemed Christian Church of God logo is instructive in the regard. Set on the wall behind the pulpit, it depicts a dove descending, symbolizing the Spirit that came upon Christ at his baptism.[80] This brand or logo, along with the theme text of Hebrews 13:8, must be prominently displayed in each Redeemed branch worldwide. At the Brooklyn parish, the focus of the Spirit is a comprehensive redemption for the born-again believer.

---

79. Emmanuel Obogbaimhe, Interview, April 10, 2005, and Omo Obogbaimhe, Interview, May 22, 2005.

80. For a thorough interpretation of the logo, see Ukah, "The Redeemed Christian Church of God," 204-7. The biblical image comes from Luke 3:22.

Speaking in tongues, a practice closely associated with Pentecostalism, can be present at any service, but is not a primary characteristic of worship services or church life as I came to know it. In descriptions of Pentecostalism, it is the Holy Spirit who is given the greatest theological and cultural emphasis. At the Brooklyn church, the Spirit is described as opening the heavens and making life anew in the church, and the fire of the Spirit is invoked as a basis for worship; yet Jesus is most central and pervades the singing, testifying, and praying of the church.[81] People sing to Jesus, pray to Jesus, exult in Jesus' victory, turn to Jesus' power, hope in Jesus, and talk to Jesus.[82] Once a year they hold a "Celebrate Jesus" Sunday where they dress their best, read the Scriptures in all the languages of church members, hire a band, dance, and feast. It is a real celebration.

The theme verse of the Redeemed Christian Church of God International Chapel, Hebrews 13:8, reads, "Jesus is the same yesterday, today, and tomorrow."[83] "Today" brings the immanence of Jesus strongly into the present. Because Jesus spans all of time, his earthly life and work bear directly on present circumstances. This may be one reason why there is little overt emphasis on millennial beliefs. There is no liturgical calendar, but instead a strong sense that the beginning of a new year brings afresh the possibility of attaining a "new level" in life.[84] As we will see in chapter four, this is part of the reason why February is a month of fasting across Redeemed churches worldwide.

Redeemed Christian Church of God International Chapel, Brooklyn, is a community in the heart of Brooklyn where people are empowered by God to move forward in their new lives in New York City. They are followers of Jesus who find their lives in the worship and life-giving power of Jesus and the Spirit of God.

---

81. I found this to be true of African Pentecostal churches inclusively.

82. This stress on worshiping Jesus resonates with New Testament patterns. See here the important work of Larry Hurtado, *Lord Jesus Christ: Devotion to Jesus in Earliest Christianity* (Grand Rapids: Eerdmans, 2003). Although not focused on Pentecostal churches, for relevant insights see the work of Diane B. Stinton, "Jesus-Immanuel, Image of the Invisible God: Aspects of Popular Christology in Sub-Saharan Africa," *Journal of Reformed Theology* 1 (2007): 6-40, and *Jesus of Africa: Voices of Contemporary African Christology* (Maryknoll, N.Y.: Orbis, 2004).

83. Hebrews 13:8 plays a role in Pentecostal theology. See, for example, Matthew Avery Sutton, *Aimee Semple McPherson and the Resurrection of Christian America* (Cambridge: Harvard University Press, 2007), 38.

84. This is confirmed by Ukah, "The Redeemed Christian Church of God," 235-38.

Globalizing Faith

In chapter one, I emphasized the global city as a primary context for locating the cross-border development of African churches in New York City. Globalization, identified here as the manner in which the histories, liturgies, and common life of the Presbyterian Church of Ghana, the Church of the Lord (Aladura), and the Redeemed Christian Church of God International Chapel, Brooklyn, circulate, occur within connected or global cities. Globalization of religion is hardly new, of course, as we know from past missionary movements.[85] But in the present episode of globalization there is a redefining of belonging and movement that takes in and moves beyond older patterns of movement. Three features of globalization illuminate how African Christianity has come to make a home in New York City.

Globalization Is Multi-Faceted

As the three churches in this chapter show us, globalization is not just economic, but religious and more as well. Despite the prominence of the economic factor,[86] a purely materialist analysis is too analytically constrictive for understanding African and world Christianity. I think it is better to speak of "economic globalization" as but one form or dimension of globalization. The emphasis on the economic dimension is frequently a way of fitting together neo-liberalism, market capitalism, transnational corporations, and American consumerism.[87] Globalization is then either something very good for the world's poor because it is equated with opportunity, or very bad because it produces new patterns of exclusion.[88]

For David Held and the co-authors of *Global Transformations*, globalization involves three dimensions: extensity, intensity, and velocity. Globalization is measured by the degree and depth of political, social, and

---

85. Webb Keane, *Christian Moderns: Freedom and Fetish in the Mission Encounter* (Berkeley: University of California Press, 2007), 41-47. See Vásquez and Marquardt, *Globalizing the Sacred*, for a discussion of episodes of globalization.

86. Teresa Okure, "Africa: Globalization and the Loss of Cultural Identity," *Concilium* 5 (2001): 67-74.

87. Cliff Marrs, "Globalization: A Short Introduction to a New World Religion," *Political Theology* 4:1 (2001): 91-116; Neil Smith, *The Endgame of Globalization* (New York: Routledge, 2005).

88. Jagdish Bhagwati, *In Defense of Globalization* (New York: Oxford University Press, 2005). Joseph Stiglitz provides a different analysis of economic globalization.

economic interconnectedness in the world, and the speed at which these exchanges occur.[89] Within this broader framework, cultures move across borders.[90] David Harvey explains globalization as the "time-space compression,"[91] the acceleration in production, capital movement, and culture along with flexibility. Manuel Vásquez helpfully refines Harvey's proposal: "Although globalization is a complex cluster of economic, socio-political, and cultural phenomena, we can heuristically characterize it as a tensile interplay between time-space compression and distanciation."[92] He continues, "At a minimum, the dialectic of time-space compression and distanciation challenges the modernist assumptions that equated territory, culture, and polity. Widespread flows of people, capital, goods, and ideas make it increasingly untenable to map the world according to the tidy logic of one nation, one culture, one language, one religion, one history, and one self-contained social formation."[93] Therefore a greater awareness of fluid identities, international movements, overlapping identities, and continually shifting borders is very important for understanding religion in a global world.[94] Globalization can be from "above" and also from "below."[95]

Globalization Is Networks

Networks, which ground globalization, are a critical factor in the dissemination of African Christianity in New York City.[96] We find this developed

---

89. David Held, Anthony McGrew, David Goldblatt, and Jonathan Perraton, *Global Transformations: Politics, Economics and Culture* (Stanford: Stanford University Press, 1999), 2, 15.

90. Arjun Appadurai, *Modernity at Large: Cultural Dimensions of Globalization* (Minneapolis: University of Minnesota Press, 1996).

91. David Harvey, *The Condition of Postmodernity* (Cambridge: Blackwell, 1990), 284-307. Conversely, one might think of globalization as the reverse, from the *compression* of space and time to the *expansion* of space and time. See Kiran Mirchandani, "Practices of Global Capital: Gaps, Cracks and Ironies in Transnational Call Centres in India," *Global Networks: A Journal of Transnational Affairs* 4:4 (October 2004): 365.

92. Manuel A. Vásquez, "Studying Religion in Motion: A Networks Approach," *Method and Theory in the Study of Religion* 20:2 (2008): 1.

93. Vásquez, "Studying Religion in Motion," 2.

94. See also José Casanova, "Religion, the New Millennium, and Globalization," *Sociology of Religion* 62:4 (2001): 415-41.

95. Gustavo Lins Ribeiro, "Non-Hegemonic Globalizations: Alternative Transnational Processes and Agents," *Anthropological Theory* 9:3 (2009) 297-329.

96. Manuel A. Vásquez, "The Limits of the Hydrodynamics of Religion," *Journal of*

Liturgy and Life

in David Maxwell's important study, *African Gifts of the Spirit: Pentecostalism and the Rise of a Zimbabwean Transnational Religious Movement*.[97] Networks are "conduits" that move religious leaders, symbols, goods, practices, and experiences — the entire spectrum of lived religion. Incorporated into this idea of networks is the construct of transnationalism, the idea that communities exist as a part of multiple settings at once.[98] As Vásquez describes networks in relationship to religion, churches are embedded in diffuse and constantly evolving informal and institutional religious networks that move across boundaries.[99] Because in a global world more than one setting is involved, Larissa Ruiz Baia is also right to suggest moving "transnationalism away from a strict bipolarity and closer to a more complex notion of multipolarity."[100] In this reality, even space itself needs to be reconceptualized as fluid and dynamic.[101] Because of networks, African churches have a "foot" in more than one world. Or put another way, religious networks distribute the transcendent in a globalized world.[102] How-

---

the American Academy of Religion 77:2 (2009): 434-45; Vásquez, "Studying Religion in Motion." See also Helen Rose Ebaugh and Janet Saltzman Chafetz, eds., *Religion Across Borders: Transnational Immigrant Networks* (Walnut Creek: Altamira Press, 2002).

97. David Maxwell, *African Gifts of the Spirit: Pentecostalism and the Rise of a Zimbabwean Transnational Religious Movement* (Oxford: James Currey, 2006).

98. For a thorough review of issues and the literature, see Peggy Levitt and B. Nadya Jaworsky, "Transnational Migration Studies: Past Developments and Future Trends," *Annual Review of Sociology* 33 (2007): 129-56. For a comprehensive source that takes religion into account, see Sanjeev Khagram and Peggy Levitt, eds., *The Transnational Studies Reader: Intersections and Innovations* (New York: Routledge, 2008). Additionally, see Peggy Levitt, "Transnational Migration: Taking Stock and Future Directions," *Global Networks* 1:3 (2001): 195-216. Levitt elaborates on the religious dimension in *God Needs No Passport: Immigrants and the Changing American Religious Landscape* (New York: The New Press, 2007). See also Aihwa Ong, *Flexible Citizenship: The Cultural Logics of Transnationality* (Durham: Duke University Press, 1999).

99. Vásquez, "Studying Religion in Motion," 27-29.

100. Larissa Ruiz Baia, "Rethinking Transnationalism: National Identities among Peruvian Catholics in New Jersey," in *Christianity, Social Change, and Globalization in the Americas*, ed. Anna L. Peterson, Manuel A. Vásquez, and Philip J. Williams (New Brunswick: Rutgers University Press, 2001), 164.

101. Huib Ernste, Henk Van Houtum, and Annelies Zommers, "Trans-World: Debating the Place and Borders of Places in the Age of Transnationalism," *Tijdschrift voor Economische en Sociale Geografie* 100:5 (2009): 577-86.

102. Thomas J. Csordas, "Introduction: Modalities of Transnational Transcendence," *Anthropological Theory* 7:4 (2007): 259-72. See the larger discussion of this theme in Thomas J. Csordas, ed., *Transnational Transcendence: Essays on Religion and Globalization* (Berkeley: University of California Press, 2009).

ever, we should also note that networks are not immune to the effects of a "gated" global world.[103]

Networks are also related to social fields or social worlds.[104] Social worlds are how people and communities situate themselves, mapping religious and moral geographies, where networks connect and ecclesial life is formed, and therefore are a source of support, power, and expansion in the global world.[105] As Vásquez puts it, "Within and through networks, actors carve out spaces to dwell, itineraries, and everyday routines, drawing from religious symbols and tropes to reflect on and orient their own praxis and to 'sacralize' nature and build environments."[106]

A discussion of globalization invariably leads to questions concerning the role and function of the state. Frequently one hears of the state's declining role in a global world, almost a prophecy of an end to the nation-state paradigm. But in another set of arguments, the state actually facilitates globalization.[107] It is obvious that I cannot thoroughly elaborate on this discussion here, but I can say that national identities appear to be retained by African Christians yet remain in negotiation as a new form of social life across borders. National borders and laws remain real for immigrants; the global world is indeed gated. In other words, the nation-state has not been transcended in globalization, but borders and places are more dynamic and open in many ways because of it.

Globalization Is Organizational

Through urban-based networks, the Presbyterian Church of Ghana, the Church of the Lord (Aladura), and the Redeemed Christian Church of God International Chapel have reproduced their organizational struc-

---

103. Vásquez, "The Limits of the Hydrodynamics of Religion."

104. Nina Glick Schiller, "Transmigrants and Nation-States," in *The Handbook of International Migration: The American Experience*, ed. Josh DeWind, Charles Hirschman, and Philip Kasinitz (New York: Russell Sage, 1999), 97-98; Glick Schiller, "Transnational Social Fields and Imperialism: Bringing a Theory of Power to Transnational Studies," *Anthropological Theory* 5:4 (2005): 439-61.

105. Joel Robbins, "Pentecostal Networks and the Spirit of Globalization: On the Social Productivity of Ritual Forms," *Social Analysis* 53:1 (2009): 55-66.

106. Vásquez, "Studying Religion in Motion," 169.

107. Saskia Sassen, *Territory, Authority, Rights: From Medieval to Global Assemblages* (Princeton: Princeton University Press, 2006).

Liturgy and Life

tures, liturgies, histories, and institutions, groups, events, rituals, and practices in New York. Scholars describe this process as the deterritorialization and reterritorialization of faith, the *"breaking down and reconstitution of spatial scales"* across space and time.[108] "Religion," Manuel Vásquez and Marie Marquardt underscore, "is one of the main protagonists in . . . [the] unbinding of culture from its traditional referents and boundaries and in its reattachment in new space-time configurations."[109] The reorganization of space and time across borders also involves the transfer of religious institutions, experiences, practices, and beliefs through networks.

There are different "types" of global structures. Afe Adogame and Gerrie ter Haar offer typologies of African churches in Europe, marking off some as branches of churches whose mother church is headquartered in Africa, others as within existing church structures, and still others are newly established.[110] For immigrant religious life, Peggy Levitt formulates the helpful model of a "transnational religious corporation."[111]

> Increasingly, religious organizations are taking their place alongside . . . global corporate and political actors. Worldwide production and distribution networks also manufacture religious goods. The local mosque or church is just one brick in this extensive global religious architecture. Some structures simply connect immigrants with people in their homelands. Others link them to fellow believers around the world. As a result, like politics and economics, domestic religion is both transnationally and nationally produced.[112]

Levitt breaks this out in greater detail, classifying three types of transnational religious corporations. First there is the "extended transnational religious organization" oriented to the Catholic Church. This enables the church to integrate migrants into existing structures where they can contribute while retaining a sense of belonging to home.[113] Second, there is the "ne-

---

108. Vásquez and Marquardt, *Globalizing the Sacred*, 51.
109. Vásquez and Marquardt, *Globalizing the Sacred*, 35.
110. Here I am combining the typologies of Afe Adogame, "The Quest for Space in the Global Spiritual Marketplace: African Religions in Europe," *International Review of Mission* 89:354 (2000): 400-401, and Gerrie ter Haar, "Strangers in the Promised Land: African Christians in Europe," *Exchange* 24:1 (1995): 7.
111. Levitt, *God Needs No Passport*, 113-35.
112. Levitt, *God Needs No Passport*, 117.
113. Peggy Levitt, "Redefining the Boundaries of Belonging," *Sociology of Religion* 65:1 (2004): 2.

gotiated transnational organization," whereby notably Protestant churches find ways to "negotiate power sharing, leadership, and financial management."[114] Third, there are "recreated transnational religious organizations," which operate like "franchises or chapters of sending country religious organizations."[115] The Presbyterian Church of Ghana in Harlem, The Church of the Lord (Aladura), and Redeemed Christian Church of God International Chapel reflect Levitt's third pattern, and generally use the term "branch" to describe their relationship to their larger organization.

In summary, "Religion's role in globalization," as Manuel Vásquez and Marie Marquardt acutely observe, "is at once . . . widespread, concrete, and vital. What interacts with globalization is lived religion — specific religious practices, discourses, and institutions which constitute the fabric of social life for large segments of the population around the world."[116] At some points we will see the activities of African churches as resisting globalization,[117] and at others times churches will be active participants in globalization. But African Christianity is not a fundamentalist reaction to globalization,[118] but a way of engaging the world with a great sense of the future, not a reaction that looks to the past.[119] Globalization creates new opportunities for the diffusion of African Christianity, even as it brings inherent contradictions.

Conclusion

Liturgy for African Christians in New York is characteristically about life — ordinary daily life. So my approach to the Presbyterian Church of Ghana, the Church of the Lord (Aladura), and the Redeemed Christian Church of God International Chapel has been to begin by setting them within the context of worship, which turns us to their histories and life to-

114. Levitt, "Redefining the Boundaries of Belonging," 3.
115. Levitt, "Redefining the Boundaries of Belonging."
116. Vásquez and Marquardt, *Globalizing the Sacred*, 51. See also Manuel A. Vásquez, "Tracking Global Evangelical Christianity," *Journal of the American Academy of Religion* 71:1 (2003): 157-73.
117. For an important study in this regard, see Timothy John Padwick, "Spirit, Desire and the World: Roho Churches of Western Kenya in the Era of Globalization" (Ph.D. diss., University of Birmingham, 2003).
118. Manuel Castells, *The Power of Identity* (Oxford: Blackwell, 1997), 5-27.
119. Marshall, *Political Spiritualities*, 17-50.

gether. I have also sought to place their experience within the complexities of a globalizing world and networks that are at the heart of religious place making. The churches are not defensive sanctuaries or enclaves, but through their liturgies, a reference point in an often unstable, confusing, and complex global world. The church is a community where God is present, saving and delivering with power. Liturgy works to form a way of life by enabling church members to understand the world and bodily participate in God's new world. Preaching, prayer, healing, community, and theological beliefs are oriented toward a way of being in the city.

III. ENGAGEMENTS

4. Praying Bodies: God and Everyday Life

Introduction: Learning to Pray

After my first few weeks at the Church of the Lord (Aladura), I was invited to offer some of the prayers that are a part of the regular Sunday liturgy. Kneeling down, as directed, I offered prayers for "the city, the world, for Christian ministers around the world, and for the leaders of the Church of the Lord (Aladura)." This invitation to pray was an act of hospitality, but also intended as formation in the practices of the church. Following the service, Sister Sarah remarked that after my time at the church, "Your wife will ask, how did you learn how to pray like that?" She laughed, but what was underneath her comment was a belief that by being part of the Church of the Lord (Aladura) I really would learn to pray differently. What I would be taught was more than vocal styles and speech patterns; it was the heart of the church's understanding of Christian faith.

What do I know without ambiguity after my years of worshiping with African Christians? They pray. They pray standing up, they praying moving around, they pray kneeling down, they pray in loud voices, they pray all night. African Christians believe in the efficacy of prayer, join it with regular and intense fasting, and offer their lives to a God who hears and acts. Life is about prayer, and prayer is life. Prayer is theology lived, embodied, and enacted in daily life.

Drawing a perhaps surprising contrast with a church Bible study, Bola Oyesanya of the Redeemed Christian Church of God International Chapel remarked in passing, "Tell them [there is] a prayer meeting, and the whole place will be filled." David Maxwell's study of Zimbabwean Pentecostals offers a concurring observation: "More important still is the power of prayer."¹ Bible reading may be essential, and its words the means of praying, but because prayer is direct and unmediated communication with the divine,² it can be a form of immediate power. "It is in the experience of vernacular prayer," Adrian Hastings observed, "both public and private, both formal and informal, and in the spirituality which grows up from such experience that the true roots for an authentic African Christianity will most surely be found."³ Afe Adogame calls prayer the "nerve-centre of Aladura spirituality,"⁴ an observation that might be extended more broadly within African Christianity. Bengt Sundkler and Christopher Steed call prayer "the very heart-beat of religion."⁵

Saskia Sassen, in her work on the global city, perceives its contradictory form. "The global city is a strategic site for disempowered actors because it enables them to gain presence, to emerge as subjects, even when they do not gain direct power."⁶ That is, if Sassen believes the global city is a limiting social form, it nonetheless can be a "strategic space"⁷ for non-state actors, transnational movements, women, and immigrants to emerge as political subjects. This is another aspect of Sassen's description of the global city, a compelling recognition that the city is potentially a site where inequality can be challenged and compelling claims for social and political rights put forward.⁸

Prayer to the God all of power is a way African believers make claims on the world in which they find themselves. In light of the pervasive inter-

---

1. David Maxwell, *African Gifts of the Spirit: Pentecostalism and the Rise of a Zimbabwean Transnational Religious Movement* (Oxford: James Currey, 2006), 197. For another concurring observation, see Cephas N. Omenyo, *Pentecost Outside Pentecostalism: A Study of the Development of Charismatic Renewal in the Mainline Churches in Ghana* (Zoetermeer: Uitgeverij Boekencentrum, 2002), 202.

2. This is basic to religious belief, as shown in Bruce Ellis Benson and Norman Wirzba, eds., *The Phenomenology of Prayer* (New York: Fordham University Press, 2005).

3. Adrian Hastings, *African Christianity* (New York: Seabury Press, 1976), 49.

4. Afeosemime Adogame, "Prayer as Action and Instrument in the Aladura Churches," in *Opfer und Gebet in den Religionen*, ed. Ulrich Berner, Christopher Bochinger, and Rainer Flasche (Gutersloh: Bertelsmann, 2005), 118.

5. Bengt Sundkler and Christopher Steed, *A History of the Church in Africa* (Cambridge: Cambridge University Press, 2000), 94.

6. Saskia Sassen, *The Global City: New York, London, Tokyo*, 2nd ed. (Princeton: Princeton University Press, 2001), xxi.

7. Sassen, *The Global City*, 319.

8. Saskia Sassen, "The Many Scales of the Global: Implications for Theory and for Politics," in *The Postcolonial and the Global*, ed. Revathi Krishnaswamy and John C. Hawley (Minneapolis: University of Minnesota Press, 2008), 82-93.

est in the New Testament on power, parallels in African Christianity should not be surprising.[9] "Anyone who wishes to make sense of the revival of religion in the world must think of spiritual power as real power," observe Stephen Ellis and Gerrie ter Haar.[10] In African Christianity, spiritual power is "enabling power," as Allan Anderson puts it.[11] Amid the torsions of powers and at the intersections of the global city's contradictions, African Christians at prayer represent a distinctive way of being in the global city. Prayer is a way of life, expressing a set of convictions about God and the world, involving mind and body.

Praying Communities

At the beginning of his *Confessions*, Augustine asks: "How shall I call upon my God, my God and my Lord?"[12] For the Church of the Lord (Aladura), the Redeemed Christian Church of God International Chapel, Brooklyn, and the Presbyterian Church of Ghana in New York, the answer begins with community. African churches are praying communities. In prayer, they individually raise their voices to God, but in community there is God's presence, and to pray as a church is to be where God is active.

Strong and Spiritual Prayers

Minister Joy, Evangelists Sarah and Eleanor, Brother David, and Mother Cooper pray at all hours of the day and for everything. There are two particular types of prayers: "spiritual prayers" and "strong prayers." Ex-

---

9. For the thematic attention to power throughout early Christianity, see Luke Timothy Johnson, *The Writings of the New Testament: An Interpretation*, rev. ed. (Minneapolis: Fortress, 1999) and *Among the Gentiles: Greco-Roman Religion and Christianity* (New Haven: Yale University Press, 2009).

10. Stephen Ellis and Gerrie ter Haar, *Worlds of Power: Religious Thought and Political Practice in Africa* (New York: Oxford University Press, 2004), 189; cf. 97-99.

11. Allan H. Anderson, "Pentecostal Pneumatology and African Power Concepts: Continuity or Change?" *Missionalia* 19:1 (1990): 68, and "African Pentecostal Churches and Concepts of Power," unpublished paper, http://artsweb.bham.ac.uk/aanderson/Publications/apcs_and_concepts_of_power.htm. Here I am following a lead suggested by Ellis and ter Haar, *Worlds of Power*, 97. See also Allan H. Anderson, *Moya: The Holy Spirit in an African Context* (Pretoria: The University of South Africa, 1991).

12. Augustine, *The Confessions* (Oxford: Oxford University Press, 1992), 3.

plained Mother Cooper, "spiritual prayers" are a "shield" against malevolent forces. Strong prayers are those you "can feel within [the] self." Spiritual prayers and strong prayers are spiritual power for whatever need is presented to God.[13] Such prayers mark the life of the community. For "all children of God" in the Church of the Lord (Aladura), not just leaders, prayer is expected to occur five times each day: at 6:00 a.m. when they awake, at 9:00 a.m. before work, at 12:00 p.m., at 3:00 p.m., and then around 9:00 p.m. before going to sleep.[14] The spirit of this program is for each member to pray without ceasing. Prayer is not simply something one does at the Church of the Lord (Aladura); it is what it means to be the church.

This is to be expected, for "Aladura," a Yoruba word, means "the praying people" or "owners of prayer."[15] J. D. Y. Peel identifies an underlying theological narrative: "Aladura churches are well-named; *adura*, prayer, is the focal point of all their doctrines and practices."[16] In the world of the Aladura, God is engaged in the world, particularly as a respondent to the prayers of the church. Peel captures the dynamic relationship between God and prayer. "Prayer may be the supplication to God to fulfil the individual's wishes and desires, or else a way of getting guidance from God, or, in religious terms, knowing His Will."[17] Robin Horton concludes similarly, "They believe that prayer to God, properly conducted, brings definite and predictable results in the world of space-time events. It cures disease, brings financial success, secures promotion, and so on."[18]

Prayer for the Church of the Lord (Aladura) in the Bronx involves the whole body, not merely the vocal cords. Prayers of great length are offered while lying prostrate on the ground, kneeling, or sometimes standing. Prayer can also be loud. As the visiting Archdeacon Lachana commented, we are "not here for meditation. . . . Let us pray . . . open your mouths. If you want a 'quiet time,' then go outside," he announced.[19] In addition to the formulaic prayers, there is a certain cadence and vocabulary

---

13. Marie Cooper, Interview, February 13, 2005.

14. Marie Cooper, Interview, October 21, 2007.

15. Adogame, "Engaging the Rhetoric of Spiritual Warfare," *Journal of Religion in Africa* 34:4 (2004): 493.

16. J. D. Y. Peel, *Aladura: A Religious Movement Among the Yoruba* (London: Oxford University Press, 1968), 119.

17. Peel, *Aladura*, 119.

18. Robin Horton, "African Conversion," *Africa* 41:2 (1971): 88.

19. Church of the Lord (Aladura), Field Notes, August 22, 2004.

Praying Bodies

Fig. 4.1 Prayer at the Church of the Lord (Aladura), facing the altar, 2005

to the prayers of the Church of the Lord (Aladura) in the Bronx that appear to have more than one source, including prayer traditions specific to Liberia and also from the liturgy of the Church of the Lord (Aladura). The charismatic, spontaneous, and ecstatic prayers have recognizable patterns and word combinations such as "Thank you, Jesus."

Few of the prayers follow a text; most are spontaneous. Yet "spontaneous" prayers in the Church of the Lord (Aladura) very much reflect repetitive linguistic and rhythmic patterns.[20] In each Sunday service, prayers of adoration, prayers of thanksgiving to God, prayers of victory, and prayers for the church are offered. Prayer as praise, intercession, and adoration is the emphasis throughout the service. There is an emphasis on confession of sin in prayer. Each service includes a recitation of the Lord's Prayer.

---

20. This observation applies to each of the three churches. Robin A. Shoaps, "'Pray Earnestly': The Textual Construction of Personal Involvement in Pentecostal Prayer and Song," *Journal of Linguistic Anthropology* 12:1 (2002): 34-71.

Fig. 4.2 Redeemed Christian Church of God workers' prayer, 2004

Sermons with God

"Redeemed is very, very prayerful," Wale Adebo, a member of the Redeemed Christian Church of God International Chapel, Brooklyn, tells me. He attends the church with his wife and young children. The practical effects of his ties to the local church are significant: "I find out that when I come to church, I have this belief and my prayers get answered." Or as he also put it, "When you pray . . . things get done."[21]

When the church prays, it is typically not one person speaking on behalf of the community to God. Instead every member prays vocally at once along with vigorous bodily gestures: hands waving, feet stomping, and movement around the room. I call this highly kinetic and emotionally charged form of prayer "preaching prayer," because it looks and sounds like each person is vigorously preaching simultaneously. The church at prayer is a preaching community. Because prayer is like a sermon addressed to God, and God is expected to answer, it appears to be a dialogical sermon with God.

21. Wale Adebo, Interview, April 10, 2005.

In a common example, the congregation is told to pray, and everyone begins to speak in voices and kinetic movements to God. A woman praying aloud next to me speaks to God in the following way:[22]

> Father God, speak. Father, do something! God Father. Once you have said it I believe it. O Lord, may it come to pass. Glorify yourself. Let your Spirit lead me. Let him lead me to my destiny.

She then speaks in tongues and adds concise lines of praise in English. Simultaneously, Pastor Nimi quotes John 3 to the congregation about the living waters of God and then declares, "It will flow to you and other people." The woman begins to pray aloud, "Let it flow." The session continues with more Bible verses and more prayers that relate to these themes.

There is no firm line between sermon and congregation-wide prayer; the two are really one activity. But at the "end" of a sermon on Jesus and the power of God, Pastor Nimi calls on the church to pray.[23] The man next to me starts loudly repeating the words, "Let your power remain in me," as he raises his hands up and down and snaps his fingers. The words vary a bit, but he continues to speak in a loud voice, "Let the seed of life, let it stream over me. Letting your power, let your power shine in me." This continues for over five minutes, with more than 150 people in the room engaged in similar preaching prayer. The prayer eventually ends with the words, "In the name of Jesus we pray, Amen."

Prayer without Ceasing

The rhythms of a life of prayer at Presbyterian Church of Ghana in New York are represented in Diana Owusu.[24] Diana works the night shift at a nursing care facility of the elderly. After a night of hard work, she returns home and sleeps briefly, waking up at 8:00 a.m. for morning prayers. But instead of travelling to the church, she dials a telephone number that switches her into a prayer meeting with between four and nine fellow members. Over the telephone, they pray for everyday needs.

---

22. Redeemed Christian Church of God International Chapel, Brooklyn, Field Notes, June 22, 2005.
23. Redeemed Christian Church of God International Chapel, Brooklyn, Field Notes, October 14, 2007.
24. Diana Owusu, Interview, July 20, 2007.

ENGAGEMENTS

Fig. 4.3 "Pray without Ceasing" uniform, 2007

Diana offers a theological and practical set of reasons for her life of prayer:

> God is our Father. Every time you wake up you know he has taken care of you. You pray to him and thank him for the day. You ask God for help, to give you good health. Every day something happens, anything can happen. In the subway, on the street, a stray bullet [could kill you]. Every time I go out, I pray. When I come back, I thank him. It's good for me [to pray]. He listens to me and helps me.[25]

Along with other members of the Bible Study and Prayer Group, Diana sometimes goes and visits the sick to pray with them. "That's how we help each other," Diana asserts.[26]

The prayer life of the Presbyterian Church of Ghana in New York provides another indication of the influence of both solemn and formal

25. Diana Owusu, Interview, March 4, 2008.
26. Diana Owusu, Interview, March 4, 2008.

Protestant prayer styles and the charismatic movement in Ghana.[27] Corporate prayer during Sunday worship service is in a solemn and formal style. Typically prayer is led by a single person and is not a vocally communal experience. For example, on Easter Sunday in 2005, a prayer was offered for visitors, the sick, and "PCG departmental directors" in Ghana. For the sick, the church was called to pray that the "Lord would strengthen and heal them," and for "departmental heads in Ghana" the prayer was, "Lord, guide them."

One of the most important groups in the church, the Bible Study and Prayer Group of the Presbyterian Church of Ghana meets on Friday evenings from 7:00-9:00 p.m. at the church's building on 123rd Street. Most of the women wear scarves on their heads with the words "Presbyterian Church Bible Study and Prayer Group" on the back and "Pray without Ceasing" on the front. Cephas Omenyo identifies the Bible Study and Prayer Group as "the main charismatic renewal group in the PCG, which has spread through the church."[28]

A typical meeting of the Bible Study and Prayer Group begins with the group gathering around a table, singing and clapping their hands.[29] If the first song is in Twi, the next is the familiar "Do something new in my life/something new in my life" sung in English. The leader directs the group to be attentive to God's involvement in their lives, "to pray and thank God for what he has done" this past week. At once, voices in English and Twi thank God. "Thank you, Father/say hallelujah/hallelujah/hallelujah be unto you," prays the leader. Then we are instructed to praise God for working in our lives and ask for forgiveness of sins, and more vocal praying goes on. "In Jesus' name we pray" is how this time ends. And then we sing, "Let the power of the Lord come down/Let the Spirit of the Lord come down." A Bible study follows, then an offering, and then a closing song.

"Prayers are the weapons of Christians," Kwabena Gyasi of the Bible Study and Prayer Group explains.[30] Prayer also has to do with the "self," showing that "more depends on you" to pray. To emphasize, he repeats

---

27. Omenyo, *Pentecost Outside Pentecostalism*, 127-53; J. Kwabena Asamoah-Gyadu, "'Christ is the Answer: What is the Question?' A Ghana Airways Prayer Vigil and Its Implications for Religion, Evil and Public Space," *Journal of Religion in Africa* 35:1 (2005): 93-117.

28. Omenyo, *Pentecost Outside Pentecostalism*, 140.

29. Presbyterian Church of Ghana in New York, Field Notes, August 20, 2004.

30. Kwabena Gyasi, Interview, August 19, 2005.

that the "most important work is you." That is, he ascribes responsibility to the individual. As a basis for this claim, he points out that Jesus "had to pray . . . otherwise he could not do it," the "it" referring to the cross. The need is great, Kwabena emphasizes, for "Satan will test you — a Christian — not those on the street."

Prayer through the Night

Night is a time of spiritual significance for African Christians. In the city that never sleeps, African Christians can be found awake at all-night fusions of prayer, singing, preaching, and healing usually accompanied by fasting. All-night prayer meetings face up to the fullness of intense spiritual struggles in the universe. Adebisi Oyesile, a member of the Redeemed Christian Church of God International Chapel, Brooklyn, describes why prayer during the night is considered so crucial:

> Before anything happens in life, [it] happened in the spiritual realm. The principalities and powers of darkness work at night, between midnight and 4:00 am. If the enemy wants to attack, it will be at night.[31]

Night vigil is important as a sustained period of prayer and praise, but also as a means of confronting the powers of evil. For this, Adebisi reports that many times he arises to pray during the hours of 3:00 and 4:00 in the morning. Dreams and "night visions" are equally part of the struggle and opportunity of these key hours.[32] While the term "warfare prayer" does not fully describe what takes place during a night vigil,[33] it does reflect an underlying concern. The struggle against the powers requires physically intense engagement. The Redeemed Christian Church of God in Brooklyn calls an all-night prayer meeting a "night vigil" or "Holy Ghost service," the Church of the Lord (Aladura) in the Bronx a "tarry," and the Presbyterian Church of Ghana often labels it a "revival." While a differentiated account of each type of vigil is helpful, they are all venues for African immigrants to praise God and bring their everyday needs to God and expect God to work "breakthroughs" in health, work, family, immigration status, fertility,

---

31. Adebisi Oyesile, Interview, January 19, 2008.
32. Adebisi Oyesile, Interview, January 19, 2008.
33. Neela Banerjee, "A Midnight Service Helps African Immigrants Combat Demons," *New York Times*, Tuesday, December 18, 2007, A-24.

and circumstances back home. They are physical acts of discipline interpreted theologically as an event in which an especially potent response is to be expected from God. Night is the time in which the struggle for life and wholeness is directly engaged.

Tarry

The "tarry" is the all-night service of the Church of the Lord (Aladura) held on the first Friday of each month. A tarry, Mother Cooper summarizes, involves "praying, preaching, all night singing . . . praise to the Lord."[34] The act of "tarrying" recalls the gospel story and belongs to the Pentecostal tradition: "In Pentecostal worship, tarrying implies travelling, waiting, prostrating, and submitting oneself before the presence of God in hopes that God's presence might break forth in the mundane and profane circumstances of life."[35] To tarry is to embrace the coming of God's new world.

I arrive at a tarry a little after 9:00 p.m., take off my shoes in the entrance area, and then join Flower and a friend who has accompanied him to the service.[36] Soon Minister Joy comes down from the upstairs apartment and begins a time of praise worship. "Glory be to God in the highest, Hallelujah," the church sings. Shortly thereafter, Mother Cooper arrives and rings the hand bell that formally gets things going. Appropriately, the next hymn begins, "Abide with me/Fast falls the eventide/The darkness deepen/Lord with me abide."[37] The slowly filling room turns to God on its knees, then the "Introit" hymn of "holy words" is sung. "Saffudda Missa Bullal/Ottass Yemi na hu/Waddarrar mi yo sulla/Wen, wen, wen, Rojjabb Ell" are the words of the first stanza.[38] "The year is coming to an end and the Lord wants us to greet him from our hearts," Mother Cooper asserts. This leads to a "three-minute secret confession of sin" that is concluded with a "prayer for cleansing."

For a stretch of over fifteen minutes, Mother Cooper recites names and descriptions of God. "Jehovah," she states, and the church responds back, "Holy, Holy, Holy." She goes on, "One in three and three in one," the

---

34. Marie Cooper, Church of the Lord (Aladura), August 29, 2004.

35. Daniel Costelo, "Tarrying on the Lord: Affections, Virtues and Theological Ethics in Pentecostal Perspective," *Journal of Pentecostal Theology* 13:1 (2004): 50.

36. Church of the Lord (Aladura), Field Notes, November 2 and 3, 2007.

37. *The Church of the Lord (Aladura) Worldwide English Hymn Book*, no. 49.

38. *The Church of the Lord (Aladura) Worldwide English Hymn Book*, no. 18.

church's common frequent reference to the Trinity. "What a God we have!" Then a new member is assigned to pray on behalf of the nations, all churches, all ministers, doctors and nurses, and prisoners. "No one knows what prayer you answer," Mother Cooper explains. There is much more singing, including "Victory Hymns" and a rousing version of "Onward Christian Soldiers." At 10:30 p.m., the singing turns to "Shouts," including "He's a miracle-working God." Minister Joy continues the theme of asking God to be present. "We have come for tarry. Lord, look down from your throne on high and grant us your presence."

As the midnight hour approaches and more people arrive, Sister Sarah delivers the first sermon. Her text is Mark 12:28, and she emphasizes the need for each member "to lend a helping hand to one another." At the midnight hour, Mother Cooper announces that now is the time for prayer. "Shout House of Prayer!" Mother Cooper exhorts. There are many prayers, and a song just for the moment: "Sweet hour of prayer!/Sweet hour of prayer!/That calls me from a world of care."

After midnight, Brother Clark preaches the second sermon from Acts 10. "Are you hungry?" he asks from the text. "Have you saved a soul?" He goes on to convey the conviction that there is "no way you can stop the Word of God," following with the need "to take the church to the people." In response to the preaching and praying of Brother Clark's sermon, the church begins to sing "Trust and Obey."

Preaching becomes prayer as Mother Cooper urges, "Pray to the Lord." The hour between 2:00 a.m. and 3:00 a.m. is largely devoted just to prayer, with members kneeling or lying prostrate before the altar. "When you pray, let it come from within." Collating the experience of the Garden of Gethsemane with the physical demands of the tarry and the tiring bodies, in her most serious voice Mother Cooper commands, "Pray, pray, pray!" Sister Lou prays during the hour: "I present barren women to you, jobless to you, the homeless to you." At 3:00 a.m., there is a rousing version of "Glory, Glory Hallelujah."

Mother Cooper provides the third sermon of the tarry, and for well over an hour she rolls through stories of the Bible, prayer in Monrovia, and the challenges of New York. It is not easy for the people in the room to stay awake, but they persist against exhaustion; the church must reach the morning hour, and Mother Cooper is winding out the stories, verses, and exhortations to get there. Prayer requires struggle, and physical denial is understood to facilitate communication with God. Following Mother Cooper's sermon are more prayers and singing, then a session of testimonies.

David Grigsby testifies about his daughter's recent wedding in Texas, Edwin Flower reports in gratitude "no sickness this week. I can walk." With the clock reaching to the 6:00 a.m. hour, Mother Cooper delivers the benediction. Seven "Hallelujahs," "Hosannas," "Urahs," and "laughters" follow, and then we file on to the Bronx streets, where the day is just beginning.

According to Daniel Costelo, "Tarrying is an embodiment and demonstration of human desire in search of being ordered by God's very presence."[39] A tarry also challenges the body with a different time, the time that awaits Christ's return yet remains filled with divine presence. Tarry time, to coin a phrase, is the time of the gospel of deliverance from the evil powers, the incursion of Jesus as victor.

Night Vigil

"Lord over every spirit, hold them bound," prays Omo Obogbaimhe. Microphone in hand she continues, "You would be Lord . . . let every tongue confess. Pray the blood of Jesus over this sanctuary."[40] As Omo is praying, others in the room are also praying aloud: "Father, you would prevail in the name of Jesus. In the mighty name of Jesus." The vocal dynamic is call and response; the spiritual effect is to sanctify the room as the presence of God.[41] It is late on a Friday night at the Redeemed Christian Church of God International Chapel, Brooklyn.[42] The first Friday of each month is Holy Ghost Night, the third Friday of each month is Workers' Vigil, and both begin at 10:00 p.m. and run into the morning.

Lacking the usual keyboard player and drummer, singing takes place to hand clapping and galloping tambourines. Omo leads the church in a series of choruses: "You are worthy, Lord," "You've been faithful, Lord," "How excellent is your name, O Lord," and the crescendo, "I lift my hands in praise to your name." When Pastor Nimi comes onto the platform, as always, he kneels down in prayer beside his chair. When he comes forward

---

39. Costelo, "Tarrying on the Lord," 50.
40. The image and power of the blood of Jesus in African Christianity and Pentecostalism is widespread and deserves further exploration and definition. In brief, the cross brings salvation that is comprehensive healing.
41. The pattern is an early and distinctive one. Larry Hurtado, *Lord Jesus Christ: Devotion to Jesus in Earliest Christianity* (Grand Rapids: Eerdmans, 2003), 140-44, 613-15.
42. Redeemed Christian Church of God International Chapel, Brooklyn, Field Notes, June 1, 2007.

to speak, he proclaims, "Your power, your presence, it would be healing, it would energize us."

It is at such night vigils that Holy Communion is celebrated, not during the morning service. Pastor Nimi points out he always "dresses his best" for Communion because he is "meeting with the King of kings and Lord of lords, the table of the Lord Almighty." He talks about love, forgiveness, and reconciliation. As the elements are taken, Pastor Nimi stresses that they are for "healing in your life, healing in your situation. If anyone is sick, let there be healing." Communion takes on an eschatological dimension, the future in the present. After everyone is served, the church kneels in prayer. A thanksgiving offering is taken. Around the room some of the children sleep on chairs made into makeshift beds, while others are curled up on the floor near their parents.

"Come see what the Lord has done" are the words of the familiar song that begins testimony time. But before people can speak, one more song, this one about success in Jesus, "Are you a winner? I am a winner." Bola Oyesanya now leads the session of testimonies. The first testimony celebrates God for preventing an accident and for vindication concerning a conflict at work. A second testimony thanks God for healing. The third testimony gives thanks to God for a family member's success back in Nigeria. Next, a woman praises God for her ministry and "for what he is." Another woman follows with a testimony in song, "In my life I see what you are doing," followed by a statement that God has "blessed and favored" her. A man provides the next testimony, telling about a change of heart by his employer that led to an increase in pay. Encouraged by the church, he spoke up and asked for a raise: "Thank God for favor with my boss." In the final testimony, a story is told about a new business. "Shall we rise," Bola asks, as she thanks God for "provision."

Sister Egbefun Adieze delivers the first sermon, based on Exodus 15:1-17, the song of Moses. "God bringing salvation" is Sister Egbefun's theme as she moves through the text verse by verse. Whether demons or enemies in life, "Drown it!" she says to God. "The Lord needs to plant you for his dwelling, in his sanctuary, in his inheritance." It is now after midnight, and Sister Omo declares, "Spirit of sleep and slumber [be] banished." More singing and Bible reading follow, but soon Sister Catherine awakens any who might be tempted to slumber with a rousing "Praise the Lord! Praise the Lord!" Sister Omo leads the congregation in singing "You are worthy, Lord."

Pastor Nimi steps to the pulpit and proclaims, "I have a mighty Father. The Lord Almighty is here! God is bigger than your problems." He recalls prophecies from last year, most prominently that God's "power will change us." In the present time, "Doors will open," a reference to opportunities. "The time of the Lord's harvest has come unto you." With emphasis he declares, "You will not remain the same. A change is coming to you." "The time has come — talk to the Lord Almighty. Be bold, stand on the Lord Jesus Christ." Such prophetic speech is seen as granting empowerment, a message of God in the context of Pentecostal worship for life in the world.

At this point Pastor Nimi begins interweaving tongues with prayer lines in English. Such language is especially familiar in times of intense prayer at the Redeemed Christian Church of God International Chapel, Brooklyn. In the New Testament, 1 Corinthians 14 describes these different forms of speech that flow from the presence of the Spirit. A summary is found in 1 Corinthians 14:26: "When you come together, each one has a hymn, a lesson, a revelation, a tongue, or an interpretation."[43] Ecstatic and expressive prayer is common in African church life, but not formally limited to speaking in tongues. In my observation, speaking in tongues is not a defining feature of African Pentecostalism. But when employed, what role do tongues play? New Testament scholar Anthony Thiselton identifies five possible meanings of tongues or *glossolalia* in 1 Corinthians: (1) angelic speech, (2) power to speak other languages, (3) liturgical rhythms, (4) ecstatic speech, and (5) release of "preconscious" or unconscious welling up.[44] Thiselton selects the last option of "release" for what occurs in 1 Corinthians 14. His conclusion is similar to a recent sociological description of tongues in global Pentecostalism as "forms of expression that bubble up out of the inner depths."[45] This may also be true of prayer generally in African churches, as David Maxwell finds.[46] Pentecostal prayer is certainly cathartic, releasing. But as I have observed the phenomenon of *glossolalia* in New York City during African church worship services, it appears first of all to reflect liturgical rhythms.

Pastor Nimi eventually begins to wind down this time of intense

---

43. NRSV.

44. Anthony C. Thiselton, *The First Epistle to the Corinthians: A Commentary on the Greek Text* (Grand Rapids: Eerdmans, 2000), 970-89, and *The Hermeneutics of Doctrine* (Grand Rapids: Eerdmans, 2007), 444-50.

45. Donald E. Miller and Tetsunao Yamamori, *Global Pentecostalism: The New Face of Christian Social Engagement* (Berkeley: University of California Press, 2007), 147.

46. Maxwell, *African Gifts of the Spirit*, 199.

prayer by proclaiming in call and response form, "Let somebody shout Hallelujah!" the signature phrase of the General Overseer of the Redeemed Christian Church of God. Pastor Nimi's sermon is from 1 Samuel 3 on the life of Samuel, and he tells it as a story of personal "destiny." Pastoral application is enfolded in the story of Samuel and Eli, "to enable people [to] come to their destiny." The same God is involved in the same way today — only the names have changed. God will "give you anointing to go the next stage." Pastor Nimi moves from Samuel to Brooklyn: "This year God will use your ministry. I will say you will not fail!" Space and time are merged as the theological dimensions of the biblical text support everyday life in New York City.

As the offering is taken, the church sings of "the sacrifice of praise." There is a final announcement reminding people that they should fast in preparation for the upcoming Redeemed Christian Church of God annual convention to be held in Dallas. It is a new day, yet still dark on the streets of Brooklyn as worshipers head home for a quick sleep before work and family duties beckon.

All-Night Revival

Many of the all-night prayer services at the Presbyterian Church of Ghana are connected with designated periods of revival. Sometimes the prayer meetings are called revivals; in other instances simply "all-night prayer services." Both are held periodically throughout the year.

By 8:00 p.m. on a Friday, the second-floor meeting room of the church building on 123rd Street begins to fill up, but it is closer to 9:00 p.m. when things start. Most of the women have their heads covered with cloth that reads simply, "Pray." Worship leader Yaw Amaning begins by inviting people to prayer with him: "Ask God for the Holy Spirit to descend on everyone so we can do God's work with all our heart and strength."

A mixture of singing and praying precede the sermon. With her strong voice, Edith Sarpong leads in praise and worship. For prayer, people stand and pray out loud. "Jesu Christou, You are Worthy" are the words that flow from the person next to me. Brother Samuel Boadu delivers the message on 1 Corinthians 4:7 and Luke 13:6-9 on the topic of "exercising your spiritual gifts to serve the church." There "are different gifts, one demand," he proclaims in a description of the work of God in believers. Overall, spiritual gifts "glorify God and serve needs of mankind," and

"God judges according to our faithfulness." The sermon, delivered in an encouraging tone, ends just after 10:00 p.m.

More praise, worship, prayer, and reading Scripture follows; three men sing a special song. Testimony time follows. The first testimony concerns a man's success in finding a job, followed by a testimony that begins with "God has done a wonderful miracle in my life" and urges the church to keep praying. A male leader in the church begins by relating a story of a son being attacked while at college. He had a dream warning it could happen, but the violence took place anyway, leaving his son with a broken jaw. In response to God beginning the work of healing his son, he gives thanks. "Only God, God, God."

"Pray, pray, pray. Yes, yes, yes. . . . In the name of Jesus. In the name of Jesus, pray, pray, pray, pray." With the distinctive cadence of a Pentecostal Christian, Kwasi Agyare of the Bible Study and Prayer Group leads a time of prayer for healing. As he says these words, the fifty people present in the room each raise their voices to God, speaking passionately to God with their bodies and words. A song breaks forth with the words, "Prayer is the master key." A declaration is given: "My problem will be solved tonight. In the name of Jesus. The Lord will bless you, touch you. Yes, yes, keep praying." And again, "Tell God if any part of your body [needs healing] and he will heal it."

Soon the white handkerchiefs are waving to shouts of "Jesu Christou." "God is at hand, so if you believe it, clap your hands for Jesus." The church sings, "Let the power of the anointing fall on me, anointing fall on me." With prayer, the service concludes after 1:00 a.m.

Praying in the Spirit

Why do African Christians pray in loud voices? Why is prayer singing to God, commanding Satan to flee, or crying out to God in need? Why can there be jumping up and down, active hand movements, or kneeling for extended periods of time? Why is there fasting? Why do people pray all night? On reflection, I have come to think that the answer to these questions can help explain how the body relates to conceptions of God and salvation. Charismatic prayer is the "attunement" of the body and senses in relationship to God.[47] African Christians use their voices *and* bodies in

---

47. On such issues, see the insightful essay by Miriam C. M. Rabelo, Sueli Ribeiro

communication with God, to the end of praising God and experiencing human flourishing. Prayer and fasting use multiple senses, a way of being receptive to God through the body that leads to joy, exultation, conviction, insight, hope, destiny, healing, visions, and dreams. Prayer is at least as much a bodily exercise[48] as it is a discursive activity.[49]

Within the three churches of this study, prayer is life-changing because it involves giving control of the individual and communal body to God. Among all these churches, the importance of physicality in praying and fasting is related to the bodily posture of being attuned to God, time, and place. Such practices are giving oneself fully over to God, and, when needed, against Satan and all evil powers. Dialogue with God, through words, gestures, and the relinquishment of food are all physical acts of attending to God and making the body open for God's presence, intervention, deliverance, healing, and empowerment. Whether jumping up and down or lying prostate on the floor, raising hands or shaking and falling, these are understood to be physical experiences of God, bringing a new apprehension of the self and world. This is powerful for understanding the world, spiritual conflict, and redemption. For African Christians in New York City, the body is the site of God's saving, intertwining the personal and the cosmic, the material and spiritual.

Three further reasons for the particular practices of prayer and fasting in African churches can be observed. The first reason is that prayer and fasting is a tradition that forms Christians; they are embodied skills. As Evangelist Sarah told me, by praying with the Church of the Lord (Aladura), I would learn how to pray in a new way. Mother Cooper indicates as much when she says it is "a habit we have formed."[50] Prayer is a tradition that members are immersed in and pass on to others; there is a bodily and linguistic competence to creating the church culture that is passed on. This is also true of fasting.

Mota, and Cláudio Roberto Almeida, "Cultivating the Senses and Giving in to the Sacred: Notes on the Body and Experience among Pentecostal Women in Salvador, Brazil," *Journal of Contemporary Religion* 24:1 (January 2009): 1-18.

48. Jürgen Moltmann, "Praying with Eyes Open," in *Loving God with Our Minds: The Pastor as Theologian*, ed. Michael Welker and Cynthia A. Jarvis (Grand Rapids: Eerdmans, 2004), 195-201.

49. Akesha Baron, "'I'm a Woman but I *Know* God Leads My Way': Agency and Tzotzil Evangelical Discourse," *Language in Society* 33 (2004): 249-83; Pieter W. van der Horst, "Silent Prayer in Antiquity," *Numen* 41 (1994): 1-25.

50. Marie Cooper, Interview, February 13, 2008.

The second reason for loud vocal prayer relates to the intimate relationship with God that believers have and are expressing. This can be crying to, singing to, or praising God. God is not "out there" but relationally present. Adebisi Oyesile explains his view of vocal prayer this way:

> Whatever you want you ask in his name. He is my Father. I will be bold enough to ask my Father. If silent, cannot ask confidently and don't have the faith. If have strong faith he will do it for you. When Jacob wrestled with God, so I am wrestling with you Daddy. I am being obedient to you. By my stripes you are healed. He died for us. It is finished. Poverty is finished and I believe you. Sickness is gone and I believe you.[51]

For this reason, as people pray to God they call out different names for God such as "Father," "Daddy," and "Jehovah Jirah." From his study of urban churches and their loud prayers and clapping, Camilo José Vergara provides an astute observation: "Persistent thanking is perhaps a form of prayer that intensifies the anointing, makes people feel the power of God, and invites the Lord to come and saturate them. Expressing gratitude . . . becomes a ritual to achieve a mystical union between the Creator and His creature."[52] Prayer and fasting bring the senses into fuller relationship with God.

The third reason is what is understood to be the biblical precedent.[53] Jesus cried out to God. For Oyesile, the biblical image is Jacob wrestling with God. It is also Pentecost.

> In the days of Pentecost people were not praying silently. The Holy Spirit will not come down when you pray quietly. When you're praising him . . . the Holy Spirit will descend on you. When we praise and worship our Father, heaven rejoices.[54]

Words have spiritual power and authority, especially in "warfare" with Satan. For Mother Cooper, praying is a physical activity that has similarities with the embodied action led by Joshua at the walls of Jericho.[55] Fasting draws from biblical texts such as Daniel and the life of Jesus.

Following suggestions of the theologian Sarah Coakley, we may come

---

51. Adebisi Oyesile, Interview, February 11, 2008.
52. Camilo José Vergara, *How the Other Worships* (New Brunswick: Rutgers University Press, 2005), 182.
53. Maxwell, *African Gifts of the Spirit*, 198-99.
54. Maxwell, *African Gifts of the Spirit*, 198-99.
55. Marie Cooper, Interview, February 13, 2008.

to think of the charismatic and ecstatic prayers of African believers not simply as praying in the Spirit, but being drawn into the Trinity.[56] For Coakley, Romans 8:26 is of particular significance: "Likewise the Spirit helps us in our weakness; for we do not know how to pray as we ought, but that very Spirit intercedes with sighs too deep for words." This verse represents for her "the experience of being prayed in."[57] There is a "divine dialogue" and "the Spirit is here seen as the current of divine response to divine self-gift in which the one who prays is caught up and thereby transformed (see again Rom. 8:9-27, 1 Cor. 2:9-16)."[58] Contemplative prayer and charismatic prayer, which share the quality of submission to God, "is strictly speaking not a simple communication between an individual and a distant undifferentiated divine entity, but rather a moment of divine reflexivity, a sort of answering God to God in and through the one who prays."[59] Such prayer can be an "experience of God who actively and always wills to be amongst us."[60] For Coakley, charismatic prayer is praying in the Spirit to God, and being drawn into the fullness of God's life. For as the Apostle Paul offers, "no one can say 'Jesus is Lord' except by the Holy Spirit."[61]

Prayer with Fasting

For African Christians, prayer is joined with fasting, combining to make a single mark of the church.[62] Religious fasting, "abstinence from certain food for a period of time,"[63] along with water and nourishment, is a lan-

---

56. Sarah Coakley, "God as Trinity: An Approach Through Prayer," in *We Believe in God: A Report by the Doctrine Commission of the General Synod of the Church of England* (Wilton, Conn: Morehouse-Barlow, 1987), 104-21, and "Why Three? Some Further Reflections on the Origins of the Doctrine of the Trinity," in *The Making and Remaking of Christian Doctrine: Essays in Honor of Maurice Wiles*, ed. Sarah Coakley and David A. Pailin (Oxford: Clarendon Press, 1993), 29-56.

57. Coakley, "God as Trinity," 108.

58. Coakley, "God as Trinity," 108.

59. Coakley, "Why Three?" 37.

60. Coakley, "God as Trinity," 109.

61. 1 Corinthians 12:3.

62. Turner comments that for the Church of the Lord (Aladura), "'prayer and fasting' are [considered] important marks of the true church." Harold W. Turner, *African Independent Church*, vol. 2: *The Life and Faith of the Church of the Lord (Aladura)* (Oxford: Oxford University Press, 1967), 79.

63. Teresa M. Shaw, *The Burden of the Flesh: Fasting and Sexuality in Early Christianity* (Minneapolis: Fortress Press, 1998), 1. Caroline Walker Bynum, *Holy Feast and Holy Fast:*

guage of the body, of desire directed to God. Informed by a holistic theology of salvation, the self-denial of fasting is not intended to turn believers away from the world as much as turn believers to God, thereby turning all of the needs of this world to God. The inspirited body goes without food to deepen participation in God's redemption. In Teresa Shaw's study of early Christian fasting, she observes that "fasting makes the body more obedient and controllable while it makes the soul lighter, quiets the restless mind, and aids in prayer and penitence."[64]

Two primary types of fasting can be identified in the churches of our study. The first type of fasting is associated with individual need and determination to address a particular problem or make progress in faith. For example, a member of the Church of the Lord (Aladura) was going through an "individual problem" and received a revelation that he should fast for seven days. He felt that fasting could bring him peace. Mother Cooper describes his solitary fast as coming from the teaching of Jesus:

> We take fasting from the Bible. When Christ sent the disciples to pray for a certain problem and they could not heal a particular person in the name of Jesus . . . Jesus told them fasting and prayer, not only prayer. . . . Fasting makes prayer stronger.[65]

The command for prayer and fasting, she holds, comes from the "gospel story."[66] The purpose of fasting is "to be strong in the spirit." Because the spirit controls the body, when the spirit is weak, the flesh moves in; "Fasting gives the spirit strength."[67] Fasting among the Church of the Lord (Aladura), as Samuel Britt observed in Liberia, has the character of struggle.[68] It is "doctrine . . . realized through a kind of 'bodily praxis.'"[69]

Mother Cooper sees an explicit link between fasting and problem solving: "If you want something to be done, if in need of deep meditation, I will take a fast and approach God on this issue." When the Faith Home faced foreclosure, for example, Mother Cooper fasted. While the motive

---

The Religious Significance of Food to Medieval Women (Berkeley: University of California Press, 1987), offers another example of relevant research on another historical period.

64. Shaw, *The Burden of the Flesh*, 9.
65. Marie Cooper, Interview, October 21, 2007.
66. Marie Cooper, Interview, February 13, 2005.
67. Marie Cooper, Interview, February 13, 2005.
68. Samuel Irving Britt, "The Children of Salvation: Struggle and Cosmology in Liberian Prophet Churches" (Ph.D. diss., University of Virginia, 1992), 648-67.
69. Britt, "The Children of Salvation," 649.

for fasting can be to address an individual desire for change, it is accomplished as a member of a community that holds both the person and practice to be important.

Michael Onyeri arrived in New York City just a few years ago and delivers dry cleaning on Manhattan's Upper East Side.[70] A quiet and impressive young man in his twenties, he goes after work to night school, where he is studying for a college degree in accounting. Michael is a worker at the Redeemed Christian Church of God International Chapel, and fasting is a regular part of his Christian life.

> I believe when you fast, you ... are focused to pray more. When you pray and fast is when you open up to God what to pray about. When I pray I speak in tongues. I have more prayer points. I pray about my job and family. God helps me to grow in His work.[71]

Like other workers in the church, Michael fasts three days every month as the anointing service approaches. During periods of fasting, he eats only once a day, after returning from work and school, between 11:00 p.m. and midnight.

A second type of fasting relates to the church calendar.[72] At the Church of the Lord (Aladura), the two primary church seasons are Lent and the Taborrar, which I will document in chapter seven. During the thirteen days of the Taborrar season in August, members are urged to join in what is called a "white fast." A white fast includes abstaining from food with salt and sugar, and no meat, fish, oil, or peppers. The Lenten season is set apart for forty days of fasting, typically from 6:00 a.m. until a set evening hour such as 3:00 p.m. or 6:00 p.m. Given the difficulty, Mother Cooper stresses participation at whatever level is possible, "so long as you serve the Lord with a pure heart."[73] Lessons for fasting are drawn from the Lenten season; "I want to believe why Jesus went, to prepare himself for ministry," Mother Cooper remarks. This entails that one "deny [the] body of certain things, a sacrifice" analogy with "Christ a sacrifice." For "if you want to get close with God in a special way, you have to deny the flesh."[74] Approaching the monthly tarry, three days of fasting are required, broken with a shared meal of fruit.

---

70. Michael Onyeri, Interviews, October 15, 2003, and October 14, 2007.
71. Michael Onyeri, Interview, October 14, 2007.
72. Shaw, *The Burden of the Flesh*, 4-5.
73. Church of the Lord (Aladura), Field Notes, February 6, 2005.
74. Marie Cooper, Interview, October 21, 2007.

The last Friday of each month is designated and encouraged as a day of fasting at the Presbyterian Church of Ghana in New York. Fasting is another example of the role played by the Bible Study and Prayer Group in the spiritual life of the church. Its members can be asked to take the lead in this practice for the church. Diana Owusu explains the church practice this way: "We fast when someone asks us to fast . . . something is in our life, or for somebody. We pray for no tragedy or sickness."[75] As an example, beginning with Lent and leading up to Easter in 2008, the pastor's wife asked the prayer group that "meets" each morning on the telephone to fast for six weeks. The hours could vary, but if possible fasting should take place between 6:00 a.m. and 6:00 p.m. There were no conditions on what foods could be eaten outside of the fast.

Across all churches of the Redeemed Christian Church of God, February is annually a month of fasting. Each year a special theme is declared for all branches of the Redeemed Christian Church of God worldwide. The year 2006 was declared by the General Overseer to be a "Year of Increase," and this was embraced at the Redeemed Christian Church of God International Chapel, Brooklyn. February 2006 was set apart as a month of prayer and fasting around that theme. In 2008, it was a year of "Greatness" and "Promotion." Ministers were to fast from February 1 to March 9, 2008.[76]

Oghogho West-Erhabor, known as Sister West, is a member of the Redeemed parish in Brooklyn.[77] Sister West lives within walking distance to the Brooklyn parish, and moves about the neighborhood with a pastoral attentiveness. She is a worker at the church, deeply committed to its life and witness. Sister West fasts for the entire month of February each year. This means she will go without food or water until the evening. What did the "year of increase" mean? Her answer was comprehensive: "spiritually, physically . . . health, wealth — everything . . . around you to do better."[78] As a testimony of what God had done in her life, Sister West revealed that she had just received her Green Card.

Adebisi Oyesile not only does the February fast, but engages quarterly in twenty-one days of fasting every March, June, September, and December. This means he abstains from food between 6:00 a.m. and 6:00

---

75. Diana Owusu, Interview, March 4, 2008.

76. Adebisi Oyesile, Interview, March 13, 2008.

77. Oghogho West-Erhabor, Interview, December 7, 2005.

78. Oghogho West-Erhabor, Interview, February 16, 2006. See Asonzeh Franklin-Kennedy Ukah, "The Redeemed Christian Church of God (RCCG), Nigeria: Local Identities and Global Processes in African Pentecostalism" (Ph.D. diss, Bayreuth, 2003), 184.

Fig. 4.4 Evangelist Sarah Richards praying, Church of the Lord (Aladura), 2005

p.m. for at least 140 days per year.[79] When he faces a significant case or problem that "ordinary prayer" cannot solve, he adds an additional fast. Fasting brings "complete concentration," the discipline to "pay more attention." The end result, Pastor Adebisi relates, is that "your course can be different," a good summary of the intent of fasting.

Prayer and the Material

African Christianity, especially Pentecostal churches and ministries like the Redeemed Christian Church of God, has come to be closely associated with what is known as the "health and wealth gospel."[80] Drawing on Paul

---

79. Adebisi Oyasile, Interview, January 19, 2008.
80. Asonzeh F-K Ukah, "'Those Who Trade with God Never Lose': The Economics of Pentecostal Activism in Nigeria," in *Christianity and Social Change in Africa: Essays in Honor of J. D. Y. Peel*, ed. Toyin Falola (Durham: Carolina Academic Press, 2005), 253-74.

Gifford's *Ghana's New Christianity: Pentecostalism in a Globalizing African Economy*,[81] the *Christian Century* in July 2007 featured a cover story by Gifford with the words "Spreading the (Prosperity) Gospel" superimposed on an image of Africa.[82] That same year, *Christianity Today* ran a cover story with the headline, "Health and Wealth in Africa: How the Prosperity Gospel Is Taking a Continent by Storm."[83] Some argue that the rise of Pentecostalism can be situated within a neo-liberal capitalist economy.[84] Pentecostal belief and practice, it is thought, fits neatly within the self-sufficiency and flexibility required for such an economy. This also links Pentecostalism's expansion to the global moment, as developed in Simon Coleman's *The Globalisation of Charismatic Christianity: Spreading the Gospel of Prosperity*.[85]

In contrast to stereotypes of a gospel of "health and wealth," I found in the churches of this study people who worked hard at often more than one job and exercised a prayerful faith in God for the present and continuing needs of life. People pray for what they need to survive — a job, a home, food, good health for their spouse and children, a better life. As Andrew Walls succinctly puts it, "The earthiness of African life demands that African salvation shall be as solidly material as biblical salvation."[86] No less is demanded of life in the global city. African Christians certainly do find in salvation a material and social dimension.[87] Being born again leads to various changes in the lives of believers.[88]

---

81. Paul Gifford, *Ghana's New Christianity: Pentecostalism in a Globalizing African Economy* (Bloomington: Indiana University Press, 2004). Whatever differences I may have with it, this book raises crucial questions about community, economics, and politics.

82. Paul Gifford, "Expecting Miracles: The Prosperity Gospel in Africa," *Christian Century*, July 10, 2007, 20-24.

83. Isaac Phiri and Joe Maxwell, "Gospel Riches," *Christianity Today*, July 2007, 20-29.

84. For example, Isabelle V. Barker, "Charismatic Economies: Pentecostalism, Economic Restructuring, and Social Reproduction," *New Political Science* 29:4 (2007): 407-27, and Jean Comaroff, "The Politics of Conviction: Faith on the Neo-liberal Frontier," *Social Analysis* 53:1 (2009): 17-38.

85. Simon Coleman, *The Globalisation of Charismatic Christianity: Spreading the Gospel of Prosperity* (Cambridge: Cambridge University Press, 2000).

86. Andrew F. Walls, *The Missionary Movement in Christian History: Studies in the Transmission of Faith* (Maryknoll, N.Y.: Orbis, 1996), 116.

87. For broader background to the theological and social issues, see Miroslav Volf, "Materiality of Salvation: An Investigation in the Soteriologies of Liberation and Pentecostal Theologies," *Journal of Ecumenical Studies* 26:3 (1989): 447-67.

88. On the ways this can work, see Ruth Marshall, *Political Spiritualities: The Pentecostal Revolution in Nigeria* (Chicago: University of Chicago Press, 2009), 173-84.

The bodily and kinetic modes of African Christians at prayer — kneeling, shouting, clapping, raising arms, moving around, and fasting — situate their stories physically in the script of salvation.[89] The emphasis is not on *how* one is saved, but on what it *means* to be saved. Afe Adogame cites the Aladura "maxim" that "a prayerless Christian is a powerless Christian, while a prayerful Christian is a very powerful Christian."[90] Put another way, as Jane Soothill observes, prayer is "more than a comfort or a refuge."[91] Spiritual power is understood to provide for human flourishing because it overcomes difficult circumstances, illnesses, negative spiritual forces, and anything that inhibits and diminishes life in its fullness. But as I learned in my research, a God who produces prosperity "on demand" is not the God represented by the churches in this study.

A brief foray into Western academic discourse on God helps to distinguish the underlying framework that is in play in African Christianity. As Thomas Torrance observes, "Where we operate within a context of epistemological and cosmological dualism . . . this involves a doctrine of the immutability and impassability of God, and what I call a deistic disjunction between God and the universe."[92] African Christianity in New York lacks such dualism. God is very much dynamic, relational, and responsive; there is no operational disjunction between God and the universe. I make this point because a Western Christian epistemological framework, with its strict division between the seen and unseen worlds, can make it difficult to understand African Christianity on its own terms. In this respect, Webb Keane's ethnography of Calvinist missionaries in what is now Indonesia provides a revealing contrast: "For strict Calvinists, prayer should express thanks to or even petition to God, but it should not undertake to direct consequences in the world."[93] For African Christians, God has already set in motion human flourishing and is involved in the course of directing daily events and overcoming powers and powerful ob-

---

89. Manuel A. Vásquez and Marie Friedmann Marquardt, *Globalizing the Sacred: Religion across the Americas* (New Brunswick: Rutgers University Press, 2003), 54; Maxwell, *African Gifts of the Spirit*, 197.

90. Adogame, "Prayer as Action and Instrument," 118.

91. Jane E. Soothill, *Gender, Social Change and Spiritual Power: Charismatic Christianity in Ghana* (Leiden: Brill, 2007), 217.

92. Thomas F. Torrance, *The Ground and Grammar of Theology* (Belfast: Christian Journals, 1980), 146.

93. Webb Keane, *Christian Moderns: Freedom and Fetish in the Mission Encounter* (Berkeley: University of California Press, 2007), 54.

Praying Bodies

Fig. 4.5 Bible Study and Prayer Group at prayer, 2005

stacles, so it is to be expected that one would through prayer seek out the Lord's favor and blessing. This assumption of God's salvation in the present grants to African Christians an authority in their prayers.

To expound this further, behind African Christian convictions concerning the efficacy of prayer stand beliefs about God and how God acts. As J. D. Y. Peel explains, "The simple claim of the Aladuras is that *God answers all prayers;* this is, of course, official Christian teaching, for it is asserted unequivocally in the Gospels, and can hardly be said to be a doctrinal assertion in itself. But when asserted with such fervour, and linked with special methods, it is a radical and liberating belief."[94] In voice and posture, African Christians at prayer in New York City have a highly personal, relational, and expectant view of God. It is here that a hermeneutics of the Psalms is prominent in the churches; the no-holds-barred language of the Psalms offers a dynamic and relational view of God in response to prayers. A similar emphasis on "results" may come from a closer reading of the New Testament materials, especially the Book of James, which puts forward a God who is "giving" in relationship to prayers rendered in

94. Peel, *Aladura*, 119.

"trust."[95] Neither in the Old Testament is God taken to be unresponsive to the prayers and actions of individuals and nations. These materials are important underpinnings for African churches at prayer. The prayers of African Christians are seen to be illocutionary — acts of speech given in expectation of their efficacy.[96]

From the prayers and testimonies conveyed in public worship settings, we can see that African Christians can be faced with nearly overwhelming challenges in areas of employment, health, and immigration matters, to name some of the recurring items.[97] To a large degree, prayer is understood to lead to change in these basic life areas. In prayers, sermons, testimonies, and Bible studies, concern for the material is for sustenance — a job, a home, a better school, health, and travel. "In prayer," David Maxwell writes of Zimbabwean Pentecostals, "their struggle for betterment is acted out both through and on the body."[98] Such bodily practice is part of the charismatic experience of God, a groaning in faith that represents vitality in the Spirit. The energy source of prayer is the Spirit, the intensifying power of life. Faith expressed through prayer brings God, the Spirit, believer, and ecclesial body into a form of community. As people pray in the Spirit, they experience God with their whole body, which is their whole life.[99] This experience of the Spirit in provision is a form of healing, especially as it addresses any blockage, spiritual or material, in the way of flourishing.

Consider the empowerment that comes through prayer in the story of David Grigsby, a clerical worker in New York state government. David credits the prayers of Mother Cooper for bringing him to the church four years ago. He also attributes to prayer success at work and the reshaping of his moral life. David first made contact with the church because he was in need of help; at the suggestion of an acquaintance, he called on Mother

95. On James 1:5-8, 4:1-3, and 5:13-20, see David R. Nienhuis, *Not by Paul Alone: The Formation of the Catholic Epistle Collection and the Christian Canon* (Waco: Baylor University Press, 2007), 199-201. See also Richard Bauckham, *James: Wisdom of James, Disciple of Jesus the Sage* (New York: Routledge, 1999), 205-8.

96. See B. Keith Putt, "'Too Deep for Words': The Conspiracy of a Divine 'Soliloquy,'" in *The Phenomenology of Prayer*, ed. Bruce Ellis Benson and Norman Wirzba (New York: Fordham University Press, 2005), 142-53.

97. Gerrie ter Haar, *Halfway to Paradise: African Christians in Europe* (Cardiff: Cardiff Academic Press, 1998), 44.

98. Maxwell, *African Gifts of the Spirit*, 197.

99. Jürgen Moltmann, *The Spirit of Life: A Universal Affirmation*, trans. Margaret Kohl (Minneapolis: Fortress Press, 1992), 267.

Cooper "to pray for me."[100] The way that David's "problem" was addressed was instrumental in his joining the church. At work David faced a conflict with a fellow employee. Mother Cooper perceived that God was testing him. Ultimately, David did not get in trouble on the job. Instead, "the man got fired. The new guy is very nice." For David, "The peace of God alone makes me think he answers my prayers."[101] Prayer is also responsible for reshaping his moral life, enabling him to avoid the use of alcohol and other temptations. David knows friends who have died or are in the hospital from alcohol abuse, and he recognizes the importance of lifestyle changes: "I'm telling you, brother, God has really been good to me these past few years. I have my mind under control."

Kwame Adom's story is a snapshot of life in the Presbyterian Church of Ghana in New York. As I got into a yellow cab on Broadway and 112th Street in early fall 2004, the driver turned out to be Kwame Adom. As fellow Kwame's, "Saturday borns," we had just celebrated "our day" together at the recent mini-harvest. Leaning back to speak through the security divider, he said, "I'm driving a taxi now, but I have a life plan to accomplish."[102] As Kwame later recalled saying, "Now I might be driving a taxi, but in a few years I will be calling the shots on Wall Street." He went to school at night to become an accountant and drove a taxi during the day to earn income. A year later, at an all-night prayer vigil described previously in this chapter, Kwame announced that he had landed a new job with KPMG, an international accounting firm.[103] By fall 2007, he had resigned from KPMG to join a private Wall Street banking firm. What made it all work? "Focus, determination, and knowing where source of inspiration is coming from — from above, from God, the bottom line."

At Redeemed Christian Church of God International Chapel, Brooklyn, prayer is believed to change circumstances directly. For example, during a testimony, a child and her mother came forward. A routine trip to the doctor turned up a condition of hyperthyroidism in the little girl. The family immediately began to pray, and people in the church joined in. A few days later, the doctor called and said it must have been an error in the lab work; she did not have hyperthyroidism. For the mother, this change in di-

---

100. David Grigsby, Interviews, March 13, 2005, and October 21, 2007.

101. David Grigsby, Interview, October 21, 2007.

102. Kwame Adom, Interview, September 1, 2007. This quote is from a recollection we both shared.

103. All-night prayer service, Presbyterian Church of Ghana, Field Notes, June 24, 2005.

Fig. 4.6 Prayer at Redeemed Christian Church of God, 2007

agnosis was the result of God's intervention in response to her prayers and those of the church, not merely a mistake in the lab work.[104]

Additional illustrations could be marshaled from any worship service or interview, but they would all point to the same belief. Prayer reflects a conviction that God continues to work among them in areas of health, employment, and relationships. Because prayer is a form of participation in the life and purposes of God, it is a form of empowerment for the requirements of daily life and the development of gifts and abilities. They are prayers for life. In Robert Orsi's words, "Prayer is a switching point between the social world and the imagination."[105] Prayer opens a world with infinite possibilities, providing freedom and empowerment to overcome any obstacle to flourishing.

A central irony is that power is achieved through the act of "submit-

104. Redeemed Christian Church of God International Chapel, Field Notes, May 1, 2005.

105. Robert A. Orsi, "Is the Study of Lived Religion Irrelevant to the World We Live In?" *Journal for the Scientific Study of Religion* 42:2 (2003): 173.

Praying Bodies

ting" to God.[106] For example, as Jane Soothill observes of Ghanaian Pentecostal women, prayer can mediate changes in gender relations.[107] Husbands and marital power dynamics can change as a result of prayer. Prayer is also a voice that impacts the personal and public spheres, because it is the divine voice.[108]

As noted at the outset of this section, there is often said to be a consumerist element in African Pentecostal prayer, linking commodities, conversion, and connection to the global economy.[109] Jean and John Comaroff present neo-Protestant religious movements as harnessing faith to global capitalism through the manipulation of God.[110] This may be true of the churches in their studies, but in my research, I did not recall hearing a prayer that suggested God would materially reward faith or prayers. Not once, either in the three focus churches or any African church in New York City, did I hear a sermon on getting rich or a reference to an American prosperity preacher. Nor did I hear anything approaching the propagation of the "spirit of neoliberalism" or a "frank embrace of worldly appetites."[111] Instead of depending on an illusion of redemption,[112] African Christians trust in a living God to provide daily bread and the means to make daily bread. It is God who saves them into a new life, they believe, not the economy. Salvation is to heaven or eternal life and also leads to transformations in this life, not one or the other.[113] In the city, indeed in the capital of capi-

---

106. While there are significant differences in conceptions of gender and power, the principle is also related to prayer in R. Marie Griffith, *God's Daughters: Evangelical Women and the Power of Submission* (Berkeley: University of California Press, 1997).

107. Soothill, *Gender, Social Change and Spiritual Power*, 218.

108. This language is from Andrea Hollingsworth, "Spirit and Voice: Toward a Feminist Pentecostal Pneumatology," *Pneuma* 29 (2007): 189-213.

109. Birgit Meyer, "Commodities and the Power of Prayer: Pentecostalist Attitudes Towards Consumption in Contemporary Ghana," *Development and Change* 29 (1998): 751-76.

110. Jean and John Comaroff, "Privatizing the Millennium: New Protestant Ethics and the Spirits of Capitalism in Africa, and Elsewhere," *Afrika Spectrum* 35 (2000): 293-312.

111. Comarorff, "The Politics of Conviction," 26.

112. Mark C. Taylor, *Confidence Games: Money and Markets in a World Without Redemption* (Chicago: University of Chicago Press, 2004).

113. In this regard, I would revisit Max Weber, *The Protestant Ethic and the Spirit of Capitalism* (London: Routledge, 2002 [1930]). Under the growing influence of African Pentecostalism in particular, the ascetic work pattern and expectation of heaven that Weber finds dividing Catholic and Protestant is being closed and remade into something new. My thanks to Carlos Eire for helping me identify this. See Carlos M. N. Eire, *A Very Brief History of Eternity* (Princeton: Princeton University Press, 2010), especially 150-56.

talism, African Christians in New York City place their trust in the certainty of God. This is countercultural on many levels. Such belief does not involve waiting for God to provide from the sky, although God certainly can; they work hard, typically two or three jobs. Africans new to New York are here for "opportunity," and believe God has brought them. But God remains ultimate, not possessions or achievements.[114]

We have seen how African Christianity in New York is a popular religion — a grassroots choice of identification. Prayer has always been powerful at the grassroots and popular level. Drawing on accounts from earlier periods of Christianity, Eduardo Hoornaert's *The Memory of the Christian People* shows that for the poor and marginalized, signs and wonders have not been viewed as something finished or located in the past, but as an ongoing part of ordinary experience.[115] A comparison between prayer and fasting in pre-Reformation Christianity and African Christianity may well be worth pursuing, with considerably broader possible implications for how we understood the world and God. A phrase on prayer from Eamon Duffy's *Marking the Hours: English People and Their Prayers 1240-1570* is meaningful: "highly supernatural, but in no sense otherworldly."[116] African prayers in New York City are highly supernatural, trusting only in God, but in no sense otherworldly, as they are focused on this life.

Here I simply offer a prayer from the Church of the Lord (Aladura) to emphasize how central is the conviction that God is the source of blessing and life. As Evangelist Sarah prayed during a service on September 10, 2006:

> Father God, we say bless us indeed. Bless us spiritually. Bless us financially. Bless us physically. My God and my Lord, you are in the blessing business. [You are] a miracle working Jesus. . . . Remember us this day.[117]

---

114. My analysis differs from that of David Tonghou Ngong, "Salvation and Materialism in African Theology," *Studies in World Christianity* 15:1 (2009): 1-21, and "The Material in Salvific Discourse: A Study in Two Christian Perspectives" (Ph.D. diss., Baylor University, 2007).

115. Eduardo Hoornaert, *The Memory of the Christian People*, trans. Robert R. Barr (Maryknoll, N.Y.: Orbis, 1988), 207-8.

116. Eamon Duffy, *Marking the Hours: English People and Their Prayers 1240-1570* (New Haven: Yale University Press, 2006), 96.

117. Church of the Lord (Aladura), Field Notes, September 10, 2006.

Praying Bodies

While Evangelist Sarah prayed, Mother Cooper began shouting, "Jesus, Jesus, Jesus. Heal, heal, heal. Spread out your healing." Evangelist Sarah continued, "Everybody who has a problem, we bring it to you today."

Conclusion: Power in the City

A life of prayer organizes a way of being in the world and city for African Christians. The character of prayer and fasting that we have examined in this chapter, including its vernacular shape, rigorous physical requirements, charismatic dynamic, and the potential for spiritual confrontation as well as festive joy, reminds us of earlier periods of revival in African history, such as that of St. Anthony (ca. 251-356).[118] For African Christians in New York City, prayer situates the body in divine power, shaping a way of life in the global city. Prayer offers a way of being in the city, the experience of freedom, hopes and joy in anticipation of God's good provision. The vivified experience of God creates communities and spaces of power and a vision of the fullness of life in the city. As they inhabit and engage the global city, there is "power from on high."[119] Prayer in African churches reflects not just a need to engage the transcendent, but also a belief that God is involved in this world.

---

118. My thanks to Andrew Walls for turning my attention to St. Anthony.
119. Luke 24:29.

5. Reading in Motion: Scripture and the Performance of Faith

Introduction: The Subway Test

The New York City subway system is the lifeblood of the city, carrying more than five million people on an average day. Standing next to a Wall Street stockbroker reading the *Financial Times* might be a homeless man singing "This Little Light of Mine" and holding out a rumpled paper bag for change. Mothers squeeze in with young children asleep in strollers, construction workers haul their bags of tools, and students shift under backpacks loaded with books. Squeezed into every nook and cranny are people of every ethnicity, from every neighborhood, and every country in the world.

While riding the subway, I devised "the subway test": how many people can I spot reading a Bible, and where do they look like they came from? I can almost always see a man or a woman reading a well-thumbed Bible. Most often he or she will have been born in Africa, Asia, the West Indies, or Latin America. And on Sundays, especially in the outer boroughs, subway cars are filled with people dressed for church with Bibles firmly in hand. The subway moves the city, and a church's location near a subway stop can be strategic for growth.[1] What the "subway test" provides is a window on the globalization of Christianity and a trope for recognizing the importance of the Bible for everyday life in the city.

In the previous chapter I began with a characterization of prayer as being seemingly more important for African Christians than reading the

---

1. Concerning the subway system as the essence of New York City, I am indebted to the insights of Kenneth Jackson. For a history of the subway system, see Clifton Hood, *722 Miles: The Building of the Subways and How They Transformed New York* (Baltimore: The Johns Hopkins University Press, 2004). A captivating take is Camilo José Vergara, *Subway Memories* (New York: The Monacelli Press, 2004).

Reading in Motion

Bible. But this does not mean that reading, hearing, and engaging the Bible is unimportant. For African Christians, the Bible provides answers to questions of how to live the Christian life and worship God; all theology is based on the Bible, the source of reflection on lived experience.[2] The way that African Christians in New York understand God is analogous to the way they read and hear the Bible.[3] Just as God is powerful and involved in all of life, the Bible is able to powerfully address all of life. Where the Word is engaged, there is divine activity.

In this chapter I examine the practice of reading, hearing, discussing, understanding, and engaging the Bible in the Presbyterian Church of Ghana in New York, the Church of the Lord (Aladura), and the Redeemed Christian Church of God International Chapel, Brooklyn. They encounter the Bible as a source of good news, of life, of direction. The Presbyterian Church of Ghana in New York stands in the tradition of the Basel Mission, which "had a firm belief in the centrality and authority of the Bible. Its commitment to the Bible is symbolically demonstrated by the large Bible which is carried in a procession at key functions of the Church."[4] At the Church of the Lord (Aladura), Mother Cooper said of the Bible, "Everything is in it" — a comment she made during a discussion of debt regulations in the Old Testament books of Deuteronomy and Leviticus.[5] Such views are in accord with the beliefs and practices of the Redeemed Christian Church of God International Chapel, Brooklyn, where belief and practice is saturated with biblical texts and the use of the Bible permeates every aspect of church life. For the three churches, belief in the Bible as God's Word is not justified with an epistemological theory or elaborate theology. Believing in God and seeing God work is all the justification that is required.

It is almost a matter of convention to cite, but no less significant with continual repeating, that the Bible has been translated and distributed into vernacular languages, which enables such rich ecclesial and theological development.[6] For all the importance ascribed to African approaches to

---

2. Andrew Walls, *The Cross-Cultural Process in Christian History: Studies in the Transmission and Appropriation of Faith* (Maryknoll, N.Y.: Orbis, 2002), 131, cf. 133; Ogbu Kalu, *African Pentecostalism: An Introduction* (Oxford University Press, 2008), 268.

3. I owe this way of putting matters to Claire Davis.

4. Cephas N. Omenyo, *Pentecost Outside Pentecostalism: A Study of the Development of Charismatic Renewal in the Mainline Churches in Ghana* (Zoetermeer: Uitgeverij Boekencentrum, 2002), 127.

5. Church of the Lord (Aladura), Field Notes, August 22, 2007.

6. The importance of the vernacular has been classically described by Lamin Sanneh,

Scripture, amply displayed in the recent publication of major works such as the evangelical *Africa Bible Commentary*,[7] Philip Jenkins's *The New Faces of Christianity*,[8] and Gerald West and Musa Dube's edited volume *The Bible in Africa*,[9] Paul Gifford's remark in a review of *The Bible in Africa* carries a ring of truth: "There is obviously a serious dearth of research on (lack of interest in?) how the Bible is actually received or understood or used on the ground."[10] Matthew Engelke concurs: "Few have turned their attention to practices of reading *per se*."[11]

Descriptions of how the Bible is engaged in local African Christian communities are largely absent in the scholarly literature, where instead professional readings of Scripture are privileged. Peter Nyende stresses the vital point in his important essay, "Institutional and Popular Interpretations of the Bible in Africa: Towards an Integration," that African scholarly readings of the biblical text are closely connected to and determined by local concerns.[12] Still, it is a different (and necessary) task to study grassroots or popular readings and uses. Thomas Kirsch's *Spirits and Letters: Reading, Writing, and Charisma in African Christianity*[13] is helpful. Matthew Engelke's ethnographic study *A Problem of Presence: Beyond Scripture in an African Church*[14] focused on the non-use of Scripture by the

---

Translating the Message: The Missionary Impact of Culture (Maryknoll, N.Y.: Orbis, 1989). For additional perspectives, see R. S. Sugirtharajah, *The Bible and the Third World: Precolonial, Colonial and Postcolonial Encounters* (Cambridge: Cambridge University Press, 2001).

7. Tokunboh Adeyemo, ed., *Africa Bible Commentary* (Grand Rapids: Zondervan, 2006). Paul Gifford in "The Nature and Effects of Mission Today: A Case Study from Kenya," *Social Sciences and Mission* 20 (2007): 119-20, notes the evangelical element of the project.

8. Philip Jenkins, *The New Faces of Christianity: Believing the Bible in the Global South* (New York: Oxford University Press, 2006).

9. Gerald O. West and Musa Dube, eds., *The Bible in Africa: Transactions, Trajectories and Trends* (Boston: Brill, 2001).

10. Paul Gifford, Review of *The Bible in Africa: Transactions, Trajectories and Trends*, *Journal of Religion in Africa* 34:3 (2004): 399.

11. Matthew Engelke, "The Book, the Church and the 'Incomprehensible Paradox': Christianity in African History," *Journal of Southern African Studies* 29:1 (March 2003): 302. For further development, see Matthew Engelke, "Reading and Time: Two Approaches to the Materiality of Scripture," *Ethnos* 74:2 (2009): 151-74.

12. Peter Nyende, "Institutional and Popular Interpretations of the Bible in Africa: Towards an Integration," *The Expository Times* 119:2 (2007): 59-66.

13. Thomas G. Kirsch, *Spirits and Letters: Reading, Writing, and Charisma in African Christianity* (New York: Berghahn, 2008).

14. Matthew Engelke, *A Problem of Presence: Beyond Scripture in an African Church* (Berkeley: University of California Press, 2007).

"Friday Masowe" Apostolics of Zimbabwe. Recently, Paul Gifford has drawn attention to Pentecostal approaches to reading the text that emphasize the action, promises, and commitments of God through words.[15] But much more attention is needed, particularly ethnographies of ways in which the Bible is engaged in communities.[16]

In this chapter, I identify and illustrate five ways that the Presbyterian Church of Ghana, the Church of the Lord (Aladura), and the Redeemed Christian Church of God International Chapel, Brooklyn, read and use Scripture. First, Scripture is an imaginative world that narrates the experiences of life. Second, it is read and heard communally to address everyday concerns and needs. Third, it is appropriated as a means of maintaining the distinct identity of transnational religious movements. Fourth, it is a basis for preaching and responding to the text. Fifth, it is received as words that have power and make commitments. Much more could be said, but in this group of themes I think we find some of the richness and uniqueness of African diaspora engagements with Scripture.

But before we examine these five ways, what is the end to which African Christians read the Bible? In New York City, members of African churches read their Bibles throughout the week, bring them to church, hold them tight during prayer, lift them high in joy during times of praise, underline them during sermons, and attend classes that discuss what they teach. In the words of their English, Yoruba, and Twi Bibles they hear teaching about God, an invitation to be born anew, good news of release for the oppressed, moral guidance, and promises of breakthroughs in this life. By and large, they do not read their Bibles to gather historical information, grow in appreciation for its literary form, compose formalized doctrines, or defend its veracity. Ultimately it is not that they are not interested in these subjects, but rather that they read the Bible, both the Old and New Testaments, with a priority to know what the Spirit is saying now, to enact it in their lives, to live as faithful disciples, and to construct theology in service of their community life and journey.

In so doing, African churches in New York City are a creative example of what Stephen Fowl believes biblical interpretation historically has

---

15. Paul Gifford, "The Bible in Africa: A Novel Usage in Africa's New Churches," *Bulletin of the School of Oriental and African Studies* 71:2 (2008): 203-19.

16. For other examples of this see Eva Keller, "Towards Complete Clarity: Bible Study among Seventh-Day Adventists in Madagascar," *Ethnos* 69:1 (2004): 89-112, and James S. Bielo, "On the Failure of 'Meaning': Bible Reading in the Anthropology of Christianity," *Culture and Religion* 9:1 (2008): 1-21.

been: "Christian interpretation of Scripture is primarily an activity of Christian communities in which they seek to generate and embody their interpretations of Scripture so they may fulfill their ends of worshipping and living before the triune God."[17] For African churches in New York City, their hermeneutical approach connects the biblical story with everyday life, but does so from the perspective of "pre-understandings" of the world, the questions and needs they bring to the text.

As Fowl does in his writings, we can compare such an approach with that of Augustine (354-430), who stands near the beginning of Africa's long Christian story.[18] For Augustine, reading Scripture is in service of a journey. In his primer on biblical interpretation titled *On Christian Teaching*, Augustine contends that there are two primary rules for the reading of Scripture. First, Scripture is to be read for the cultivation of love of God, and second, it is to be read in loving service of one's neighbor.[19] As Augustine approaches the reading of Scripture, he finds in it not an end in itself, but a means to end. A correct reading of Scripture for Augustine leads to love for God and neighbor. The Word then becomes embodied in the reader.[20] At that point, the need for the Christian to read Scripture would cease, except as a means to educate others.[21] The Bible, in other words, is a travel guide for pilgrims.

Augustine's approach to Scripture aptly describes the Bible for African Christians in New York: the Bible is traveling truth that is performed in everyday life as it is experienced before God. Reflecting such an Augustinian outlook, Kwame Bediako considers the Bible for African believers a "road map," linking the stories of believers on their journey of faith to the living God and the story of Scripture.[22] This emphasis dovetails with the emphasis on narrative and script developed in earlier chapters.

---

17. Stephen E. Fowl, *Engaging Scripture: A Model for Theological Interpretation* (Malden: Blackwell, 1998), 161.

18. For my reading of Augustine I am indebted to Stephen Fowl. In addition to *Engaging Scripture*, see Stephen E. Fowl, "Further Thoughts on Theological Interpretation," in *Reading Scripture with the Church: Toward a Hermeneutic for Theological Interpretation*, ed. A. K. M. Adam, Stephen E. Fowl, Kevin J. Vanhoozer, and Francis Watson (Grand Rapids: Baker, 2006), 125-30.

19. Saint Augustine, *On Christian Teaching*, trans. R. P. H. Green (Oxford: Oxford University Press, 1997), 27.

20. Augustine, *On Christian Teaching*, 28-29.

21. Augustine, *On Christian Teaching*, 28-29.

22. Kwame Bediako, "Scripture as the Hermeneutic of Culture and Tradition," *Journal of African Christian Thought* 4:1 (2002): 2-11.

As Gerrie ter Haar summarizes, the Bible is "the book of life for believers."[23] Allan Anderson, speaking of Pentecostals but in ways that characterize a more pervasive emphasis, states that "Their purpose in reading the Bible is to find there something that can be experienced as relevant to their felt needs."[24] Thus the hermeneutic of New York's African churches converges with a reading of the Bible that is concerned with providing for life needs and human flourishing. For African Christians, this means that the Bible still "speaks" today; it is not just a book about the past. African Christians in New York City read the Bible as God's story of salvation, past, present, and future — for self, community, and family.

In these African churches, mentalist and discursive readings take a secondary place to readings that are embodied and materialized — marking another difference with Enlightenment-shaped religion. While some theologians may argue that reading the Bible in such a focused and pragmatic way is problematic, I think it is much closer to patterns of interpretation that have long proceeded in the Christian church. Theology in African churches, to use the terminology of Anthony Thiselton, is "action-oriented" and related to the "contingencies" of everyday life.[25] "Action-oriented" theological convictions about God, Jesus, and the Holy Spirit are the most prominent features of African churches in New York City.

Living in the World Imagined by Scripture

For the Presbyterian Church of Ghana in New York, the Church of the Lord (Aladura), and the Redeemed Christian Church of God International Chapel, Brooklyn, the Bible is first of all not a book of moral precepts or doctrinal teachings, but an imaginative world.[26] The Bible's description of the world is embraced as the story of the world. Luke Timothy Johnson, a

---

23. Gerrie ter Haar, *Halfway to Paradise: African Christians in Europe* (Cardiff: Cardiff Academic Press, 1998), 49.

24. Allan Anderson, *An Introduction to Pentecostalism* (Cambridge: Cambridge University Press, 2004), 225.

25. Anthony C. Thiselton, *The Hermeneutics of Doctrine* (Grand Rapids: Eerdmans, 2007), 21. See also Margaret M. Mitchell, *Paul, the Corinthians and the Birth of Christian Hermeneutics* (Cambridge: Cambridge University Press, 2010).

26. Simon Coleman, *The Globalisation of Charismatic Christianity: Spreading the Gospel of Prosperity* (Cambridge: Cambridge University Press, 2000), 117-42.

New Testament scholar at Emory University, argues that the Bible presents a world that is more expansive and more complex than what we see. It is the world created by God, a world where God's power is at work, where grace transforms: "By imagining the world as always and essentially related to God, Scripture reveals the world and at the same time reveals God."[27] From this flow a number of implications. "People act on the basis of the imagined world in which they dwell," Johnson observes, "and by acting on what they imagine, they help establish their worlds as real."[28] Like a city that is intuitively known and lived in, Johnson suggests that the world of Scripture can also be inhabited.[29]

The Presbyterian Church of Ghana in New York, the Church of the Lord (Aladura), and the Redeemed Christian Church of God International Chapel, Brooklyn, share in common themes, albeit with divergent emphases, in how they engage the world of Scripture. For all three churches, the defining feature of the imaginative world of Scripture is Christ, and particularly God as triumphant in Christ over powers seen and unseen. The narrative life and actions of Jesus present themselves here. In the Pentecostal telling, the resurrection of Jesus is at the forefront, revealing God's ultimate power over human frailty, barrenness, sickness, and death. During his life he also ministered to the sick and announced good news. Church life is the experience of the resurrected Lord who still heals, ministers, and proclaims.

At the Redeemed Christian Church of God International Chapel, Brooklyn, Pentecost introduces a new reality into the world. "Like the day of Pentecost, fire fall on me" is a song that is often part of worship. With Pentecost, the Spirit came upon persons; the words of the song are often sung today directly to invoke the Spirit's presence and activity. But equally in the Christian story, Pentecost involves the living powers of the future manifest in the present, "the powers of the age to come."[30] Not only does the "fire" fall in Brooklyn; so do the energies of the Spirit. A new world of eternal joy is also created. What is invisible, the new life of

---

27. Luke Timothy Johnson, "Imagining the World Scripture Imagines," *Modern Theology* 14:2 (1998): 166.

28. Johnson, "Imagining the World Scripture Imagines," 166.

29. Johnson, "Imagining the World Scripture Imagines," 167-69.

30. Hebrews 6:5. This is a major emphasis in Jürgen Moltmann's work on the Holy Spirit. See Moltmann, *The Spirit of Life: A Universal Affirmation*, trans. Margaret Kohl (Minneapolis: Fortress, 1992), among his most enduring contributions; see also Moltmann, *The Source of Life: The Holy Spirit and the Theology of Life* (Minneapolis: Fortress, 1997).

God that *is* God, is rendered visible in miraculously healed bodies and born-again hearts. The conditions that give rise to faith are essentially empirical — God is still active in healing and transforming. How do you know Jesus' presence and power is real? By testing it, seeing it, and experiencing it.[31]

For the Presbyterian Church of Ghana, Jesus is the Savior, guiding and instructing the Christian life, but he is also the life-giver. The unseen world is also very active, and God protects and leads in this area. For the Church of the Lord (Aladura), the imaginative narrative rests prominently on a conflict between God and Satan, in which God has achieved a victory. But a conflict remains with evil forces, requiring a life of prayer, fasting, and the use of Scripture to combat the forces. There is also a strong pneumatological emphasis.

African Christians in New York City assume the potential for ill in witchcraft, spirits, and possessions as a matter of course.[32] Wayne Meeks effectively describes the early Christian viewpoint: "From the beginning of their movement, it seems, the Christians live in a world with demons filled. Paul, explaining a change of plans, can say, 'Satan prevented me' (1 Thess. 2:18) as casually as we might say, 'My car had a flat tire.'"[33] The unorganized world of spirits, powers, and demons recognized in the Bible remains real,[34] not collapsed under the inactive cosmology of the West. But Christ controls the world, and faith in God engages the world with power and authority. Reading Scripture is an act of interpretation of this world and also a dimension of spiritual conflict and victory.

As Teresa Okure indicates, biblical interpretation is often divided between exegesis (the meaning of the text in its original context) and hermeneutics (the meaning of the text in its contemporary setting). Okure questions this fissure, arguing that there are "natural limitations" to objectivity

---

31. I owe this way of putting things to a comment made by Professor David Kerr during a seminar on the New Testament scholar Charles Dodd at the Centre for the Study of Christianity in the Non-Western World.

32. See Walls, *The Cross-Cultural Process in Christian History*, 116-35. On the "primal" substructure of African Christianity, see Kwame Bediako, *Christianity in Africa: The Renewal of a Non-Western Religion* (Edinburgh: Edinburgh University Press and Maryknoll, N.Y.: Orbis, 1995), 91-108. See also Ogbu U. Kalu, "Preserving a Worldview: Pentecostalism in the African Maps of the Universe," *Pneuma* 24:2 (2002): 110-37.

33. Wayne A. Meeks, *The Origins of Christian Morality: The First Two Centuries* (New Haven: Yale University Press, 1993), 112.

34. Karel van der Toorn, Bob Becking, and Pieter W. van der Horst, eds., *Dictionary of Deities and Demons in the Bible* (Leiden: Brill and Grand Rapids: Eerdmans, 1999).

in every reader and that we all read in terms of our cultural and social realities.[35] For African Christians, the imaginative world of Scripture provides a better description of the world as it is.[36] In this world, God does intervene, protect, lead, heal, and speak.

African Christians, especially Pentecostals, are often charged with being caught up in the promises of modernity, but their appeal to the world of Scripture is an important rebuttal to the charge. Assuming that the scriptural world is the primary setting, African Christians recognize that they also live within other settings and communities. They live in the world, but it is a world in which Christ has entered and brought conversion. The church inhabits the culture and the city, and does so in Christ.

Reading in Community

The imaginative world of Scripture African Christians live in comes to them by reading and hearing that Scripture together in community. In Fowl's characterization of reading the Bible, the text is not self-generating in its "meaning," but depends on a communal process that discerns a faithful reading for a specific context.[37] This is evidenced in both sermons and Bible studies in the three churches studied here.

In the previous chapter I introduced the Bible Study and Prayer Group of the Presbyterian Church of Ghana in New York. One of their meetings, led by Kwabena Gyasi, illustrates how they read scriptural texts.[38] This evening there are eight women and four men. After praying for twenty minutes, Matthew 17 is the first text they read together for their discussion of "praying to receive something special from God." They are seated around a table, and the format is primarily teaching with some discussion. Five ways are given. First, "pray to the Father in Jesus' name." From John 16, the group speaks of Jesus as advocate. Second, "when we pray, believe and you shall receive," with Matthew 24 providing a basis. Third, forgiveness is required — forgiveness from God. Fourth, the Holy Spirit must help. Fifth, "you must build yourself up by prayer in the Holy Ghost." As the study con-

---

35. Teresa Okure, "I Will Open My Mouth in Parables (Matt. 13:35): A Case for Gospel-Based Hermeneutics," *New Testament Studies* 46:3 (July 2000): 445-63.
36. Johnson, "Imagining the World Scripture Imagines," 167.
37. Fowl, *Engaging Scripture*.
38. Presbyterian Church of Ghana in New York, Field Notes, August 19, 2005.

Reading in Motion

Fig. 5.1 Bible Study, Mother Cooper and Minister Joy, Church of the Lord (Aladura), 2005

cludes, the group brings John 14:16 into the discussion. The Holy Spirit is a personal "advocate" and "comforter," they stress.

The Bible Study and Prayer Group is studying biblical texts without engaging in concerns of critical scholarship. Instead they connect biblical texts together to inform Christian living and thought. The Bible Study and Prayer Group read together in friendship, prayer, and worship.

When two or three gather at the Church of the Lord (Aladura) in New York to discuss the Bible, the readings address everyday life. At the church's founding, Wednesday evening was set apart for Bible study — the day and time are still posted on their sign. But it became apparent that work obligations and travel distances precluded regular attendance on Wednesday evening, so Mother Cooper incorporated the Bible study into Sunday worship. Every Sunday afternoon, midway through the service, the liturgy is paused and the leaders come down from the platform and sit on folding chairs among the congregation. Reading Scripture now takes place within a worship setting, which for the ends of the Church of the Lord (Aladura) is perhaps the best possible setting.

Typically, Minister Joy sits on a folding chair front and center, with Mother Cooper seated to her right. To select a text, either a guide produced by the Church of the Lord (Aladura) is consulted, or one of the leaders proposes a biblical text. In a typical format, first someone is asked to read the text aloud, and then over the course of approximately one hour an exchange of questions, answers, and viewpoints takes place. In one service, Deacon David is asked to read Matthew 24, identified as a discussion on "Signs of the Coming of Christ." Mother Cooper begins the discussion by sharing that she "heard on the radio Christ is coming that September." However, it is now October. Christians need to read the Bible, she insists: only "Christ — no one [else], not even angels — knows when he is coming." Christ is, however, announcing signs, and they are related to mission: "When God says, go. Whenever he is in my spiritual imagination, he is getting ready. When [the] Father says move . . . we must know when the time is getting close." How will we know when the time is close? "Strange things, false prophets," Mother Cooper ruminates.

Someone then asks: what is the gospel message to be applied? At this point Mother Cooper reads Matthew 24:14, which in her King James Version reads, "And this gospel of the kingdom shall be preached in all the world for a witness unto all nations; and then shall the end come." Reference is made to the importance of the open air preaching in the Church of the Lord (Aladura) in Liberia, speaking the gospel in the subway, the use of different languages to communicate the gospel. But what is given most attention is the story of a woman in the Church of the Lord (Aladura) who could not read and write to whom "God gave her knowledge of the Word of God." Mother Cooper comments, "God will give people different gifts." Indeed, "God raises up people to speak to the poor and Ph.D.s."

After a while, the discussion turns back to Matthew 24:13 and the notion of service. Along the way, Mother Cooper comments that the "love of flesh is a transitory love" and reminds the community not to "let anybody shake your faith." The Christian life, she offers, is "a day to day business. He doesn't want us cold, or lukewarm. God is so hot. God wants strong people. God wants committed people." She brings up the powerful presence of the Spirit: "The Holy Ghost . . . like fire, a mighty wind is the day of Elijah." As the hour of Bible discussion comes to a close, the topic turns to Liberia, to "wars and rumors of war." "Look what happened to our country," laments someone in the group. What to do? Mother Cooper exhorts, "Keep steady, fasting and praying." The Bible lesson over, Mother Cooper and Minister Joy return to the platform, and soon a "strong prayer" brings the liturgy back into focus.

In another service, during the Bible lesson on John 14, Deacon David asks to discuss verse 3, which reads, "And if I go and prepare a place for you, I will come again, and receive you unto myself; that where I am, there ye may be also."[39] "What does this mean?" he asks. Mother Cooper pauses to think, and then provides a profound theological commentary on social reality. It is "not the kind of selfish mansion we have here . . . a very expensive house" where you can "walk in and feel satisfied." In heaven, "these mansions are not houses set aside" but "a peaceful place . . . of love . . . where everyone will have a share and there will be no segregation." Here "everybody will have no need" and "there will be an equal share, no time to envy [the] next [mansion]." Further, she reasons, "if no sin, no selfishness . . . nobody will be [sick], nobody will be homeless." Instead, "there is togetherness." Expands Mother Cooper, "white, black, pink . . . all of them who believe in Jesus Christ will rejoice together." In the new world, there is "no hunger . . . because there will be no need to cook." Instead of work, the community will "just [be] singing and praising God like the angels." Imagining such a world as this, says Mother Cooper, takes a certain God. "God is one God, one in three, three in one."

What takes place in these gatherings is that as communities are reading the Bible they share experiences, questions, and ideas. They work with one another toward transformation after Christ. Women and men bring their knowledge of the world, the city, and their faith together. When read in community, the texts are not in free play without reference to their original settings, but by the workings of the Spirit merged with the present horizon.

Biblical Texts and Identity

The biblical text plays a significant role in shaping the identity of African congregations in New York. For a precedent, we need only look to the development of early Christianity, where textual identity came to be an important element in communal self-understanding.[40] Today an emphasis on

---

39. King James Version.
40. Judith M. Lieu, *Christian Identity in the Jewish and Graeco-Roman World* (Oxford: Oxford University Press, 2004).

a textually inscribed identity for African immigrant churches forms believers in a way of life and helps connect between two cultural worlds. For the "Mother churches," distance and expansion lead to constant change and new leadership. The need to have mechanisms to shape a common identity can be urgent. Scripture and doctrine help fulfill this role. This finding suggests that global diffusion of charismatic and Pentecostal movements is not simply based on the physical and ritual components,[41] but also on biblical texts and doctrine.

A good picture to introduce this phenomenon is found in the Children's Service at Presbyterian Church of Ghana. During the service Julie Agyemang leads over twenty children in the following song:[42]

> Read your Bible
> Read your Bible
> Read your Bible
> In the morning
> In the afternoon
> In the evening
> In the night
> Read your Bible everyday

After singing this song through a number of times in English, the children sing the same song in the Twi language, reinforcing the emphasis on the Bible in two languages. Church and home, Julie Agyemang explains later, are the only two places where they can learn to speak the Twi language. While the children have all been born in the United States and English is or will be their primary language, Twi is important culturally, and by extension religiously.[43] Through the Bible as medium, they will gain knowledge of their Ghanaian culture.

On the face of things, J. Kwabena Asamoah-Gyadu is certainly correct in his observation that "Pentecostalism is itself a movement that relies on direct experience of the divine rather than on codified beliefs, creeds or philosophies."[44] Yet whether one attributes it to an inevitable process of

---

41. Joel Robbins, "Pentecostal Networks and the Spirit of Globalization: On the Social Productivity of Ritual Forms," *Social Analysis* 53:1 (2009): 55-66.

42. Service, November 25, 2007.

43. Julie Agyemang, Interview, November 25, 2007.

44. J. Kwabena Asamoah-Gyadu, *African Charismatics: Current Developments within Indigenous Pentecostalism in Ghana* (Leiden: Brill, 2005), 17; cf. 54.

institutionalization or to other factors and dynamics,[45] there is indication that a set of codified beliefs is considered essential to maintain the identity of the far-flung operations of Redeemed Christian Church of God, the largest Pentecostal church in Nigeria and one of the fastest growing churches worldwide. Religious faith can be mediated through what Thomas Kirsch terms "print globalization";[46] in Redeemed Christian Church of God congregations, pastors select their sermon texts and topics themselves, but Digging Deep and Sunday school instruction is the same in every parish in every part of the world. Sunday school instruction is more widely attended than Digging Deep, at least in Brooklyn. Attendance is strong, and the classes are broken into three groups, each with a leader. Local practice reflects a global organizational mandate. As an indication of the growth of the Redeemed Christian Church of God, instead of importing the books from Nigeria, the North American office now reprints the booklet developed by its Directorate of Christian Education in Lagos; it is also available on their Web site at no charge.[47] Digging Deep material is now available only on the church's Web site.[48]

Writing in the preface to the 2006-2007 Sunday school manual, General Overseer E. A. Adeboye instructs:

> The Redeemed Christian Church of God has witnessed a lot of growth and God has been gracious to us in many ways. Many of our parishes have joined the wise ones who are growing through Sunday Search the Scriptures. No doubt, Search the Scriptures on Sunday is one avenue or means to teach biblical doctrines to match the speed of our growth. Being a formal school, therefore, its syllabus, as it were, needs to be tailored towards presenting undiluted biblical teachings, which must consider the different categories of people in the church, the young Christians, the middle aged and the matured ones.[49]

Adeboye's words indicate how the Sunday school manual is designed to help unite a global organization with an increasing variety of parishes, but

---

45. Kirsch, *Spirits and Letters*, has developed important leads here on the relationship between charismatic authority and routinization that might be related here.
46. Thomas G. Kirsch, "Ways of Reading as Religious Power in Print Globalization," *American Ethnologist* 34:3 (2007): 509-20; see also *Spirits and Letters*.
47. See http://ss2007.rccg.org/.
48. See http://diggingdeep.rccg.org/.
49. *Search the Scriptures* (Redeemed Christian Church of God North America, 2006), 6.

Fig. 5.2 Segun Oyesanya teaching Sunday school, Redeemed Christian Church of God International Chapel, Brooklyn, 2005

they also show his authority as a reader of the biblical texts and their meaning for the church.

Organized quarterly and by themes, the manual begins with a ten-part study on "Foundational Truths" that includes Jesus, the Holy Spirit, and sanctification. The manual goes on to teach on other topics such as ministry, healing, apostles, prophets, divine favor, holiness, faith, marriage, money, victorious living, prosperity, soul saving, and restitution. The earlier 2002-2003 Sunday school manual begins with a history of the church. The themes of this manual are "readiness for the King," "Jesus our Baptizer," and what are called "revelation," "inspirational," and "power" gifts as well as marriage, home life, the Great Commission, and prayer. While there are many similarities between the two manuals, the more recent of the two is even more intentional about doctrine and formation.

With a uniform reading of Scripture, the Redeemed Christian Church of God is using its Sunday Bible classes as a form of global catechesis. In so doing, the church is establishing moral and theological boundaries. Put another way, the Sunday school manual is building tradition into a charismatic movement. As a church with an increasingly global operation and an aggressively decentralized approach to growth, the Redeemed Christian Church of God is seeking uniformity in identity through normative readings of Scripture.[50]

Like the Redeemed Christian Church of God, the Presbyterian Church of Ghana headquarters provides direction and material on what to study in the local parish. A good example of this is the church-wide Bible study that takes place monthly during the Sunday worship service. Midway into one Sunday service, the church breaks into three language groups for Bible study: Twi, Ga, and English. Each group meets in a different portion of the sanctuary and is led by a different lay leader. For almost an hour, the study follows a Bible study booklet published by the Presbyterian Church of Ghana headquarters and imported for use in the church. "This is a Bible church," the leader of the English group proclaims as he encourages people to bring their Bibles to church. The topic of this session is "repentance," and Isaiah 55:7, Psalm 38:18, 2 Samuel 12, and Luke 19:8 are read and discussed in this regard. The groups wrap up and return to their pews. Summarizing what has been discussed, Rev. Asiedu tells the church: "May He help us choose between the world and Him." Soon the Singing Band has the church joyously praising God.

Reading Scripture is a mark of identity in the Church of the Lord (Aladura) as well. As Harold Turner notes, "The constitution declares that the Scriptures are the official basis of the Church, and an effort is made to support practice and teaching by biblical references. The Church desires to be a biblical church and holds the Bible in great reverence."[51] Peter Probst connects this emphasis on the Bible with an early stress on literacy and written texts[52] in the Church of the Lord (Aladura), including Josiah Ositelu's "holy words" committed to writing.[53]

---

50. Put another way, the global use of Sunday school and related materials could be seen as reflecting the role of doctrine as keeping church members "spiritually fit," to use the formulation in Kevin Vanhoozer, *The Drama of Doctrine: A Canonical-Linguistic Approach to Christian Theology* (Lousiville: Westminster John Knox, 2005).

51. Harold W. Turner, *African Independent Church*, vol. 2: *The Life and Faith of the Church of the Lord (Aladura)* (Oxford: Clarendon Press, 1967), 83.

52. Peter Probst, "The Letter and the Spirit: Literacy and Religious Authority in the History of the Aladura Movement in Western Nigeria," *Africa* 59:4 (1989): 479.

53. Probst, "The Letter and the Spirit," 489-90, 492.

ENGAGEMENTS

Preaching for Life

As I began this project, I expected to hear sermons on the diaspora, messages that find in Abraham, Sarah, or Ruth analogues for faith in a foreign land. This was not the case. Rather, there is a sense that all of Scripture, understood as the story of God's work of redemption, continues to be experienced in everyday life. Preaching in the three churches is intended to shape a way of seeing and living in the world.

At the Presbyterian Church of Ghana in New York, the pulpit is recognized as holding great consequence, and ministers undertake formal theological training, which in part forms them in correct ways of reading the text. Preaching calendars in Ghana and New York are linked together. Each week the selection of texts follows an "almanac," meaning that preaching texts are assigned even for visiting preachers. A sermon delivered by Rev. Asiedu on Easter Sunday is based on readings from Acts 10:34-43, 1 Corinthians 5:6-11, and Matthew 28:10.[54] Rev. Asiedu starts off with a question: "What is new for us today?" The message of the resurrection for those who "have Christ" should lead, in the words of John's Gospel, to "go . . . and tell them about Jesus Christ. He is risen!" For Rev. Asiedu, "Jesus rose from the grave so that we might have faith. Salvation is for everybody . . . we need salvation." From the Corinthians reading he makes the point that "church discipline is needed" because "one bad apple spoils a bunch of apples." In conclusion, he emphasizes that if you believe or have faith, you will "prevail," you will be a "conqueror," you will be a "victor." The sermon is delivered in English, but he stops along the way to provide short summaries in Twi.

Sermons are just a part of a complex and multifaceted worship service at the Church of the Lord (Aladura), but they provide an opportunity to speak a prophetic word to the congregation. Consequently, preaching is based on gifts and their acknowledgment by the community. The Evangelist Eleanor Campbell is one of the regular preachers at the Church of the Lord (Aladura). One sermon she delivers on Matthew 5:1-10 hones in on the saying, "blessed are the poor in spirit."[55] "This is how I want to explain it," she says.

> When [there is] no where else to turn . . . look to your left, right, backwards, and forwards. You feel like you're in another world. . . . When you've lost a loved one . . . you have to come to the Lord.

54. Presbyterian Church of Ghana in New York, Field Notes, March 27, 2005.
55. Church of the Lord (Aladura), Field Notes, February 6, 2005.

Reading in Motion

To this end Sister Eleanor quotes Psalm 37:11, which reads, "But the meek shall inherit the earth; and shall delight themselves in the abundance of peace." David's story offers an example: "You have to humble yourself before the Lord and he will lift you up." She then talks about the white garments that members wear, including head coverings for women. Recalling the practice in Liberia, she says the white garments represent spirituality.[56] "You have to humble yourself to ask for prayer. Right now, ask for salvation of your soul," she concludes.

Harold Turner has analyzed the distribution of biblical texts across a wide selection of sermons in the Church of the Lord (Aladura).[57] Like Turner, I heard a wide range of Old Testament and New Testament texts preached on. However, whereas Turner raised concerns about a "muted testimony to Christ,"[58] nearly five decades later I heard much attention and devotion to Christ. The full canon is employed in the church's preaching.

At the Redeemed Christian Church of God International Chapel, Brooklyn, the sermon is a nexus in which the Spirit fills the congregation with power for life. When Nimi Wariboko comes to the pulpit to preach at the Redeemed Christian Church of God International Chapel, Brooklyn, he brings his Bible and a notebook containing his sermon points. In one instance, he preached on the topic of revival, based on Acts 2:1-8. Typically, Pastor Wariboko has a number of points to each sermon, and James Adieze or another worker, sitting to the side, types verses and an outline into a laptop computer that projects onto a screen for the congregation to view. Pastor's Wariboko's sermon on revival has seven points.[59] First, "there is a turning to Christ in holiness." Second, "here is a manifestation of the gifts of the Holy Spirit" that offers the hope of a church where "there is no discrimination and racism in the midst of God's people." This applies to other possible divisions: "a Green Card doesn't make you better. God has brought us here to our destiny." Third, "emotional and physical healings take place in our midst." Fourth, "there is a strengthening of faith." Fifth, "there is unity in the

---

56. For further background see Elisha P. Renne, "'Let Your Garments Always Be White . . .': Expressions of Past and Present in Yoruba Religious Textiles," in *Christianity and Social Change in Africa: Essays in Honor of J. D. Y. Peel*, ed. Toyin Falola (Durham: Carolina Academic Press, 2005), 139-63.

57. Harold W. Turner, *Profile Through Preaching: A Study of the Sermon Texts Used in a West African Independent Church* (London: Edinburgh House Press, 1965).

58. Turner, *Profile Through Preaching*, 79, cf. 12-13.

59. Because it appeared that Pastor Nimi Wariboko combined a number of points along the way, I recognize that the numbering may vary.

church" through grace that abounds. Sixth, there is a "missionary drive." Seventh, there is "prophetic criticism" that applies to all of society. He explains that fasting is part of social criticism. Pastor Nimi closes by summoning people to "stand up and speak unto Christ."

Words with Power

Christian Scripture in African churches "does things" — it produces concrete change. For African Christians, while God urges and instructs in the Scriptures, more attention is given to how God performs actions through the Bible. The Bible is considered the Word of God, and hence an active power in every setting, making possible all things. Indeed, biblical words are seen to have within them the capacity of spiritual power, an attribute bound up with divine authority. What African Christians believe about God is reflected in their view of the Bible. As Paul Gifford observes, the Bible is seen as contemporary, for its past promises and commands, its covenant commitments, are realized in the present.[60]

The power conveyed in biblical texts — repeating them, reading them, and praying them — assists in pastoral needs. For example, the text has performative ability in the area of deliverance, healing, and power that connects to life needs in the city.[61] It is not so much that the biblical text "speaks" to persons, but rather that when its words are invoked, they carry power. For the biblical writers, for example, the proclamation of the cross brings redemption; it does not simply transmit information. In speech-act theory, as Nicholas Wolterstorff develops in *Divine Discourse,* God does things by illocutionary acts — words do things when God speaks them.[62] As Anthony Thiselton argues, "*Illocutions* transform worldviews not merely *by* rhetorical utterance but *in* their very utterance."[63] "The proclamation of the cross is a speech-act to promote a new way of being in the world."[64] African Christians

---

60. Paul Gifford, "The Bible in Africa."
61. In the "Bible in Africa," Gifford also calls this a "declarative use" (p. 206).
62. For a leading discussion on speech-act theory in relationship to the Bible, see Nicholas Wolterstorff, *Divine Discourse: Philosophical Reflections on the Claim that God Speaks* (Cambridge: Cambridge University Press, 1995).
63. Anthony C. Thiselton, *The First Epistle to the Corinthians: A Commentary on the Greek Text* (Grand Rapids: Eerdmans, 2000), 51.
64. Brevard S. Childs, "Speech-act Theory and Biblical Interpretation," *Scottish Journal of Theology* 58:4 (2005): 389.

have developed a hermeneutical framework with affinities to speech-act theory: God's words do things when spoken by persons. They heal, deliver, promise, and direct. Yet the biblical words themselves have strength only within God and, in a secondary manner, through the agency of faith.

The name of Jesus is frequent invoked as a means of receiving God's influence in all areas of life. "In the name of Jesus!" one is healed and delivered, a phrase drawn from Acts in the New Testament.[65] Here the continual repetition of Jesus' name aloud is crucial. A related theme is the "blood of Jesus," understood to protect, cover, and heal persons. Asamoah-Gyadu draws these elements together as they are found in Ghanaian neo-Pentecostalism: "the deployment of divine resources, that is, power and authority in the Name or Blood of Jesus — perceived in pneumatological terms as the intervention of the Holy Spirit."[66] The underlying image of atonement is not judicial in its emphasis, but experiential; salvation is healing that comes continually into the believer's life through Christ's death.

At the Church of the Lord (Aladura) in the Bronx, the reading of particular psalms is a factor in many occasions of divine involvement. Psalm 24 is used for consecration, for example, and Psalm 121 for protection. Like other Aladura, Mother Cooper and the church ascribe particular powers to the Psalms.[67] When a person presents a problem, she says, "I refer them to the book of Psalms," which focuses on "prayer and supplication."[68] The words of the Psalms are understood to make claims and produce specific actions. In the Aladura tradition, words are considered to have power.[69]

As observed in chapter one, Grace Presbyterian in Ghana yearly sends a healing team to New York. A core element of the healing process involves "the client" reading lines from Scripture. The protocol on healing, a typed sheet with the heading "Healings," has twelve lines from Scripture.[70] It begins, "God's ideal way of creation was to be devoid of evil including sickness. Genesis 1:31." There are different causes of sickness, not always but possibly including sins, which require confession. Line eleven is

---

65. Acts 3:6.
66. Asamoah-Gyadu, *African Charismatics*, 165.
67. David Tuesday Adamo, "The Use of Psalms in African Indigenous Churches in Nigeria," in *The Bible in Africa*, ed. West and Dube, 336-49.
68. Marie Cooper, Interview, March 15, 2005.
69. Peter Probst, "The Letter and the Spirit," 478-95.
70. "Healing," no date.

"MAINTAINING the healing is also heavily dependent upon your CONTINUED ASSOCIATION with Jesus Christ. John 15:4-7." Overall, the protocol asks, "What is the relevance of Jesus Christ (the healer) to your life?"

An accompanying sheet of "Prayer Lines" directs an additional step in the healing process. The prayer lines begin with "Give thanks to [the] Lord who came to bind the broken hearted, free the captives and release prisoners." Other lines that can be assigned for prayer include, "Bind every spirit of infirmity in the name of Jesus," "Pray in the name of Jesus to release yourself from every hereditary sickness," "Ask the Lord to perform a divine surgery in every area of your body, which requires such an operation," and "Pray that you would always enjoy a good health, body, soul and spirit." The standard interpretation would be that these words are to be applied to the problem in question. But that alone does not help; the words and their objectives must be voiced and therefore embodied.

At the Redeemed Christian Church of God International Chapel, Brooklyn, one can hear worship leaders direct the entire church to "prophesy to yourself," with each person then filling in some words from Scripture such as "blessing" or "success." For example, "God, I prophesy blessing into my life today." Blessing, which presupposes God's active engagement as a life-changing force for good, brings about certain results understood to be the logic of promise and holiness.

Conclusion: The Word Abides

After the sermon at the Church of the Lord (Aladura) is concluded, the congregation sings: "The living words of God/The living words of God/The living words of God/Abide within me." For emphasis, it is sung through three times. This is a fitting way to conclude this chapter on the Bible in African churches in New York City. For the Presbyterian Church of Ghana in New York, the Church of the Lord (Aladura), and the Redeemed Christian Church of God International Chapel, Brooklyn, Scripture is viewed as living, powerful, and relevant, especially when it inhabits the bodies of believers and communities of worship to which they belong. Reading is not required, but hearing and abiding is. The Bible speaks to the totality of everyday life, to family life, to employment, to politics, and to school. It is not information, but a story to dwell within congregants as they also dwell in the world. In a global setting, reading the Bible together provides continuity of belief and continually shapes self-understanding.

6. Witnesses in the City: Dynamics of a New Missionary Movement

Introduction: New Patterns

Where Nostrund and Parkside Avenues meet in Brooklyn is a jumble of everything — pharmacy, childcare center, grocery store, mosque, bodega, restaurant, and a stop for the 2 and 5 trains. Also located in this cultural and interreligious zone is the Redeemed Christian Church of God International Chapel. As people are coming up out of the subway and into daylight, Bola Oyesanya, a minister at the church, a lawyer by training, and a corporate vice-president at a global financial institution, greets people, offers an evangelistic tract, and then asks if they have a few minutes to talk about Jesus. Later Minister Bola explains that she begins by asking, "Do you have a few minutes for me to share with you about the love of God?" Then she shares that Christ died for them and invites them into a relationship with God. "Sometimes a soul is won, sometimes just a seed is planted," Bola reflects.[1]

"Christianity," observes Andrew Walls, "has throughout its history spread outwards, across cultural frontiers, so that each new point on the Christian circumference is a new potential Christian centre."[2] In a global urban world, new frontiers and encounters are occurring resulting in new centers. Following migration, the growth of African churches in New York is quite in line with developments in the early Christian story when "those who were scattered went from place to place, proclaiming the word."[3] Ob-

---

1. Bola Oyesanya, Interview, September 23, 2007.
2. Andrew F. Walls, *The Missionary Movement in Christian History: Studies in the Transmission of Faith* (Maryknoll, N.Y.: Orbis, 2000), 22.
3. Acts 8:4. For a fuller background, see Wayne Meeks, *The First Urban Christians: The Social World of the Apostle Paul* (New Haven: Yale University Press, 1983). See also

serves Paul Freston, "Christianity has become a truly global religion, and this applies to its mission dimension as well."[4] We speak not of a "reverse mission," but of a mission in a new key, for African Christianity, as Ogbu Kalu writes, has a long history of missionary enterprise: "missionary work within a nation, within Africa, and cross-culturally outside Africa."[5] It is the third phase of mission where we now pick up the story.[6]

There is no single definition or practice of mission.[7] In the New Testament, the very act of establishing a new church was mission, as was a commitment to Christ's lordship in the culture.[8] In this chapter I describe and analyze the mission discourse, beliefs, institutional capacities, and practices found in the churches and membership of the Presbyterian Church of Ghana, Church of the Lord (Aladura), and the Redeemed Christian Church of God International Chapel, Brooklyn. The context is a religiously pluralistic and culturally heterogeneous city. Because I did not hear the discourse of "reverse mission" (a re-evangelization of the West) in the churches, and because I think something new with its own identity and integrity is taking place, I do not find this term to be apt. In my reading, the basic picture of mission that emerges is less one of sending missionaries from Africa to New York City and more one of a mission intertwined with migration;[9] not as

---

Rodney Stark, *The Rise of Christianity: A Sociologist Reconsiders Christianity* (Princeton: Princeton University Press, 1996).

4. Paul Freston, "Globalization, Southern Christianity, and Proselytism," *The Review of Faith and International Affairs* 7:1 (2009): 3.

5. Ogbu U. Kalu, "Pentecostalism and Mission in Africa, 1970-2000," *Mission Studies* 24 (2007): 36. See further Matthews A. Ojo, "The Dynamics of Indigenous Charismatic Missionary Enterprises in West Africa," *Missionalia* 25:4 (December 1997): 537-61.

6. On the "back story," see Lamin Sanneh, *Disciples of All Nations: Pillars of World Christianity* (Oxford: Oxford University Press, 2008); Andrew F. Walls, *The Cross-Cultural Process in Christian History: Studies in the Transmission and Appropriation of Faith* (Maryknoll, N.Y.: Orbis, 2002); and Dana L. Robert, *Christian Mission: How Christianity Became a World Religion* (Malden: Wiley-Blackwell, 2009).

7. For a discussion of different views see the important work by Stephen B. Bevans and Roger P. Schroeder, *Constants in Context: A Theology of Mission for Today* (Maryknoll, N.Y.: Orbis, 2004).

8. C. Kavin Rowe, *World Upside Down: Reading Acts in the Graeco-Roman Age* (New York: Oxford University Press, 2009).

9. Peter Beyer sees these as two choices in *Religion in a Global Society* (London: Routledge, 2006), 146-47. For a fuller discussion of mission and migration, see Andrew F. Walls, "Mission and Migration: The Diaspora Factor in Christian History," *Journal of African Christian Thought* 5:2 (December 2002), 3-11, and "Migration and Evangelization: The Gospel and Movement of Peoples in Modern Times," *The Covenant Quarterly* 63:1 (2005): 3-

much the result of a grand strategy as it is the ways in which people freely live and name what is Christian in the city; a movement not driven by missionary organizations but rooted in church-based initiatives; not an outreach linked to political reach, but one imbued with the Spirit.

A Global Vision

African churches do not have small visions. Their vision of the missionary nature of the church is longstanding, expansive, and comprehensive: the entire globe covered with disciples of Jesus Christ. In this ambition they exhibit what Arjun Appadurai identifies as a "global imagination"[10] and Simon Coleman speaks of as a "global orientation" and "global consciousness."[11] Crossing spatial and cultural borders has always been a vital part of the Christian story, but globalization and immigration have made it even more central to that story.

An international sensibility is part of the history of the Presbyterian Church of Ghana going back to the beginnings of the church with the Basel Mission,[12] but the church has expanded on this global outlook in ways almost certainly unforeseen by the Basel Mission. October 24, 2004, was a watershed day in the history of the Presbyterian Church of Ghana. On this day, over 500 members of congregations of the Presbyterian Church of Ghana traveled from Chicago, Maryland, Virginia, Houston, Dallas, Newark, Worcester, and New York to the Bronx. Here the churches gathered in the expansive building of the First Ghana Seventh Day Adventist Church for the purpose of officially organizing the Overseas Mission Field of the Presbyterian Church of Ghana.

The two highest officials of the Presbyterian Church of Ghana, Reverend Dr. Samuel Prempeh, the moderator of the General Assembly, and Reverend Dr. Charles Gyang-Duah, the clerk of the denomination, led the vibrant service. Also present from Ghana was Catechist Abboah-Offei. Ac-

---

28. See also Jehu J. Hanciles, *Beyond Christendom: Globalization, African Migration, and the Transformation of the West* (Maryknoll, N.Y.: Orbis Books, 2008).

10. Arjun Appadurai, *Modernity at Large: Cultural Dimensions of Globalization* (Minneapolis: University of Minnesota Press, 1996).

11. Simon Coleman, *The Globalisation of Charismatic Christianity: Spreading the Gospel of Prosperity* (Cambridge: Cambridge University Press, 2000), 51, 58.

12. Noel Smith, *The Presbyterian Church of Ghana, 1835-1960: A Younger Church in a Changing Society* (Accra: Ghana Universities Press, 1966).

Fig. 6.1 Banner in Harlem announcing Mission Convention of the Presbyterian Church of Ghana, 2007. Note the citation of the "Great Commission," Matthew 28:19.

cording to Prempeh, the purpose of organizing the Overseas Mission Field was to "acknowledge this number of congregations with us and . . . get better organized."[13] Remarked Prempeh to the congregations, "[We] want you to be assured [that we] remember you and pray for you." Visiting many of the churches in North America, he explained, the church officials "have come to say hello, see how you are getting along."

On the day prior to the service, a meeting of the Overseas Mission Field (OMF) was held at the church offices in Harlem, attended by church leadership from Ghana and the United States. Here they discussed plans and budgets. With a small office in the back of the New York church building on 123rd Street, Rev. Moses Biney, then a doctoral student at Princeton Theological Seminary, served as acting director from 2003-2006. Upon his retirement as clerk of the Presbyterian Church of Ghana, Reverend Dr. Charles Gyang-Duah was appointed head of the office, moving to New York to assume the role and raising its profile.

13. Samuel Prempeh, Interview, October 24, 2004.

Witnesses in the City

The history of the OMF is in measure shaped by a story of divergent choices. Initially the OMF was an umbrella group for "all Presbyterian churches in the United States with Ghanaian membership."[14] However, some of the churches determined instead to become part of the Presbyterian Church USA, dividing the Ghanaian Presbyterians into two groups. In 2004, ten churches operated together in the Presbyterian Church of Ghana fold. Finances were often given as a reason for more closely aligning with the American mainline denomination, but certainly other factors were involved. One report indicated that "After the split, the PCG Overseas Mission Field in USA was formed to serve as a de facto presbytery for the churches operating under the administrative and ecclesiastical leadership of the Presbyterian Church of Ghana."[15] If there were local wounds resulting from the split, at the denominational level the Presbyterian Church of Ghana and the Presbyterian Church USA continued in conversation.

The Church of the Lord (Aladura) emphasized an expansive view of its mission reach from its earliest days, its universal trajectory ultimately leading to the Bronx in 1994, as described in chapter two. "The Church has never regarded itself as merely one small denomination among others, or confined to one West African tribe or territory,"[16] according to Harold Turner. According to the texts of Church of the Lord (Aladura) founder Josiah Ositelu, among his early revelations in 1927 were included "a promise that 'the fame of the glory of my God's name shall spread up to Syria and America.'"[17] As a child, Ositelu reportedly had "prophesied the future, revealed unknown secrets of the past, read signs in the sky, been able to detect witches, and to have had unusual dreams of being taught by holy beings."[18] His parents, whom Turner describes as "illiterate pagan farmers," turned to an Ifa priest in Ogere for counsel, and were told "these were signs of a great future, when he would lead both Europeans and Africans."[19]

---

14. Presbyterian Church of Ghana, Overseas Mission Field in USA, 2004 Clerk's Report.

15. Presbyterian Church of Ghana, Overseas Mission Field in USA, 2004 Clerk's Report.

16. Harold W. Turner, *African Independent Church*, vol. 2: *The Life and Faith of the Church of the Lord (Aladura)* (Oxford: Oxford University Press, 1967), 93.

17. Harold W. Turner, *African Independent Church*, vol. 1: *History of an African Independent Church* (Oxford: Oxford University Press, 1967), 44, cf. 45.

18. Turner, *African Independent Church*, vol. 1, 35, cf. 35-39.

19. Turner, *African Independent Church*, vol. 1, 35.

As noted in chapter three, spreading the Church of the Lord (Aladura) in Africa began with sending missionaries to Sierra Leone in 1947,[20] Liberia in 1947,[21] and Ghana in 1953.[22] There was also expansion within Nigeria to the north and east.[23] By 1964, the church was first established in Europe with the opening of a branch in London.

Pressing this global sensibility, Oduwole, in a 1960 sermon quoted by Turner, commented: "It is time for Africa to get up, and this Church is going to show the world and the white men that Africa has the Holy Spirit."[24] For Turner, this assessment is borne out: "It is because the Church of the Lord has discovered its peculiar Africanness as a church, and so becomes a real church within its context, that it also feels compelled to a universal mission; for, as the world church has been discovering afresh in our time, mission is of the *esse* of the church."[25] Today the full name found in official publications and Web sites is the Church of the Lord (Aladura) *World-Wide* (italics mine), underscoring a renewed global vision for the twenty-first century. In line with the global view of God's work, Mother Cooper looks to God, who "will put all nations together."[26]

When Primate Rufus Ositelu came to the Bronx parish on October 8, 2006, he did so while on a mission called the "U.S.A. for Christ" crusade. Along with his message of encouragement in faith, he brought with him material from headquarters: cassette tapes of Tabborrar music, programs from major events, calendars with photographs of church life, and copies of his book. Also during his visit he met privately with the Bronx branch and members of a new branch getting off the ground in Brooklyn. There was an air of familiarity among all, and the transnational ties between the Bronx and Nigeria were reinforced.

Click on the Redeemed Christian Church of God Web site in 2007 and you are immediately introduced to a global vision. Beneath a photograph of the General Overseer, E. A. Adeboye, is a map of the world that stretches from the United States to Africa.[27] The "Parish Directory" link on the home

20. Turner, *African Independent Church*, vol. 1, 114.
21. Turner, *African Independent Church*, vol. 1, 137.
22. Turner, *African Independent Church*, vol. 1, 161.
23. Turner, *African Independent Church*, vol. 1, 72-88.
24. Turner, *African Independent Church*, vol. 2, 93.
25. Turner, *African Independent Church*, vol. 1, 322.
26. Marie Cooper, Interview, February 13, 2005.
27. See http://www.rccg.org (accessed August 26, 2006). By January 1, 2008, the Web site design was altered. Adeboye remains prominent on the home page, which features his

page has a globe with flags from around the world.[28] This links the viewer to the International Directory page. While the heading includes a globe of the world, more to the point is a flat map of the world that is the main design on the page. On this map, Africa is at the center. A red circle is found where Nigeria is located, and another concentric red circle concentrically reaches outward to the rest of the world.[29] There are two directories and headings that link to Africa/Nigeria, North America/South America, UK/Europe, and Asia/Australia. As noted previously, the total number of Redeemed parishes worldwide is unclear, but estimates place it at over five thousand.[30]

Symbolized by the globe on the home page, the church's planetary aspirations are also emphasized throughout the Web pages of the Redeemed Christian Church of God in North America. Their mission is described as follows:

> As received by the General Overseer (G.O.), Pastor E. A. Adeboye, and communicated to the Headquarters leaders, our vision and mission statement shall remain intact, with a qualifying addendum in view of the peculiarity of the demography in the North American region. They are as follows:
>
> - To make heaven.
> - To take as many people with us.
> - To have a member of RCCG in every family of all nations.
> - To accomplish No. 1 above, holiness will be our lifestyle.
> - To accomplish No. 2 and 3 above, we will plant churches within five minutes walking distance in every city and town of developing countries and within five minutes driving distance in every city and town of developed countries.
>
> We will pursue these objectives until every Nation in the world is reached for the Lord Jesus Christ.
>
> ADDENDUM: For planting new parishes in North America & Caribbean countries, the location to any existing parish must be at least 10 minutes driving distance.[31]

---

prophecies for the new year and links to Redeemed Christian Church of God in North America and the United Kingdom.
    28. http://home.rccg.org/home.html (accessed August 26, 2006).
    29. http://directory.rccg.org/home.html (accessed August 26, 2006).
    30. James Fadele, Interview, March 21, 2004.
    31. http://www.rccgna.org/mission.asp (accessed February 26, 2008).

It is noteworthy that it begins with what the G.O. has "received." In conversations at church events, I heard that the G.O. seeks a member of the church in every household in the world; here it is publicly stated. Another goal one hears for the United States is a Redeemed parish in every zip code.

The following "Purpose Statement" presented in 2007 captures another facet of the Redeemed Christian Church of God's mission dynamic: "To bring people from all nations to Jesus, continually growing and abiding together in the Lord by the teaching of the Word of God and the kingdom principles; Receiving the power of the Holy Spirit for effective witnessing to the world. . . . We are world changers!!!"[32] Just as in the previous statement, there is a global perspective in outlook and call to action, but in this context the power of the Holy Spirit and change are emphasized. The Redeemed seem to be seeking on the global scene a mix of "universalism and particularism."[33]

In supporting this mission the Redeemed Christian Church of God has established an ambitious operation in North America, with headquarters in Detroit and a large tract of land in Dallas, Texas, for a "Redemption Camp." James Fadele is Chairman of Redeemed Christian Church of God in North America, which oversees around 300 parishes. At the Annual Convention in 2004 held at the Secaucus Convention Center in New Jersey, he introduced a plan for each branch to work with the "purpose-driven church" model associated with the American evangelical Rick Warren. Other topics Fadele spoke of were financial records, visas for ministers, and new church development. Here he laid out a vision for establishing the church's identity in North America:

> Let's Position our Church as a Distinct Class
>
> For people who care about their Spiritual diet and won't compromise on ambiance, message and standard of worship, RCCG NA must transcend traditional 'churching' by offering a variety of events that meet the different demographic classes living in our society
>
> Let's make every program an experience they'll ever desire to relive![34]

32. James Fadele, "Visit to Zone 18" Presentation Packet, 2007.
33. Paul Freston, "Globalisation, Religion and Evangelical Christianity: A Sociological Meditation from the Third World," Position Paper 151, Currents in World Christianity Project, 2001, 23.
34. James Fadele, 8th Annual RCCG North American Convention, PowerPoint presentation.

Fadele's emphasis on reaching a broader American culture is clear; he makes no reference to reaching Nigerians or any African immigrants. This is important for Redeemed, who do not want to be limited to being a "Nigerian church."

Such expansion fits within a network culture. In Mark C. Taylor's *The Moment of Complexity: Emerging Network Culture,* he argues that a cultural shift is taking place whereby the world is moving from being organized on the basis of a "grid" to the basis of a "network."[35] With globalization, as Taylor shows, society is more complex, the rate of change more propulsive, and inter-relationships more pervasive: "Whereas walls divide and seclude in an effort to impose order and control, webs link and relate, entangling everyone in multiple, mutating, and mutually defining connections in which nobody is really in control. As connections proliferate, change accelerates, bringing everything to the edge of chaos."[36] While Taylor's networks and webs are not grounded in migration, he can help us see African churches in New York City as part of a global Christianity that is dynamic and in tune with a period of cultural change.

Phillip Berryman's essay "Churches as Winners and Losers in the Network Society," focused on Pentecostal religious development in Latin America, offers a useful point of reference.[37] In Berryman's reading of the Latin American church scene, the fastest growing churches are Pentecostal and operate on a decentralized model; the historical churches where growth is at best stagnant reflect a more traditional and bureaucratic structure.[38] Pentecostal pastors are free to focus on their parishioners, provide locally determined leadership, and do what is required to sustain their churches.[39] Yet they also remain accountable to local leadership and draw strength from their fellow pastors. A network model emphasizes "horizontal integration, flexibility, adaptability, rapid and context-specific responses."[40] In a centralized model of church life, decisions concerning resources, strategy, and leadership are determined from the top down.

---

35. Mark C. Taylor, *The Moment of Complexity: Emerging Network Culture* (Chicago: University of Chicago Press, 2001).

36. Taylor, *A Moment of Complexity,* 23; cf. 157-94.

37. Phillip Berryman, "Churches as Winners and Losers in the Network Society," *Journal of Interamerican Studies and World Affairs* 41:4 (1999): 21-34. My thanks to Manuel Vásquez for pointing me to this essay.

38. Berryman, "Churches as Winners and Losers in the Network Society," 25-26, 30.

39. Berryman, "Churches as Winners and Losers in the Network Society," 26-27.

40. Berryman, "Churches as Winners and Losers in the Network Society," 24.

Given the hierarchical leadership of the Redeemed Christian Church of God, beginning with the General Overseer, it would appear that the church is a classic example of a bureaucratic organization. However, in a mission context, it is not.[41] Thus far the church's growth has reflected a decentralized structure, exemplifying the model of a network organization outlined by Berryman. For example, the church has divided North America into 22 zones, each with its own coordinator, who is also a parish pastor.[42] Included among the zonal pastors in 2007 were two women — the first in North America to fill this role. In 2006, New York City, which had been established as Zone 1, was divided, splitting Brooklyn, Long Island, and New Hampshire into a new Zone 18, with Nimi Wariboko as coordinator.[43] Each zonal pastor keeps in close contact with all the pastors, but each branch pastor has the full responsibility for growth, leadership development, and resource gathering.[44] Individual innovation, direction, and creativity are required for success, while collaboration and mutual care among leaders also takes place at the local level.

While in his public presentations James Fadele, the chairman of Redeemed Christian Church of God in North America, is seeking to centralize core practices such as accounting procedures and visa applications — "putting our house in order," as he puts it — he is simply trying to impose some order on the church's decentralized growth. As the church grows, the pendulum may continue to swing from decentralization to more top-down, centralized organization.

On a smaller scale, Mother Cooper and the Church of the Lord (Aladura) also represent a decentralized model, with responsibility related to the local level. Within the framework of a network analysis, the Presbyterian Church of Ghana operates in a more formally structured way. Decisions and processes move slower, and must directly involve leadership in Ghana. This pattern fits the identity of the denomination, even with its increasing charismatic influences. Notably, the different headquarters in Africa all retain control over one important facet in each of the three churches: ordination of leadership.

---

41. For an apparent contrast see Opoku Onyinah, "Pentecostalism and the African Diaspora: An Examination of the Missions Activities of the Church of Pentecost," *Pneuma* 26:2 (Fall 2004): 216-41.

42. By 2007, there were twenty-two zones in North America, a number that is growing.

43. Zone 18 includes Brooklyn and beyond to New Hampshire.

44. Nimi Wariboko, E-mail Correspondence to Zone 18, November 6, 2006.

Three Mission Strategies

There is no single model of mission strategy of African churches in New York City. There are, of course, several features that all three churches have in common.[45] Still, each church has a unique emphasis.

Mission as Member Care

Member care as mission is key to each of three churches, but it is a point of emphasis for the Presbyterian Church of Ghana as it provides pastoral accompaniment for its scattered membership. Member care and institutional maintenance appear to be the backbone of their mission strategy, representing a primary mission focus on the Ghanaian Presbyterian community in the city.

As relayed to me during an interview by then-Moderator of the Presbyterian Church of Ghana Samuel Prempeh, pastoral care and social support for their church members is the denomination's principal mission concern in New York City.[46] Over time, he indicates, attention might be given to other groups, starting with the wider Ghanaian population. If this strategy is limited to one group of people and sounds exclusive, it may simply be a realistic appraisal of time and resources. The mission model here is similar to international chaplaincies, and Prempeh drew an analogy with the international churches of the Church of Scotland.[47] The regular visits from Catechist Abboah-Offei and Evangelist Samuel Asare, framed as missionary in nature, reinforce this dimension of member care.

Each church service involves the use of three languages: English, Twi, and Ga. Language is a marker of identity but in practice it is a means of pastoral care for the Presbyterian Church of Ghana. Language can be a major concern for many African immigrant churches, as W. David Stevens explains in his doctoral thesis on Ghanaian churches in the Chicago area.[48]

---

45. For an important discussion, see Allan Anderson, "Towards a Pentecostal Missiology for the Majority World," *Asian Journal of Pentecostal Theology* 8:1 (2005): 29-47.

46. Samuel Prempeh, Interview, October 24, 2004.

47. Samuel Prempeh, Interview, October 24, 2004.

48. W. David Stevens, "'Taking the World': Evangelism and Assimilation Among Ghanaian Pentecostals in Chicago" (Ph.D. Dissertation, Northwestern University, 2003), and "Spreading the Word: Religious Beliefs and the Evolution of Immigrant Congregations," *Sociology of Religion* 65:2 (2004): 121-38.

Fig. 6.2 Representatives of the Presbyterian Church of Ghana participate in the inauguration of the Overseas Mission Field, 2004. Standing in the background, from left to right, are Catechist Abboah-Offei and the stated clerk, Dr. Charles Gyang-Duah

Should the service be in an African language, enabling people to feel at home, or in English as a common language that will allow for broader participation? Splitting the difference, many African immigrant churches have chosen to add a service in English.[49] But is the use of a culturally dominant language different from one's primary linguistic allegiance a rejection of one's own culture?[50] Indeed, do words by themselves represent a culture?[51]

The importance of the vernacular for Christian faith has been previously noted, and language will be a theme I pick back up in chapter eight on the second generation. Here I am asking questions related to mission.

49. Stevens, "Spreading the Word," 132.
50. Laila Lalami, "Native Speaker," *Boston Review*, September/October 2006, online at http://bostonreview.net/BR31.5/lalami.php.
51. On some of the broader theoretical linguistic issues, see Fred E. Jandt, *An Introduction to Intercultural Communication: Identities in a Global Community*, 4th ed. (Thousand Oaks: Sage, 2004): 149-51.

In practice, language is among the factors in limiting who associates with the church. Taking the point of view of linguistic theory applied to the new African charismatic churches, Moradewun Adejunmobi in *Vernacular Palaver* argues for a reconsideration of the relationship between language and identity in the postcolonial world.[52] The "territorially-fixed community, with claims to common origins, a common history and cultural specificity is only one of many possible types of community,"[53] and represents but one type of belonging. This type of community, however, can be a barrier to other language groups.

However, with a change in denominational leadership the overarching mission outlook may be evolving. "You are the ones to carry the message of salvation to people around you. That's why you're here," sermonized the Right Reverend Dr. Yaw Frimpong-Manso in 2005, visiting the Harlem church as the new moderator of the Presbyterian Church of Ghana. Having come to New York City, he declared it a "missionary visit," ministering to his scattered flock.[54] There is the diaspora, the flock that are far-flung members of their denomination, but there is also a larger mission.

During the summer of 2007, the Presbyterian Church of Ghana in New York held a missions conference that underscored its belief in the universality of the gospel. Stretched out across the front of the Presbyterian Church of Ghana building on 123rd Street was a banner announcing the annual convention of the Presbyterian Church of Ghana Overseas Mission Field (USA District) in July 2007. In large type across the bottom of the banner were words from the Gospel of Matthew: "Go therefore and make disciples of all nations." Under the aegis of the Spirit, the church is calling its members to proclaim good news outside of Ghana to the world, to the streets of New York City and beyond. The propulsive command of Matthew is publicly urging members to fill the space of the world with disciples of Jesus. However, the emphasis of the church remains solidly on providing pastoral care for the Presbyterian Church of Ghana members who are living, working, and raising their families in New York City.

---

52. Moradewun Adejunmobi, *Vernacular Palaver: Imaginations of the Local and Non-Native Languages in West Africa* (Clevedon: Multilingual Matters Ltd., 2004), vii.

53. Adejunmobi, *Vernacular Palaver,* 164.

54. Presbyterian Church of Ghana, Field Notes, September 18, 2005.

ENGAGEMENTS

Mission as Intercession

"Don't be selfish . . . let your prayers extend far and wide to the world," members of the Church of the Lord (Aladura) are exhorted. "The responsibility is ours, the praying people." [55] The model of mission of the Church of the Lord (Aladura) in New York is one of prophetic and prayerful intercession for the world.

I asked Mother Cooper what she calls herself. Her answer is descriptive: "I do a lot of counseling and a lot of praying, asking the Lord to help us solve whatever problem. I don't know what you'd call [that]."[56] On another occasion, Mother Cooper elaborates, "Ministers stand in the gap" for those who need prayer, such as people in hospitals and prisons, those who need a lawyer, and world leaders.[57] She understands her ministry as faithfully following a call to proclaim the Christian message. "Even if it's to one person, even if it's a child, the gospel must be preached," Mother Cooper holds.[58] Mission for the Church of the Lord (Aladura) resembles a struggle on behalf of people in need.[59]

A good example of the prominence given to intercession is provided by what occurred at the end of the "tarry" I described in chapter four. As the tarry is ending, Mother Cooper has a prophecy that somewhere in the world there will be "a terrible plane crash."[60] In response, the church is called to pray: "Let us ask God to reverse this terrible plane crash . . . whether in Europe, America or Africa." She continues, we are "asking you for mercy. Reverse. You can stop it. Mercy, mercy, mercy. Pray." She leads the church in intercession for the pilot and passengers. "You can stop it," she prays to God — though the meaning of "you" may also be stretched to include the church at prayer. Mission is elevated to the global, and involves the prophetic and revelatory dimension of the church. During the same service, Mother Cooper prays, "Someone is in the operating room right now. Help them. Pray for the sick, the shut-ins. Pray for the prisoners."[61] Similar prayer concerns could be heard in nearly any service. The pattern

---

55. Church of the Lord (Aladura), Field Notes, February 6, 2005.
56. Marie Cooper, Interview, January 12, 2006.
57. Marie Cooper, Interview, February 6, 2005.
58. Marie Cooper, Interview, October 17, 2004.
59. Samuel Irving Britt, "The Children of Salvation: Struggle and Cosmology in Liberian Prophet Churches" (Ph.D. diss., University of Virginia, 1992), 291.
60. Church of the Lord (Aladura), Field Notes, November 2, 2007.
61. Church of the Lord (Aladura), Field Notes, November 2, 2007.

Witnesses in the City

of praying for people in need of the gospel also reflects a prominent concern for the poor, the sick, the incarcerated, and the marginalized.

The missional attraction to outsiders is spiritual power and its intercessory effect upon their lives. After living in New York for a number of years, David Grigsby found himself in need of effective prayers, too personal to openly share with me. It is a story he related to me on more than one occasion, and I wrote of it in chapter four. What he emphasizes in its telling is that as he called on Mother Cooper to pray with and for him, his needs were fulfilled.[62]

As I interpret the mission of the Church of the Lord (Aladura) in the Bronx, prayer is both their identity and mission. As Stephen Bevans and Roger Schroeder emphasize in *Constants in Context,* prayer and liturgy are rightly considered forms of action.[63] At the Church of the Lord (Aladura), intercession touches the broken world of the sick, the imprisoned, and the lost. God is acting, the church believes, outside the boundaries of their fellowship for the salvation of the world.

Mission as Church Planting

Pastor Nimi has a plan to bring Christ to New York City, and it is found on a street map of Brooklyn that hangs in his church office.[64] A red marker divides the map into seven sections, each area designating where a new Redeemed parish has been started or is planned. With his Parkside branch as nucleus, members and leaders would be sent out to launch or "plant" new churches in each of the designated sections, covering all of Brooklyn. Within a few years, the plan was completed, and there was a Redeemed church within a few subway stops, short bus ride, or walking distance of Brooklyn's 2.5 million residents. By way of the map and a strategy, local spaces of the city become sites of mission outreach and global advance.

Mission for the Redeemed Christian Church of God International Chapel, Brooklyn, is very much focused on the development of new churches or branches, expanding the work of God one new church at a time.[65] For now at least in New York City, the idea is not to build one

---

62. David Grigsby, Interview, March 13, 2005.
63. Bevans and Schroeder, *Constants in Context,* 368.
64. Kim Knibbe, "'We Did Not Come Here as Tenants, But as Landlords': Nigerian Pentecostals and the Power of Maps," *African Diaspora* 2:2 (2009): 133-58.
65. For more on Pentecostal motivation in church planting, see Julia C. Ma, "Pentecostalism and Asian Mission," *Missiology* 35:1 (2007): 32.

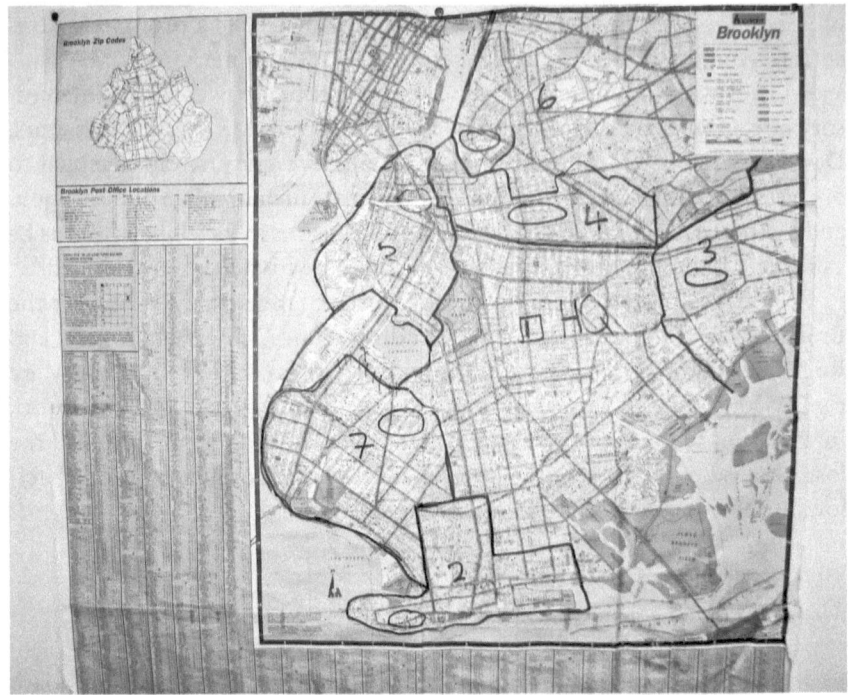

Fig. 6.3 Church-planting map of Brooklyn, Redeemed Christian Church of God International Chapel, 2004. "HQ" is the International Chapel.

megachurch, but to create as many branches as possible. Because they are seeking to cover the whole borough and not just ethnic communities, it also represents the practice of mission at the local level. Evangelism is an underlying passion and driving force as the church seeks to build the kingdom not only one church at a time, but also one new convert at a time. Church members hand out tracts on street corners, preach on buses, and go into the community to engage in personal evangelism. While the residency of membership can be distributed around the city, most live in Brooklyn, reinforcing the parish concept as a mission in itself.

This vision for Brooklyn is fulfilled through church planters like Adebisi Oyesile, who, with a Ph.D. in management, by day works on Wall Street for a global insurance firm but devotes the rest of his time to build and pastor his church, Chapel of Hope. On the day before the official end of summer 2006, when most New Yorkers were squeezing in one last day at the beach, Adebisi Oyesile was planning a new church. A worker in Re-

Witnesses in the City

Fig. 6.4 Pastor Adebisi Oyesile with the choir at the Chapel of Hope, 2007

deemed Christian Church of God International Chapel, Brooklyn, Adebisi was challenged by Pastor Wariboko to plant a new congregation. At first he resisted, but a dream confirmed his call. "God told me to move," Adebisi recalled, by which he means make a "move" to start a new branch of Redeemed. To prepare, he traveled via Paris to the Redeemed "camp" (headquarters), where he spent a week in prayer.[66]

Returning to New York, he started the Redeemed Christian Church of God International Chapel of Hope in a storefront located on Lafayette Avenue in the Bedford-Stuyvesant section of Brooklyn. Fully responsible for its growth, pastoral care, financing, and operations, Pastor Adebisi received from the Brooklyn "mother church" a gift of $10,000 to pay the first months of rent, purchase sound equipment and music instruments, and support a few members, including his wife, Abosede Oyesile, daughters Kemi, Tola, Tosin, son Ade, and sister-in-law Bisola Onayemi. His wife and family play key roles in providing spiritual and other leadership, to-

66. Adebisi Oyesile, Interview, September 3, 2006.

Fig. 6.5 Anniversary service announcement, Chapel of Hope

gether making incredible sacrifices of time and financial resources to build the church.

A year later, on October 7, 2007, Pastor Adebisi and the Chapel of Hope celebrated their first anniversary. To accommodate members and guests, they rented a school auditorium across the street from the church. As they outgrow their storefront, they planned to begin another church in Brooklyn, leaving the Chapel of Hope in place.

Pastor Adebisi doesn't just talk or pray about his mission; he lives it continually. The model is self-funded by the church in New York and based on the production of leaders in the local parish. Funding comes through the pastor and his family, who frequently pay the church's rent with their tithes and offerings, tithing among church members, and special offerings; no grants are garnered from fundraising, no "denominational" finances are made available.[67] Instead, as part of the Redeemed network, for the first two years the church is mandated to pay 10 percent of its tithes and offerings to the Redeemed Christian Church of God, North America, with an increase to 20 percent after year two. Other offerings, such as the "First Fruit In-

---

67. This stands in contrast to the ongoing Western missionary involvement in Africa as shown by Paul Gifford, "The Nature and Effects of Mission Today: A Case Study from Kenya," *Social Sciences and Mission* 20 (2007): 117-47.

> My Friend, what will you do with JESUS CHRIST.
> **Will You ACCEPT Him, or REJECT Him?**
> To accept Him means everlasting life. If you reject Him, you will perish, and serve eternal punishment. Jesus said, "Verily, Verily I say unto you, he that believeth on Me hath everlasting life" John 6:47 The wages of sin is death; but the gift of God is eternal life through Jesus Christ our Lord. Rom 6:23 If thou shalt confess with thy mouth Jesus as Lord and shalt BELIEVE IN THINE HEART that God hath raised Him from the dead, thou shalt be saved. For with the heart man believeth unto righteousness and with the mouth confession is made unto salvation
>
> THE REMEEMED CHRISTIAN CHURCH OF GOD
> 672 Parkside Avenue, Brooklyn, NY 11226

Fig. 6.6 Evangelism Card, Redeemed Christian Church of God International Chapel, Brooklyn

crease," which is a percentage of salary given at the beginning of the year, are paid to the parish and then also go to the North American office.

Church planting skills are developed on the job and in the context of workers' meetings and regional pastors' meetings. Knowledge comes through reflection on praxis. Mix this funding model and leadership strategy together with a robust faith, a handful of willing church members, an entrepreneurial drive, an intuitive sense of how the systems of the city work, and it is easy to see how African mission comes together in New York City. There is no how-to textbook or seminary with experts that prepares — just the local church. Peggy Levitt has shown how, in similar transnational church planting movements, such an approach is far more successful — and, I would add, far more in tune with the logic of the city — than more heavily programmed and financed Western counterparts.[68]

Pastor Adebisi's work in Brooklyn is an example of the network and decentralized approach discussed earlier in this chapter. He files reports, attends ministers' meetings locally and nationally, fulfills tithing requirements, and has his first point of contact in the Zonal Coordinator, Nimi Wariboko. Other contact with Redeemed leadership is through e-mail, con-

---

68. Peggy Levitt, *God Needs No Passport: Immigrants and the Changing American Religious Landscape* (New York: The New Press, 2007), 132-33.

ference calls, and meetings. But ultimately Pastor Adebisi has the sole responsibility to meet the needs of the congregation and determine strategy.

The worship service itself is a missionary enterprise.[69] Project 500, Project 600, and Project 700 were a series of special Sunday services at the Redeemed Christian Church of God International Chapel in 2005 that sought to bring 500, 600, and 700 people to worship. Greater attendance in turn would grow the church and fuel expansion. But at the same time, people who attended the special services would benefit from an encounter with the Spirit's power that would be present. The power of life is attractive, and the festive celebration of Jesus inviting. Although salvation is always presented as personal, one of the most striking aspects is the way salvation is understood as fully realized in the church. Therefore, becoming a Christian means joining and participating in a body where God is present, Christ is alive, and the Spirit is active.

Pastor Wariboko insists that English is the exclusive language of the church. The use of English as a more global language is a way of transcending locality. Like the array of African and Caribbean flags in the front, the use of language is intended to make a mission statement. There is a striving after what John Burdick refers to in a Brazilian setting as "pneumatic egalitarianism."[70] That is, the Spirit makes all persons equal, breaking down barriers of ethnicity, race, and gender. This does not mean that ethnic groups have broken down all barriers at Redeemed Christian Church of God International Chapel, or that culture is denied. The annual "Celebrate Jesus" event, naming ceremonies, and weddings are indicators that Nigerian culture remains a part of the church's identity. Internally at the church, the possibility of marriage across ethnic lines remains an area of concern. But there is a real commitment to be a church that transcends ethnic, cultural, and linguistic differences for the sake of the gospel.

---

69. Bevans and Schroeder, *Constants in Context*, 362-65; Dana L. Robert and M. L. Daneel, "Worship among Apostles and Zionists in Southern Africa," in Charles E. Farhadian, ed., *Christian Worship Worldwide: Expanding Horizons, Deepening Practices* (Grand Rapids: Eerdmans, 2007), 70.

70. John Burdick, *Blessed Anastácia: Women, Race, and Popular Christianity in Brazil* (New York: Routledge, 1998), 119-48. See also Mathijs Pelkmans, "'Culture' as a Tool and an Obstacle: Missionary Encounters in Post-Soviet Kyrgyzstan," *Journal of the Royal Anthropological Institute* 13:4 (2007): 881-99.

Mission and the Charismatic Powers of Life

In line with a holistic understanding of salvation, a ministry of healing is an active commitment of the Presbyterian Church of Ghana in Harlem, the Church of the Lord (Aladura), and the Redeemed Christian Church of God International Chapel, Brooklyn. Typically this means that in the name of Jesus they bring the Christian gospel to bear on spiritual forces that inhibit life to all persons in need. Mission is evangelism, and evangelism is healing in the authority of Jesus and in the power of the Spirit. Healing is a powerful encounter with forces, ills, authorities, and structures that hold people back from life abundant. As J. Kwabena Asamoah-Gyadu emphasizes, this "supernatural" and "interventionist" approach to evangelism and mission is both common and grounded in the New Testament.[71] The experience of God that African Christians have encountered — the divine power of deliverance, heightened sensitivity to the presence of God through prayer and fasting, and an open imagination to the work of the Spirit — helps give shape to a mission to bodies in need of wholeness in the city.

How is it possible that African Christians and Americans, Christian or otherwise, have such different views on miracles, healing, prayer, and the spirituality of the universe? For children of the Enlightenment, including Western evangelicalism, "God" only rarely touches down in this world. Miracles, visions from the Lord, healings, and other miraculous encounters are rare occurrences. But for non-Enlightenment Christians, what is real is more layered. As we have seen in chapters one and four, African maps of a spiritually active universe continue into the diaspora. God is not one step removed from the world, but dynamically involved at all levels of life. African Christians see God's full involvement as essential to human flourishing. They know that they are not in charge, and they find security in God, who is with them and in control.

This is a crucial question in the crossover work of mission, for the African churches not only believe in the power of Christ to bring about healing and deliverance, but also situate their mission movement within this expectation. In pastoral ministry as in mission, healing touches people at their point of daily life and need. Just as healing and a spirituality of the charismatic powers of life represent the face of popular religion in Latin

---

71. J. Kwabena Asamoah-Gyadu, "Pulling Down Strongholds: Evangelism, Principalities and Powers and the African Pentecostal Imagination," *International Review of Mission* 96:382/383 (2007): 306-17.

America[72] and Asia — and a key source of its growth — the same is true of the African story.

In New York City, churches that provide healing help African immigrants on the journey in ways that are constructive and not compensatory. Salvation is inseparable from social, economic, physical, and spiritual flourishing. This is a message of hope in uncertain economic and political times.[73] But a religion of healing is for all, regardless of economic means. In my observation, healing involves emancipation and protection from the "powers" that oppress, cause illness, block success, and inhibit life, bringing forth flourishing.[74] In the context of New York City, this message can make the gospel real, leading to the expansion of Christianity.

Throughout Christian history and across its traditions, healing has a special relationship to Christian expansion.[75] A western reader would likely be surprised to read Adolf Harnack's treatment of healing in *The Mission and Expansion of Christianity in the First Three Centuries*. Here Harnack devotes significant attention to the roles of conflict with demons, healing, and the place of the miraculous in the advance of the early church.[76] He recounts, for example, that "with regard to his own church, Irenaeus . . . was convinced that the very dead were brought back to life by its members."[77] Some members have healing gifts, "others possess a foreknowledge of the future, with visions and prophetic utterances."[78] Early Christians also believed in "innumerable hosts of demons"[79] and the "possibility of possession."[80] In the first century of early Christianity, the

---

72. Relevant comparative examples include R. Andrew Chestnut, *Competitive Spirits: Latin America's New Religious Economy* (Oxford: Oxford University Press, 2003), and Candy Gunther Brown, ed., *Global Pentecostal and Charismatic Healing* (Oxford: Oxford University Press, 2011).

73. See Ruth Marshall, *Political Spiritualities: The Pentecostal Revolution in Nigeria* (Chicago: University of Chicago Press, 2009).

74. J. Kwabena Asamoah-Gyadu identifies these themes in "Mission to 'Set the Captives Free': Healing, Deliverance, and Generational Curses in Ghanaian Pentecostalism," *International Review of Mission* 93:370/371 (July/October 2004): 389-406.

75. Amanda Porterfield, *Healing in the History of Christianity* (Oxford: Oxford University Press, 2005).

76. Adolf Harnack, *The Mission and Expansion of Christianity in the First Three Centuries*, trans. James Moffatt (Gloucester: Peter Smith, 1972 [1908]), 125-46.

77. Harnack, *Mission and Expansion of Christianity*, 135.

78. Harnack, *Mission and Expansion of Christianity*, 135-36.

79. Harnack, *Mission and Expansion of Christianity*, 136.

80. Harnack, *Mission and Expansion of Christianity*, 142.

relationship between healing, deliverance, and the very real physical and social afflictions of people, as well as the social context of magic and healing, are integral to the story.[81] Given this background, the widespread belief in African religion and African Christianity that the etiology of illness is a result of outside supernatural forces[82] is hardly strange within Christian tradition.

Healing is at the forefront of the mission of the Redeemed Christian Church of God International Chapel, Brooklyn. With "the class of Joshua," a row of seven workers about to be consecrated before him, Nimi Wariboko turns to Matthew 10:1: "And when he had called unto him his twelve disciples, he gave them power against unclean spirits, to cast them out, and to heal all manner of sickness and all manner of disease."[83] Healing is part of salvation, and salvation is the message of the gospel for Pastor Wariboko. "The word salvation means healing. . . . 'Christ came to save' means Christ came to heal." This healing of Jesus is multidimensional: Jesus came to "heal physical sickness, emotional sickness, and spiritual disease." In the prior chapter of Matthew, Jesus has performed a number of healings, including that of a demonically possessed man who was also mute. As interpreted by Wariboko, "The man is sick, his tissues separated from normal body function." The separation is "demon influenced," "splits a person in two," the "inner mind is not united," and there is a "condition of estrangement." But "when the Holy Spirit comes upon you, [there is] a reconnection."

The workers' foremost responsibility, Wariboko tells them, is to realize that "the power of God comes to you to connect for a purpose." In other words, consecration to being a worker brings an anointing of power, a "destiny" to bring reconnection and healing. But in order to do that, they must recognize their mission context: "Americans will say [we] don't need healing. But you know there is estrangement in America." This means they will hear, "All you Africans want to do is talk about healing." But as he sees it, the challenge remains, particularly in one area: "Many people in America need [their] past healed . . . things they have done in the past — always

---

81. Justin Meggitt, "Magic, Healing and Early Christianity: Consumption and Competition," in *The Meanings of Magic: From the Bible to Buffalo Bill*, ed. Amy Wygant (New York: Berghahn Books, 2006), 89-114.

82. Matthews Ojo, "Healing in Sub-Saharan Africa," in *The Encyclopedia of African and African-American Religions*, ed. Stephen D. Glazier (New York: Routledge, 2001), 139.

83. Redeemed Christian Church of God International Chapel, Brooklyn, Field Notes, March 20, 2005.

curses and blessings." In other words, "How do you forget about [the] past and move out to blessing?" Their message must be one of repentance and forgiveness, announcing that the "curse [and] sins of the past . . . have been forgiven." Wariboko urges the workers to recognize that they are being charged with a "power to heal the sick" and a call to "remove separation." Separations can also be "racial," the other side of Galatians 3:28. Healing is "physical, spiritual." But it is not connected to their agency alone; "God will do it."

In a similar way, Mr. Asare of the healing team from Ghana insisted that Westerners do not fully recognize the powers that afflict our culture. On more than one occasion, I tried to get a sense of whether any particular territorial spirits or curses travelled with Ghanaian Christians to New York. Were health-related complaints in New York linked to traveling spiritual forces and powers? Was there durability to African "spiritual exposures" in New York? I found it difficult, if not impossible, in the context of such a line of inquiry, to come across as anything but suspicious of the African worldview. During one such attempt, Mr. Asare turned the tables on my question: Westerners don't believe in the powers, so the powers take on new forms in order to blind them to their influence. Disbelief and self-sufficiency can be their own forms of enthrallment.[84]

Healing is very much part of the life of the Church of the Lord (Aladura). A participant at the Tabborrar festival in 2007, an event I describe in the next chapter, asked me after the service what most "attracted me to the church." My reply was their understanding of God and practice of prayer. He didn't seem sure of my answer, but he went on to say, "We are a people who take prayer to be our business, healing the sick, raising the dead, and performing miracles."[85] The mission of healing is closely related to Mother Cooper's early commitment to open a faith home. The living quarters and sanctuary of the church building in the Bronx are not simply a house or sacred sanctuary, but a faith home and place of prayer. As Mother Cooper explains, the faith home is for "people in need, [the] sick." "Enter with faith and things go well," she observed.[86] The transformation of this house into a place where healing through intercession can take place is a significant mission initiative of the Church of the Lord (Ala-

---

84. Samuel Asare, Interview, December 13, 2006. His point brings to mind the late French philosopher and social prophet Jacques Ellul.

85. David Agbaye, Interview, August 13, 2007.

86. Mother Cooper, Interview, June 23, 2005.

dura). Mother Cooper's vision for ministry in New York was not simply to begin the first branch of the church in North America, but to open a faith home, a place of healing.

As Gerrie ter Haar explains, "Christian miracles in Africa combine effectively the 'sign' and the 'proof' character of Biblical miracles. They are seen both as proof of the power of God and as a sign of his kingdom to come."[87] She observes that this framework also carries over to the diaspora context.[88] Behind such an expectation of God's presence and involvement in the world is a conceptualization of the "miraculous" that paradoxically may reframe miracles from extraordinary to ordinary. Jürgen Moltmann powerfully portrays a view where the charismatic powers of life are at work in the world:

> Jesus does not bring the kingdom of God only in words that awaken faith; he also brings it in the form of healings which restore health. God's Spirit is a living energy that interpenetrates the bodies of men and women and drives out the germs of death. Jesus' miraculous healings are what Christoph Blumhardt called "miracles of the kingdom." In the dawn of the new creation of all things, they are not really "miracles" at all. They are completely natural and just what we have to expect. It is only if this eschatological hope is lost that these "wonders" appear to be miracles in an unchanged world. But in the framework of hope for the kingdom of God, Jesus' healings are reminders of hope. They justify expectations brought to the Spirit of Jesus now, in the present.[89]

There is a sense that charismatic powers of life, the miracles of the kingdom, are part of everyday life. It is what is expected, for the kingdom of God is not just in the future, but in the here and now.

A traditional understanding of Christian mission involves crossing boundaries and translating the gospel into a new culture.[90] However, the concept of a single "host culture" does not apply to New York City, which is populated with many cultures. Certainly the communication of the gospel

---

87. Gerrie ter Haar, "A Wondrous God: Miracles in Contemporary Africa," *African Affairs* 102 (2003): 427.

88. ter Haar, "A Wondrous God," 427.

89. Jürgen Moltmann, *The Spirit of Life: A Universal Affirmation*, trans. Margaret Kohl (Minneapolis: Fortress, 1992), 190.

90. For a discussion on the many meanings of mission, see Bevans and Schroeder, *Constants in Context*.

must of necessity be "multi-lingual" in the deep sense.[91] But the message of healing, wholeness, flourishing, and deliverance proclaimed by the three churches in this study represents a holistic or integrative worldview that meets significant needs. Such practices as healing may provide a countercultural witness amid a diversity of religious, social, intellectual, and economic needs.[92]

Mission as a Way of Life

Early on in my research I started asking questions about the role played by Christian faith among church members at work. My interest was in the relationship between vocation and Christian commitment, and the way in which the two relate to one another. But no matter how I framed the subject or tried to clarify the question, the answers I received turned to descriptions of the opportunities that work afforded people to witness to Jesus and the gospel. This points to a significant and neglected perspective on the African missionary movement. Rather than measuring cross-cultural and inter-ethnic mission success through church attendance by non-Africans,[93] we should recognize that mission primarily takes place where people are. And in New York, that is at work, on the streets, and in their communities — the daily situations and encounters of human relationship that define urban life. This is what Helen Liggett calls the "lived space" of the city.[94] In this sense, I think the relationship between a movement's mission discourse, local church strategies, and individual praxis can sometimes be in tension.[95] Mission is not neat and clean in a pluralistic and heterogeneous city; it must be contextually flexible.

An example is Segun Oyesanya, a vice president at an international

---

91. John Howard Yoder, "On Not Being Ashamed of the Gospel: Particularity, Pluralism, and Validation," *Faith and Philosophy* 9:3 (1992): 285-300.

92. I am adapting terminology proposed by Octávio Velho, "Missionization in the Post-Colonial World: A View from Brazil and Elsewhere," *Anthropological Theory* 7:3 (2007): 282.

93. Stevens, "Spreading the Word."

94. Helen Liggett, *Urban Encounters* (Minneapolis: University of Minnesota Press, 2003).

95. The results may be different in Europe. See Danielle Koning, "Place, Space, and Authority: The Mission and Reversed Mission of the Ghanaian Seventh-Day Adventist Church in Amsterdam," *African Diaspora* 2:2 (2009): 203-26.

bank in New York City.[96] Tall and always dressed in a suit and tie, Segun Oyesanya exudes confidence and poise. He became a "born again" Christian at university, through Ogun State University Fellowship, a Pentecostal student group in Nigeria. After a brief stay in Los Angeles with family, Segun and his wife, Bola, moved to New York in 1999. Having been a member of the Redeemed Christian Church of God in Nigeria, he made inquiries online and was directed to the nascent Brooklyn parish. Soon Segun and Bola became highly dedicated workers in the church. Segun has a strong sense of God's calling on his life, and consequently he teaches and practices evangelism at church. Yet he sees the workplace as his primary mission context. Referring to the role his faith has at his place of employment, Segun explains, "I do let it show. I say it. I share it with persons. I try to minister to people at work." Even still, Segun's evangelism is less spoken than lived: "how I do my work and how I deal with pressure," and how he performs his responsibilities with absolute "integrity" is his witness. "At work I'm a Christian first," he states. Making a connection between faith, work, and evangelism represents a pattern of living faith in the public realm.

Other stories also point to work as a mission context. Prince Asante, a member of the Presbyterian Church of Ghana in Harlem, is a taxi driver in New York City. As Prince drives his shift, "I put on Christian music [for my passengers], and it's calming. Sometimes they even thank me for it."[97] When Joy Cooper managed a daycare center for children, she would open staff meetings with prayer. It was not a Christian or religious daycare center, but she felt it was important.[98] Sarah Richards remarked how important it was that she would stop to share the goodness of Jesus to a coworker. Kwasi Agyare, who "came here to look for the future, to take care of family,"[99] works in a restaurant. When taking his break, Kwasi uses the time to read his Bible. People often approach him with their problems, and he is able to offer "some prayers and encouragement."[100]

Matilda Oyeyemi of the Redeemed Christian Church of God provides another variation on this theme of mission within the structure and routines of the city. Deeply involved in her church, Matilda has created her own ministry that combines prayer, healing, and church planting. A regis-

96. Segun Oyesanya, Interview, June 11, 2006.
97. Prince Asante, Interview, August 6, 2006.
98. Mother Cooper, Interview, January 16, 2005.
99. Kwasi Agyare, Interview, July 30, 2004.
100. Kwasi Agyare, Interview, July 30, 2004.

tered midwife in New York, she works part-time at her own pace so she can dedicate time to her ministry.

> I thank God for my ministry. Many are called, few are chosen. God has really established me in the ministry of praying. I do intercession, I do counseling. I visit people in the hospital and have a ministry of healing. I counsel pregnant women near delivery and I continue to pray for families. I am a missionary person because God has used me in many years of church planting. God has connected me to so many churches, in partnerships. I have a giving ministry to them. In the Bible this is talked about. I give for the kingdom of God. Being led by the Spirit of the Lord, I [look] to be in charge of a parish. God has given me the name of the parish: the Rose of Sharon Sanctuary. I have made this intention known to Zonal Coordination. God gives the addition and God will surely provide.[101]

A member of the Redeemed Christian Church of God International Chapel, Brooklyn, in 2006 Sister Matilda joined with one of the parish's new church initiatives, the Chapel of Love, in downtown Brooklyn.

"Migration mission," a term used by John Howard Yoder, may be the best label for the paradigm of mission that we are seeing. Yoder, a Mennonite theologian who emphasized the narrative life of Jesus as a basis for Christian discipleship, was in the 1960s a mission executive who saw "fundamental change" coming to "world missions" entering into a postcolonial period. In his book *As You Go: The Old Mission in a New Day*,[102] Yoder proposed that instead of a perpetuation of traditional missionary patterns, a day was coming when Christians would migrate to strategic parts of the world, live as residents, become employed in their vocations, and have a long-term impact on their adopted culture. He called this "migration evangelism."[103]

In a series of descriptions that sound remarkably descriptive of African Christians in New York City, Yoder locates a precedent for this pattern in the early church.

---

101. Matilda Oyeyemi, Interview, February 12, 2008, and interviews in January and June 2004.

102. John Howard Yoder, *As You Go: The Old Mission in a New Day* (Scottsdale: Herald Press, 1961). I am grateful to Joon-Sik Park's essay "'As You Go': John Howard Yoder as Mission Theologian," *Mennonite Quarterly Review* 78:3 (2004): 378-79, for first drawing my attention to this publication.

103. Yoder, *As You Go*, 17.

> Where they went, they took their faith with them, and new Christian cells were planted. . . . This church growth was not a matter of organized "mission." Christians, often serving as artisans or merchants, following the ordinary lines of travel and commerce, established themselves farther and farther from their original homes, taking their faith with them and making an economic contribution to the society into which they moved.[104]

> Today such "missionaries" from Nigeria, Ghana, Liberia require no financial support, no language training, do not send out missionary letters, and will not go home on furlough.[105] They take their own initiative and develop their own leadership.[106]

Yoder was pointing to a shift away from the West as missionary "sending" to a more pluralistic and different type of mission movement altogether. In a global world and church marked by motion, terminology such as "reverse flow" reflects an older paradigm of mission, one that inordinately emphasizes the West. Migration mission presses church members in a dynamic world to come to terms with their "missionary obligations." Although Yoder's emphasis was on Western churches, he recognized a non-Western story beginning to take place.[107] For Yoder, the cross-cultural witness rested on a distinctive social and ethical way of life.[108] More recently, Jehu Hanciles has pointed out that, "With millions of non-Western Christian migrants fulfilling a 'missionary' function within their own continents and in Western societies, the inattentiveness within Christian historiography to the role and significance of migrants as key actors in the Christian missionary movement translates into a major analytical flaw — a deficiency evident in ongoing efforts to calculate the comparative numerical strength of the Western and non-Western missionary movements."[109]

---

104. Yoder, *As You Go*, 12, 13. The seeds of migration mission are often traced to the narrative impulse of Acts. For this and other relevant themes in Luke-Acts see Dana L. Robert, "Encounter with Christ: Luke as Mission Historian for the Twenty-first Century," in *Evangelical, Ecumenical and Anabaptist Missiologies in Conversation: Essays in Honor of Wilbert R. Shenk*, ed. James R. Krabill, Walter Sawatsky, and Charles E. Van Engen (Maryknoll, N.Y.: Orbis, 2006), 19-27.

105. Yoder, *As You Go*, 15.

106. Yoder, *As You Go*.

107. Yoder, *As You Go* 10-25.

108. Yoder, *As You Go*, 27, cf. 24-25.

109. Jehu J. Hanciles, "God's Mission through Migration: African Initiatives in Globalizing Mission," in *Evangelical, Ecumenical, and Anabaptist Missiologies in Conversation*, 65.

If mission is a way of life and not a specialized calling, it is not surprising that African Christians in New York City rarely describe themselves as "missionaries." Instead, there is an underlying assumption that every Christian is to share, proclaim, and witness to Jesus Christ. They are Christians and New Yorkers, living accordingly. As they proclaim the gospel in New York City, they are certain of their convictions but do not share in the rhetoric of spiritual crisis and peril found in much of American evangelicalism and fundamentalism. Nor do they share in a spiritually negative view of the city that is so characteristic of American evangelicals. Rather, they graft their faith onto the pluralistic culture and everyday encounters that shape life in New York City. In a global and information age, African Christians practice mission and evangelism foremost through relationships. By reaching into the circles and networks in the city, the members of African churches recall the migration pattern of early Christianity.

Mission Back to Africa

African initiatives in mission are not only impacting New York City, but continue to move in many directions, and one significant direction is back to Africa, through the sharing of resources and the development of ministries.

Migrant remittances help address the economic needs of families and churches back home in Nigeria, Liberia, and Ghana. Research indicates that remittances are a major component of global economics, often surpassing other types of economic development.[110] Every person I interviewed in every church sends money home via Western Union or similar service. With mobile telephone technology increasing, people speak of receiving telephone calls wherever they are in the city from family and friends at home in Africa seeking help.[111] And help they do. One church member casually mentioned staying in a high-paying job she did not enjoy to earn more money to send home. Typically money goes to support parents and put siblings through school. Western Union advertisements in African newspapers and bodega windows are reminders of the corporate

---

110. For a journalistic account with reference to relevant literature, see Jason DeParle, "A Good Provider Is One Who Leaves," *New York Times Magazine,* April 22, 2007, 50-57, 72, 122-23.

111. This is part of a much wider dimension of globalization. See Steven Vertovec, "Cheap Calls: The Social Glue of Migrant Transnationalism," *Global Networks* 4:2 (2004): 219-24.

Witnesses in the City

Fig 6.7 Mother Cooper with supplies for the James E. Cooper Child Foundational Academy and Smiling Face Orphanage, 2005. Note the blue barrels for shipping.

competition for the money transfer market.[112] Given the great economic and social needs of Africa, remittances from the West may be an important expression of holistic mission "under the radar."[113]

Mother Cooper runs an orphanage in Monrovia, basing her resource gathering in the Bronx. Filling the room where I met with Mother Cooper were blue barrels, well-travelled suitcases, and taped-up boxes that towered to the ceiling. These were supplies for the orphanage and school in Monrovia that by force of will and prayer Mother Cooper opened in 2002. Soon the blue containers would be filled and shipped by boat to Liberia, the suitcases repacked for the journey by plane. It is not unusual for people to arrive with twenty pairs of shoes or clothing to be added to the barrels and boxes.

---

112. Jason DeParle, "Western Union Empire Moves Migrant Cash Home," *New York Times,* November 21, 2007, A-1, 20.

113. For a proposal of mission in Africa today that addresses everyday needs, see Philomena Njeri Mwaura, "Integrity of Mission in the Light of the Gospel: Bearing Witness of the Spirit among Africa's Gospel Bearers," *Exchange* 35:2 (2006): 169-90.

ENGAGEMENTS

Liberia faces the legacy of two brutal regimes and wars. Following Samuel Doe and Charles Taylor's violent regimes, which left the economy and infrastructure destroyed, Ellen Johnson Sirleaf was elected the president of Liberia in 2005.[114] As a response to the conditions in Liberia, Mother Cooper opened the James E. Cooper Child Foundational Academy and Smiling Face Orphanage.[115] Founded by Mother Cooper in 2000 and opened officially in 2002, the school is named after her late husband. For Mother Cooper, the school and orphanage represent her personal calling, not an official church ministry. But church members all seem to find ways to help. In the spring of 2006, there were 15 children in the orphanage and 222 children in the school, with ages ranging from four to twelve. A principal and business manager oversee the school in Monrovia, and there are ten teachers and teacher aides, three matrons who help with the orphans, and a janitor that draws water and occasionally turns on the generator. Because in 2006 there was still no electricity in much of the city, the school was using lanterns at night.

Mother Cooper maintains constant contact with the school and orphanage by occasional visits and regular telephone calls. In 2006, she went for more than three months to Monrovia to oversee the construction of a new two-story building. The first floor was to function as a classroom and the second as an addition to the orphanage. This would enable her to double the number of children she is able to care for. All the children from the orphanage attend the school, and some of the other orphans of the war, "living with grand aunts, uncles, living with relatives but not able to do for them," are provided scholarships. A small fee is charged to other children in the neighborhood, and basic supplies like pencils, perhaps a uniform, and some meals are provided. When children from the orphanage outgrow their care, "they remain there until I [know] what God has planned for them."[116]

Mother Cooper somehow cobbles the funding together to keep the school going. In the fall of 2006 she was working to fill a shipping container with "school materials, chairs, tables, and school supplies." With plans to finish the new building, she intended to go back in January to Monrovia. If the James E. Cooper Child Foundational Academy and Smiling Face Or-

114. Jon Lee Anderson, "After the Warlords: Can Ellen Johnson Sirleaf Remake Her Nation?" *The New Yorker*, March 27, 2006, 58-65.
115. Mother Cooper, Interview, September 18, 2006.
116. Mother Cooper, Interview, September 18, 2006.

phanage was founded to heal some of the wounds of violence, it now plays a role in the hopeful rebuilding of Monrovia and the nation.

With a concern for pastors in Nigeria, Nimi Wariboko and Elsie Obed decided to organize and fund a conference in Port Harcourt, Rivers State, Nigeria. Pastor Elsie Obed founded and is president of Lilies International Christian Outreach, which has offices in New York City and Lagos.[117] Along with her husband Olu Obed, Elsie Obed laid the groundwork for Redeemed Christian Church of God in New York and North America. Given their history and shared concerns for mission, Wariboko and the Obeds have remained in contact over the years. Expending their own funds, Wariboko and Obed rented a conference room and provided accommodations to the pastors and their spouses in a hotel. The idea, Wariboko explained, was to encourage pastors, to let them know they are not alone.

Wariboko's motive was "giving something back": "I felt like I'm [returning] to my roots where I'm from."[118] Through the conference, he found himself "pleasantly surprised" to see Christian developments in the Niger delta. Rather than just giving, "I learned more from them." In particular, he gained respect for the "high price" that the pastors pay for ministry. The needs he encountered were great; pastors asked for financial help, for Bible education, and for Christian books. To be unable to help is "painful." But the meeting of pastors would go on in locally initiated gatherings.

In all of this, globalization is a factor. Distances are bridged with phone cards, airplane travel, and Western Union. Mission meets the range of needs of family and community. People, spiritual gifts, and money are channeled to Africa in a globalized approach to faith in the world. Mission calling is strongly felt and practiced, with models of community work and pastoral training generated based on need, relationships, and opportunity.

Conclusion: Mission in the Way of Christ

In this chapter I have sought to show the historical context, convictions, and practices of mission found in Church of the Lord (Aladura), the Presbyterian Church of Ghana in New York, and the Redeemed Christian Church of God International Chapel. Of course, mission includes the work of each church in preaching, healing, praying, and evangelism. This, however, seemed to me to only partially capture their mission influence. In-

117. See http://www.liliesinternational.org/.
118. Nimi Wariboko, Interview, November 15, 2006.

stead, the fullest expression of mission can be found in everyday life. What is being fulfilled among African Christians in New York is a mission without imperial power; it is a mission in the power of the Spirit in line with the peaceable kingdom.

To understand why this represents mission in a new key, we can examine the work of Chinua Achebe in dialogue with Philip Jenkins. Chinua Achebe's novel *Things Fall Apart* tells the story of Okonkwo, and in so doing renders a much larger story of social and cultural change among the Igbo.[119] The first part of the novel tells of his life and exile from his village; the second part records his return and encounter with Western missionaries and colonizers. "The white man had indeed brought a lunatic religion, but he had also built a trading store and for the first time palm-oil and kernel became things of great price, and much money flowed into Umuofia."[120] At first the arrival of missionaries is about "the strange faith and the white man's god,"[121] but soon religion and colonization run together: "But apart from the church, the white man had also brought a government."[122]

Mr. Brown, the first missionary, would sit and dialogue about God and religion,[123] but he is succeeded by the Reverend James Smith, "a different kind of man." It is Rev. Smith's actions that will lead directly to the destruction of Okonkwo. Achebe's textured picture of the missionaries is notable.[124] Yet the two missionaries are separated only by degree; Mr. Brown and Rev. Smith are both complicit in the colonial government and the havoc it brings. Of the "white man," the view is:

> He came quietly and peaceably with his religion. We were amused at his foolishness and allowed him to stay. Now he has won our brothers and our clan can no longer act like one. He has put a knife on the things that held us together and we have fallen apart.[125]

White people here are like "locusts,"[126] a plague and not agents of Good News.

---

119. Chinua Achebe, *Things Fall Apart* (New York: Everyman Library, 1992 [1958]).
120. Achebe, *Things Fall Apart*, 153.
121. Achebe, *Things Fall Apart*, 124.
122. Achebe, *Things Fall Apart*, 150.
123. Achebe, *Things Fall Apart*, 153-56.
124. Alison Searle, "The Role of Missions in *Things Fall Apart* and *Nervous Condition*," *Literature and Theology* 21:1 (2007): 53.
125. Achebe, *Things Fall Apart*, 152.
126. Achebe, *Things Fall Apart*, 120.

Witnesses in the City

Philip Jenkins's widely discussed *The Next Christendom: The Coming of Global Christianity*[127] offers evidence for the church as now globally diverse, with Africa, Asia, and Latin America at the forefront. But Jenkins wants to do more than speak of a shift in Christian demographics; he wants to speak of the meaning of this development. If Achebe's accomplishment is to view the Anglican mission from inside the standpoint of the Igbo,[128] and in so doing teach us much about community, life, God, and the power of the West,[129] Jenkins approaches the non-Western advance of Christianity from inside the Western point of view.

Jenkins's interpretive proposal is not in the image of the old Christendom,[130] but the image of a "new Christendom."[131] "Worldwide," Jenkins believes, "religious trends have the potential to reshape political assumptions in a way that has not been seen since the rise of modern nationalism."[132] Jenkins is right on many fronts, including his sense that the changes taking place in the church represent a major development in the world and in the history of the church. But Jenkins's Christendom template is a category error, because the Christianity emerging in Africa, Asia, and Latin America is not projecting a new territorial imperialism like the European powers of the past.[133] There is no state, military, or economic apparatus behind African mission to New York. African missionaries are not installing a new government. Instead, they come in the way of Christ, with healing and a message of new life, not with violence and an imperial army. African mission is taking place without the affluence or influence that characterizes mission rooted in the West. It is a movement marked by incarnation, vulnerability, and dependence on God. The power that accompanies them is not the state, but the Holy Spirit.

Emmanuel Katongole argues that Jenkins's conception of Christian-

---

127. Philip Jenkins, *The Next Christendom: The Coming of Global Christianity* (Oxford: Oxford University Press, 2002). For a wider interaction with his work, see Frans Wijsen and Robert Schreiter, eds., *Global Christianity: Contested Claims* (Amsterdam: Rodopi, 2007).

128. Searle, "The Role of Missions in *Things Fall Apart* and *Nervous Condition*," 50-51.

129. For a discussion of *Things Fall Apart* in relationship to theology, see Agbonkhianmeghe E. Orobator, *Theology Brewed in an African Pot* (Maryknoll, N.Y.: Orbis, 2008).

130. Jenkins, *The Next Christendom*, 209.

131. Jenkins, *The Next Christendom*, 10-13.

132. Jenkins, *The Next Christendom*, 13, cf. 192.

133. For a different assessment, however, see Nina Glick Schiller, "Transnational Social Fields and Imperialism: Bringing a Theory of Power to Transnational Studies," *Anthropological Theory* 5:4 (2005): 439-61.

ity is that of a faith without a social imagination. He offers the trenchant criticism that "*The Next Christendom* is bad news for Christians not simply because it assumes the existing North-South dichotomies shaped by the economic and political realities of late capitalism, but because it seeks to secure this current vision of the world against any possible interruption from Christianity."[134]

No one knows whether African mission in New York City is at the beginning, at its midpoint, or near its end. Because it is a movement initially rooted in migration, its future is open. Christian movements historically have a serial character, with political, economic, and other developments playing a role.[135] There are questions about the religious expectations for converts, the future cultural identity of churches, the adaptability of the message in a pluralistic setting, and the development of leadership outside the founding communities.[136] As we see in the mega-church Embassy of God in Kiev, Ukraine, under the leadership of the Nigerian Pentecostal pastor, Rev. Sunday Adelaja, African Christianity can cross cultures to grow to great heights.[137] Of course, just being a church that worships God across borders, whatever the size of its membership, is a witness.[138] One thing is certain: the story of African Christian mission in New York City is still being written by the churches and in the lives of "new missionaries."

---

134. Emmanuel M. Katongole, "Hauerwasian Hooks, Stories, and the Social Imagination of the 'The Next Christendom,'" in *A Future for Africa: Critical Essays in Christian Social Imagination* (Scranton: Scranton University Press, 2005), 24. See further Peter C. Phan, "A New Christianity, But What Kind?" *Mission Studies* 22:1 (2005): 59-83.

135. Walls, *The Cross-Cultural Process*, 27-48.

136. These are classic questions that I draw and adapt from Richard Fletcher, *The Barbarian Conversion: From Paganism to Christianity* (Berkeley: University of California Press, 1997), 6-9.

137. J. Kwabena Asamoah-Gyadu, "An African Pentecostal on Mission in Eastern Europe: The Church of the 'Embassy of God' in the Ukraine," *Pneuma* 27:2 (Fall 2005): 297-321.

138. For reflection on this, see Stanley Hauerwas, "Beyond the Boundaries: The Church Is Mission," in *Walk Humbly with the Lord: Church and Mission Engaging Plurality*, ed. Viggo Mortensen and Andreas Osterlund Nielsen (Grand Rapids: Eerdmans, 2010), 53-69.

IV. DIRECTIONS

7. Moveable Pilgrimages: Relocating Sacred Geographies

Introduction

This part of my book is entitled "Directions" because it concerns the future of African Christianity in New York City. I employ direction in two different but related ways. The first sense is temporal, describing how the three churches are moving into the future, and the second is spatial, concerning the continuing flow of faith across borders. How will a movement based on global migration fare in future years? What will be the relationship between the New York City churches and the original center? In this chapter, I begin to offer an answer by recounting what I call reverse pilgrimages, the movement of spiritual geographies to serve communities unable to travel to Africa. In the subsequent chapter I will focus on an additional dimension of the future, the perspective and involvement of the second generation.

Pilgrimage is a long-standing form of popular Christian spirituality. In general terms, pilgrimage is a practice that links mobility together with a place, object, or person that holds out some hope of change. A pilgrimage involves an encounter that seeks transformation and healing; it relates once again to divine power. Protestants have traditionally been ambivalent at best about such religious expressions, but there is increasing emphasis on pilgrimage in modern society and all parts of the world.[1] Surely Charles Taylor is correct in pointing out that "people still seek . . . moments of fusion, which wrench us out of the everyday, and put us in contact with something beyond ourselves."[2] Through pilgrimage or encounters, African

---

1. For an example, see John Inge, *A Christian Theology of Place* (Aldershot: Ashgate, 2003).

2. Charles Taylor, *A Secular Age* (Cambridge: The Belknap Press of Harvard University Press, 2007), 516-17.

Christians seek the power of God in their lives. But how does pilgrimage work in African Christianity in New York? Can the category of a transformed or moveable pilgrimage be accepted?

Following the lives of three focus churches, I came to appreciate the role of pilgrimage-type events, experiences, spaces, and histories that had been relocated to New York. While I identify these events as "moveable" pilgrimages, other terms that apply include "reverse," "transformed," or "reframed." Globalization promotes the wider coverage for these pilgrimages. Thomas Tweed speaks of "sacroscapes," the flows of religion across global landscapes[3] and dynamism across space and time.[4] The scenario is one of deterritorialization and reterritorialization, the components of a spiritual event or space moved or extracted to a new globalized location.[5] Global networks are the linkage between sites of assembly.[6] This relocated spiritual geography comes into being through acts of the imagination, discourses, and bodily practices. In the instances detailed below, each pilgrimage increases the global scope of African churches.[7]

A range of pilgrimages is found across Christian tradition. In their *Pilgrimage in Graeco-Roman and Early Christian Antiquity: Seeing the Gods*,[8] Jas' Elsner and Ian Rutherford suggest a typology of over twenty different types of pilgrimages.[9] Their typology includes pilgrimages of healing and initiation in classical Greek culture[10] and scriptural, relic, icon, and living-saint pilgrimages in Christian culture.[11] Pilgrimage, Victor and Edith Turner maintain in their benchmark study, is a "universal drama, cutting across cultures, societies, polities, language groups and ethnicities."[12]

---

3. Thomas Tweed, *Crossing and Dwelling: A Theory of Religion* (Cambridge: Harvard University Press, 2006), 61.

4. Tweed, *Crossing and Dwelling*, 61-62.

5. This language comes from Gilles Deleuze and Felix Guattari, *A Thousand Plateaus: Capitalism and Schizophrenia*, trans. Brian Massumi (Minneapolis: University of Minnesota Press, 1987).

6. Manuel A. Vásquez, "Studying Religion in Motion: A Networks Approach," *Method and Theory in the Study of Religion* 20:2 (2008): 151-84.

7. Peter Beyer, *Religions in Global Society* (London: Routledge, 2006), 24.

8. Jas' Elsner and Ian Rutherford, eds., *Pilgrimage in Graeco-Roman and Early Christian Antiquity: Seeing the Gods* (Oxford: Oxford University Press, 2005).

9. Elsner and Rutherford, "Introduction," 12-30.

10. Elsner and Rutherford, "Introduction," 16-18.

11. Elsner and Rutherford, "Introduction," 28-30.

12. Victor Turner and Edith L. B. Turner, *Image and Pilgrimage in Christian Culture* (New York: Columbia University Press, 1978), 16.

Moveable Pilgrimages

Leaving aside the critique that the Turners' model requires more historical context,[13] it points to important universal concerns and the possibility of liminal experience. In pilgrimage, a theology is not so much defined as experienced.

Simon Coleman and John Eade speak instructively of reframing pilgrimage, of "implicit stories of movement"[14] that can also be different modes of travel, "embodied, imagined, metaphorical."[15] Pilgrimage provides an analytical construct for a type of travel that "seeks."[16] The object of seeking is the destination. Unprecedented developments in the growth of Christianity in Africa have not only produced new churches, ministries, and movements, but also introduced a range of spiritual geographies, with new sites of "pilgrimage."[17] Within this new range of spiritual geographies, how are boundaries crossed within constraints and limits?[18] What is the relationship of the diaspora to the center?[19] One answer is found in the examples I recount in this chapter. My framework in this chapter is first of all descriptive, examining the reproduction of sacred spaces and pilgrimages in New York City. This enables me to develop the concept "pilgrimage" in a flexible manner and take account of its interplay with globalization. As a matter of the research "field," pilgrimage adds to the diversity of ethnographic sites.[20] These pilgrimages are an important example of the mobility of African Christianity and demonstrate the continued importance of sacred topography and religious events across borders.

---

13. Manuel A. Vásquez and Marie Friedmann Marquardt, *Globalizing the Sacred: Religion Across the Americas* (New Brunswick: Rutgers University Press, 2003), 67.

14. Simon Coleman and John Eade, "Introduction: Reframing Pilgrimage," in *Reframing Pilgrimage: Cultures in Motion*, ed. Simon Coleman and John Eade (London: Routledge, 2004), 1.

15. Coleman and Eade, "Introduction: Reframing Pilgrimage," 3.

16. Coleman and Eade, "Introduction: Reframing Pilgrimage," 6.

17. In addition to the example I develop in this chapter, see André Mary, "Pilgrimage to Imeko (Nigeria): An African Church in the Time of the 'Global Village,'" *International Journal of Urban and Regional Research* 26:1 (March 2002): 106-20; and John Eade and David Garbin, "Reinterpreting the Relationship Between Centre and Periphery: Pilgrimage and Sacred Spatialisation Among Polish and Congolese Communities in Britain," *Mobilities* 2:3 (2007): 413-24.

18. Tweed, *Crossing and Dwelling*, 123-63.

19. Vida Bajc, Simon Coleman, and John Eade, "Introduction: Mobility and Centring in Pilgrimage," *Mobilities* 2:3 (2007): 321-29.

20. Mary, "Pilgrimage to Imeko (Nigeria)," 108.

DIRECTIONS

"Let Somebody Shout Hallelujah"

"Anywhere [General Overseer E. A. Adeboye] is, the Redeemed Christian Church of God headquarters is. New York City is the headquarters of the Redeemed Christian Church of God."[21] These words, spoken at Madison Square Garden, highlight the globalization of a key event and person in the Redeemed Christian Church of God. From June 15 through 17, 2005, the Theater at Madison Square Garden hosted the Ninth Annual North American Convention of the church, gathered this year under the theme of "Pillars of Greatness." At great expense, the most recognizable public space in New York was rented for the event, which attracted members from over two hundred churches in North America but also Europe and Africa, spotlighting the Redeemed Christian Church of God in the global public sphere.

In Nigeria, the Annual Convention is considered "the most important event in the liturgical calendar"[22] of the church. Its basic features are replicated each summer in the United States. During the daytime, leaders based in Nigeria ordain women and men into new leadership offices, and church members from over two hundred parishes in North America conduct church business and attend seminars on topics ranging from marriage to prayer to money. Special rooms are curtained off for prayer, and teams are scheduled to be praying throughout the conference. James Fadele, chairman of the Board of Coordinators for the Redeemed Christian Church of God North America, gives a PowerPoint presentation on the church, its plans for growth, and the obligations of ministers.

In the evenings are large meetings featuring magnificent choirs, guest speakers, and the General Overseer ("G.O.") of the Redeemed Christian Church of God, E. A. Adeboye. On the final night of the convention, an overflow crowd of some five thousand people attend the Holy Ghost service, an event renowned in Lagos for attendance that is reported to regularly exceed one million, with some placing attendance at over four million.[23] People come just for the evening from nearby parishes of the Redeemed Christian Church of God, but I was told that a large number of

---

21. Words from a speaker, June 17, 2005.
22. Asonzeh Franklin-Kennedy Ukah, "The Redeemed Christian Church of God (RCCG), Nigeria: Local Identities and Global Processes in African Pentecostalism" (Ph.D. diss., Bayreuth, 2003), 217.
23. Based on Ukah's description, "The Redeemed Christian Church of God," 217-28, there are some differences, but the general format, emphases, and outcomes are the same.

Moveable Pilgrimages

Fig. 7.1 Pastor E. A. Adeboye, General Overseer, Redeemed Christian Church of God, at Madison Square Garden, 2005

Nigerian Pentecostals from other churches in New York were in attendance as well. It was a good example of multiple networks intersecting — in this instance, Nigerian Pentecostal networks. (Many members of the Brooklyn parish described themselves to me first as Pentecostal rather than as members of the Redeemed denomination.)

For Redeemed Christian Church of God parishes in Zone 1, which in 2005 included the New York area, a year of work went into preparation for the Annual Convention. At the Brooklyn church, members were enlisted in a variety of tasks and many volunteered their time for more than one year. Segun Oyesanya was on the organizing committee; Pastor Nimi was in charge of protocol, enlisting members with cars to transport leaders from the airport; leaders like Ossai Chegwe made sure members were registered; Wapaemi Wariboko was in charge of childcare. Everyone seemed to be contributing prayers, time, and resources.

The culminating event of the Annual Convention is the Holy Ghost service. The Holy Ghost service, which took place on June 17, 2005, is a combination of singing, special choir performances, preaching, praying, healing,

Fig. 7.2 Egbefun Adieze (left), first member of Redeemed in New York City, being served lunch at the Pillars of Greatness Convention, 2005. Note Madison Square Garden in the background.

spiritual pronouncements, multimedia participation, and offerings.[24] The scale of the Holy Ghost service in North America may be smaller than what occurs in Lagos, but it reproduces an important if not essential component of the Redeemed Christian Church of God spiritual experience.

Different stages mark the Holy Ghost service, all of which build to the climactic sermon and declarations of the G.O. Praise and worship begin the evening, with corporately sung songs such as "Worthy is the Lamb." From the podium, the speaker announces the expectation to "heal America, to heal Nigeria, to heal Africa." Continuing the theme of a global impact, the hope is conveyed: "Starting from New York City, three days of meeting, let it end in . . . revival." It soon feels like a revival service, complete with mass choir, special music, prayer, and a youth dance choreographed like it belonged on Broadway.

At significant expense, guest preachers from outside Redeemed

24. Field Notes, June 17, 2005.

Moveable Pilgrimages

Fig. 7.3 Bola Oyesanya, Minister at Redeemed Christian Church of God International Chapel, Brooklyn, at Pillars of Greatness Conference, Madison Square Garden, 2005

Christian Church of God are brought in to participate in the Holy Ghost service. Guest preachers perform two functions. First, they indicate connection to a global Pentecostal culture. Second, they act as warm-up for the G.O. Pastor William "Bill" Winston is the first guest speaker, and he wants the audience to know that he arrived in New York on his own private jet, part of a fleet of airplanes he controls. After he finishes speaking, he informs the crowd that he will fly back to Chicago where he is based, and then to South Africa. Winston emphasizes his travels around the world, and names himself "a revelation preacher" who addresses "obstacles, breakthroughs." Regarding the finances of those gathered, Pastor Winston commands, "In the name of Jesus Christ of Nazareth, be paid off!" The phrase "With God all things are possible" frames this command.

"Pastor Paula" White is the next speaker, and like Bill Winston, she comes from the American Pentecostal circuit.[25] Because she has a television program, "introducing the next speaker would be a waste of time," the Master of Ceremonies states. However, the people that I canvas around me have not heard of her, and until this event, neither have I. People stand and cheer for her, but it appears from her introductory remarks that she has little awareness about the people or scale of the group she is speaking to. Somewhere I hear a rumor that upon arriving in New York City, she had a personal meeting with Donald Trump, or that she stayed in one of his hotels. True or false, it goes to the perception of a certain form of success. Pastor Paula, as she is called, brings a "Rhema" word, not a sermon, a distinction that seems to accent the special spiritual power to her words. "Are you ready for favor? God is getting ready to change some things," she declares. Among her prophecies, she declares that listeners' "season of struggle is over," that there are "blessings all around you."

One of the jobs of the "warm-up" preachers is to set the stage for the offerings. As the second offering of the evening is taken, the Jesus House Mass Choir, from a Redeemed branch congregation, sings "Shabach Hallelujah" with great polish and enthusiasm. Before the General Overseer is introduced, the worship leader states, "Prophesy into your life," which leads to a room packed with people prophesying aloud. This is followed by the sweeping chorus "Holy, holy, holy."

From the moment Adeboye says, "Let somebody shout hallelujah" and the response is a booming "hallelujah," the Holy Ghost service is in its climactic hours. Relatively speaking, the G.O. does not deliver the oratorical fireworks of the prior speakers brought in to "warm up" the crowd. But from the moment he begins to speak, it is clear he has charismatic authority that situates him in an altogether different category than the previous speakers.[26] Sharply dressed in a green suit with white shoes, Adeboye projects confidence in his role as General Overseer. In many ways, Adeboye is central to the pilgrimage, his charismatic and prophetic authority at the heart of the Redeemed movement. Adeboye begins to speak around 1:30 a.m., and continues conducting ministrations until he declares the North American convention over just after 4:00 a.m.

Upon hearing his signature phrase, "Let somebody shout hallelujah,"

25. Her Web site is http://www.paulawhite.org/.

26. For an insider story of his life, see Tony Ojo, *Let Somebody Shout Hallelujah! The Life and Ministry of Pastor Enoch Adejare Adeboye* (Lagos: Honeycombs Cards and Prints, 2001). At the time of the book's publication, the author was described as a pastor in the Redeemed Christian Church of God.

with a roar five thousand people at the Theater at Madison Square Garden do just that. Adeboye then falls to his knees and prays, with more prayer and choruses like "Glory, glory, glory" to follow. He then gives a string of declarations to the people gathered: "The Almighty God is here to answer prayer. . . . Father, send your word to me." Together, the room is asked to repeat, "Father, do something new in my life." A call to prayer is issued, "Now whatever you want God to do for you tonight, talk to him now," at which thousands of people fill Madison Square Garden with preaching prayer.

Adeboye's message is on the topic of ten "Pillars of Greatness," also the name of this Annual Convention. The ten "pillars" are divine favor, dedication unto God, humility, loyalty, focus, "hot" prayers, rugged determination, right connection, faith, and holiness. Accompanying his recitation of each pillar is a series of verses and an exposition. Throughout the course of his message, Adeboye cites some eighteen texts from the Old Testament and six from the New Testament, with an emphasis on 1 and 2 Kings. Topical concerns blend with biblical instruction to situate listeners in not just a way of life but a world of faith.

At 3:00 a.m., Adeboye introduces a video that appears on two large screens. The video is of a worship service that Adeboye has conducted at the Redemption Camp in Lagos. So while he is speaking at Madison Square Garden, simultaneously there are two large video screens playing an earlier event in Nigeria. The specifics are unclear to me, but in the video Adeboye is holding a long pole and swinging it around as he turns. As soon as Adeboye moves the rod in the video, people in New York begin to clap, louder and louder. By now he is physically standing to the side as the video screen images become more prominent. The room is filled with people clapping on the video screens and clapping at the Garden, with Adeboye holding forth in both worlds simultaneously. Rapturous prayer envelops the Garden as everyone is speaking aloud to God with the kinetic force of preaching. Images, sounds, prayers, and visions are circulating back and forth across borders in a powerful sensory effect.[27]

The image is Moses-like in transference: the General Overseer part-

27. On the relevance of such issues, see Birgit Meyer, ed., *Aesthetic Formations: Media, Religion, and the Senses* (New York: Palgrave Macmillan, 2009), particularly in the same volume her "Introduction: From Imagined Communities to Aesthetic Formations: Religious Mediations, Sensational Forms, and Styles of Binding," 1-28. See Patrick Eisenlohr, "Technologies of the Spirit: Devotional Islam, Sound Reproduction and the Dialectics of Mediation and Immediacy in Mauritius," *Anthropological Theory* 9:3 (2009): 273-96.

Fig. 7.4 Pillars of Greatness Poster, 2005

ing the figurative sea.[28] Through his physical presence in New York City, he declares, "From tonight forward all the Pharaohs and his hosts in your life [are] defeated." Adeboye imparts spiritual power by enacting the experience of a biblical figure, drawing in a global community to a transnational event. Part of Adeboye's leadership involves story telling, placing the church into a biblical narrative event. In the space-time merging of the biblical allusion, video event, and live encounter, horizons past and present merge.

This experience confirms Arjun Appadurai's observation that "collective experiences of the mass media, especially film and video, can create

---

28. Ukah, "The Redeemed Christian Church of God," 246, mentions that Adeboye's personal office in Nigeria is considered a sacred space; pastors remove their shoes during visits, reminiscent of the "holy ground" theme in Exodus 3:5.

Moveable Pilgrimages

Fig. 7.5 "In Two Places at Once" — the General Overseer in a pre-recorded video from Nigeria, projected at Madison Square Garden while he speaks in person, 2005

sodalities of worship and charism"[29] in which a consciousness of the "Global Now"[30] operates on many levels at once. Ruth Marshall-Fratani describes Pentecostalism in Nigeria as "part of a transnational movement, one in which the circulation of narrative via the media plays a central role."[31] Global media, images, and ideas have the power to mediate a movement beyond Nigerian borders, with effects on the identity of participants.[32] Electronic means of global connection, including Web pages, vid-

    29. Arjun Appadurai, *Modernity at Large: Cultural Dimensions of Globalization* (Minneapolis: University of Minnesota Press, 1996), 8.
    30. Appadurai, *Modernity at Large,* 2-11.
    31. Ruth Marshall-Fratani, "Mediating the Global and Local in Nigerian Pentecostalism," *Journal of Religion in Africa* 28:3 (1998): 280, cf. 278-81, 293-99.
    32. See further Rosalind I. J. Hackett, "Charismatic/Pentecostal Appropriation of Media Technologies in Nigeria and Ghana," *Journal of Religion in Africa* 28:3 (1998): 258-77; J. Kwabena Asamoah-Gyadu, "Of Faith and Visual Alertness: The Message of the 'Mediatized' Religion in an African Pentecostal Context," *Material Religion* 1:3 (2005): 336-56; Birgit Meyer, "Impossible Representations: Pentecostalism, Vision, and Video Technology in Ghana," in *Religion, Media and the Public Sphere,* ed. Birgit Meyer and Annelies

eos, and tapes used by the Presbyterian Church of Ghana and the Redeemed Christian Church of God in Brooklyn in particular, are modest and often event-specific. In Brooklyn the church makes CDs and tapes of its weekly services — mostly, it seems, for members. Still, it should not be overlooked that the use of media is secondary to the actual message communicated. Generally speaking, African churches do not yet appear to be posting blogs or enlisting newer platforms such as Facebook, YouTube, or Flickr, although this is changing. Ogbu Kalu describes the relationship between ministry and the use of media in a way that fits the New York component: "African Pentecostals used media as complementary to their ministries, extending their public presence, and signifier of the relative importance of a ministry."[33]

Near the end of the Holy Ghost service, Adeboye summons those who have been healed during the service to come forward. "I see some people healed who are sitting down," he announces as the space near the stage floods with people. Rental arrangements at Madison Square Garden are expensive and time overruns costly, and Adeboye voices frustration. The same Garden employees that work the Knicks' basketball games are stationed at various points around the room. It is announced that the next Annual Convention will be in Dallas, Texas, where the church has purchased land to build a permanent reproduction of Redemption Camp.[34] It is just after 4:00 a.m. when everyone spills out onto Broadway and underground to the subways and trains.

In ways imaginative, spatial, and spiritual, the Holy Ghost service of Lagos "travelled" to New York so its membership could continue to share in the experience.[35] Both the people (including the G.O.) and the institution (the Holy Ghost service) are mobile.[36] Following patterns established in Lagos, the Holy Ghost services promise a special encounter with God, mediated through the entire evening's events but particularly through

---

Moors (Bloomington: Indiana University Press, 2006), 290-312; and Charles Hirschkind, "Media, Mediation, Religion," *Social Anthropology* 19:1 (2011): 90-97.

33. Ogbu U. Kalu, "Pentecostalism and Mission in Africa, 1970-2000," *Mission Studies* 24 (2007): 30.

34. The plans for the Dallas property include a conference center, fish farm, recreational facilities, and large pavilion. See Afe Adogame, "Contesting the Ambivalences of Modernity in a Global Context: The Redeemed Christian Church of God, North America," *Studies in World Christianity* 10:1 (2004): 32-35.

35. Coleman and Eade, "Introduction: Reframing Pilgrimage," 3.

36. Coleman and Eade, "Introduction: Reframing Pilgrimage," 17.

Moveable Pilgrimages

Fig. 7.6 Celebrating 175 years of the Presbyterian Church of Ghana, anniversary uniforms, 2004

Adeboye. Moreover, they provide a ministry encounter with the General Overseer. The global flow of religious goods meets the global dispersion of people in New York City, resulting in an encounter of the body.[37] The divine encounter aids the "pilgrims" in the United States on their journey to greatness.

During interviews, people recounted their experiences of attending the Holy Ghost service in Nigeria. It involved arduous travel, time, and expense. As with pilgrimages of the past, significant expense can be involved in traveling to a Holy Ghost service.[38] Here the event has come to them in New York City, greatly reducing the cost to American members. People still journey to the service from far parts of the United States, but this is much more feasible than a trip to Nigeria. Locally, instead of returning home to Brooklyn or Queens, many take rooms in local hotels, just to be

37. Coleman and Eade, "Introduction: Reframing Pilgrimage," 16.
38. Turner and Turner, *Image and Pilgrimage in Christian Culture*, 231.

near the event. Matilda Oyeyemi's convictions represent what many told me: "[I came] for signs and wonders, for testimonies, for miracles."[39]

"Let Us Walk in the Light of the Lord"

While a major celebration of the Presbyterian Church of Ghana's 175th anniversary took place in Ghana, a smaller parallel version was held in New York during the week of May 17-23, 2004, complete with special imported cloth, a week of revival, and a Sunday anniversary service featuring a denominational leader from Ghana. The anniversary celebration was intended as an encounter with God, not merely a catalogue of historical events. Like all pilgrimages, this one required an act of imagination.[40] Participants needed to remember the past, the people whose sacrifices made this anniversary possible.

The week of May 17-23, 2004, begins with evening "revival" services led by different groups within the church. The first revival service is led by the "Osofo Group." The intense multi-vocal prayers of the charismatic tradition are in full swing,[41] focused on the church. Thelma Annan delivers the sermon on the theme "That All May Be One," words that come from John 17:21. "Oneness" can be traced back to the church's earliest days, she remarks, including the renaming of the church in 1957 with national independence:[42] "They didn't fight about the name." With an eye on the present, Annan observes, "Real love overcomes mistakes." Through their experiences, "God is telling us we should be responsible to [our] pastors and leaders. God blesses churches that are united. . . . [In] 175 years, this is how far God has taken us." Her words were in English, with brief summaries in Twi.

Friday brings an "all-night service" at the church building on 123rd Street. The event is being videotaped, and with the extra lights and people, the room is hot. Nearly everyone has on Presbyterian Church of Ghana t-shirts, many with the words "Pray Without Ceasing" inscribed on the back. Others say "Presbyterian Women's Fellowship U.S.A." As people pray, there are the loud voices of "preaching prayer" and shouts of "In Jesus' Name." In the spirit of a Pentecostal revival, the worship leader declares: "Before you leave here you have to be a different person." A biblical reflection, a special song, testimonies, and more prayers are offered.

---

39. Matilda Oyeyemi, Interview, June 22, 2005.
40. Coleman and Eade, "Introduction: Reframing Pilgrimage," 6.
41. Presbyterian Church of Ghana, Field Notes, May 17, 2004.
42. It had been the Presbyterian Church of the Gold Coast.

Moveable Pilgrimages

The evening's centerpiece is a historical overview of the Presbyterian Church by Rev. Asiedu, beginning with the Basel missionaries. "Some people somewhere, they left everything, all the pleasures, came to us, taught us what we have now — 175 years, a very long journey." To tell this story, Rev. Asiedu distributes and explains photocopies of the "Basel missionaries who left everything behind to travel to Africa." He describes the death of the early missionaries and the later use of Jamaicans. There would be no "Presbyterian Church of Ghana if those men and women had not come." Rev. Asiedu talks about Rev. Ramsayer, illustrated by a picture of him preaching at Abetifi. He mentions the first baptism in 1847, the development of the seminary in Akropong in 1848, the introduction of the Salem system, and the role of Scottish missionaries. When Rev. Asiedu mentions Peter Hall, the first moderator, "a descendent of pioneer Jamaican missionaries," he establishes the context as "local leadership right from [the] beginning." "Today," Rev. Asiedu comments, "the Presbyterian Church of Ghana is a key player in Ghanaian society." For evidence he cites 1,907 schools, a university, 37 health institutions, 7 agricultural programs, a prison ministry, and 23 congregations in Western Europe and North America. Yet there are "still people in Ghana and elsewhere who [need] to trust in Christ." Then, Rev. Asiedu makes the connection to the history of the church here in New York. Casting the challenges they face in spiritual terms, he says that "all obstacles . . . help us grow spiritually." With an offering and prayer, the service ends.

Some weeks prior to the 175th anniversary of their denomination, there was a blessing during the service of "the anniversary cloth." Large rolls of the green, blue, red, white, and yellow cloth with sketches of church leaders from their history had been shipped to New York, where members purchased sections and make clothing for the grand day. One section featured Isaiah 2:5, "Come let us walk in the light of the Lord," words that encircle "175th Anniversary 1828-2003." The parallel section features photographs of fourteen "Moderators," including Samuel Prempeh.

The anniversary clothing of the Presbyterian Church of Ghana presents a glimpse into the material dimension of religion.[43] Webb Keane is certainly right in pointing out that clothing "has an indisputably intimate

---

43. For the importance of material culture in the urban church context, see Camilo José Vergara, *How the Other Worships* (New Brunswick: Rutgers University Press, 2005), 265-70. More generally, see Colleen McDannell, *Material Christianity: Religion and Popular Culture in America* (New Haven: Yale University Press, 1995).

relationship to persons"[44] and can be deeply meaningful, not superficial.[45] If clothing can be a "text"[46] — and in this instance it is literally imprinted with a text — then it shows a reading of their story. One of the interesting features of the entire anniversary is the difference between the story Rev. Asiedu tells at the all-night service and the story told by the anniversary cloth.[47] While at no point is anything but a positive interpretation given to the work of the Basel missionaries, the anniversary cloth that is used to make uniforms for the anniversary celebration exclusively emphasizes Ghanaian figures and contributions. More than a cultural object, the anniversary cloth communicates a certain authority and narrative. Through the materiality of the cloth, a story circulates across borders.

"Pass on the word to those afar: [we] will raise our voices, Lord, to proclaim thy glory," Rev. Asiedu offers in his opening prayer of the climactic anniversary service on Sunday. He prays "for those who have gone out to proclaim thy word all around the world." The leaders in the churches today, "evangelists, catechists, pastors," are also prayed for. Together the church recites in English the Lord's Prayer. To the beat of a hand bell, the Women's Fellowship sings, waving white handkerchiefs. The Men's Fellowship gathers and performs a special song.

The Reverend Dr. Yaw Frimpong-Manso, chairperson of the Ashanti Presbytery and a lecturer in Old Testament at Trinity College, Legon, is introduced as the guest preacher (later in the year he will become the moderator of the Presbyterian Church of Ghana). "Greetings from Ghana, your friends and relatives," he begins. His theme is "Come let us walk in the light of the Lord," words taken from Isaiah 2:1-5, the theme of the denomination for this occasion. Linking the story of Isaiah with the life of the church, he notes the "heavy responsibility of [the] people of Israel." In this telling, "Missionaries came to our part of the world" and "passed responsibility on to local people." The implication is that the mission continues in New York. "Walk in [the] light," he exhorts, "all those around you will see." Here in New York, "remain united and love one another." He also appeals to the church in New York to support the work of the church back home. Rev. Asiedu delivers greetings from Mama Ohemeng, the founder of the church, who is homebound. Framed certificates honor members who have

44. Webb Keane, "Signs Are Not the Garb of Meaning: On the Social Analysis of Material Things," in *Materiality*, ed. Daniel Miller (Durham: Duke University Press, 2005), 183.
45. Keane, "Signs Are Not the Garb of Meaning," 196.
46. Keane, "Signs Are Not the Garb of Meaning," 196-97.
47. Presbyterian Church of Ghana in New York, May 20, 2004.

Moveable Pilgrimages

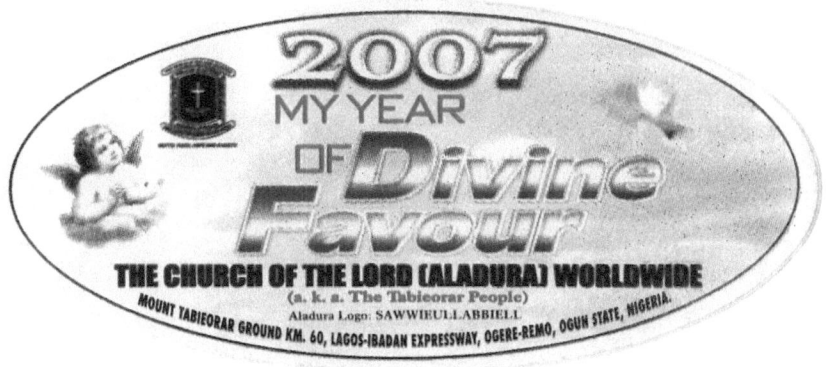

Fig. 7.7 Church of the Lord (Aladura) sticker, "a.k.a. The Tabieorar People." 2007

provided leadership over the years. It is nearly 7:00 p.m. when the service ends with an offering taken for the Presbyterian Church of Ghana.

In this celebration of the history of the Presbyterian Church of Ghana, people and place are recalled and situated in a spiritual narrative; church membership is a community that crosses borders. In marking out the early Mission House in Akropong, in recalling the work of Rev. Ramsayer, and in connecting this story to their own journey in New York, they are shaping their own memorial across borders. Rev. Dr. Frimpong-Manso came to New York, enlarging the sacred circuit of remembrance for a future of mission. Ghana is a place of spiritual meaning for these New Yorkers, and by travel as well as the mediums of photographs, friends, blessed cloth, and prayer, it has journeyed to their new home.

"We Are on Mount Tabborrar"

Over five thousand miles from the Bronx, Mount Tabborrar[48] stands on a patch of land in Ogere, Nigeria. The Tabborrar was inaugurated in 1937 in Ogere, Nigeria, when the founder of the Church of the Lord (Aladura), Josiah Ositelu, reported that he was given a vision to go to a site and pray and fast, during which time he received revelations.[49] The site of these rev-

---

48. As I earlier noted, there are a variety of spellings to Tabborrar. Unless citing a source that spells it alternatively, I use "Tabborrar."

49. Rufus Okikiolaolu Olubiyi Ositelu, *African Instituted Churches: Diversities,*

Fig. 7.8 Mother Marie Cooper leading Tabborrar worship, 2004

elations in Nigeria was given the name Mount Tabborrar, a word with biblical connotations to Mount Tabor, but of course mountain imagery is crucial in the biblical narrative. According to a seventieth-anniversary program published in Ogere, "the name stands for the mountain of power, victory, and blessings. The mount where the Holy Spirit will be disseminated upon all and sundry from all the remotest parts of the world."[50] Thereafter Josiah Ositelu designated it a site of yearly August pilgrimage for the leadership and membership of the Church of the Lord (Aladura). While not an event in commemoration of the founder of the Church of the Lord (Aladura), the Tabborrar is very much an event that keeps the role of the founder, Josiah Ositelu, before the wider church.

Large numbers of pilgrims continue to journey each year to the

---

Growth, Gifts, Spirituality and Ecumenical Understandings of African Initiated Churches (Hamburg: LIT, 2002), 138; H. W. Turner, *African Independent Church*, vol. 2: *The Life and Faith of the Church of the Lord (Aladura)* (Oxford: Clarendon Press, 1967), 221-30.

50. "Tabieorar @ 70 Programme," The Church of the Lord (Aladura) Worldwide, Tuesday, August 22, 2006.

Moveable Pilgrimages

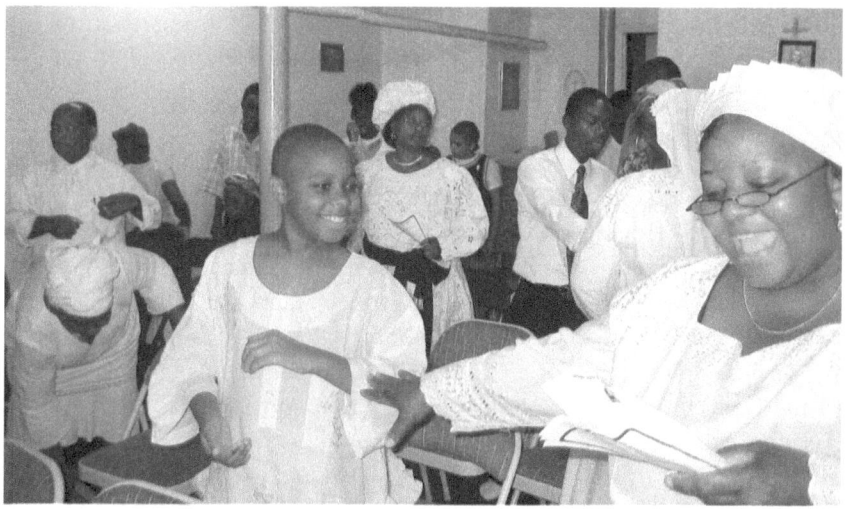

Fig. 7.9 Celebrating the Tabborrar, Church of the Lord (Aladura), Bronx, 2004

mountain for healing, renewal, prophecies, and proclamations.[51] For the Church of the Lord (Aladura), the Mount Tabborrar season or festival is its most distinctive and important communal event. Held annually in August, the Tabborrar involves thirteen days of praying and fasting, culminating on August 22 with a "finale" service that pronounces the thirteen blessings of Tabborrar, after which everyone breaks their fast.

Instead of having its members travel to Ogere for the Tabborrar festival, the church relocates its practice to New York. In New York, not only are its disciplines of fasting and prayer kept, but the discourse of the finale service suggests that the sacred topography of Ogere has been transferred or relocated. That is, the world created in marking the Tabborrar — fasting, prayer, worship on the mountain, healing, blessings, and breaking the fast — is experienced on Mount Tabborrar in New York. I participated in two Tabborrar festivals, the first in August 2004 and the second in August 2007. The description that follows is from 2004.[52]

In New York City, Tabborrar pilgrims arrive from New Jersey, New

---

51. Olatunji F. Aina, "'Psychotherapy by Environmental Manipulation' and the Observed Symbolic Rites on Prayer Mountains in Nigeria," *Mental Health, Religion and Culture* 9:1 (2006): 1-13; J. Kwabena Asamoah-Gyadu, "'On the Mountain of the Lord': Healing Pilgrimages in Ghanaian Christianity," *Exchange* 36:1 (2007): 65-86.

52. Field notes, August 22, 2004.

York, Atlanta, and Rhode Island. Outside in the hot summer evening the teenagers talk about sports and music. Inside, bottles and gallon jugs of water are being placed in the front altar area, in preparation for the Tabborrar blessing.

Prayers, ecstatic shouts, and loud exclamations of "Thank you, Jesus" emanate from the prayer room located behind the altar area. By 7:00 p.m., with hand bells ringing, five calabashes swirling, and hand drums catching the rhythms, the service begins with a congregation that will reach sixty pilgrims elatedly singing the processional song, "Tabborrar De o, Tabborrar De o Halleluyah o," which means "Tabborrar Day Hallelujah." Officiating the service along with Mother Cooper is the representative of the Primate of the Church of the Lord (Aladura), Archdeacon John Lachana, who is based in Atlanta.[53] The hymns, prayers, readings of psalms, and a sermon all lead to the liturgical apex: the thirteen blessings of Tabborrar. Yet for all the liturgical order, a fluid dynamic characterizes the service.

Following the processional song, we sing the introit hymn, a nineteenth-century hymn known by its opening line, "Immortal, Invisible, God only wise." Next in order is a reading of Psalm 51, leading to a confession of sin. "Holy Spirit move! Move in thy Holy Ghost power!" the worship leader pleads, and a woman in front falls over under the influence of the Spirit. More hymns and singing follow. Then Mother Cooper asks, "Who wants a Tabborrar blessing?" to which the congregation replies, "I do!" For the next thirty minutes praise and worship take place, beginning with "What a mighty God we serve" and including "Amazing Grace." Kneeling, Sister Sarah then offers a prayer focused on God: "Our God, help in ages past . . . God who never fails, God of Tabborrar. . . ."

Archdeacon Lachana preaches a sermon from Judges 14:1-14 that underscores how God blesses. As he recounts the story, it pivots around honey and the lion. For Lachana, the lion is a symbol of "power . . . the devil, enemy, adversary." We may face "difficult lions" such as at work and sickness, but there is the possibility of honey. Honey in the Bible, he states, can mean wealth, riches, and the good. For reference, he cites the land of milk and honey in Exodus 3, Isaiah 7:14, Mark 1:6, and 1 Samuel 14:24-29: "Honey is a symbol of blessing." "On Mount Tabborrar tonight there is honey in the lion." A principle follows: "After every attack comes a promotion." Human action is required in response: "If you obey God and listen to his word, take a bold action and see what he will do."

---

53. John Lachana, Interview, August 22, 2004.

Moveable Pilgrimages

Fig. 7.10 Archdeacon John Lachana, blessing the Tabborrar fruit and water, 2007

Biblical interpretation leads to immediate results in the Tabborrar service. Lachana proclaims, "If you believe, you will not go away empty." Just as "the lion had become food for him [Samson]," so we have an "inheritance." If God gave to Samson, he will give to you. The language of portion, inheritance, and possession overflows. What is our possession distributed from God? "Healing, deliverance, joy, peace, favor, the power of the Holy Ghost, mercy, riches, prophecy . . . that is God's will for you." "Have you ever been blessed by your enemies?" Ultimately, the God of Tabborrar "will tell your enemy to be a blessing." "In the name of Jesus I declare healing . . . I bind every spirit of sickness, I command it to leave."

After the sermon it is time for the thirteen blessings of Tabborrar. We are "on Mount Tabborrar," Archdeacon Lachana announces during a Tabborrar service. In Liberia, congregations of the Church of the Lord (Aladura) construct a small version of the holy mountain.[54] Land becomes sacred ground. In New York City, the Tabborrar arrives in spiritual, almost Eucharistic form.[55] The merging of sacred time and sacred space[56] is spiritually manifested in the worshiping community. In the trans-temporal ritual action they follow, as their hands are lifted up in prayer, the mountain becomes present. A gesture of prayer, not a shovel, creates the sacred mountain.

Inside the Bronx church, Archdeacon Lachana begins a liturgy of the Tabborrar:

> QUESTION: Whence commeth ye thou hither ye pilgrims in white robes?
> ANSWER: Tabborrar, Tabborrar, the mountain of the Lord.
> QUESTION: What is your first request here ye pilgrims in white robes?
> ANSWER: (First blessing) Forgiveness of sins from King Olufiji, that God of Tabborrar may forgive all our sins.

Thirteen Tabborrar blessings are pronounced: forgiveness of sins, God's cleansing, God's mercy, God's blessing, perfect peace, good children, victory, salvation, God's healing, joy, God's favor, the mighty power of the Holy Spirit, and steadfastness. After the recitation of each blessing follows a similar rhythm of call and response, singing, prayer, sermonic exhortation, and a declaration of blessing. It is nearly thirteen liturgical services bound into one. In response to each of the thirteen blessings of Tabborrar, from the congregation there are a series of choruses and shouts, special intercessory prayers, vows, and testimonies. Voiced as a vow for individuals are the words, "Lord, I come to the Holy Mountain of Tabborrar and I make this vow." The service throughout is punctuated with the phrase, "God of Tabborrar, manifest your power." As the service ends, Lachana and the other ministers on the platform bless the fruit and collected water bottles and jugs. Then everyone goes upstairs to break the fast with Jamba rice, fruit, soft drinks, and juices. It is into the morning hours.

Back on Mount Tabborrar in Ogere, the head of the Church of the Lord (Aladura) is receiving a set of prophecies that will be distributed

---

54. Samuel Irving Britt, "The Children of Salvation: Struggle and Cosmology in Liberian Prophet Churches" (Ph.D. diss., University of Virginia, 1992), 280, 297, 308.
55. My thanks to Alan Jacobs for suggesting this possible representation.
56. Britt, "The Children of Salvation."

around the world via paper pamphlet and the Internet. The paper copy I obtained was sent via postal mail to Mother Cooper and the church. Titled "Divine Revelation for the Year 2005 from Holy Mount of Tabieorar,"[57] it is dated "18.8.2004," corresponding to the Primate Rufus Ositelu's time on the Mountain. The preface of the 2005 booklet opens with "Sawwiellakkabie" and "Happy Tabieorar," followed by thirty-eight pages of revelation and prayers. There are "Divine Revelations and Prophecies for Each Month" in 2005, monthly prayers, divine revelations and prophecies for each month, general and country-specific revelations, and divine revelations to those in specific occupations, such as drivers and computer scientists. The revelation regarding the United States reads,

> The Lord said, the Nation of America should be careful and pray so that their political activities would not cause commotion. Pray against things that could bring set-back to the economy of this country. The deception of many prominent personalities in the society will be exposed. The Lord said, let this Nation not relent in their prayer because of enemies that pretend to be their friends. There will be a new beginning that will usher in hope and stability to the country. The Lord said, the end of the year will bring peace to the Nation.[58]

There is a prophetic character to the revelation; it provides a critical analysis of the United States along with encouragement.

Throughout the whole Tabborrar season of thirteen days, but especially in the finale night, there is a conviction that participants "will not leave here the same." Mother Cooper refers to "a new life" that is operative in people. She also notes that no one became sick or ended up in the hospital as a result of the fasting. If the process of keeping the Tabborrar involves sacrifice and discipline, the intended outcome is human flourishing.[59] As evident in the testimonies and comments, Tabborrar blessings are responsive and adaptive to the context of life in New York.

In Harold Turner's earlier assessment of the Tabborrar, he finds that "it is difficult to come to clear conclusions about the Taborar development and why it has occurred."[60] He concludes, "The ambiguous nature of its chief liturgical creation is a token of the uncertainty attending its own fu-

---

57. Church of the Lord (Aladura).
58. Church of the Lord (Aladura), 24.
59. Programs, 2004 and 2007.
60. Turner, *African Independent Church*, vol. 2, 230.

ture."⁶¹ Forty years since Turner's study, with a view from the Bronx, its value is much clearer. The Tabborrar is a religious event that holds out the promise of flourishing and preserves the unique identity of the Church of the Lord (Aladura) as a global church.

Conclusion: Moving Expectation

Historically, pilgrimage involves planned travel to a specific site for an encounter of deep meaning. Following Simon Coleman and John Eade, I have reframed pilgrimage to include movement along "new modes of travel."⁶² In describing pilgrimage this way, I have sought to show how through the annual convention and Holy Ghost service of the Redeemed Christian Church of God, the Tabborrar festival of the Church of the Lord (Aladura), and the 175th anniversary of the Presbyterian Church of Ghana, sacred geographies and events are moved across borders. These transported events enable each of the larger church movements to break down constraints of distance and provide a crucial experience of faith for their dispersed membership.⁶³

The three pilgrimages that I experienced share at least four features. First, the pilgrimages maintain core religious identities through highly identifiable rituals, narratives, and experiences. Each event helps ensure people stay involved across borders. Second, the events demonstrate the power of memory and imagination, recalling home and establishing community. The preaching, the music, the participants, the textiles and clothing all help move people into this transformed space. Third, each event reinforces the importance of religious networks. This is true for both leaders and participants. Each event links the participants to religious networks around the globe. Fourth, each gathering places front and center the primacy of the celebratory religious experience.

Whether it is for healing or remembrance, empowerment or hope, in each pilgrimage event there is an encounter, an expectation, and a change that is sought. The shared features of each pilgrimage — maintaining identity, nurturing memory and imagination, staying connected to religious networks, and celebrating faith — demonstrate the global direction of African Christianity.

61. Turner, *African Independent Church*, vol. 2, 230.
62. Coleman and Eade, "Introduction: Reframing Pilgrimage," 1, 3.
63. Coleman and Eade, "Introduction: Reframing Pilgrimage," 6.

8. Handing Off:
Faith in the Second Generation

Introduction

For sheer joy, few days surpass a confirmation Sunday. August 14, 2005, was confirmation day at the Presbyterian Church of Ghana in New York, one of the most significant events in the life of the church.[1] For months if not years, fifteen young men and women had been instructed in the beliefs and practices of the church — the nature of Christ, the Holy Ghost, and the Ten Commandments. As they knelt one by one before Pastor Yaw Asiedu, he laid his hands upon them and they affirmed the vows of membership. Then, beginning with the elders, followed by the whole of the church, a line stretched around the sanctuary to shake hands with, hug, and celebrate each new member. "First communion" followed for only the new members. Rev. Asiedu remarked, "On [this] day he [Jesus] is dining with you, same as the disciples." The service was followed by a celebration of eating and dancing in the basement of the church. For the fifteen young people, this public commitment was not simply a gesture of faith; it was an affirmation of their parents' history and tradition, a participation in a story that usually runs many generations.

In Latin, "translation" means "to transfer," to hand off. Translating faith from one generation to the next is of perennial concern for all religious traditions.[2] As the author of Deuteronomy wrote, "But take care and watch yourselves closely, so as neither to forget the things that your eyes

---

1. Presbyterian Church of Ghana in New York, Field Notes, August 14, 2005.
2. James L. Heft, ed., *Passing on the Faith: Transforming Traditions for the Next Generation of Jews, Christians, and Muslims* (New York: Fordham University Press, 2006); Carolyn Chen, "From Filial Piety to Religious Piety: Evangelical Christianity Reconstructing Taiwanese Immigrant Families in the United States," *International Migration Review* 40:3 (2006): 573-602.

have seen nor to let them slip from your mind all the days of your life; make them known to your children and your children's children."[3] Today there are new challenges to raising children in a particular faith tradition. Pluralism and its options join with social pressures and changes in moral standards to challenge African families as they raise children in global New York City. Away from the reinforcements of culture and tradition, these concerns are compounded.

As I have emphasized throughout this book, New York City is an immigrant city, and this is perhaps most evident in its youth: "among New Yorkers under age eighteen, 62.4 percent are second- or 1.5-generation."[4] Here "second-generation" is a term for children born in New York City to new immigrant parents, and "1.5-generation" are youth born in a "home" country but raised in New York City. If in immigrations past an assimilation model of incorporation prevailed, children of global migrations today live in more than one world. Issues of identity, home, belonging, and faith span borders.

Supplementing my general observations and personal interviews, near the end of my research I conducted two focus-group sessions with young people of the Presbyterian Church of Ghana in New York and the Redeemed Christian Church of God International Chapel, Brooklyn. No area of research drew more encouragement by the congregations themselves than this topic. And perhaps no area is of more determinant value in life outcome than religion and family, as Christian Smith argues in *Soul Searching: The Religious and Spiritual Lives of American Teenagers*.[5] Of the many notable conclusions produced in this study, two are particularly relevant for the present inquiry. First, Smith's research indicates that teenagers are most significantly influenced by the religious beliefs and practices of parents.[6] The influence of other adults is important, but parents matter most. Second, the study found a correlation between religious belief, practice, and positive life outcomes.[7] (All too much of the literature on the sec-

---

3. Deuteronomy 4:9.

4. Philip Kasinitz, John H. Mollenkopf, and Mary C. Waters, "Worlds of the Second Generation," in *Becoming New Yorkers: Ethnographies of the Second Generation*, ed. Philip Kasinitz, John H. Mollenkopf, and Mary C. Waters (New York: Russell Sage Foundation, 2004), 2.

5. Christian Smith with Melinda Lundquist Denton, *Soul Searching: The Religious and Spiritual Lives of American Teenagers* (New York: Oxford University Press, 2005).

6. Smith, *Soul Searching*, 56, 120, 261.

7. Smith, *Soul Searching*, 218-58.

ond generation of immigrant families leaves out religion, emphasizing instead race and ethnicity.[8] On the other hand, the literature on youth and religion is largely incomplete due to its omission of immigrants, Pentecostal settings, and global expressions of Christianity. This points to the need for significant further research and generally much greater attention to the "spiritual lives" of children and youth.[9])

It Takes a Church

Drawing on an ancient Christian practice, on Easter Sunday Rev. Asiedu of the Presbyterian Church of Ghana in New York calls forward a group of parents and children to be baptized.[10] Both parents and children are mostly dressed in white. The elders stand behind Rev. Asiedu; parents are positioned to his front left and right. Rev. Asiedu reads the Scriptures and recites a series of questions — in English. As an elder — not the pastor or parent — holds each child, Rev. Asiedu baptizes the children "in the name of the Father, Son, and Holy Spirit." In his prayer for the parents raising children, Rev. Asiedu acknowledges that the work of parents "is not easy ... especially in this country." Nothing symbolizes that the parents are not alone in this challenge more than what happens next. The elders proceed to carry the newly baptized children up the center aisle so the congregation "learns them," as it is put. With this act, the church is proclaiming that it takes a community of faith to raise a child for Christ, not simply a nuclear family.

With its pronounced connection to history and culture, the continuation of faith for the Presbyterian Church of Ghana is not simply a religious concern; it holds cultural and institutional importance as well. Rev. Asiedu said that if the church had the funding, they would begin a Saturday school for youth that taught Ghanaian languages, culture, and history. Instead the youth meet together during the regular church service. Neither the "Brigades" nor the "Young People's Guild" (YPG), groups functioning

---

8. On this development generally, see Gerrie ter Haar, *Halfway to Paradise: African Christians in Europe* (Cardiff: Cardiff Academic Press, 1998), 164-65.

9. For the kind of listening that is important, see Robert Coles, *The Spiritual Life of Children* (Boston: Houghton Mifflin, 1990). For an account that helps to shift the debate, see Janice A. McLean, "Living Their Faith: Identity and Mission among West Indian Immigrants in Pentecostal Churches in New York City and London" (Ph.D. thesis, University of Edinburgh, 2009).

10. Presbyterian Church of Ghana in New York, Field Notes, March 27, 2005.

in Ghana, are in full swing; what takes place on Sundays seems to function as a youth group. At Mount Morris Church, they meet in the basement, a room with flickering fluorescent lighting, ceilings with peeling paint, floors encrusted with dirt, and a door with no spring that booms shut. With the sanctuary above, the ceiling pulsates as music is played.

Their de facto leader is Rex Agyemang, a faithful member of the church who week after week "pastors" the youth of the church. Rex has done this for years without a title, salary, or official position in the church. He does it with passion, commitment, and contextual sensitivity. Rex is "always trying to help them understand the meaning of being a Christian" and especially urging them to live as a "Christian among their friends." Rex has bigger dreams for the group: "I would love for us to get to the point where we can call on one another, pray for one another."[11] As a good youth leader, Rex is trying to foster spiritual maturity and community.[12]

This is a challenge, as I found during a focus group meeting on December 2, 2007. Here I was able to hear directly from a group of sixteen young people approximately ages 13-18 about their faith and church life. Before we talked, as is their standard practice, they had a time of worship that alternated between praying and singing. The songs, such as "He is Lord" and "We May Magnify Your Name," are sung first in English and then Twi.

They are an active group of young persons, the vast majority of whom live in the Bronx, where they also attend school. While a few of the young women keep in contact during the week by mobile phone, they mostly see each other only in church or special church activities such as "outdoorings." So it is on Sundays that the group primarily meets together. Their closest friends are not necessarily fellow church members.

Racial and ethnic identity are on the surface of their daily lives in New York City.[13] When I asked how they identified themselves, I suggested as possible categories "Ghanaian," "African American," or "Christian." At first, eight people responded they considered themselves to be "African American," six "Ghanaian," and one "Christian." One person, who had been born in Japan, preferred being recognized as Japanese. After some discussion, it became clear that in their minds "African American,"

11. Rex Agyemang, Interview, May 31, 2006.
12. Smith, *Soul Searching*, 261-62.
13. Alejandro Portes and Rubén G. Rumbaut, *Legacies: The Story of the Immigrant Second Generation* (Berkeley: University of California Press and New York: Russell Sage Foundation, 2001), 147-91.

Handing Off

Fig. 8.1 Youth Service, Presbyterian Church of Ghana, 2007, with leader Rex Agyemang at the right

as I was using the term, meant "Black American." As they discussed terms, there was consensus for something like "Ghanaian American." They were Americans, but also quite pointedly Ghanaian.

Along this line, I asked their assessment of the Democratic presidential candidate Barack Obama, whose father was Kenyan and mother was white. Because of Obama's race, they give a decidedly tepid review of his ability to get elected in America. From their personal experience in New York City, they know there is "still racism" in America. At school they are often taunted with "you look like a gorilla" and "you don't have no clothes." Perhaps because of this they expressed pride in and affirmation of their Ghanaian identity. But overall, school is not only a place for achievement;[14] it is also where identity comes into question.[15]

All of the youth attend church because a parent or family member brings them. However, the Presbyterian Church of Ghana places great stress on the role of the institution in religious formation, an example of

14. Portes and Rumbaut, *Legacies*, 192-268.
15. Portes and Rumbaut, *Legacies*, 192-268.

how "it takes a church" to raise a Christian. Through participation[16] in the life of the church, "spiritual capital" is passed on from generation to generation. At the same time, for parents, church participation is part of a strategy for maintaining transnational identity.[17]

When I inquired about the youths' personal religious practices, such as praying and reading the Bible, church, not home, was primarily where this occurred. But overall, as one young woman put it, they seek to put "Christ first." This faith guides them through life. Overall, they felt that their parents held them to higher standards than the parents of friends outside of church. "Come try that at my home," one person reported telling a friend who said and did things they never would. A number of children attend parochial (Catholic) schools because parents view it as a more "ordered" environment. No matter their age, parents continue to play a major role in their social life.

There appears to be a significant disconnect between parents and youth concerning the worship service. Part of the gap involves language. As one person muses, language has "always been my insecurity." The youth do not always understand Twi (few reported being fully bilingual). There is an irony here in that the use of Twi and Ga represents stability for the parents. Youth enjoy listening to Ghanaian music, which they are able to purchase at Ghanaian markets in the city; they also hear Ghanaian music at parties with friends. But the message they hear from the adults is that the traditional hymns of the church "are closer to Scripture" than more contemporary musical forms.

The search for the self among Ghanaian youth is apparent in Rex Agyemang's story.[18] Born at Harlem Hospital, he was raised in the community, and has only been to Ghana once. Yet "I'm Ghanaian," he asserts, and "I feel more African and proud of it." He recognizes that there is a concern on the part of some African Americans that "Africans have come here to take their jobs." Here Rex also identifies another group of African Americans which sees itself "as more African" and by implication, more welcoming of newcomers. "I feel sometimes caught in the middle. I can feel what African Americans are going through and think. And to some degree I can think through what Africans are thinking." He uses the word "passionate" to describe his positive feelings toward Martin Luther King Jr. But no matter his subjectivity, Rex realizes that he remains "black" to the

---

16. Joanna L. Waters, "Transnational Family Strategies and Education in the Contemporary Chinese Diaspora," *Global Networks* 5:4 (2005): 359-77.

17. Peggy Levitt, "Roots and Routes: Understanding the Lives of the Second Generation Transnationally," *Journal of Ethnic and Migration Studies* 35:7 (2009): 1225-42.

18. Rex Agyemang, Interview, August 29, 2006.

Handing Off

Fig. 8.2 Confirmation meal with church and family, Presbyterian Church of Ghana, 2005

police and others. He lives in multiple worlds, moving among a diverse "black" community and city, yet also affected by the potentials of racial discrimination. "Complex" does not begin to describe it.[19]

From the outset of my time at the church, it was evident that for parents it was a matter of paramount importance that as their children become adults they would become confirmed as members of the church. It is, I think, most profoundly a sign of their care for their children.[20] For parents much more than the youth, joining the church is not simply about beliefs; it is a means of connecting generations. It is grandparents, schools, and communities — in other words, memory.[21] For the youth, it is about making their way in New York City and honoring their parents. But as one

---

19. Philip Kasinitz, John H. Mollenkopf, and Mary C. Waters, "Identity," in *Becoming New Yorkers*, 281-87, and Natasha Warikoo, "Cosmopolitan Ethnicity: Second-Generation Indo-Caribbean Identities," in *Becoming New Yorkers*, 361-91.

20. Smith, *Soul Searching*, 259.

21. Mary Chamberlain and Selma Leydesdorff, "Transnational Families: Memories and Narratives," *Global Networks* 4:3 (2004): 227-42.

youth told me, confirmation was perceived as more important for the parents, at least at that point in time. The parent-child relationship continues to be prominent even if movement across borders has strained it.

As in Ghana,[22] it is not unheard for grown children in New York City to switch from the Presbyterian Church to a Pentecostal church. I ran into a few people who did just this during a visit to a Ghanaian Pentecostal church in New York City. Still, some youth return to the Presbyterian Church of Ghana in New York on certain Sundays to please their parents.

On a number of occasions I spoke with Eric Gyasu.[23] From college he was going to law school; he is on his way up in the United States, with many professional options before him. Did Eric expect to be attending this church or another Presbyterian Church of Ghana in ten years? As he was leaving to catch his ride back to college, he paused to think about it, then replied, "The short answer: yes."[24] His parents and church would be relieved to hear the answer, for Eric and others like him represent the continued flourishing of the church and its traditions.

Children of the Lord

Because of the size of the Church of the Lord (Aladura), my review is necessarily briefer than for the other two churches. There is, however, a clear pattern to be seen in the church: children learn the ways of the Church of the Lord (Aladura) by fully participating in the life of the church. Alana is now ten, and her participation is indicative of this process. In the first few years that I was part of the church, during the Sunday service she distributed the hymnals, Bibles, and offering envelopes. More recently, she is reading the Bible before the congregation. Alana actively participates in the Sunday Bible study and prayer meetings, asking questions and offering prayers. There is no separate space or activity for Alana and the other children who visit from time to time; they are an integral part of the service and life of the church. Some families also consider sending children "back home" to attend school or to stay with family. Expense can make this difficult, but it is an option some consider.

---

22. Cephas N. Omenyo, *Pentecost Outside Pentecostalism: A Study of the Development of Charismatic Renewal in the Mainline Churches in Ghana* (Zoetermeer: Uitgeverij Boekencentrum, 2002), 131.

23. Interviews, Eric Gyasu, August 29, 2004, and August 6, 2006.

24. Interview, Eric Gyasu, August 6, 2006.

Handing Off

Fig. 8.3 Alana, Church of the Lord (Aladura), 2007

Sons and Daughters of Pentecost

During my years of attending the Redeemed Church of God International Chapel, Brooklyn, I observed that children are given a special place in the life of the church. Pastor Nimi travels to people's homes for naming ceremonies, conducts baby dedications in church services, and prays regularly for the "fruit of the womb." Parents of new children are given money from the church to open a savings account. Children go to their own room during the sermon, but otherwise they are active in the service. There is also a new mothers' room for feeding adjacent to the sanctuary. After Sunday worship has ended, children play together in the main room as their parents engage in meetings or conversations.

I met with a focus group of eight young people at the Redeemed Christian Church of God International Chapel, Brooklyn, on October 14,

Fig. 8.4 Praying for children and youth, Church of the Lord (Aladura), 2005. Note the cross in Minister Joy's hand.

2007. They ranged in age between 18 and 24, with one person soon turning 18. During the time at the church, I had frequently seen many of them at a diverse array of services and activities. What I found in my focus group was a religiously intense and personally committed group of young people who held strongly to the practices of Pentecostal faith but also had independent ideas about ministry. They are what Christian Smith might call the "highly devoted."[25]

Before I had an opportunity to ask a question of the focus group, they wanted to know if I was a Christian. What is striking is that I had been in regular attendance for years. It didn't matter. They wanted to know if I

25. Smith, *Soul Searching*, 110.

Handing Off

Fig. 8.5 Baby dedication of a child of James and Egbefun Adieze by Pastor Wariboko, 2005

was "born again." They were not taking for granted any general impression church members may have had of me; they wanted a personal conversation. Significantly, baptism for Pentecostals comes only with conversion, not because of a family's membership. At Redeemed, baptism takes place from age thirteen onwards. If one was baptized as an infant, rebaptism also takes place with conversion.

Church life is seen as a very important factor in their daily lives, with prayer at the forefront. Like most of her peers in the group, Stephanie West-Erhabor has been a member of the Brooklyn church for a number of years. She and her family pray together every morning from 6:00 a.m. to 7:00 a.m. I came to understand that family devotions are a common activity; doubtless they play a key role in forming the religious devotion of youth, confirming Smith's conclusions.[26] Theological identity is passed on through learning the practices of prayer.

26. Smith, *Soul Searching*, 261.

Fig. 8.6 Youth of Redeemed Christian Church of God International Chapel, Brooklyn, 2007

Bola Ogungbuyi daily prays the Lord's prayer; Kimberly Jean Baptiste prays each morning before leaving home, for the "transportation" she will take and for "guidance." She also writes poems to God. Lashe Davies prays each day and also sings to God: "Guide me, Jesus," she asks. A few indicated praying before exams, not for "success," but that their "potential" would be evident in results. Youth are highly engaged in worship as a "collaborative process,"[27] with music as an attraction point and outlet.

In other words, the youth at the Redeemed Christian of God International Chapel, Brooklyn, do not just hold spiritual values, but seek to incorporate the Christian tradition and its practices in their daily lives. As Lashe Davies put it, "church helps [when] you're going through stuff" and helps her "find a solution." Others affirmed this perspective. Church is where "God addresses" people. Or as Stephanie West-Erhabor puts it, "stuff happens" in life and church helps her "remember" God in the midst. Bola Ogungbuyi frames it simply: "Jesus is [the] example." There-

---

27. Donald E. Miller and Tetsunao Yamamori, *Global Pentecostalism: The New Face of Christian Social Engagement* (Berkeley: University of California Press, 2007), 132.

fore, Christians are not to worship what they call idols, such as "cars" and "sex" and "lust."

This sense of moral commitment fits within what David Martin calls the Pentecostal narrative.[28] From my conversations, it is evident that Pentecostal youth have a particular way of speaking theologically about their faith; they appear very comfortable and confident in doing so. The youth also exhibit confidence in the area of leadership. This came through particularly as they expressed a desire to develop a greater ministry to their Brooklyn community than presently exists. Bola is clear that "when we grow up, we will be the next leaders."

Perhaps not surprisingly, the youth of Redeemed Christian Church of God International Chapel, Brooklyn, report they are friends in and outside of church. In youth sessions, they discuss and "understand things different than adults." They share with one another how they are "going through things." What appears to unite them the most is not an ethnic or racial culture, or even a church tradition, but a culture of faith — of being born again.

Underlining all of this is the cosmopolitan outlook one might expect from New York kids raised in two worlds, but it is not where I initially began. When I began my conversation with this group of young adults at the Redeemed Christian Church of God International Chapel, Brooklyn, I thought of them as the next generation of New Yorkers. That may be true, but most expressed a strong desire to visit more of the world before they consider settling in New York City. This sense of the world correlated to how long they had lived in New York City; the longer they lived in the city, the more of the world they wanted to see. It also follows their parents, who continue to live in multiple worlds.

I expected a high percentage would see their faith journeys as continuing in the Redeemed Christian Church of God, wherever they located. This was true for some, of course. But what was more important for most was their identity as Christian and Pentecostal, of belonging to a church that fits their devotion to God. This was about neither "brand loyalty" nor negative feelings toward the church. Rather, it appears to reflect their commitment to follow and worship God faithfully wherever they are, as well as their embrace of the Pentecostal narrative. If they are not the children of Pentecost in Brooklyn, they will be children of Pentecost in the wider world.

---

28. David Martin, *On Secularization: Towards a Revised General Theory* (Aldershot: Ashgate, 2005), 141-54.

Conclusion: Conversion and Community

In this chapter we have seen diverse examples of "handing off" faith to the next generation. As the discussion revealed, this transfer is closely bound up with diverse notions of conversion and the meaning of community.

For the Presbyterian Church of Ghana in New York, confirmation is linked to both personal faith and the tradition to which generations of their family have often belonged. It is what one is expected to do. Membership joins family, cultural, and faith obligations. Confirmation is a public recognition of faith and belonging to a very specific faith community, the Presbyterian Church of Ghana. At the Church of the Lord (Aladura), belonging is linked to a spiritual community that works to protect, guide, and provide for its children.

For young people at the Redeemed Christian Church of God International Chapel, Brooklyn, the starting points are conversion and then the practices of faith that include prayer, fasting, and a disciplined moral life. An active faith can help lead the young people, they believe, to success in life; a moral life can lead to flourishing. Wherever they go, they intend to keep faith, and certainly plan to continue in their Pentecostal tradition. They may or may not attend a Redeemed parish; what matters to them is being born again and living the life of faith.

Passing on faith is an act of translation. It is one of the most important things that a church does. No church assumes the process is simple, particularly with the divergent forces that can impinge upon the life of faith in New York City. Living between worlds, African families in New York put great emphasis upon church life as a space of moral and spiritual guidance.

Conclusion: Giving and Receiving

Crossing Over

When Nimi Wariboko of the Redeemed Christian Church of God International Chapel, Brooklyn, preaches, it is more than a spoken "message." In every service you expect his opening words to be "Let somebody shout hallelujah," the biblical texts to be crunched together at lightning pace, the practical points to be many, and the prayers of the congregation to extend his preachments. But often something new and unexpected happens. At that moment, not only is the Word expounded, but the Spirit comes alive in the community.

It is summer 2005 and the sermon, based on Matthew 6:9-13, is on debt.[1] In the years to come, Wariboko's words would have a prophetic and global relevance. But for now the immediate situation of his parish is in view. Wariboko explains that debt is a spiritual power that can infiltrate the lives of African immigrants, snaring them in a lure of credit card companies that can leave them with nothing. With his business background, Pastor Nimi provides a miniature lecture on types of debt, blending the spiritual and material together. His declaration that "God will set you free" means many things. In an altar call, Pastor Nimi tells the church, "If you are not born again, I want to pray with you." Then he summons people in need of having debt paid off forward for prayer. As a stream of more than one hundred people move forward to receive the anointing of the Spirit, the choir sings, "He is able, abundantly able, to deliver and to save," and "Jesus is a winner man, a winner man all the time. I am on the winning side all the time."

1. Redeemed Christian Church of God International Chapel, Brooklyn, Field Notes, June 5, 2005.

CONCLUSION

This is where the sermon event usually ends, but this time it continues, because in Pastor Nimi's words, "The anointing is in the house!" The choir begins to sing, "I am what I am by the grace of the Lord. I've crossed over to destiny. I will never fail by the grace of the Lord." With these words repetitiously looped over in the background, the entire church sings and dances along, laughing and sharing embraces. In the moment, Pastor Nimi beckons Segun Oyesanya and another member forward, where arm in arm, shoulder to shoulder, they walk across the platform. The idea is that they are crossing over to their destiny together, the individual and the church together. No one doubts that "this is the day that the Lord has made."

In this book I have sought to show how dynamic movements of African Christianity have "crossed over" through the globalization of faith and proliferation of networks, primarily through the pairing of Christian expansion in Africa with migration to global New York City. African Christianity in New York City is not merely a numerical development, but a combination of people and institutions, experiences and practices, convictions about God and ways of narrating salvation, and liturgies and dances. Each of the three churches in this study have created a new social space in the city and constructed a common life rooted in Jesus and the abundance of the Spirit.

Each church embodies and emphasizes multiple identities at once, including ancient and future, local and global, cognitive and affective, body and spirit, material and immaterial. For all of the differences among the three churches, which I do not want to minimize, they share much in common, including a focus on worshiping God, an active interpretation of the world, a comprehensive understanding of salvation related to Christ's ongoing victory over evil powers, a repertoire of rigorous spiritual practices, and attendant pastoral strategies. This common sensibility paints a picture of a single story of African Christianity with connections still to be made. It may well be fair to speak of African Christianity *and* African Christianities.

Through African Christianity in New York, we can see the city and church in new ways. Each congregation can help us to remap the city and understand its imaginaries, communities, links, and hopes.[2] The cutting edge of Christian faith in New York City is flourishing in the overlooked

---

2. Mary Hancock and Smriti Srinvas, "Spaces of Modernity: Religion and the Urban in Africa," *International Journal of Urban and Regional Research* 32:3 (2008): 617-30.

Giving and Receiving

and neglected parts of the city, the margins. Here the substantial yet largely unrecognized presence of African Christianity in New York reflects a perennial theme, highlighted by Andrew Walls, of Christian history in which the "margins" are the key site for the growth, creativity, and energy of the church. The African churches of New York City are representatives of post-Western Christianity in the global city that also includes churches from Asia, Latin America, and the West Indies. In this global dimension African churches are to be seen as a "sign" of contemporary religious development more than simply measured by size or impact, as Peter Beyer observes.[3]

Living Faith

As part of the first section, in chapter one, I surveyed the landscape of Ethiopian Orthodox, Catholic, Protestant, independent, Pentecostal, Francophone, Liberian, and other African churches in New York City, arguing that the clustering of congregations, branches, communities, and overseas headquarters is related to the global city and the convergence of Christian expansion in Africa with migration. From this slice of the religious life of the city, we can see that faith is growing in the city. African churches in New York are global — Gerrie ter Haar calls them African International Churches.[4] They are also, I suggest, essentially New York City churches, a part of the social and religious landscape that pushes past the language of "immigrant churches."

While globally related via networks and circulations, each church is also locally inspired, calibrated to its context. They show a close relationship between religion, the city, globalization, and multi-directional networks. Following Saskia Sassen, I have noted the city as a switching point for global networks, a relay in the global diffusion of African Christianity. While the potential for uniformity and homogeneity is ever present with globalization, the results presented here give every indication that the globally connected city facilitates religious ferment, expansion, and diversity. That bodies of faith, reliant on the Spirit, are moving across borders at such a rate may be due to the spirituality and bodily adaptability to multi-

---

3. Peter Beyer, *Religion in a Global Society* (London: Routledge, 2006), 146-47.
4. Gerrie ter Haar, *Halfway to Paradise: African Christians in Europe* (Cardiff: Cardiff Academic Press, 1998), 191.

ple scales.[5] New York City's history with its long-established commitment to religious tolerance provides a unique and receptive space for African Christianity to flourish.

With the second part, chapters two and three, I characterized and discussed African churches in New York City as "formations," by which I mean the development of communities. In chapter two I provided a description and analysis of the pastors or spiritual leaders of the Presbyterian Church of Ghana in New York, Church of the Lord (Aladura), and the Redeemed Christian Church of God International Chapel, Brooklyn. Each leader is developing new leaders and communities across borders. The four domains of ministry — spiritual direction, healing, institution building, and cultural bridge building — bring a spiritual, social, physical, and material focus to pastoral activity, reflective of a narrative of salvation. African Christians in New York City have not moved away from a spiritually active universe, and church leaders function within this range. Rather than offer theologies of communion, pastors mediate theologies of life and for life. This is meeting a spiritual and intellectual challenge.

In chapter three, I emphasized the way that liturgy forms persons in a way of life before God. In describing the history and character of the three churches in this study, I emphasized that the experiences, practices, and beliefs of each church are shaped by personal and communal histories. In the genesis of each church, women played particularly important roles, sharing in all aspects of ministry and leadership with men. In the formulation I offered, globalization is not new or exclusively economic, but a radical space-time compression. Through connection across borders, religion in a global world provides stability, identity, meaning, direction, and power. However, the rise of African Christianity, and in particular Pentecostal modes, should not be reduced to a response to globalization and neo-liberalism.

Through the networks of people and institutions, experiences and practices from Accra, Monrovia, and Lagos, the local turns global and becomes reconstituted as a new local in New York City. Here the local stories of the Presbyterian Church of Ghana in New York, the Church of the Lord (Aladura), and the Redeemed Christian Church International Chapel, Brooklyn, exist in multiple layers, moving from New York City's history as

---

5. For a discussion, see Manuel A. Vásquez, "The Global Portability of Pneumatic Christianity: Comparing African and Latin American Pentecostalisms," unpublished paper, 2009.

New Amsterdam, to the spatial level of the boroughs of the Bronx, Brooklyn, and Manhattan. Clearly the local that is uniquely New York City is not a hermetically sealed space, but exists in continual construction within a world that is globally connected and influenced.[6] To recognize this is to also place African churches within New York City's historic trajectories of immigration, religious diversity, economic drive, and global relationship. Conceptualized this way, the local story also benefits from being placed within urban history.

As I have described throughout this study, African churches in New York City create and participate in a variety of religious and social networks. The notion of networks both grounds and contextualizes the movement of churches in a global world. In light of what we have seen, "transnationalism" should be understood to encompass religious networks that are multi-directional, rather than limited to two "national" worlds.[7] Religious networks are not limited to two sites — between, for example, Lagos and New York City — but circulate in multiple directions simultaneously. Such multi-directionality is represented in the Redeemed Christian Church of God, which is building dense networks throughout New York City and across North America, connected to a now-global church. A larger Pentecostal world of networks is also found in New York City, as evidenced by the diverse Nigerian churches in attendance at the Holy Ghost service at Madison Square Garden. Churches act as nodes in this dynamic world of religious movements and activities. In a world of global networks, it is possible to argue that African Christian geography has no single fixed point, but many connection points.

The third part of this book, chapters four through six, documented a series of central practices of the three churches. Emerging out of the experience and worship of the risen and living Lord Jesus Christ, the practices of prayer, engaging Scripture, and mission are brought into the global city. These practices at once sustain people while projecting a universal vision of life in God. Faith is not forced into a niche, but engages the city as public sphere.

In chapter four, I portrayed each church as a community immersed in the life of prayer. In prayer African Christians look to God to lead, deliver, open up new opportunities, and achieve destinies. Presence in the

---

6. Manuel A. Vásquez, "Studying Religion in Motion: A Networks Approach," *Method and Theory in the Study of Religion* 20:2 (2008): 151-84.

7. Vásquez, "Studying Religion in Motion."

global city is accompanied by "power from on high" that comes when personal stories are placed within the larger narrative of God's saving activity. Prayer is embodied, its kinetics and disciplines frequently accompanied by fasting. In its participation in the Trinitarian life of God, the life of prayer in the three churches illustrates the connection between God and the world, the spiritual and material, that is so deeply held by African believers. In chapter five, I examined how the Bible is read for life, for its living message. Scriptural texts shape communal identity, but even more than that, they bring faith into home life, the doctor's office, work, and other areas of ordinary life. The hermeneutical paradigm of thee churches brings together daily needs with a strong conviction that the Bible is powerful. The Bible is filled with promises about salvation, words that accomplish the intentions of God for life in the here and now.

In chapter six, I sought to identify the similarities and differences in the three churches' approach to mission. African churches have a strong global consciousness but diverse primary models of mission. Rather than locating their primary mission influence in intentional activities, I argued that a more diffuse urban "evangelization" is taking place in the encounters of everyday life. Healing, prayer, evangelism, and worship are its main components. In the name of Jesus, they offer a holistic and integrative soteriology that suggests human flourishing through the energies of the Spirit. Drawing on John Howard Yoder, I contended that a "migration mission" model is more operative than an institutionally driven "great commission" model. There is no indication of any dependence on the financial or strategic resources of the West for their mission work. With this vulnerability and power that comes only from the Spirit, such mission is post-Christendom.

Historically, New York City is a city of opportunity, a place where people from around the world come to build a better life. Even in difficult economic times, this remains true. However, New York City is not an urban utopia for African immigrants; it is often a site of hardship, struggle, and peril as well as opportunity. Yet they believe that God promises new life found in Jesus, evidence of which is shared in testimonies. Such positive faith in God grounds education, raising and supporting families, work, and sharing faith. Spiritual energy produces social consequences.

It is in the experiences, practices, and beliefs that operate in everyday life that we encounter something of the relevance of faith in the city. For immigrants in the global city, as Saskia Sassen reminds us, presence can be a platform for recognition. But I have argued that African Christians understand themselves to have achieved not only presence but also power.

Giving and Receiving

The power they have is found in the life of the Spirit — power from above. There is no shortage of "testimonies" to God's provision of personal and family "breakthroughs" in the global city, whether socially, economically, or even politically. Praying communities, I find, are a particular expression of such agency in the city. This is a reading of "tactics" over "strategy," to borrow from Certeau. It is social and cultural change not from the top down, but percolating from the bottom up.

Person by person, act by act, we can see African Christians helping to shape, build, and maintain New York City. First, there is the role that church members play as New Yorkers, each contributing to the building of a city endlessly under construction. Whether as a student, taxi driver, health care worker, social service provider, banker, accountant, or parent, each contributes to the economic and social fabric of the city. Second, their collective physical presence has an economic and community impact. For example, by reclaiming a vacant building and bringing business to the community, the Redeemed Christian Church of God International Chapel, Brooklyn, has played a role in the economic revitalization of their immediate geographical community. Third, there are the ethics, ideas, and hopes for life that they contribute to the city. This is a model of Christian life that goes back to the Scriptures.

In chapters seven and eight, the fourth part, I posed the natural question of the future of African churches in New York. First I developed the idea of "reverse pilgrimages" as a form of spatial connection from Africa to New York. The "mother churches" are relocating key geographies and experiences to New York, expanding the scale and scope of the church. This brings a festiveness and expectation to life in God across borders. In the final chapter, I concluded with reflections on the second generation and the manner in which faith is "translated" and identity is formed. A key component appears to be the influence of parents and adults, the community of faith. One can see how transferring faith involves transferring practices. I also noted the importance of language. The influence of baptism and church membership play differing roles not only in church attendance, but also in the way faith is given verbal expression.

In retrospect we can see how "cultural incarnations" of faith, in Kwame Bediako's turn of a phrase, have been a durable factor of African Christian migration to New York City.[8] One place we can see such transla-

---

8. Kwame Bediako, *Christianity in Africa: The Renewal of a Non-Western Religion* (Edinburgh: Edinburgh University Press and Maryknoll, N.Y.: Orbis, 1995), 109-25.

tion and enculturation continued is in the ongoing importance of African "maps of the universe." Such maps, according to our study, have been maintained as part of the "script of salvation" that guides pastoral ministry and conceptions of everyday life. There is divine protection while traveling in the city, openings for employment that only God could produce, and answers to prayers concerning immigration status. Faith is understood to lead to new life in the city. For Pentecostal and independent believers in particular, the importance of representing a trans-cultural faith is considerable. Yet in the end, cultural particularities, from language to material symbols to prayer traditions, are resources that all African believers draw upon in their global journey. As religious and other forms of African culture relocate to New York City, the potential of disruption is ever present. However, as I have followed the stories of church life, I have seen that continuities of faith are maintained and applied to new challenges. Traditions are always evolving, and as African Christianity encounters New York City, new dynamics of faith and ecclesial life will be the result.

Catholicity in the City

> .... Africa has not become the subject of serious theological inquiry in the United States, or generally in the West. On the contrary, by and large, African issues and concerns remain peripheral to the theological project in the West. In theology, just like in other disciplines, no serious attempts are made to engage Africa's history, traditions, and the historical challenges facing African Christians. In the absence of serious inquiry, engagement with Africa comes to be reduced to Christian activism grounded in some form of sentimental humanitarianism. This is particularly disastrous for the future of World Christianity; for in the absence of serious intellectual/theological engagement, talk about the growing significance of Africa within World Christianity sounds hollow, or at best it is a hope based on the usual misleading generalizations and outdated clichés.[9]

These challenging words from Emmanuel Katongole lead me to ask how the Presbyterian Church of Ghana in New York, the Church of the Lord (Aladura), and the Redeemed Christian Church International Chapel,

---

9. Emmanuel Katongole, "A Tale of Many Stories," in *Shaping a Global Theological Mind*, ed. Darren C. Marks (Aldershot: Ashgate, 2008), 89.

Giving and Receiving

Brooklyn, can interrupt our imagination in the West. How do they help us take seriously the theological and spiritual significance of African Christianity? How do they help us understand a way of being in the city and world? And how do we do so in a way that does not, as Gerrie ter Haar warns, "distance [us] from African Christians and . . . classify them as a different type of Christian"?[10]

We need a framework that opens the door for mutuality in a shared quest for faithful discipleship, of "exchange" in the global city, one that arises from an expectation that true ecclesia is intercultural. To say this is to believe that the particularities of Christian faith, reflected in stories of translation across space and time, ultimately affirm a universal faith. If we are open, we can learn in unexpected ways. While offering no quick and easy formulations, this approach may lead to rich and unexpected outcomes. Here we can benefit from the work of Emmanuel Katongole and Andrew Walls. Andrew Walls is widely recognized as the leading interpreter of world Christianity in its encounter with culture. A historian trained in Patristics, Walls found himself relearning church history while living in Africa.[11] Emmanuel Katongole is a priest from the diocese of Uganda, trained in philosophy, and now teaching theology in the United States.[12] Through the unique perspectives of Walls and Katongole, we can move from segregation and division in Christian faith to mutuality and interconnection.

For Emmanuel Katongole, African Christianity is one part of the single story of Christian faith. As I indicated in chapter six, he questions the legitimacy of "Western/non-western" and "North/South" divisions within Christianity.[13] Katongole's basic concern is that such distinctions, present for example in Philip Jenkins's work, feed Christian assent to geopolitical divisions.[14] In their place Katongole proposes the lens of catholicity, a return for the church to its origins and identity in Christ, so that

---

10. ter Haar, *Halfway to Paradise*, 161.

11. For biographical background, see Mark R. Gornik, "Andrew Walls and the Transformation of Christianity," *Catalyst* 31:3 (2005): 5-6.

12. For autobiographical background, see Katongole, "A Tale of Many Stories," 89-93, and Katongole, *The Sacrifice of Africa: A Political Theology for Africa* (Grand Rapids: Eerdmans, 2011).

13. Emmanuel Katongole, Review of Lamin Sanneh, *Whose Religion Is Christianity? The Gospel Beyond the West*, *Pro Ecclesia* 15:1 (2006): 143.

14. Emmanuel M. Katongole, "Hauerwasian Hooks, Stories, and the Social Imagination of the 'The Next Christendom,'" in *A Future for Africa: Critical Essays in Christian Social Imagination* (Scranton: Scranton University Press, 2005), 231-52.

we may see the churches of Africa as part of the "universal communion of discipleship":[15]

> For what a radical notion of Catholicity names is not mere geographical distribution of Christians but the presence of concrete communities and practices that are at once local and global in their very nature and way of life. It is through concrete church communities, made possible through such practices as baptism, that the local and universal can be seen to penetrate each other and to exist as internal one to another.[16]

While Katongole urges a framework of catholicity, Andrew Walls offers what he calls "Ephesian Christianity" as a way of seeing the wider church. Ephesian Christianity comes from Walls's reading of the New Testament story as one of cross-cultural movement, as described in the Epistle to the Ephesians.[17] For Walls, the story in Ephesians 2–4 is a moment when two culturally distinct Christian cultures, Jewish and Hellenistic, could have formed two different churches, but instead together they formed one new community. The result was not the erasure of difference, but a richness of cultural mutuality that birthed a deeper comprehension of Christ. Looking over Christian history, Walls believes the experience described in Ephesians was a brief episode that soon passed, but that such a time may now have come again:

> Like the old Jerusalem Christians, Western Christians [have] long grown used to the idea that they were guardians of a "standard" Christianity; also like them, they find themselves in the presence of new expressions of Christianity, and new Christian lifestyles that have developed or are developing under the guidance of the Holy Spirit to display Christ under the conditions of African, Indian, Chinese, Korean, and Latin American life.[18]

Walls identifies two likely Western responses to the current Ephesian moment: one is to seek to protect or even try to establish its position as

---

15. Katongole, Review of Lamin Sanneh, *Whose Religion Is Christianity?*, 144.
16. Katongole, Review of Lamin Sanneh, *Whose Religion Is Christianity?*, 144.
17. Andrew F. Walls, *The Cross-Cultural Process in Christian History: Studies in the Transmission and Appropriation of Christian Faith* (Maryknoll, N.Y.: Orbis, 2002), 72-81.
18. Walls, *The Cross-Cultural Process*, 78.

normative; the other is to acknowledge other viewpoints but ignore any deep engagement.[19] A very different approach is presented in Ephesians:

> The Ephesian metaphors of the temple and the body show each of the culture-specific segments as necessary to the body but as incomplete in itself. Only in Christ does completion, fullness, dwell. And Christ's completion, as we have seen, comes from all humanity, from the translation of the life of Jesus into the lifeways of the world's cultures and subcultures through history. None of us can reach Christ's completeness on our own. We need each other's vision to correct, enlarge and focus our own; only together are we complete in Christ.[20]

When different cultures together form a complete body of Christ, Walls suggests that growth in theological knowledge and comprehension will occur, along with material sharing.[21] As Walls has long argued, diffusion is the lifeblood of Christian faith;[22] with "diffusion across cultural lines" has always come the salvation of Christianity.[23] Herein is also the possibility of the realization of the full body of Christ.[24]

Katongole and Walls have similar approaches to Christianity and the church: each underscores the mutual enrichment that can come to the whole body of Christ. They both seek alternate ways of speaking about "world Christianity," and stay far away from categories like "Christendom." Both scholars also look at the church from the ground up. Katongole is looking for signs of the new social imagination, giving attention to what is taking place in daily life; Walls seeks to understand theology, discipleship, and Christian life through the phenomena of local translations.[25]

Neither Walls nor Katongole tries to fit faith into a neat ecclesiastical box, instead allowing concrete ecclesial communities (as opposed to abstract concepts of the church) to animate a wider conversation involving

---

19. Walls, *The Cross-Cultural Process*, 78-79.
20. Walls, *The Cross-Cultural Process*, 79.
21. Walls, *The Cross-Cultural Process*, 79-81.
22. Andrew F. Walls, "Converts or Proselytes? The Crisis over Conversion in the Early Church," *International Bulletin of Mission* 28:1 (January 2004): 2-6.
23. Andrew F. Walls, *The Missionary Movement in Christian History: Studies in the Transmission of Faith* (Maryknoll, N.Y.: Orbis, 1996), 2.
24. Walls, *The Cross-Cultural Process*, 69.
25. James L. Cox, *A Guide to the Phenomenology of Religion: Key Figures, Formative Influences and Subsequent Debates* (London: Continuum, 2006), 153-59, describes Walls as a phenomenologist of religion.

social imagination and theological renewal. In other words, for Walls and Katongole much more is at work than a "comparative ecclesiology."[26] While comparative ecclesiology implies that churches learn about each other simply for the purpose of maintaining a kind of enlightened tolerance of each other's traditions — a dynamic that could well leave cultural and theological divisions intact — Walls and Katongole emphasize mutuality, mission, catholicity, and reconciliation. Culturally diverse forms of Christian faith are a gift to be celebrated, not a problem to be resolved.

Surely this approach has relevance for examining our New York City churches. Differences can lead to divergence, but in recognizing differences there is also an opening for growth.[27] In New York City, with its many churches from around the world and a diversity of itineraries, experiences, practices, and beliefs, there is the possibility of new theological conversations, breakthroughs, and constructions. Because none of us can reach Christ's completeness without one another, there is a great need for reading the Scriptures together, praying together, and celebrating a common faith in Jesus. So these churches do not simply present us with an opportunity for observation; they present us with a far richer gift.

Gifts and Challenges

I have primarily focused on providing a description and contextual interpretation of African churches in New York. But I think more is possible, with the potential for great enrichment to the West. This cannot be done in the abstract. Rather, as Emmanuel Katongole emphasizes, the resources required for strengthening faith are to be drawn from ecclesial communities that live and imagine the gospel; they come from lives dedicated to God and dependent upon the Spirit.[28] The lived theologies and ethnographies of diverse world Christianities should therefore be our teachers. What do the particular stories, people, and leaders of the Presbyterian Church of Ghana in New York, the Church of the Lord (Aladura), and the

---

26. Nicholas M. Healy, "'By the Working of the Holy Spirit': The Crisis of Authority in the Christian Churches," *Anglican Theological Review* 88:1 (2006): 13.

27. John Howard Yoder, "On Christian Unity: The Way from Below," *Pro Ecclesia* 9:2 (2000): 178-79.

28. Emmanuel M. Katongole, "Prospects of Ecclesia in Africa in the Twenty-First Century," *Logos* 4:1 (2001): 193, and *A Future for Africa: Critical Essays in Christian Social Imagination*.

Giving and Receiving

Redeemed Christian Church of God International Chapel, Brooklyn, offer to enrich the life of the churches of the West? How can they contribute to a larger inter-cultural conversation? Building on the sacramental character of catholicity and the theology of Ephesians, we can look for gifts to be given and embraced.[29] In Christian theology, led by the Spirit, every gift from God is to be shared with others in Jesus' name.

A first gift of African churches is that they can help the churches of the West to see themselves within a larger story. We live in a time of monumental transitions, and one of the most important is the shifting center of Christian gravity. African churches in New York can help the churches of the West see themselves as interdependent, not as mission leaders or theological standard bearers. This involves learning church history again, changing the curriculum from a Western-centered one to one that begins in Africa and moves to all the continents. It means new maps, mental and real.

A second gift of African churches is an invitation to name ourselves by Pentecost. A primary gift of African Christianity to the West, and to the church as a whole, is the Holy Spirit. Through the name of Jesus, African Christians believe the Spirit brings forth new birth, heals the sick, makes days new, conquers the past, casts out evil spirits, answers prayers, speaks in dreams, and raises to new life. Ecstatic praise is another element of an ecclesiology of the Spirit. The lengthy worship services of African churches may be difficult for western Christians to understand and participate in, but if theological works can be lengthy because "theological praise of the eternally bounteous God is never-ending,"[30] I know African Christians would say the same applies to worship in the Spirit.

Jürgen Moltmann's reflections on the Spirit offer theological bridges among diverse ecclesiastical traditions and cultures. I found that his theological description of the Spirit's work in *The Spirit of Life* matches the church life I experienced, confirming his constructive "universal affirmation."[31] As

---

29. Emmanuel Katongole, "The Tales of African Christianity: Singing a New Song in the Midst of Africa's Histories," unpublished paper, 2005. As inspiration for making this list, I celebrate the late David A. Shank's pioneering work; see Shank, "What Western Christians Can Learn from African-Initiated Churches," in *Mission from the Margins: Selected Writings from the Life and Ministry of David A. Shank,* ed. James R. Krabill (Elkhart: Institute for Mennonite Studies, 2010), 219-30.

30. Jürgen Moltmann, *Experiences in Theology: Ways and Forms of Christian Theology,* trans. Margaret Kohl (Minneapolis: Fortress Press, 2000), 14.

31. Jürgen Moltmann, *The Spirit of Life: A Universal Affirmation,* trans. Margaret Kohl (Minneapolis: Fortress, 1992).

CONCLUSION

Ogbu Kalu's *African Pentecostalism: An Introduction* points out, Pentecostalism is a dynamic movement.[32] Viewed this way, African Christianity represents one strand of a global pneumatology. Theologians Amos Yong, J. Kwabena Asamoah-Gyadu, and Sarah Coakley are also important in opening up new horizons in this direction.[33]

A third gift of African Christianity is a sacramental imagination. From birth to death, African Christians believe that their lives are in the hands of God. In tangible, everyday ways, they believe that in God they "live, move and have [their] being."[34] Life is filled with sacramental value; the Spirit's presence is not confined to the Eucharist or the occasional miracle that is a sign of God, but fills all of life and all of creation.[35] Ultimately, I would describe African Christianity as a theology of life, of human flourishing. The world is place of spiritual conflict, and Christ is powerful over all powers and forces. In the West, this can help us recover a sense of the spiritual in the physical and material, of the eternal in the present.

African Christians do not have a small God. Historically, significant theologies are often responses to times of instability, struggle, and anxiety in the world. In a global age, this is true of African Christianity, with its understanding of a free and all-powerful God that goes hand in hand with an expectation of redemption in this unstable and divided world. African Christians stake their claims to life in the reality of God, Jesus, and the Spirit, and for this reason, testimony is crucial.[36] They know God to be true in their lives — this is what they testify. But they also read about similar activity in Scripture, locating their story in God's story. In the Book of Acts Philip said to Nathanael, "Come and see," so African Christians continue to offer their testimonies as reason for faith.[37]

A fourth gift of African churches is a holistic anthropology and ap-

---

32. Ogbu Kalu, *African Pentecostalism: An Introduction* (Oxford: Oxford University Press, 2008), 288.

33. Amos Yong, *The Spirit Poured Out on All Flesh: Pentecostalism and the Possibility of Global Theology* (Grand Rapids: Baker Academic, 2005). See also Kirsteen Kim, *The Holy Spirit in the World: A Global Conversation* (Maryknoll, N.Y.: Orbis, 2007).

34. Acts 17:28, cf. 17:26.

35. For historical factors, see Regina Mara Schwartz, *Sacramental Poetics at the Dawn of Secularism: When God Left the World* (Stanford: Stanford University Press, 2008).

36. For the important place of testimony in theology, see Walter Brueggemann, *Theology of the Old Testament: Testimony, Dispute and Advocacy* (Minneapolis: Fortress Press, 1997), 119-20.

37. John 1:46. This is a ground of evangelism in Africa, as noted by John S. Mbiti, *Bible and Theology in African Christianity* (Nairobi: Oxford University Press, 1986), 8-9.

proach to Christian practice. Prayer, fasting, reading Scripture, and worship are all linked to the embodiment of Christian faith, an emphasis that can help the West especially recover the body in intrinsic relationship to God and formation. As James K. A. Smith observes of Pentecostalism, the "emphasis on the healing of the body is an affirmation of the goodness of embodiment."[38] This is also true, as we have seen, in the spirituality of worship, prayer, and fasting. The goodness of embodiment affirms God's creation and world.[39] The contrast with many Western expressions is significant. In *A Secular Age,* Charles Taylor sees real differences between embodied and intellectualistic versions of Christianity in their encounters with modernity.[40] For Taylor, "official Christianity has gone through what we can call an 'excarnation,' a transfer out of embodied, 'enfleshed' forms of religious life, to those which are more 'in the head.'"[41] Taylor goes on to emphasize, "The issue here is not how many positive invocations of the body we hear.... The issue is whether our relation to the highest — God for believers ... is mediated in bodily form."[42]

A fifth gift is an enlarged reading of Scripture. African churches, belonging to a global communion, can offer all of us new readings of the Biblical text. They can help the West recover long-neglected themes of deliverance, healing, release, power, and the Spirit. African Christians can also help the West recover the Gospels and Acts — the *stories* of the New Testament — and not just privilege Paul, as is so often the case. They can help us read the whole canon without a rational filter that limits the ongoing work of God in the world. Overall emphasis is placed on not just reading but living within the narrative that Scripture records. This is a powerful hermeneutical approach, with obvious affinities to narrative and biblical-theological readings, and able to impact many areas of ecclesial and mission life.

A sixth gift is resources for ecclesiology. We have seen how African churches offer models of praise and worship. There are other areas where their spirituality and common life are a challenge, and contribute to ad-

---

38. James K. A. Smith, "Teaching a Calvinist to Dance," *Christianity Today,* May 2008, 45.

39. Smith, "Teaching a Calvinist to Dance."

40. Charles Taylor, *A Secular Age* (Cambridge: The Belknap Press of Harvard University, 2007), 71, 554.

41. Taylor, *A Secular Age,* 554.

42. Taylor, *A Secular Age,* 554, See also Troels Engberg-Pedersen, *Cosmology and Self in the Apostle Paul: The Material Spirit* (Oxford: Oxford University Press, 2010).

vances in global ecclesiology. In African churches, even with their different polities, everyone has a gift and calling, with barriers to ministry broken down between men and women at every level. Ministry does not pivot on an academic model; it is shared and shaped by the Spirit. The extended festive celebration of God at the start of the week, bodies and the body of Christ offering praise to God, reading the Bible through the Spirit for hope and direction — all this should be a challenge to us. Andrew Walls writes of the African Independent Churches, "One of the remarkable features of the independent churches for a westerner is their combination of the ritual and hierarchical with the charismatic and spontaneous. The West knows both types of religion, but — at least until recently — identifies them with different traditions. The independents combine them in the same tradition."[43] Is there not also here a pattern for community life to be guided by both freedom and the structures necessary for institutional life? How does the pneumatic and scriptural imagination work in worship?

As a worshiping community, we encounter in African churches an extended family, a community across borders that shares in a journey of life from birth to death. During a conversation, Rev. Asiedu remarked of Angelina Akiwumi, an elder in the church, "You know she's my sister." I didn't know that, and it turns out, as far as I can tell, they are family members only "in Christ." Members of the three churches have found, in Afe Adogame's words, "places to feel at home" and a "home away from home."[44] To be "home away from home" is also a theological function, as M. L. Daneel has stressed.[45] But more practically, African churches in New York City are about a family that will care for your children, help with a job lead, praise God for your success, and carry burdens that no one else can.[46]

A seventh gift is a model of mission. Situated in global networks, these three churches are on the cutting edge of urban ministry in the twenty-first century. Models more of being than of doing, of witness rather than of moral transformation, these churches' mission practice is holistic — heal-

---

43. Walls, *The Missionary Movement in Christian History*, 118.

44. Afe Adogame, "The Quest for Space in the Global Spiritual Marketplace," *International Review of Mission* 89:354 (2000): 407.

45. M. L. Daneel, *Quest for Belonging: Introduction to a Study of African Independent Churches* (Zimbabwe: Mambo Press, 1987), and F. B. Welbourn and B. A. Ogot, *A Place to Feel at Home: A Study of Two Independent Churches in Western Kenya* (London: Oxford University Press, 1966). Both talk about the African independent church life as a place to feel at home, socially and theologically.

46. ter Haar, *Halfway to Paradise*, 43, 107.

Giving and Receiving

ing, delivering, and praying — because salvation is comprehensive. If the location of mission is the city, the mode is the displaced body of Christ. Recalling the ecclesial location marked out in 1 Peter, addressed to the "exiles of the dispersion,"[47] African churches are both fully present to the local and ever in motion within the global. It is the church that is in mission, not a mission organization. As John Howard Yoder contended, exile serves to provide normative direction for a faithful mode of social existence.[48] This theme is highly relevant for our global moment. They are announcing good news and working to see persons, families, and communities become whole in Christ. In the name of Jesus they are proclaiming life, eternal and without fear, yet with vulnerability. They are not seeking the transformation of others or systems as much as witnessing to new life.

Through their involvement in the economy and social fabric they are contributing to the overall flourishing of New York, thereby witnessing to God's peace for the city.[49] Like in the Old Testament, the common life and commitments of the people of God can be a light among the nations.[50] African Christians in New York model the Jeremiah paradigm, found also in 1 Peter and elsewhere in the New Testament, which urges the people of God in exile to "seek the peace and prosperity of the city to which I have carried you into exile. Pray to the Lord for it, because if it has peace, you too will have peace."[51] No city is ever finished, and the African Christians who live in its buildings, walk its streets, travel its subways, raise their families in it, and contribute to its economic life are ever renewing New York City.[52] Here is a model of urban ministry, one that is contextual and without pretense, fitting ideally within pluralistic New York City. Diaspora is

---

47. 1 Peter 1:1.

48. John Howard Yoder, *For the Nations: Essays Public and Evangelical* (Grand Rapids: Eerdmans, 1997), 51-78. For a larger discussion, see Jonathan Boyarin and Daniel Boyarin, *Powers of Diaspora: Two Essays on the Relevance of Jewish Culture* (Minneapolis: University of Minnesota Press, 2002); Edward Said, *Reflections on Exile and Other Themes* (Cambridge: Harvard University Press, 2000); and Daniel L. Smith-Christopher, *A Biblical Theology of Exile* (Minneapolis: Fortress Press, 2002).

49. Here once again I have great appreciation for the argument of John Howard Yoder in *As You Go: The Old Mission in a New Day* (Scottdale: Herald Press, 1961).

50. James Chukwuma Okoye, *Israel Among the Nations: A Mission Theology of the Old Testament* (Maryknoll, N.Y.: Orbis, 2006), 129-43. This is of course a theme also found in the New Testament, but it rests on the Old Testament.

51. Jeremiah 29:7; cf. 1 Peter 1:1, 2:8-12.

52. Michael de Certeau, "Walking in the City," in *The Practice of Everyday Life*, trans. Steven Rendall (Berkeley: University of California Press, 1984), 91-110.

not as much a mission as the mission itself.⁵³ African churches in New York City offer creative and relevant examples of what a "missional church" can be like in a post-Christendom setting,⁵⁴ and point to broader ways of engaging a world in need of healing.⁵⁵

*An eighth gift is a repositioning of the concept of citizenship and concern for immigrants.*⁵⁶ We need a theology of migration.⁵⁷ To start, African Christians remind the church it is first of all an international body with a distinctive set of moral and political outlooks and obligations. We may not live in a post-national age, but the lens of religion can help us see the importance of denationalizing social rights and obligations, moving toward greater protection for all immigrants. African churches can help churches of the West see themselves as but one member of a global body, and in a post 9/11 world, this has fresh importance. Herein lies the task of learning a new narrative, and unlearning a politically dominant one.⁵⁸ With this, Christian faith can come to be defined more by its interdependencies than by borders or nationalities. Indeed, these African churches can help us live more completely in a world where space and place are in continual motion.

We should have great appreciation for the entrepreneurial, spiritual, and social energy immigrants bring to the West.⁵⁹ Without drawing attention to themselves or taking credit, immigrants are at the forefront of renewing neighborhoods throughout New York City. All of this should be recognized in any discussion of public policy, which should now take into account the role of networks in a global age.⁶⁰ Immigration policy needs

---

53. Yoder, *For the Nations*, 51-78.

54. An introduction to key issues is found in Wilbert R. Shenk, "New Wineskins for New Wine: Toward a Post-Christendom Ecclesiology," *International Bulletin of Missionary Research* 29:2 (2005): 73-79.

55. For reflections on mission, see Marthinus L. Daneel, *African Earthkeepers: Wholistic Interfaith Mission* (Maryknoll, N.Y.: Orbis, 2001).

56. For an excellent discussion, see Manuel Vásquez, "Dispatches from the Borderlands: The Immigration Impasse: How Did We Get Here," online at http://www.religiondispatches.org/Gui/Content.aspx?Page=AR&Id=92&SP=1 (accessed Feb. 27, 2008).

57. See the work of Daniel Groody, "Theology in the Age of Migration," *National Catholic Reporter*, September 14, 2009.

58. Katongole, *A Future for Africa*.

59. Fiscal Policy Institute, "Working for a Better Life: A Profile of Immigrants in the New York State Economy," 2007, available at http://www.fiscalpolicy.org/publications2007/FPI_ImmReport_WorkingforaBetterLife.pdf.

60. See Saskia Sassen, "Regulating Immigration in a Global Age: A New Policy Landscape," *Parallax* 11:1 (2005): 35-45.

Giving and Receiving

reframing. More immediately, diversity and chain migration should be considered important in any new legislation. Christian thought and language in the areas of the immigrant, the stranger, hospitality, and justice are especially important to invoke in a time of economic crisis and reactionary politics. At the very least, African immigrants can remind Americans that each of us is part of an immigrant story, and remind Christians that we are all aliens and strangers. We must remember our calling and identity that moves beyond borders, working toward active theologies of welcome, hospitality, and migration.

In summary, as Rowan Williams underscores, learning from the body of Christ where there are differences touched by history and culture is hard and risky work.[61] Therefore, it will require "listening" and perhaps "doing nothing but sharing the contemplation of Christ."[62] But such work is the gift of the gospel as the church shares in the ongoing extension of the Christian story.

Of course, in a global world, listening is beneficial in all directions. It is not my place to seek in any way to correct, reformulate, or supplement the theology and practice of African churches of New York. Still, from time to time members and leaders in the three churches expressed a desire to hear from me any potentially critical observations or questions that arose during my research. So in a spirit of mutuality, I offer three areas for further exploration on the part of the churches.

A first area for consideration is the relationship between the resurrection and the cross, power and suffering. How does spiritual power come to express itself in self-giving love for the other? Is there a place for weakness, vulnerability, and struggle? A theological emphasis on the resurrection produces a powerful way of being in the world, yet there can be a lack of vulnerability among members. J. Kwabena Asamoah-Gyadu thinks that in the case of barrenness, for example, the cross could add empathy to the Pentecostal movement in Ghana.[63] What would happen if the dynamism of resurrection power also brought a pastoral theology of the cross to bear on personal struggle and suffering? Such a combination of the self-giving of the cross with the renewal of the resurrection could provide a new theo-

---

61. Rowan Williams, "On Making Moral Decisions," *Anglican Theological Review* 81:1 (1999): 295-308.

62. Williams, "On Making Moral Decisions," 308.

63. J. Kwabena Asamoah-Gyadu, "'Broken Calabashes and Covenants of Fruitfulness': Cursing Barrenness in Contemporary African Christianity," *Journal of Religion in Africa* 37:4 (2007): 458.

logical paradigm. Of course, the cross is a form of power, the power of costly self-giving. And being with us in our suffering is for the Apostle Paul a key element of the Spirit's work. Power and its relationship to service will also influence models of church leadership. Spiritual authority and the ways of negotiating difference can profoundly impact church life.[64]

A second area for renewed thinking is the relationship between new African immigrants and African Americans. New African immigrants and African Americans both came to New York City as part of "great" migrations, the former from the global south, the latter from the American south.[65] But in the crucible of seeking scarce housing and jobs in, for example, Harlem or the Bronx, there can be a distance and even tension between these two communities.[66] Different histories can bring different politics, social perspectives, and religious practices.[67] In matters of identity and drawing in African and West Indian communities to the larger black community, there will discussions around the meaning of diaspora. But on the ground, there are stereotypes that prevent relationships and friendships. What is required is bridge building, and a good place to start is at the church level. Intentional involvement is crucial.

A third area for exploration involves the relationship to history. The more a church can learn of its own story and Christian past, the more it can appreciate its understanding and practice of Christian life in the present. History also connects to the catholicity of the church. From the Patristic period to the present, history can provide different ways of seeing African church life, evaluating influences, or considering theological challenges. For example, the classic study by Kwame Bediako, *Theology and Identity*,[68] brings contemporary African questions into conversation with

---

64. For larger concerns in this area, see Emmanuel Katongole, "Kannungu and the Movement for the Restoration of the Ten Commandments of God in Uganda: A Challenge for Christian Social Imagination," *Logos* 6:3 (2003): 108-43.

65. See Isabel Wilkerson, *The Warmth of Other Suns: The Epic Story of America's Great Migration* (New York: Random House, 2010).

66. Sam Dolnick, "For African Immigrants, Bronx Culture Clash Turns Violent," *New York Times*, October 19, 2009, http://www.nytimes.com/2009/10/20/nyregion/20africans.html?scp=1&sq=africans%20bronx%20african%20americans&st=cse.

67. Yvette M. Alex-Assensoh, "African Immigrants and African-Americans: An Analysis of Voluntary African Immigration and the Evolution of Black Ethnic Politics in America," *African and Asian Studies* 8:1-2 (2009): 89-124.

68. Kwame Bediako, *Theology and Identity: The Impact of Culture Upon Christian Thought in the Second Century and in Modern Africa* (Oxford: Regnum Books, 1992).

Giving and Receiving

early Christianity. History can open new windows on the social identity of the church, moral economy, and political thought. History can shed new light on political life for a multi-religious world. Overall, such a deepening of historical perspective at the grassroots level offers a basis for enhanced inter-cultural learning.[69]

Christian faith is dynamic, not static. The Spirit still leads the church into transformation through the ongoing story of salvation. In inter-cultural mutuality, a charismatic community across borders, there is great hope for new insight in Christian thought and life for the twenty-first century.

The Word Made Global

Perhaps the place to end is where we began, with a return to the metaphor of the Word made global. Running through John's Gospel are a series of emphases: the experience of the Spirit through the gift of Jesus, the centrality of new life in God, an assumption of Christ's extension to all of creation, and the expectation that wonders are yet to be performed by every disciple.[70] In John's Gospel, the resurrection story of Jesus continues in the presence of communities that, having encountered the body of the One who is risen, rise up to new lives of forgiveness, hope, sharing, and witnessing. It is through the community of those touched by the power of God that the Spirit is encountered.[71] The Word made flesh is found in vulnerable bodies that testify to the power of the risen Christ.

The stories of the Church of the Lord (Aladura), Presbyterian Church of Ghana in New York, and Redeemed Christian Church of God International Chapel, Brooklyn, show how faith that worships the Lord Je-

---

69. Michael N. C Poon, "Patristic Theology," in *Global Dictionary of Theology*, ed. William R. Dyrness and Veli-Matti Kärkkäinen (Downers Grove, Ill.: IVP Academic, 2008), 630.

70. In addition to John 1:14, see John 1:1, with its correlation to Genesis 1:1 and creation, John 14:12, with its expectation that "you will do greater things," and the promise of the Spirit in John 16:7. Jesus is interpreted as the Word made flesh and then transferred to the Spirit dwelling in flesh. On the Spirit in John's prologue, see David F. Ford, *Christian Wisdom: Desiring God and Learning in Love* (Cambridge: Cambridge University Press, 2007), 53-56.

71. For these reflections, focused on John 20–21, I am indebted to Harold W. Attridge, "Resurrection in the Fourth Gospel," unpublished paper, SNTS Johannine Literature Seminar, Aberdeen, 2006. I thank my friend Skip Masback for sharing this paper with me.

sus Christ has traveled with them from Monrovia, Accra, and Lagos. Each ecclesial narrative is a unique and imaginative rehearsing of the gospel, but all three point to an energizing vision and experience of God global in scale, local in practice, and Catholic in character. Indeed, this is what it means to be the body of Christ. If Christian faith requires witnesses before reasons, testimonies of resurrection life before arguments, then the truth of the gospel is in evidence in these churches.

I began this study wanting to learn about African Christianity, New York City, and the two together. In the pilgrimages of faith, struggle, and joy found in the three churches of this study along with the scores of other African communities of faith present in New York City, I also found an opening for a fresh encounter with the Word made flesh. In a global world of "uncertainty and instability," African churches preach dependence upon God while living the risks of faith.[72] Read against the claims of Christ on our bodies, individual and communal, the African churches of New York offer new invitations for discipleship. But while gifts can be offered, receiving them requires another journey.

---

72. For a significant analysis but a different response, see Mark C. Taylor, *After God* (Chicago: University of Chicago Press, 2007).

Epilogue: The Word Keeps Moving

It has been the burden of this book to demonstrate that African Christianity in New York City is a significant, dynamic, and globally circulating movement. This potential continues to develop, as I found in the three churches following the major period of my participation and research.

Change is the only constant of life in a globalizing world. This thought comes to mind on Sunday June 24, 2007, Nimi and Wapaemi Wariboko's last Sunday as pastors of the Brooklyn parish they had poured their lives into for nearly a decade. With his Ph.D. from Princeton Theological Seminary in hand, Nimi accepted a fulltime academic position in ethics at Andover-Newton Theological Seminary. They were moving in a few weeks, their life built in New York uprooted for new opportunities.

Ever the business school professor, Pastor Nimi put a succession plan in place before making an announcement to the church. He first informed the Redeemed Christian Church of God North American Chairman, James Fadele, and then the workers. Pastor Nimi wanted the new pastor to succeed, for the church to realize it was at "the beginning of the beginning." In a religious environment where pastoral departures often represent divisions, he was determined that this church would be different. When internal choices turned down the position, Fadele and Wariboko selected Pastor Dolapo Osinfade. A pastor of a Staten Island branch of the Redeemed Christian Church of God, Pastor Dolapo had been in New York City for three years.

The Waribokos' final Sunday was an anointing service, and it seemed that the teaching, singing, preaching, praying, and testifying stayed decibels above any other service. Shifting from the sermon to a season of anointing, Pastor Nimi summoned people forward — those in need of fruit of the womb, those starting a business, those in need of the gift of prophecy and

EPILOGUE

Fig. A. Pastor Dolapo Osinfade receiving the Spirit of leadership, Pastor Nimi Wariboko's last service as pastor in Brooklyn, 2007

wisdom. Person by person he laid hands on and prayed for them, some swooning in the Spirit, others simply returning to their seats. Pastor Nimi was not leaving them behind; he was simply ready to go to the "next level," empowered by the Spirit.

On this day, beneath the shadows of the wide-brimmed hats of the women were hidden many a tear-stained face. When Wapaemi Wariboko stood before the congregation, she brought the new pastor's two sons forward and asked the church to make a place for them, just like they did for her family. Her voice barely held together. "We are family," she stated simply. The room was painfully silent except for the sound of crying.

The concluding act of Pastor Nimi's final service as pastor was not a charge or public word to his successor. Instead, as Pastor Dolapo lay on the floor of the sanctuary, arms open before both God and the congregation, Pastor Nimi passed on what he called the "flow," transferring the Spirit and passing on the mantle of leadership. Herein is an image that captures African Christianity in a global world. Just as the Spirit "flows" from one pastor to another, so does the Word keep moving, a global migration of the

The Word Keeps Moving

Spirit that started on the streets of Lagos and moves through global urban networks to the streets of Brooklyn.

Under the leadership of Pastor Dolapo, the work of Redeemed Christian Church of God International Chapel, Brooklyn, carries on in new ways. Her theme for the church is "Changing Lives . . . Empowering Generations," emphasizing to her members that "there is a better life for them in Christ Jesus. In Christ, you are a new creation."[1] While some members would leave after Pastor Nimi, including Segun and Bola Oyesanya, two workers who were an integral part of the church, new members arrive and are helping to lead the church. The "international" commitment of the church is being underscored, and Saturday mornings an evangelism team goes out in the neighborhood, knocking on doors and meeting new people with whom to share the gospel. The result, Sister Catherine reports, is new church members — and not just Nigerians, but Haitians and West Indians. The building they rent is still for sale, but the façade has been rebuilt. With faith, prayer, and every dollar they can put together, they expect one day to purchase it — or something better.

A move was in the works for some years for the Presbyterian Church of Ghana. In July 2007 they traded the pews of the Mount Morris Church for the folding chairs of their new building on 123rd Street. In the beautifully retrofitted gym, basketball hoops are now joined with colorful fabrics that wave across the room, pictures of Jesus, inspiration banners, and the flags of America, Ghana, and the Presbyterian Church of Ghana.

Present to inaugurate the new sanctuary in 2007 was the Catechist Abboah-Offei, who led a revival. In the summer of 2009, once again the Presbyterian Church was having a revival with Catechist Abboah-Offei and Evangelist Samuel Asare. As I walked up the stairs of the church, a member related that the "Bishop is here." Had the Catechist received a promotion, I asked. "No, that's just the way we think of him."[2] Whether in the morning, afternoon, or evening, church members turned out in great numbers to praise God, learn about healing, testify to spiritual realities, and participate in deliverance sessions. The team from Ghana is more engaged than ever in training local leaders in the ways of healing ministry intended to serve the church as "humanity."

For the youth program, the new building means more space. Rex Agyemang and the youth no longer must meet in the basement, but in-

---

1. Interview, Pastor Dolapo Osinfade, May 10, 2009.
2. June 30, 2009.

stead gather in their own room. Rex steadily continues to urge the youth along on their Christian walk and leads activities such as summer camp.

Rev. Asiedu's office remains always open, his mobile phone ready to receive a call for prayer and assistance at any time of the day or night. Trips to Ghana continue, of course, as do visits from Ghana by church leaders who bring the Word and healing. People are being helped and healed on their journeys of faith, and the message of Jesus and grace is proclaimed across borders. Through prayer and mutual support, the church family continues to care for one another.

In 2008, Mother Cooper was officially promoted to the Overseer of the American Diocese of the Church of the Lord (Aladura). Drawing together her two life passions, she continued to make plans to return to Monrovia to dedicate a new building for the orphanage in 2010, coinciding with a Church of the Lord (Aladura) assembly meeting planned for Monrovia.

For the Church of the Lord (Aladura) in the Bronx, the yearly Tabborrar festival in August continues to be a benchmark. Heartbreak struck, however, during the 2009 Tabborrar season. Minister Joy was not feeling well, and her family took her to a Manhattan hospital. She improved briefly, but early on a Sunday morning, Mother Cooper received a telephone call from the hospital that Joy had died in her sleep. Through their tears, the church came to see that Joy had been getting ready to leave them. In the months before, her prophecies had been even more strong and forceful than usual. Within hours of her death, Joy appeared to Alana in a dream. With a glow around her head symbolizing that she had gone to heaven, Joy told Alana that everyone should stop crying; she was now with God. Through the course of her life, the Church of the Lord (Aladura) had "prepared her for heaven," Mother Cooper reflected. More than ever, one could see that the Bronx church was a family, as people cried together and held one another up. After a wake and funeral, Mother Cooper and Eleanor took her body back to Liberia for burial.

"You have to keep dancing," one member of the Redeemed Christian Church of God, Chapel of Hope in Brooklyn, said to me, a word that felt like it applied to this moment in history. By fall 2008, the globe was under the cloak of the worst financial crisis since the Great Depression. As New York City employers shed jobs and the city shook, members of the three churches worked harder than ever. Prayers were offered to God, the giver of life, for the preservation of employment. Sermons that spoke to the crisis made no promise of easy returns, but encouraged diligent and creative faith, the seed of faith and talents. With a tenacity born of great adversity

The Word Keeps Moving

Fig B. Minister Joy Cooper, 2005

and an imagination that saw the world through the eyes of God's salvation, the churches held ground and moved forward. Christ was their "sufficiency." In such difficult global economic conditions, the resources to come to New York City from Africa were more difficult to gather, and immigration appeared to be slowing in general. But as throughout its history, New York City remains a point of aspiration for people from around the world seeking the opportunity for a better life.

On November 4, 2008, Barack Obama, the son of a Kenyan father, was elected President of the United States. Not a single African immigrant I had interviewed before the election believed Obama would become president. With racism, about which they spoke very little publicly but recognized as persistent, the election of an "*African* American" president seemed impossible. Following his historic election, there was extraordinary excitement that "a son born of African soil," as Mother Cooper put it, was leading the United States. To Pastor Dolapo, Obama's election provided a pastoral message for her members: "do not give up on yourself."[3] In

3. Interview, Pastor Dolapo Osinfade, May 10, 2009.

ways that have perhaps just begun to unfold, Obama is a "game changer" not only for the nation, but also for African immigrants to the United States. In every African church, Obama had their prayers.

Visibility for African Christianity in the West continues to grow. In 2009, the *Newsweek* cover story on Obama and the new global elite featured Redeemed Christian Church of God General Overseer E. A. Adeboye.[4] Adeboye was listed forty-ninth of "the fifty most powerful people in the world," a fact featured on the Redeemed North American Web site. Such media accolades match aspirations for growth as the work on the ground continues. Not surprisingly, in 2009, the Waribokos launched Living Christ Chapel, a new parish in the Boston area.

The signs of the Spirit are embodied in the faithful — Presbyterian, Aladura, Pentecostal, and more; this is the dynamic of African Christianity moving through the twenty-first century. Imprinted upon the African churches of New York City is the story of salvation, the born-again bodies of saints resisting the powers and reaching for life abundant. They are praising Jesus, building new lives, healing the sick, preaching the gospel, and burying the dead. As New Yorkers, they are creating jobs, raising their families, going to school, graduating with advanced degrees, and moving to the "next level." The world, and the Word, keep moving. The Spirit, the gift of God, is ever in motion.[5]

---

4. *Newsweek*, December 29, 2008/January 5, 2009.

5. I am thinking here of the wonderful imagery in the song "The Gift," by Bruce Cockburn (*Big Circumstance*, 1998). The "gift" as Cockburn describes it cannot be controlled, and as such it moves and is shared in unexpected ways. African churches have been this to me, a gift. No doubt the Spirit will continue to surprise us all.

Afterword

Mark Gornik's *Word Made Global: Stories of African Christianity in New York City* not only makes a significant contribution to the conversation of world Christianity; it reframes the conversation and points it in a fresh and innovative theological direction. Reflecting his own itinerant life and drawing on his innovative leadership as a pastor, pilgrim, and scholar — and on his research with African immigrant churches in New York — Gornik provides us in this book with a good lens into the social, theological, and ecclesiological significance of "journey" and its implications for world Christianity. That this is the case reflects Gornik's own deep appreciation of Christian life as a journey. To be honest, I know very few people who allow the theological conviction of Christian life as a journey to shape their lives, social engagement, and scholarly pursuits as profoundly as does Gornik. That is why, in order to appreciate the fresh voice and innovative direction that *Word Made Global* brings into the conversation of world Christianity, one must first place the book within the context of Gornik's own journey.

Gornik is always on the move — both literally and figuratively — and that is part of what is refreshing about his work. In 1986, inspired by the vision and leadership of John Perkins — the civil rights activist and founder of the Christian Community Development Association, whose theology developed around the "3 Rs" of Reconciliation, Relocation, and Redistribution — Gornik relocated from his suburban neighborhood of Baltimore to the inner-city neighborhood of Sandtown. Here, together with his friends Susan and Allan Tibbels, they established the New Song Community Church, of which Gornik became the pastor, and which still continues today to be the engine behind impressive efforts of inner-city revitalization.

In 1998, at the height of New Song's Sandtown success, Gornik left

Baltimore and moved to New York City, where he and his wife Rita helped found a New Song community in Harlem similar to the one in Sandtown. Soon Gornik was taking classes at Princeton Theological Seminary with Andrew Walls before turning to the University of Edinburgh Ph.D. program in world Christianity. His contact with a number of immigrant churches, brought about by his relocation to New York, only deepened his interest in the significance of these communities for world Christianity. It was also the contact with immigrant communities that opened Gornik's eyes to the need for theological education in a new way, and that led to the establishment of the City Seminary of New York, which was formally launched in 2003.

A key component of the seminary curriculum is the annual global pilgrimage, during which Gornik travels with the seminary community to different cities in the world. Another distinctive feature of the seminary is the teaching that takes place (mostly in the evenings and weekends) at different locations and churches within the city. I note this in order to highlight the fact that traveling to and within world cities, as well as around neighborhoods and churches in New York City itself, is part and parcel of what Mark Gornik is and does. *Word Made Global* not only reflects this reality, but much of its conceptualization and writing took place "on the way" — on the Metro between stops in New York boroughs, on the train between New York and Baltimore, on the plane between Edinburgh and New York, and within churches across the world.

Drawing attention to these contexts helps to explain why, as a book, *Word Made Global* is born out of journeys, and reveals its deep connection with Gornik's earlier work *To Live in Peace: Biblical Faith and the Changing Inner City* (Eerdmans, 2002) — which is about the New Song Community of Sandtown in Baltimore. For at the heart of both books is a key theological conviction that drives Gornik's life, work, and scholarship: namely that journey and traveling are the unique means by which the God whom Christians worship saves the world. Thus "journey" in its many forms — traveling, pilgrimage, relocation, migration, exile, and dispersion — is deeply connected to the mystery of the Incarnation, the drama of the Word Made Flesh, which is nothing but the story of a God who comes (again, on a "journey") to dwell among us. Gornik not only gets this foundational theological conviction right; he explicates it to show that the Good News of the God who lives among us is not geographically bound, but "circulates through inspired bodies in a global world." And, ironic as it might sound, the logic of the Incarnation means that the Word who "dwelt among us" did not do so simply for the sake of making us feel at home or successful in the world as we know it, but also to "displace" us and render us homeless, as it draws us within the drama of its circulating logic. The church's calling within this circular logic is thus to be a community committed to "seek the peace of the city to which I have exiled you" (Jer. 29:7).

Once one notes this inner theological architecture that informs Gornik's work, then the connection between the reality of the immigrant churches in New York (under investigation in *Word Made Global*) and the New Song Community Church in Baltimore (the subject of *To Live in Peace*) becomes clear. For what makes the New Song Community in Sandtown a vibrant ecclesiological experiment is the realization that "seeking the peace of the city" cannot be separated from participation in the whole range of social, cultural, economic, and political realities that constitute success and well-being in a city. Thus, the different programs of New Song Community in Baltimore — reconstruction, drug rehabilitation programs, Habitat for Humanity home ownership, job and daycare centers, and a charter-type school — are not simply development projects or mere service programs, but integral elements of a robust ecclesiological vision in a local place.

Word Made Global is grounded within and pursues the same ecclesiological vision. That partly explains why Gornik spends a considerable amount of time exploring ways in which the beliefs, practices, and networks of the African immigrant congregations in New York help the members adapt, manage, and become successful in the global city — all part of what it means to "seek the peace of the city." But what *To Live in Peace* also shows is that if to "see the peace of the city" is about flourishing in the city, it is also about interrupting the flow, rhythm, and logic of the city with the reality of a community that lives by and draws from a different, even strange account of what constitutes success and well-being. This I take to be the *unique* significance of the New Song Community in Baltimore: a strange and odd presence, a refreshing interruption within the once-abandoned community burdened by violence and drugs, the neighborhood of Sandtown. This is what constitutes the "new song" of the New Song Church community.

It is this same quest for "new song" that drives Gornik in *Word Made Global*. Or, to put it differently, what Gornik is driving at in *Word Made Global* is the same ecclesiological vision of the church as a community, whose gift and calling in the world is to "sing" — nay, *be* — "a new song" within the local places in which it finds itself within the Word's orbiting circuit, which constitutes God's movement of salvation. Accordingly, the primary interest behind Gornik's extensive descriptions of the immigrant churches in the book is not sociological. His primary interest is not to display how African Christians in New York are drawing on the social, personal, spiritual, liturgical, and ritual heritage of their African Christian faith to succeed in that city — although that is definitely the case. His primary interest is ecclesiological, whether and to what extent these immigrant communities represent an "odd" and yet liberating presence — a fresh interruption that is a microcosm of the gifts and prospects of world Christianity.

Read in this context, *Word Made Global* becomes less a book about African immigrant churches in New York and more an argument and quest for the gift of a "new song" that the movement of world Christianity makes possible, or at least ought to make possible. This is what I find to be particularly fresh and exciting about *Word Made Global:* it draws our attention to the unique phenomenon of immigrant churches as the locus and site of a fresh conversation for world Christianity. If, as we noted, it is through journey and traveling that God saves the world, immigration represents a unique moment in that movement — a way in which God forms a new people in the world. "Immigrant" congregations, to the extent they belong neither totally here nor there, at once local and global, both indigenous and foreign, at home here and yet not at home, are thus communities that represent something of this new creation. Accordingly, they illumine possibilities of personal and ecclesial identity beyond geopolitical boundaries, and in this way help to press against and redefine the notions of citizenship and belonging in a way that foreshadows that great assembly of Revelation 7:9 (drawn from all nations, tribes, and races . . .). And to the extent that they do, they represent a true "Ephesian moment" (to use Andrew Walls's famed expression), and thus help to illumine a new future made possible by the Word Among Us, which is the ultimate end — the telos — of world Christianity.

In a conversation about world Christianity that is so often framed around stable geopolitical poles of North/South, old/new, us/them, *Word Made Global* offers not only a fresh perspective, but a helpful reminder that one gift of the movement of world Christianity is to help to create a new people in the world for whom these geopolitical frames of reference become increasingly inadequate and eventually irrelevant.

EMMANUEL KATONGOLE
Kampala Archdiocese in Uganda
Duke Divinity School

APPENDIX 1

Where the Spirit of God Is:
Notes on Ethnography and Global Theology

"For where the Church is, there is the Spirit of God; and where the Spirit of God is, there is the Church," observed Irenaeus.[1] Christian faith is neither unchanging nor static, but living and breathing in the Spirit of God. As Jürgen Moltmann writes of Pentecostalism, but with equal relevance to the range of churches that have been written of in this study, "This is not a religion *for* the people; it is a religion *of* the people."[2] Rooted in local communities, theology is not what is found in libraries or study carrels, but what occurs as persons and communities seek to turn all of life to Christ.

Ethnographic practice, attending to concrete Christian communities, is necessary to understand the questions and answers of faith at the heart of theological activity. Such ethnographic practice is crucial not only for understanding the global city or African Christianity, but more broadly, for understanding Christian faith itself. Moreover, it is a crucial resource for the mission of the church.[3]

"Ecclesiological ethnography"[4] takes seriously accounts of Christian living, thereby adding to a wider understanding of the ways by which concrete ecclesial communities and their understandings of Christian life have

---

1. Quoted in Michael N. C. Poon, "Patristic Theology," in *Global Dictionary of Theology*, ed. William R. Dyrness and Veli-Matti Kärkkäinen (Downers Grove, Ill.: IVP Academic, 2008), 633.

2. Jürgen Moltmann, Preface, In *The Spirit in the World: Emerging Pentecostal Theologies in Global Contexts*, ed. Veli-Matti Kärkkäinen (Grand Rapids: Eerdmans, 2009), x.

3. Wilbert R. Shenk, "Recasting Theology of Mission: Impulses from the Non-Western World," *International Bulletin of Missionary Research* 25:3 (2001): 98-107.

4. Nicholas Healy, *Church, World and the Christian Life: Practical-Prophetic Ecclesiology* (Cambridge: Cambridge University Press, 2000).

been established and maintained. Such an approach does not begin with answers, but is open to learning and understanding in new ways.[5] Now that we can speak of "world Christianity" once again, ethnography is a way into learning what is occurring in global theology. It also picks up on a growing and important interest in the anthropology of Christianity.[6]

Theology in African churches is reflection on God's presence and power in the world and creation.[7] African Christianity is a dynamic reality that entails songs, dances, values, prayers, material representations, sermons, meals, baptisms, and communal reflections in relationship to God and God's purposes in Christ. These are practices, creative activities that are learned and participated in over time. They are passed on through the generations, and they are also adaptable. Knowing and responding to God can take the form of singing, praying in loud voices, and dancing. This is why attending to practices is so essential in the study of African Christianity.

Because Christianity is a salvation faith for African believers, prior to practice and belief is the experience of God the Creator, Jesus the Redeemer, and the Spirit of life, which in turn shapes practice, belief, and life.[8] If such experience is central in African Christianity, it is not at odds with holding strong theological beliefs — and indeed, the contrary may well hold true. Many in the West are wary of religious experience, granting little credence to dreams, healings, deliverance, visions, and prophecy.[9] Yet

---

5. Harri Englund and James Leach, "Ethnography and the Meta-Narratives of Modernity," *Current Anthropology* 41:2 (2000): 225-39.

6. Among the expanding literature, see Jon Bialecki, Naomi Haynes, and Joel Robbins, "The Anthropology of Christianity," *Religion Compass* 2:6 (2008): 1139-58; Fanella Cannell, ed., *The Anthropology of Christianity* (Durham: Duke University Press, 2006); Joel Robbins, "Anthropology and Theology: An Awkward Relationship?" *Anthropological Quarterly* 79:2 (2006): 285-92; Joel Robbins, "Continuity Thinking and the Problem of Christian Culture: Belief, Time, and the Anthropology of Christianity," *Current Anthropology* 48:1 (2007): 5-38, with comments; Debra McDougall, "Rethinking Christianity and Anthropology: A Review Article," *Anthropological Forum* 19:2 (2009): 185-94; Chris Hann, "The Anthropology of Christianity per se," *European Journal of Sociology* 48:3 (2007): 383-410; and Frederick Klaits, *Death in a Church of Life: Moral Passion during Botswana's Time of AIDS* (Berkeley: University of California Press, 2010).

7. See Gerrie ter Haar, *How God Became African: African Spirituality and Western Thought* (Philadelphia: University of Pennsylvania Press, 2009).

8. Another way of putting this might be that for Christian theology the Spirit is privileged over practices. See Nicholas M. Healy, "Practices and the New Ecclesiology: Misplaced Concreteness?" *International Journal of Systematic Theology* 5:3 (2003): 287-308.

9. For a review of many of the current academic issues, see Ann Taves, *Religious Ex-*

such an emphasis on experience is not at odds with the biblical material. For example, New Testament scholars Luke Timothy Johnson[10] and Larry Hurtado[11] draw attention to the importance of the experience of Jesus in the early Christian story. Just as religious experience is internally tied to theological accounts and the worship of Jesus in the early church, and not simply "emotions," "personal feelings," or "intuitions," the same holds true for African Christians. Claims about God's work are related in testimony, giving public witness to the experience of God's everyday involvement in lives and events. At the same time, the experience of God, relational in character, can convey theological beliefs, convictions, and propositions.

In an overarching sense, the reason there is not a single expression of church, but Christian faith expressed in a vast diversity of languages, cultures, and practices, is the particularity and universality of Christ. This represents, as Andrew Walls, Lamin Sanneh, Kwame Bediako, and others describe, a "translation" of Christian faith, giving rise to a multiplicity of indigenous responses.[12] Translation is the full experience of a community as it encounters the gospel, as opposed to contextualization, a process of adaptively transferring a theology more associated with the work of a missionary or cross-cultural ministry.[13]

The translation of Christian faith is more than a linguistic activity; it is formation in Christ, the "incarnation of the word in a people."[14] Joan Burke cites a number of texts that help build a solid ground for understanding what as a Catholic she calls inculturation, but also expresses what

---

perience Reconsidered: A Building-Block Approach to the Study of Religion and Other Special Things (Princeton: Princeton University Press, 2009).

10. Luke Timothy Johnson, *Religious Experience in Earliest Christianity: A Missing Dimension in New Testament Studies* (Minneapolis: Fortress, 1998).

11. L. W. Hurtado, "Religious Experience and Religious Innovation in the New Testament," *Journal of Religion* 80:2 (2000): 183-205.

12. Andrew F. Walls, *The Missionary Movement in Christian History: Studies in the Transmission of Faith* (Maryknoll, N.Y.: Orbis, 1996) and *The Cross-Cultural Process in Christian History: Studies in the Transmission and Appropriation of Faith* (Maryknoll, N.Y.: Orbis, 2002); Lamin O. Sanneh, *Translating the Message: The Missionary Impact on Culture* (Maryknoll, N.Y.: Orbis, 1989).

13. Andrew F. Walls, "Inculturation," in *Encyclopedia of Protestantism*, vol. 2, ed. Hans J. Hillerbrand (New York: Routledge, 2004), 932-35. For an explication of the experience of Christ as an individual and communally forming activity, see Hendrikus Boers, *Christ in the Letters of Paul: In Place of Christology* (Berlin: Walter de Gruyter, 2006).

14. Joan F. Burke, *These Catholic Sisters Are All Mamas! Towards the Inculturation of Sisterhood in Africa, an Ethnographic Study* (Leiden: Brill, 2001), 196.

we have discussed as translation: "In our becoming one with this same Jesus Christ, the incarnation continues . . . and in each of us there will be a unique reflection — revelation — of the God in whose image we have been fashioned."[15]

Through the mediation of the Spirit, the Word becomes flesh in community. This is not a simple adaptation to culture, but a critical interaction and reinterpretation that involves both affirmation and transformation. The call to translation is a call to growth, to "living into the incarnation."[16] Conversion, as Walls has stressed, is turning to Christ from all that is within, not being proselytized into conformity from without.[17] No tradition holds the final word on God, but all have a word for each other; no single center exists for Christian faith, but instead there is a multiplicity of points of reference.

Not only is the encounter of cultures with the gospel diverse; the results produce new configurations. Therefore I agree with Michael Scott "that the anthropology of Christianity must begin on the ground with the ethnography of the unpredictable ways in which Christians continuously select and reinterpret the content of Christianity."[18] In a globalized world, such terms are also stories of faith in motion, and we can see in them encounters of the gospel with the world, marked by awareness that there is no single delineation of this encounter. Our information may be imperfect, but any understanding requires listening and sensitivity to multiple ways of knowing. Epistemology belongs to the body and the mind.

As Dietrich Bonhoeffer offers in *Sanctorum Communio*, to see Christ one must see the church in its social form, and in the church as social form one should be able to view Christ.[19] Each church has a story to tell, a calling to offer, a description and interpretation of the faith that has taken root in their experience of Christ. To write about a church's history, story, and the people who make it alive is to be entrusted to tell it as much as possible on their terms. It is also to tell the story of Christ, the Word made flesh.

---

15. Burke, *These Catholic Sisters Are All Mamas!*, 197.

16. Burke, *These Catholic Sisters Are All Mamas!*, 7-10.

17. For an introduction to this theme in his work, see Andrew F. Walls, "Converts or Proselytes? The Crisis over Conversion in the Early Church," *International Bulletin of Mission* 28:1 (January 2004): 2-6.

18. Michael W. Scott, "'I Was Like Abraham': Notes on the Anthropology of Christianity from the Solomon Islands," *Ethnos* 70:1 (March 2005): 118.

19. Dietrich Bonhoeffer, *Sanctorum Communio: A Theological Study of the Sociology of the Church*, trans. Reinhard Krauss and Nancy Lukens (Minneapolis: Fortress, 1998), 190.

Where the Spirit of God Is

This approach can be aided by the turn toward the body in religious studies. In this vein, Manuel Vásquez provides an incisive and constructive series of contributions.[20] Rather than developing formulations in abstract, a focus on the body involves all of the senses,[21] being engaged by what is actually occurring in church life in the city. This approach challenges theology to be more critically reflective in the areas of epistemology, paradigms of body and spirit, dynamics of place and displacement, and practices in relationship to the development of doctrine.

Camilo José Vergara's *How the Other Half Worships* is a unique document that with depth and imagination opens space for seeing the urban church.[22] Vergara tells the stories of urban churches on the margins, recording the words and images of their church life as he documented them. It works "from the bottom up," building on the particular, what is living and active. Numerous questions emerge: Who is Christ for the community? How are they living their faith, and why? What are the foundational questions they are answering, and what is ecclesial formation? In contrast, ecclesiology all too often is composed "from the top down" and seeks to impose its particular history and understanding of the Christian life on others.

It is not true that the West does "theology," therefore, while other communities have "contextual theologies." Rather, all theology is "inculturated" or "contextual" within a historical, political, and social moment, and the West's theologies are no exception. "Theology" is better understood and interpreted as the history of the development of Christian faith, discipleship, and confession in relationship to questions, needs, aspirations, and struggles of people across cultures and generations, not as the production and maintenance of definitions shaped and determined by the West.[23] This is why mutuality is so important: Christian churches belong to one another, and can only understand Christ through the eyes, voices, and experiences of one another. In this view of Christian faith, there is an experience of the church "from every nation, from all tribes and peoples

---

20. Manuel A Vásquez, *More Than Belief: A Materialist Theory of Religion* (Oxford: Oxford University Press, 2011).

21. Paul Stoller, *Sensuous Scholarship* (Philadelphia: University of Pennsylvania Press, 1997).

22. Camilo José Vergara, *How the Other Half Worships* (New Brunswick: Rutgers University Press, 2005).

23. Harvie M. Conn, "The Missionary Task of Theology: A Love/Hate Relationship," *Westminster Theological Journal* 45 (1983): 1-21.

and languages, standing before the throne and the Lamb," as John's Revelation describes it.[24]

N. T. Wright offers an example of this in a popular summary of what it means to be "simply Christian," where he speaks of a Christianity that "belongs to all."[25] While any definition of the gospel will contain universal or constant elements around the story of Jesus and salvation, as Wright emphasizes, every Christian community also displays in their reading of the gospel a response to the questions and spiritual struggles of their world.[26] Christian faith "makes sense" and is good news to African Christians for reasons different than for Wright. Although he does not present his argument as such, Wright is reflecting the apologetic concerns facing the church in western culture, and his work would have a different impact read in other cultural and social settings. The Christian gospel is both profoundly universal and highly particular. Jesus is Lord and Savior of the world, but he also speaks to African believers in ways that meet their needs,[27] as he does to every community.

Close attention to theology in a lived mode can facilitate theological renewal "from above" by introducing new ways of being church. Christian Scharen's important appeal for drawing ecclesiology and ethnography together creates room for such a concrete approach to the church within the academy and beyond.[28] The Project on Lived Theology, directed by Charles Marsh, is a major development and ongoing initiative in this area.[29] With a particular interest in the Civil Rights movement, exemplified in Marsh's classic study *God's Long Summer: Stories of Faith and Civil Rights*,[30] the Project on Lived Theology highlights theology as grassroots action.

Viewing African Christianity abstractly through its numerical growth or meta-themes is not unimportant, but is in the end limiting. This is why, for Emmanuel Katongole, the church as local community is the "method-

24. Revelation 7:9.

25. N. T. Wright, *Simply Christian: Why Christianity Makes Sense* (San Francisco: HarperSanFrancisco, 2006).

26. The approach of Stephen B. Bevans and Roger P. Schroeder, *Constants in Context: A Theology of Mission for Today* (Maryknoll, N.Y.: Orbis, 2004), appears to be influenced by Walls. See their argument on pages 32-33 in particular.

27. Diane B. Stinton, *Jesus of Africa: Voices of Contemporary African Christology* (Maryknoll, N.Y.: Orbis, 2004).

28. Christian Batalden Scharen, "'Judicious Narratives,' or Ethnography as Ecclesiology," *Scottish Journal of Theology* 58:2 (2005): 125-42.

29. www.livedtheology.org.

30. Charles Marsh, *God's Long Summer: Stories of Faith and Civil Rights* (Princeton: Princeton University Press, 1997).

ological starting point" for theological reflection.³¹ "African theological reflection," he offers, "must be grounded in, and seek to shape, the life and practice of concrete church communities. In this way, theological reflection will reflect the concerns, anxieties, aspirations, hopes, and frustrations of the ordinary African Christians in their everyday struggle in the world."³² Similarly, Isabel Mukonyora voices the concern that "a great deal of time has ... been spent setting up an agenda for the development of an authentic African theology rather than in carrying out in-depth theological enquiries of the various ways in which Africans have interpreted Christianity."³³ Scharen, Marsh, Katongole, and Mukonyora's emphases on local appropriations and concrete communities offer constructive directions for the theological enterprise. I would simply underscore that churches are "primary sources," so the data from ethnographic research may well take us in new and surprising directions.

While religious narratives and practices are closely linked to communities of belief, experience, and practice, basing a study largely in congregational forms of African Christianity requires some justification and methodological elaboration. Vásquez and Marquardt emphasize the varied, lived experience of religion that exists extra-congregationally.³⁴ Among the extra-congregational modes that African Christianity uses in New York are the radio, Internet, music, revivals, prayer bands, and faith instilled into everyday life and activities. Practices that occur outside of a church community are indeed crucial, but the church remains central to the spiritual lives of believers. The practices of faith are inseparable from the social body and activities of the church.

Theology is performed and enacted in service of life. For this reason, I did not place adjectives such as "informal," "folk," and "oral" before the theology of churches in this study. Nicholas Healy's "ordinary theology" rightly takes aim at the problem.³⁵

---

31. Emmanuel M. Katongole, "A Different World Right Here, A World Being Gestated in the Deeds of the Everyday: The Church within African Theological Imagination," *Missionalia* 30:2 (2002): 207.

32. Katongole, "A Different World Right Here," 206-7.

33. Isabel Mukonyora, "The Dramatisation of Life and Death by Johane Masowe," *Swedish Missiological Themes* 88:3 (2000): 410.

34. Manuel A. Vásquez and Marie Friedmann Marquardt, *Globalizing the Sacred: Religion across the Americas* (New Brunswick: Rutgers University Press, 2003).

35. Healy, *Church, World and the Christian Life*; see also John S. Mbiti, *Bible and Theology in African Christianity* (Nairobi: Oxford University Press, 1986), 46-47.

APPENDIX 1

Learning about local theology requires knowledge of all the senses. Being able to reflect critically on communities of faith involves a way of being present, of listening, hearing, being self-aware, and most of all being open to what is taking place. The story that gets told needs to come out of being present and open to pieces of a narrative that will emerge over time.[36] A preset process will produce much that can be expected, but not the unexpected. In Isaiah we read, "I am about to do a new thing; now it springs forth, do you not perceive it?"[37] This is an evaluative question in prophetic mode, a reminder to attend to God's ongoing activity. Because African Christianity is very much a faith that makes use of the body, it is important for a researcher to be present not just in mind but also in body; this research is a "bodily craft."[38] Being present is also about being open to apprehending the world in a new way.[39] It requires a holistic engagement and epistemology. Just as knowledge does not come about in a singular way, learning is not rote, but involves different styles and approaches. The body is important, but it is not the only vehicle for knowing.[40]

Rather than thinking of ethnographies as limited to "thick descriptions," finely tuned accounts of social life and practice that contribute to a body of knowledge,[41] Paul Stoller, the anthropologist whose work on West African traders in New York I earlier discussed, proposes the category of "witness." A personal experience with cancer led him to

36. For relevant reflections, see Paul Rainbow and George E. Marcus with James D. Faubion and Tobias Rees, *Designs for an Anthropology of the Contemporary* (Durham: Duke University Press, 2008), 116.

37. Isaiah 43:19.

38. Loïc Wacquant, *Body and Soul: Notebooks of an Apprentice Boxer* (New York: Oxford University Press, 2004), 3-11. Compare Robert A. Orsi, *Between Heaven and Earth: The Religious Worlds People Make and the Scholars Who Study Them* (Princeton: Princeton University Press, 2005).

39. Valentina Napolitano, "Of Migrant Revelations and Anthropological Awakenings," *Social Anthropology* 15 (2007): 71-87.

40. Again, I am seeing the imagination, practice, the body, and experience as part of a holistic epistemology. For a contribution to this discussion, see Lyle Yorks and Elizabeth Kasl, "Toward a Theory and Practice for Whole-Person Learning: Reconceptualizing Experience and the Role of Affect," *Adult Education Quarterly* 52:3 (2002): 176-92; and James K. A. Smith, *Thinking in Tongues: Pentecostal Contributions to Christian Philosophy* (Grand Rapids: Eerdmans, 2010). We would also do well to recall wider traditions and histories. For example, see Susan Ashbrook Harvey, *Scenting Salvation: Ancient Christianity and the Olfactory Imagination* (Berkeley: University of California Press, 2006).

41. Paul Stoller, *Money Has No Smell: The Africanization of New York City* (Chicago: University of Chicago Press, 2001), 200.

Where the Spirit of God Is

this reconsideration of his craft: "I now believe that the anthropologist's fundamental obligation is to use her or his repertoire of skills to bear witness. In so doing we are compelled to tell stories about kinship as well as cancer that shed light on social realities."[42] There is for Stoller a nearly revelatory dimension to ethnography, a witness to a greater reality: "In the end this turn may take us to that elusive and oft forgotten end of scholarship: wisdom, the knowledge that enables us to live well in the world."[43]

Witness is also a key concern of the New Testament, as exemplified in Acts 15, where the Jerusalem council discusses the appropriation of faith by Gentile converts. What would it mean to be Christian? Would the past or present dominate the future of the church? By deciding to withdraw the imposition of Jewish cultural standards on Gentiles, chief among them circumcision, the council released the church for cross-cultural expansion, as Andrew Walls points out.[44] As Stephen Fowl shows in his study of Acts 10–15, this change came to depend on the witness of Peter to the Spirit's work among the Gentiles.[45] Fowl observes, "Christians must not only become and learn from people of the Spirit, we must also become practiced at testifying about what the Spirit is doing in the lives of others."[46]

Taking an approach that emphasizes concrete communities for theological development makes it very important to consider one's point of view. As Afe Adogame and Ezra Chitando emphasize, theoretical reflection and grounded research in fieldwork are important for the study of the "African religious Diaspora."[47] In *Crossing and Dwelling: A Theory of Religion*, Thomas Tweed[48] argues that religion is concerned with location, but also with motion. For Tweed, religion involves spatial practices of crossing and dwelling.[49] In this respect, Tweed's proposal resembles the centerpiece

---

42. Stoller, *Money Has No Smell*, 200.

43. Paul Stoller, *Stranger in the Village of the Sick: A Memoir of Cancer, Sorcery, and Healing* (Boston: Beacon Press, 2004), 200.

44. Walls, *The Cross-Cultural Process in Christian History*, 75-78.

45. Stephen E. Fowl, *Engaging Scripture: A Model for Theological Interpretation* (Malden: Blackwell, 1998), 97-127. See Acts 15:8.

46. Fowl, *Engaging Scripture*, 117.

47. Afe Adogame and Ezra Chitando, "Moving among Those Moved by the Spirit: Conducting Fieldwork within the New African Religious Diaspora," *Fieldwork in Religion* 1:3 (2005): 253-70.

48. Thomas A. Tweed, *Crossing and Dwelling: A Theory of Religion* (Cambridge: Harvard University Press, 2006).

49. Tweed, *Crossing and Dwelling*, 79-85, 123.

of Walls's thought that Christianity continually translates the gospel. As religion is practiced "en route," the practices of homemaking and movement of religious flows are twinned.[50] So the study of African Christianity in New York City, with its flows of people, beliefs, practices, and experiences, should attend to its new location as well as its former one.

Tweed goes on to suggest that just as religion is characterized by itineraries in a global age, so a researcher should also find a position within an itinerary.[51] No single place finalizes the position or sight of the researcher, Tweed reasons. Therefore all interpretations are positioned sightings.[52] Such "positioned locations," whether professional, epistemological, or cultural, situate the researcher in multiple webs of interpretative frameworks.

Post-colonial, liberationist, and feminist voices remind us that the process of seeing, experiencing, and interpreting the world always involves a point of view or position. Just as culture, economic status, and gender are foundational ways of encountering and interpreting the world, so also is religious faith and commitment. One cannot fully suspend "belief" or be against it; rather, within ethnographic practice it is important to recognize and be critical about what we take for granted.[53] In the Reformed tradition, for example, knowledge is always considered positional, situated in a prior religious commitment. For Deidre Crumbley, Linda Thomas, and Benetta Jules-Rosette, Christian faith is a recognizable and integral part of their approach to ethnographic study among African independent churches.[54]

Rose Mary Amenga-Etego expands the "insider/outsider" terminology to describe herself as an insider-outsider — first an insider, but also an outsider.[55] I would classify myself as an outsider-insider to my research

---

50. Tweed, *Crossing and Dwelling*, 54-79.
51. Tweed, *Crossing and Dwelling*, 20-25.
52. Tweed, *Crossing and Dwelling*, 20-28, 165.
53. For some of the issues involved, see Galina Lindquist and Simon Coleman, "Introduction: Against Belief," *Social Analysis* 52:1 (2008): 1-18.
54. Deidre Helen Crumbley, "Indigenous Institution Building in an Afro-Christian Movement: The Aladura as Case Study" (Ph.D. thesis, Northeastern University, 1989), and *Spirit, Structure, and Flesh: Gendered Experiences in African Instituted Churches among the Yoruba of Nigeria* (Madison: University of Wisconsin Press, 2008); Benetta Jules-Rosette, *African Apostles: Ritual and Conversion in the Church of John Maranke* (Ithaca: Cornell University Press, 1975); Linda Elaine Thomas, *Under the Canopy: Ritual Process and Spiritual Resilience in South Africa* (Columbia: University of South Carolina Press, 1999). Similarly, see Marla F. Frederick, *Between Sundays: Black Women and the Everyday Struggles of Faith* (Berkeley: University of California Press, 2003).
55. Rose Mary Amenga-Etego, "Mending the Broken Pieces: Religion and Sustainable

Where the Spirit of God Is

topic. As one formed in the cosmology and epistemology of the West, formally trained in the Reformed theological tradition, and placed by the privileges of my whiteness, I was very much an outsider. Yet as a Christian, ordained minister, and New Yorker, I could be something of an insider. Before moving to New York, for more than a decade I had been a minister in an inner-city African American community in Baltimore. These are factors that position me as a researcher. Over the course of several years, the three focus churches became my "home," and whenever it was offered that I was home, I received such words and acts of hospitality as a gift.

A number of basic research challenges within African Christianity are raised in Harold W. Turner's essay "Problems in the Study of African Independent Churches,"[56] and they have both continued and wider salience. Turner, an early student in the study of new religious movements and author of a seminal study on the Church of the Lord (Aladura), begins with issues related to participatory research. Turner first argues that the study of religion should not be displaced by anthropology or sociology. Religion, he states, involves "inner spiritual life,"[57] an "inner reality"[58] or an "inner religious reality,"[59] and therefore cannot mean only its exterior "expressions or manifestations,"[60] such as rituals and traditions. Turner's division between "inner" and "outer" forms of religion and experience is neither possible nor even desirable, as scholars of religion such as Talal Asad have shown,[61] but his concern to take what might be called the "life of the Spirit" seriously is important.

A second challenge that Turner names concerns "the student of the Christian church . . . [who] is a member of some Christian communion, and makes this explicit in his relationship with the group he is investigating."[62] One should assume, Turner proposes in more than an ecumenical

---

Rural Development Among the Nankani of Northern Ghana" (Ph.D. thesis, University of Edinburgh, 2007), 221-48.

56. H. W. Turner, "Problems in the Study of African Independent Churches," *Numen* 13:1 (1966): 26-42. For other research challenges, see Tinyiko Sam Maluleke, "Theological Interest in AICs and Other Grass-Root Communities in South Africa: A Review of Methodologies," in *Journal of Black Theology in South Africa* 10:1 (1996): 18-48.

57. Turner, "Problems in the Study of African Independent Churches," 28.

58. Turner, "Problems in the Study of African Independent Churches," 31.

59. Turner, "Problems in the Study of African Independent Churches," 32.

60. Turner, "Problems in the Study of African Independent Churches," 31.

61. Talal Asad, *Genealogies of Religion: Discipline and Reasons of Power in Christianity and Islam* (Baltimore: The Johns Hopkins University Press, 1993).

62. Turner, "Problems in the Study of African Independent Churches," 27.

gesture, "that God is at work there through the Holy Spirit."[63] If one starts with the Spirit, then the welcome of a researcher can be an act of pneumatic hospitality.

Turner identifies four problems in participatory research. First is the problem of *participation*, the requirement of not being a "tourist who will try anything quaint once."[64] Positively, one should participate in the liturgy and activities of the church when called to do so, and learn with openness,[65] for "academic enquiry becomes inevitably also a personal discovery."[66] A second problem is in the area of *commitment*, which emerges because "the investigator who participates in the life of an African independent church becomes personally involved. . . . Here one is involved with other people and with their expectations and needs, and at the deepest level of all, and under a divine constraint."[67] Farewells and departures are not predetermined, for "the situation is completely different from that of the entomologist who concludes his studies of beetles and decides he will turn to spiders, and it is very different from that of the sociologist who lives a while in a mining village to study its social structure and attitudes, presents his report, and moves to another task."[68] Indeed, the "report" produced by the researcher becomes a bond of "deep and permanent commitment"[69] and requires various levels of interaction.

Having established such a research approach, it follows for Turner that *objectivity* is the third challenge to be faced, especially if one has bonded with a church. Objectivity is in itself impossible, but how this impossibility encumbers research requires clarification. Researchers, Turner explains, can impose their views of ecclesial practice, such as the sacraments, on the church. Still, "at a deeper level the observer will tend to analyse, classify, and interpret African religious existence in terms and forms developed in the West and built into the very structure of his thinking — the rational, critical, conceptualized systems of Western Christian thought which may not be adequate to embrace all Christian existence, and may falsify the understanding of African religious movements if they are imposed. The result may be an impasse where only African-type answers are

---

63. Turner, "Problems in the Study of African Independent Churches," 36.
64. Turner, "Problems in the Study of African Independent Churches," 35.
65. Turner, "Problems in the Study of African Independent Churches," 34.
66. Turner, "Problems in the Study of African Independent Churches," 34.
67. Turner, "Problems in the Study of African Independent Churches," 35.
68. Turner, "Problems in the Study of African Independent Churches," 35.
69. Turner, "Problems in the Study of African Independent Churches," 36.

answered to Western-type questions."[70] "Objectivity" is best understood as seeking to understand a church on its own terms, and therefore requires reflection on one's own ecclesiology.[71]

As a related concern, the fourth and final problem Turner names is forming a responsible *detachment* from the church in question, thus enabling the researcher to render an academic form of analysis. Such evaluation requires "considerable skill . . . if the investigator is to speak the truth in love and retain the confidence of those about whom he writes."[72] This tells us something of a major goal of Turner's research: the determination for a wider world that an independent church such as the Church of the Lord (Aladura) was really a Christian church.[73] Yet at least implicitly, this could be construed as assuming a Western-based theological test.

In summary, Turner urges a certain form of participatory research, one marked by mutuality, open-endedness, learning in community, and discernment. Not incidentally, for Turner friendship stands as a guide for relationships,[74] which in principle renders an "exotic other" untenable. Turner also correctly emphasizes the human encounter with God as central for the congregations and their lived narratives. Participant research, as Turner suggests and other scholars such as Vásquez and Tweed concur, can bring about a level of understanding that a textual reading could never provide. Burke approaches it as a spiritual calling: "The call of the hour to foster inculturation of the Christian Church is a call to be open to the ever-living mystery of the Incarnation unfolding in us and our peoples . . . revealing both who we are as human beings and who our God is in whose image we have been made."[75]

From this discussion, I draw a further conclusion: there is no single way to describe my point of view. This became especially clear as I found myself changing through the process and period of research. Initially I wanted to understand the global circulations of prayer, yet increasingly I also found myself in need of prayer and called to prayer in ways that were different than where I began. The closer I came to becoming a part of a praying community, the more ways my experience pressed my Western-shaped presuppositions about God and faith.

70. Turner, "Problems in the Study of African Independent Churches," 38.
71. T. Jack Thompson, "A Place to Feel at Home," *Studies in World Christianity* 10:2 (2004): 156.
72. Turner, "Problems in the Study of African Independent Churches," 41.
73. Turner, "Problems in the Study of African Independent Churches."
74. Turner, "Problems in the Study of African Independent Churches," 31.
75. Burke, *These Catholic Sisters Are All Mamas!*, 204.

APPENDIX 1

In effect, over the course of my study, I frequently moved from personal interest to personal implications, from documenting theological contributions to encountering theological challenges.[76] This did not displace critical reflection and evaluation, but enriched it and required it to be more reflexive. Looking back, my experience with African churches provided "a critical comparative perspective"[77] on my own culture and understanding and practice of Christian faith. By helping me identify my experience of God in relationship to my own theological environment,[78] my study raised personal tensions and questions about how I have come to live and relate my faith to everyday life. As a result, through African churches I have come to appreciate new ways of thinking about faith as an integral way of life, the "imperative" to "know God in all your ways" (Proverbs 3:6).[79]

---

76. As Benetta Jules-Rosette wrote in *African Apostles:* "The critical transition for me was that from an outsider observer looking for general descriptions of the church and its worship to that of a full member for whom all descriptions had their own personal implications and sense of urgency" (96).

77. Lamin Sanneh, *Translating the Message: The Missionary Impact on Culture,* revised and expanded ed. (Maryknoll, N.Y.: Orbis, 2009), 35.

78. Burke, *These Catholic Sisters Are All Mamas!,* 198, speaks of "inner listening to outer experiences."

79. This translation is from Michael Fishbane, *Sacred Attunement: A Jewish Theology* (Chicago: University of Chicago Press, 2008), 111.

APPENDIX 2:
Survey Data on African Churches in New York City

Church	Primary Country of Origin	Borough
Abundant Life Christian Ministries Worldwide (Abundant Life Christian Center)		
Victory Center	Nigeria	Bronx
Winners House	Nigeria	Brooklyn
Alive Chapel International	Ghana	Bronx
Apostolic Church International		
Bronx	Ghana	Bronx
Bronx	Ghana	Bronx
Brooklyn	Ghana	Brooklyn
Staten Island	Ghana	Staten Island
Bethel Ethiopian Evangelical Church	Ethiopia	Manhattan
Bethel Outreach	Liberia	Staten Island
Calvary First Nigerian Seventh Day Adventist Church	Nigeria	Brooklyn
Celestial Church of Christ		
Calvary Parish	Nigeria	Queens
Coney Island Parish	Nigeria	Brooklyn
Illeri Oluwa Parish	Nigeria	Brooklyn
New York Parish	Nigeria	Brooklyn
Promise Land Parish	Nigeria	Brooklyn
Queens Parish	Nigeria	Queens
Rock of Ages	Nigeria	Queens
Staten Island Parish	Nigeria	Staten Island
Thy Will Be Done	Nigeria	Brooklyn
Winners Parish	Nigeria	Brooklyn
Cherubim & Seraphim Movement Church (The Holy Order of)		
#1 — Radde Place	Nigeria	Brooklyn
#2 — Rockaway Avenue	Nigeria	Brooklyn
#3 — Glory Star	Nigeria	Bronx

APPENDIX 2

#4 — Ogo-Oluwa	Nigeria	Brooklyn
#5 — Church of Jesus Christ	Nigeria	Bronx
Christ Apostolic Church		
"Agbala-Itura, International Miracle Center"	Nigeria	Brooklyn
First in the Americas	Nigeria	Brooklyn
Christ Apostolic Church of America (W.O.S.E.M.)	Nigeria	Queens
Christ Assembly Lutheran Church	Liberia	Staten Island
Christ Deliverance and Healing Ministries	Nigeria	Brooklyn
Christ Life Ministries Worldwide —		
Uncommon Champion's Cathedral	Nigeria	Brooklyn
Christ Memorial Christian Church (closed in 2009)	Liberia	Staten Island
Christ Pentecostal International Church	Nigeria	Bronx
Church of Pentecost		
Bronx Assembly	Ghana	Bronx
Brooklyn Assembly	Ghana	Brooklyn
International Worship Center (Harlem)	Ghana	Manhattan
Queens Assembly	Ghana	Queens
Staten Island Assembly	Ghana	Staten Island
Church of the Lord Aladura		
Bronx	Liberia	Bronx
Brooklyn	Nigeria	Brooklyn
Dayspring Glory Ministries	Ghana	Bronx
Deeper Life Bible Church		
Bronx	Nigeria	Bronx
Brooklyn	Nigeria	Brooklyn
Queens	Nigeria	Queens
Staten Island	Nigeria	Staten Island
Diocese of Brooklyn (Brooklyn, Queens)		
Ghanaian Apostolate/ St. Benedict the Moor	Ghana	Brooklyn
Ghanaian Apostolate/ St. Catherine of Genoa	Ghana	Brooklyn
St. Fortunata	Nigeria	Brooklyn
St. Paul	Nigeria	Brooklyn
St. Stanislaus Bishop and Martyr	Nigeria	Queens
St. Xavier	Nigeria	Brooklyn
"Diocese of New York (Bronx, Manhattan, Staten Island)"		
Angela Merici Parish	Nigeria	Bronx
Ghanaian Catholic Community of Christ the King	Ghana	Bronx
St. Margaret Mary Parish	Ghana	Bronx
Eglise Evangelique "Amour Du Christ"	Congo	Manhattan
Emmanuel Presbyterian Reformed Church	Ghana	Bronx
Emmanuel Worship Center/ Ethiopian Evangelical	Ethiopia	Bronx
Ethiopian Orthodox Tewahedo Church		
Holy Trinity	Ethiopia	Bronx
Medhane Alem	Ethiopia	Manhattan
St. Mary of Zion	Ethiopia	Manhattan
First Ghana Seventh Day Adventist	Ghana	Bronx

Survey Data on African Churches in New York City

First United Christian Church	Liberia	Staten Island
French Ministry of Lexington Avenue United Methodist	Congo	Manhattan
Gethsemane House of Prayer	Liberia	Queens
Ghana Wesley United Methodist Church	Ghana	Brooklyn
Ghanaian Reformed Presbyterian Church of Brooklyn	Ghana	Brooklyn
Hill of the Lord Ministries Glory Temple	Ghana	Brooklyn
International Central Gospel Church		Bronx
Light of God International Miracle Center	Nigeria	Brooklyn
Lighthouse Chapel International		
Bronx	Ghana	Bronx
Bronx (Akan)	Ghana	Bronx
Brooklyn	Ghana	Brooklyn
Manhattan	Ghana	Manhattan
Queens	Ghana	Queens
Mountain of Fire & Miracles Ministries		
Bronx	Nigeria	Bronx
Brooklyn	Nigeria	Brooklyn
Queens	Nigeria	Queens
Staten Island	Nigeria	Staten Island
Presbyterian Church of Ghana		
Bronx	Ghana	Bronx
Harlem	Ghana	Manhattan
Redeemed Christian Church of God		
Chapel of Hope	Nigeria	Brooklyn
Chapel of Love	Nigeria	Brooklyn
Chapel of Praise	Nigeria	Brooklyn
Chapel of Restoration	Nigeria	Bronx
Covenant Chapel (Castleton Ave)	Nigeria	Staten Island
Covenant Chapel (Cebra Ave)	Nigeria	Staten Island
Destiny Sanctuary For All Nations	Nigeria	Queens
Divine Restoration Chapel (East Elmhurst)	Nigeria	Queens
Divine Restoration Chapel (Elmhurst)	Nigeria	Queens
Freedom Court	Nigeria	Staten Island
House of Prayer	Nigeria	Manhattan
International Chapel Brooklyn	Nigeria	Brooklyn
International Chapel Coney Island	Nigeria	Brooklyn
International Chapel East New York	Nigeria	Brooklyn
International Chapel Queens	Nigeria	Queens
International Chapel Roosevelt Island	Nigeria	Roosevelt Island
Rehoboth Chapel	Nigeria	Brooklyn
Restoration Family	Nigeria	Bronx
Restoration Springs	Nigeria	Queens
Solid Rock	Nigeria	Staten Island
Refined Holy Fire of Zion Church	Nigeria	Bronx
Royal House Chapel International	Ghana	Bronx
Spirit and Life Bible Church	Nigeria	Brooklyn

APPENDIX 2

The Eternal Sacred Order of Cherubim & Seraphim Abgo-Jesu	Nigeria	Brooklyn
The Gospel Faith Mission International, New York	Nigeria	Brooklyn
The Grace of God Ministries Inc.	Nigeria	Bronx
The Sacred Cherubim & Seraphim Church	Nigeria	Bronx
Trinity Baptist	Liberia	Staten Island
United Methodist Church Ghana	Ghana	Bronx
Vineyard International Christian Ministries	Nigeria	Bronx
Winners' Chapel International, New York	Nigeria	Queens
Zion Sanctuary	Nigeria	Queens

Sources

INTERVIEWS

Name	Church	Office/Title	Date
Ademola Adeabenro	RCCG	Member	06/05/05
Wale Adebo	RCCG	Member	04/10/05
Solomon Adelaja	Celestial Church of Christ	Senior Evangelist, New York Branch	03/12/06
Egbefun Adieze	RCCG MSG	Deaconess, Founding Member, RCCG New York City	07/16/05
Jimmy Ado	PCG	Choir President	08/13/06
Kwame Adom	PCG	Member	09/01/07
Nana A. Afwireng	PCG	Choir Member	08/13/06
Kwasi "K.B" Agyare	PCG	Bible Study and Prayer Group	07/30/04
Rex Agyemang	PCG	Youth Pastor	08/15/04 08/14/05 05/31/06 08/29/06
Julie Agyemang-Du[o]ah	PCG	Member	08/21/05 11/25/07
Angelina Akiwumi	PCG	Women's Fellowship Bible Study and Prayer, Elder	08/20/04
Dave Francis Ali	Diocese of Brooklyn	Assistant Director, Migration Office	08/04/06
George Kofi Amankwah	PCG	Member	08/21/05
Isaac Amissah	PCG	Session Youth Representative	08/14/05
Apostle Amonah	Church of Pentecost	Leader	04/14/04
Amma Amponsah	PCG	Member	08/07/05
Oheneba Amponsah	PCG	Member	08/14/05
Prince Asante	PCG	Member	08/06/06

SOURCES

Ebenezer Asare	PCG	Member	08/21/05
Kwame Asare (pseudonym)	PCG	Member	08/05/05
Samuel Asare	PCG	Member and team mission, Catechist Abboah-Offei	10/27/05 12/13/06 12/14/06
Mindy Asiedu	PCG	Member, Youth Program	08/14/05
Yaw Asiedu	PCG	Pastor	03/09/04 04/18/04 07/16/05 08/09/05 11/08/05 12/06/06 09/13/07
Seth Atakora	PCG	PCG Bronx Leader, Ebenezer	04/18/04
Benjamin Ayeh	Apostolic Church International	Member	08/27/06
Moses Biney	PCG	OMF Director	06/10/05
"Bisolani, Sis." (pseudonym)			06/05/05
George Asbe Boafu	PCG	OMF Meeting	10/23/04
Eleanor Campbell	CLA Bronx	Evangelist	12/12/04
Ossai Chegwe	RCCG	Worker	05/01/05
Harold Clarke	CLA	Member	10/21/07
Joy Cooper	CLA	Minister	01/16/05
Marie (Mother) Cooper	CLA Bronx	Founder and Leader	09/30/04 10/17/04 12/12/04 02/13/05 03/13/05 05/12/05 06/23/05 01/12/06 10/21/07 02/13/08
Rakiya Dada	RCCG	Member	08/11/04
Nana Darko	PCG	Catechist in Ghana	08/13/04
Daniel Diakanwa	Congolese Church	Pastor	02/15/08
Olumuyiwa Durodola	RCCG at MSG		06/16/05
Prince Edosa	RCCG	Member	05/29/05
Justin Emineke	RCCG	Member, Worker	10/19/03 10/10/04
Nosa Evbuomwan	Texas RCCG		07/16/05
James O. Fadele	RCCG	Chairman, North America Board of Coordinators	03/21/04
Grace Fakeye	RCCG	Minister	04/10/05

Sources

Edwin Flower	CLA	Member	11/28/04
			10/21/07
David Grigsby	CLA	Member	03/13/05
			10/21/07
Eric Gyasu	PCG	Member	08/29/04
			08/06/06
Kwabena Gyasi	PCG	Member	08/19/05
Tobias Haller	St. James Episcopal Church	Pastor	03/14/08
Dorcas Idemudia	RCCG	Member	04/10/05
Tolashe Jaiyeoba	RCCG	Member	04/17/05
Olubunmi (Elizabeth) Kadiri	RCCG	Worker	04/17/05
			06/22/05
Emmanuel Katongole	Duke Divinity School		11/19/04
Alfred Kissiedo	PCG	Member	07/31/05
John Lachana	CLA	Archdeacon, Rep of Primate based in Atlanta	08/27/04
Opanin Kwabena Mensah	PCG	Member	08/14/05
Prince Nyrako	Central Gospel Church	Church leader	01/04/06
Elsie Obed	Lillies International	Evangelist, RCCG Missionary to North America	04/14/07
Olu (Olusegun) Obed	Dayspring Church	Pastor, RCCG Missionary to North America	02/18/04
Emmanuel Obo	RCCG	Member	04/10/05
Omo Obogbaimhe	RCCG	Choir, Worker	05/22/05
Catherine (Idusuyi) Obohidusuyo	RCCG	Minister	07/14/04
			06/22/05
Agatha Ofori-Mankata	PCG	Member	10/27/05
Lona Ojedapo	RCCG	Worker	05/29/05
Bola Olalade	RCCG	Member	06/05/05
Kola Olaleye	RCCG	Member	04/10/05
Tunde Olaose	RCCG	Musician, Member	06/05/05
Olesegun Olowolabi	MFM		02/19/06
Olakunle Onaleye	Winners' Chapel International, New York	Pastor	12/31/06
Michael Onyeri	RCCG	Member, Worker	10/15/03
			10/14/07
Dolapo Osinfade	RCCG	Pastor	05/10/09
Rufus Ositelu	CLA	Primate	10/08/06

SOURCES

Diana Owusu	PCG	Member, Bible Study and Prayer Group	07/20/07 03/04/08
Kwaku Owusu	Lighthouse Chapel	Manhattan Branch Ministry Leader	06/25/06
Bola Dyesanya	RCCG	Deacon	09/23/07
Segun Oyesanya	RCCG	Deacon	06/11/06
Adebisi Oyesile	RCCG Brooklyn	Minister	04/03/05 09/03/06 01/19/08 02/11/08 03/13/08
Matilda Oyeyemi	RCCG	Minister	01/30/04 06/05/04 06/22/05 01/12/08
Samuel Prempeh	PCG Ghana	Moderator of the General Assembly (Bronx)	10/24/04
Sarah Richards	CLA Bronx	Evangelist	12/12/04
Bisola Rotimi-Omodehin	RCCG	Worker/minister	08/25/04 04/17/05
David Rquarm	CLA Bronx	Deacon	12/19/04
Sandra Ukoh	RCCG	Member	09/01/04
Austin Umanmielen	RCCG	Member	04/17/05
Nimi Wariboko	RCCG	Pastor	08/25/04 11/15/06
Wapaemi Wariboko	RCCG	Assistant Pastor	05/29/05
Sister West-Erhabor	RCCG	Minister	12/07/05 02/16/06

FOCUS GROUPS

Redeemed Christian Church of God International Chapel, Brooklyn Youth–October 14, 2007

    Kimberly Jean Baptiste
    Lashe Davies
    Idowu
    Nita Idusuyi
    Bola Ogungbuyi
    Cyril Osinfade
    Sena West-Erhabor
    Stephanie West-Erhabor

Sources

Presbyterian Church of Ghana in New York Youth–December 2, 2007

Abena	Fanny	Phyllis
Abby	Gifty	Rosemary
Barbara	Kevin	Samuel
Debora	Kofi	Selonma
Eleanora	Mimi	
Ernest	Papa	

BOOKS AND ARTICLES

Abbl, Martin C. "'Are Any Among You Sick?' The Health Care System in the Letter of James." *Journal of Biblical Literature* 121:1 (2002): 123-43.

Abdullah, Zain. *Black Mecca: The African Muslims of Harlem.* Forthcoming, Oxford University Press.

―――. "Sufis on Parade: The Performance of Black, African, and Muslim Identities." *Journal of the American Academy of Religion* 77:2 (2009): 199-237.

Abu-Lughod, Janet L. *New York, Chicago, Los Angeles: America's Global Cities.* Minneapolis: University of Minnesota Press, 1999.

Achebe, Chinua. *Things Fall Apart.* New York: Everyman Library, 1992 [1958].

Adamo, David Tuesday. "The Use of Psalms in African Indigenous Churches in Nigeria." In *The Bible in Africa: Transactions, Trajectories and Trends,* edited by Gerald O. West and Musa W. Dube, 336-49. Boston and Leiden: Brill, 2001.

Adams, Michael Henry. *Harlem Lost and Found: An Architectural and Social History, 1765-1915.* New York: The Monacelli, 2002.

Adeboye, Olufunke. "'Arrowhead' of Nigerian Pentecostalism: The Redeemed Christian Church of God, 1952-2005." *Pneuma* 29 (2007): 24-58.

Adejunmobi, Moradewun. *Vernacular Palaver: Imaginations of the Local and Non-Native Languages in West Africa.* Clevedon: Multilingual Matters Ltd., 2004.

Adeyemo, Tokunboh, ed. *Africa Bible Commentary.* Grand Rapids: Zondervan, 2006.

Adichie, Chimamanda Ngozi. *The Thing around Your Neck.* New York: Knopf, 2009.

Adogame, Afe. "Ranks and Robes: Art Symbolism and Identity in the Celestial Church of Christ in the European Diaspora." *Material Religion* 5:1 (2009): 10-13.

―――. "HIV/AIDS Support and African Pentecostalism: The Case of the Redeemed Christian Church of God." *Journal of Health Psychology* 12:3 (2007): 475-84.

―――. "Prayer as Action and Instrument in the Aladura Churches." In *Opfer und Gebet in den Religionen,* edited by Ulrich Berner, Christopher Bochinger, and Rainer Flasche, 115-31. Gütersloh: Bertelsmann, 2005.

―――. "Contesting the Ambivalences of Modernity in a Global Context: The Redeemed Christian Church of God, North America." *Studies in World Christianity* 10:1 (2004): 25-48.

―――. "To Be or Not to Be? Politics of Belonging and African Christian Communities in Germany." In *Religion in the Context of African Migration,* edited by Afe Adogame and Cordula Weisskӧppel, 95-112. Bayreuth: Bayreuth African Studies, 2005.

SOURCES

———. "Engaging the Rhetoric of Spiritual Warfare: The Public Face of Aladura in Diaspora." *Journal of Religion in Africa* 34:4 (2004): 493-522.

———. "Betwixt Identity and Security: African New Religious Movements and the Politics of Religious Networking in Europe." *Nova Religio: The Journal of Alternative and Emergent Religions* 7:2 (November 2003): 21-41.

———. "The Quest for Space in the Global Spiritual Marketplace: African Religions in Europe." *International Review of Mission* 89:354 (2000): 400-409.

Adogame, Afe, and Ezra Chitando. "Moving Among Those Moved by the Spirit: Conducting Fieldwork within the New African Religious Diaspora." *Fieldwork in Religion* 1:3 (2005): 253-70.

Adogame, Afe, ed. *Who Is Afraid of the Holy Ghost? Pentecostalism and Globalization in Africa and Beyond*. Trenton: Africa World Press, 2011.

Adogame, Afe, Roswith Gerloff, and Klaus Hock, eds. *Christianity in Africa and the African Diaspora: The Appropriation of a Scattered Heritage*. London: Continuum, 2008.

Adogame, Afe, and Cordula Weisskӧppel, eds. *Religion in the Context of African Migration*. Bayreuth: Bayreuth African Studies, 2005.

Aina, Olatunji F. "'Psychotherapy by Environmental Manipulation' and the Observed Symbolic Rites on Prayer Mountains in Nigeria." *Mental Health, Religion and Culture* 9:1 (2006): 1-13.

Akrong, Abraham. "Salvation in African Christianity." *Legon Journal of the Humanities* 12 (1991-2001): 1-29.

Alex-Assensoh, Yvette M. "African Immigrants and African-Americans: An Analysis of Voluntary African Immigration and the Evolution of Black Ethnic Politics in America," *African and Asian Studies* 8:1-2 (2009): 89-124.

Alter, Robert. *The Book of Psalms: A Translation with Commentary* (New York: W. W. Norton, 2007).

Amenga-Etego, Rose Mary. "Mending the Broken Pieces: Religion and Sustainable Rural Development Among the Nankani of Norther Ghana." Ph.D. thesis, University of Edinburgh, 2007.

Ammerman, Nancy Tatom. *Pillars of Faith: American Congregations and Their Partners*. Berkeley: University of California Press, 2005.

Anderson, Allan H. "Towards a Pentecostal Missiology for the Majority World." *Asian Journal of Pentecostal Theology* 8:1 (2005): 29-47.

———. *An Introduction to Pentecostalism: Global Charismatic Christianity*. Cambridge: Cambridge University Press, 2004.

———. "The Newer Pentecostal and Charismatic Churches." *Pneuma* 24:2 (2002): 167-84.

———. *African Reformation: African Initiated Christianity in the Twentieth Century*. Trenton: Africa World Press, 2001.

———. "Stretching the Definitions? Pneumatology and 'Syncretism' in African Pentecostalism." *Journal of Pentecostal Theology* 10:1 (2001): 98-119.

———. *Moya: The Holy Spirit in an African Context*. Pretoria: The University of South Africa, 1991.

———. "Pentecostal Pneumatology and African Power Concepts: Continuity or Change?" *Missionalia* 19:1 (1990): 65-74.

———. "African Pentecostal Churches and Concepts of Power." Unpublished paper. Available at http://artsweb.bham.ac.uk/aanderson/Publications/apcs_and_concepts_of_power.htm.

Anderson, Jon Lee. "After the Warlords: Can Ellen Johnson Sirleaf Remake Her Nation?" *New Yorker,* March 27, 2006.

Appadurai, Arjun. *Modernity at Large: Cultural Dimensions of Globalization.* Minneapolis: University of Minnesota Press, 1996.

Asad, Talal. *Genealogies of Religion: Discipline and Reasons of Power in Christianity and Islam.* Baltimore: The Johns Hopkins University Press, 1993.

Asamoah-Gyadu, J. Kwabena. "'Broken Calabashes and Covenants of Fruitfulness': Cursing Barrenness in Contemporary African Christianity." *Journal of Religion in Africa* 37:4 (2007): 437-60.

———. "'Get on the Internet!' Says the Lord: Religion, Cyberspace and Christianity in Contemporary Africa." *Studies in World Christianity* 13:3 (2007): 225-42.

———. "'On the Mountain of the Lord': Healing Pilgrimages in Ghanaian Christianity." *Exchange* 36:1 (2007): 65-86.

———. "Pulling Down Strongholds: Evangelism, Principalities and Powers and the African Pentecostal Imagination." *International Review of Mission* 96:382/383 (2007): 306-17.

———. "An African Pentecostal on Mission in Eastern Europe: The Church of the 'Embassy of God' in the Ukraine." *Pneuma* 27:2 (Fall 2005): 297-321.

———. *African Charismatics: Current Developments within Independent Indigenous Pentecostalism in Ghana.* Leiden: Brill, 2005.

———. "'Christ is the Answer: What is the Question?' A Ghana Airways Prayer Vigil and Its Implications for Religion, Evil and Public Space." *Journal of Religion in Africa* 35:1 (2005): 93-117.

———. "Of Faith and Visual Alertness: The Message of the 'Mediatized' Religion in an African Pentecostal Context." *Material Religion* 1:3 (2005): 336-56.

———. "Mission to 'Set the Captives Free': Healing, Deliverance, and Generational Curses in Ghanaian Pentecostalism." *International Review of Mission* 93:370/371 (July/October 2004): 389-406.

Attridge, Harold W. "Resurrection in the Fourth Gospel." SNTS Johannine Literature Seminar, Aberdeen. Unpublished paper, 2006.

Augustine, Saint. *On Christian Teaching.* Translated by R. P. H. Green. Oxford: Oxford University Press, 1997.

———. *The Confessions.* Oxford: Oxford University Press, 1992.

Baia, Larissa Ruiz. "Rethinking Transnationalism: National Identities among Peruvian Catholics in New Jersey." In *Christianity, Social Change, and Globalization in the Americas,* edited by Anna L. Peterson, Manuel A. Vásquez, and Philip J. Williams, 147-64. New Brunswick: Rutgers University Press, 2001.

Bajc, Vida, Simon Coleman, and John Eade. "Introduction: Mobility and Centring in Pilgrimage." *Mobilities* 2:3 (2007): 321-29.

Banerjee, Neela. "A Midnight Service Helps African Immigrants Combat Demons." *New York Times,* December 18, 2007, A-24.

Barker, Isabelle V. "Charismatic Economies: Pentecostalism, Economic Restructuring, and Social Reproduction." *New Political Science* 29:4 (2007): 407-27.

Baron, Akesha. "'I'm a Woman but I *Know* God Leads My Way': Agency and Tzotzil Evangelical Discourse." *Language in Society* 33 (2004): 249-83.

SOURCES

Barrett, David B., George T. Kurian, and Todd M. Johnson. *World Christian Encyclopedia.* Vol. 1, 2nd ed. New York: Oxford University Press, 2001.

Bateye, Bolaj Olukemi. "Forging Identities: Women as Participants and Leaders in the Church among the Yoruba." *Studies in World Christianity* 13:1 (2007): 1-12.

Bauckham, Richard. *James: Wisdom of James, Disciple of Jesus the Sage.* New York: Routledge, 1999.

Baumann, Martin. "Diaspora: Genealogies of Semantics and Transcultural Comparison." *Numen* 47 (2000): 313-37.

Bediako, Kwame. "Worship as Vital Participation: Some Personal Reflections on Ministry in the African Church." *Journal of African Christian Thought* 8:2 (2005): 3.

———. "African and Christian: Recovering an Ancient Story." *Princeton Seminary Bulletin* 25:2 (2004): 153-61.

———. *Jesus and the Gospel in Africa: History and Experience.* Maryknoll, N.Y.: Orbis, 2004.

———. "Scripture as the Hermeneutic of Culture and Tradition." *Journal of African Christian Thought* 4:1 (2002): 2-11.

———. "Africa and Christianity on the Threshold of the Third Millennium: The Religious Dimension." *African Affairs* 99:395 (2000): 303-23.

———. *Christianity in Africa: The Renewal of a Non-Western Religion.* Edinburgh: Edinburgh University Press and Maryknoll, N.Y.: Orbis Books, 1995.

Benjamin, Walter. "The Work of Art in the Age of Its Technological Reproducibility: Second Version." In *Selected Writings.* Volume 3, *1935-1938*, translated by Edmund Jephcott, Howard Eiland, et al., edited by Howard Eiland and Michael W. Jennings. Cambridge: Belknap Press of Harvard University Press, 2002.

Benson, Bruce Ellis, and Norman Wirzba, eds. *The Phenomenology of Prayer.* New York: Fordham University Press, 2005.

Benton-Short, Lisa, Marie D. Price, and Samantha Friedman. "Globalization from Below: The Ranking of Global Immigrant Cities." *International Journal of Urban and Regional Research* 29:4 (2005): 945-59.

Bergner, Daniel. "The Call." *New York Times Magazine*, January 29, 2006.

Berlin, Ira, and Leslie M. Harris, eds. *Slavery in New York.* New York: The New Press, 2005.

Berryman, Phillip. "Churches as Winners and Losers in the Network Society." *Journal of Interamerican Studies and World Affairs* 41:4 (1999): 21-34.

Bevans, Stephen B., and Roger P. Schroeder. *Constants in Context: A Theology of Mission for Today.* Maryknoll, N.Y.: Orbis, 2004.

Beyer, Peter. *Religion in a Global Society.* London: Routledge, 2006.

Beyer, Peter, and Lori Berman, eds. *Religion, Globalization, and Culture.* Leiden: Brill, 2007.

Bhagwati, Jagdish. *In Defense of Globalization.* New York: Oxford University Press, 2005.

Bialecki, Jon Naomi Haynes, and Joel Robbins. "The Anthropology of Christianity." *Religion Compass* 2:6 (2008): 1139-58.

Bielo, James S. "On the Failure of 'Meaning': Bible Reading in the Anthropology of Christianity." *Culture and Religion* 9:1 (2008): 1-21.

Bilger, Burkhard. "Mystery on Pearl Street." *New Yorker*, January 7, 2008, 56-65.

Binder, Frederick M., and David M. Reimers. *All the Nations Under Heaven: An Ethnic and Racial History of New York City.* New York: Columbia University Press, 1995.

Biney, Moses. "Singing the Lord's Song in a Foreign Land: Spirituality, Communality, and Identity in a Ghanaian Immigrant Congregation." In *African Immigrant Religions in*

America, edited by Jacob K. Olupona and Regina Gemignani, 259-78. New York: New York University Press, 2007.

———. "Singing the Lord's Song in a Foreign Land: A Socio-Ethical Study of a Ghanaian Immigrant Church in New York." Ph.D. thesis, Princeton Theological Seminary, 2005.

Boers, Hendrikus. *Christ in the Letters of Paul: In Place of Christology*. Berlin: Walter de Gruyter, 2006.

Bonhoeffer, Dietrich. *Sanctorum Communio: A Theological Study of the Sociology of the Church*. Translated by Reinhard Krauss and Nancy Lukens. Minneapolis: Fortress, Press, 1998.

Bourdieu, Pierre. *Outline of a Theory of Practice*. Cambridge: Cambridge University Press, 1977.

Boyarin, Daniel, and Jonathan Boyarin. *Powers of Diaspora: Two Essays on the Relevance of Jewish Culture*. Minneapolis: University of Minnesota Press, 2002.

Britt, Samuel Irving. "The Children of Salvation: Struggle and Cosmology in Liberian Prophet Churches." Ph.D. thesis, University of Virginia, 1992.

Brodwin, Paul. "Pentecostalism in Translation: Religion and the Production of Community in the Haitian Diaspora." *American Ethnologist* 30:1 (2003): 85-101.

Brown, Candy Gunther, ed. *Global Pentecostal and Charismatic Healing*. Oxford: Oxford University Press, 2011.

Brown, Karen McCarthy. *Mama Lola: A Vodou Priestess in Brooklyn*. Berkeley: University of California Press, 2001.

Brueggemann, Walter. *Theology of the Old Testament: Testimony, Dispute and Advocacy*. Minneapolis: Fortress Press, 1997.

Buama, Livingstone. "The Worship Experience of the Reformed Family in Ghana, West Africa: The Cry and Quest for Liturgical Reform." In *Christian Worship in Reformed Churches Past and Present*, edited by Lukas Vischer, 216-23. Grand Rapids: Eerdmans, 2003.

Burawoy, Michael. "Manufacturing the Global." *Ethnography* 2 (2): 147-59.

Burdick, John. *Blessed Anastácia: Women, Race, and Popular Christianity in Brazil*. New York: Routledge, 1998.

Burke, Joan F. *These Catholic Sisters Are All Mamas! Towards the Inculturation of Sisterhood in Africa, an Ethnographic Study*. Leiden: Brill, 2001.

Burrows, Edwin G., and Mike Wallace. *Gotham: A History of New York City to 1898*. New York: Oxford University Press, 1999.

Butler, Jon. "Theory and God in Gotham." *History and Theory* 45 (2006): 47-61.

———. "Religion in New York City: Faith that Could Not Be." *U.S. Catholic Historian* 22:2 (2002): 51-61.

Bynum, Caroline Walker. *Holy Feast and Holy Fast: The Religious Significance of Food to Medieval Women*. Berkeley: University of California Press, 1987.

Cage, Wendy, and Elaine Howard Ecklund. "Immigration and Religion." *Annual Review of Sociology* 33 (2007): 359-79.

Caglar, Ayse. "Hometown Associations, the Rescaling of State Spatiality and Migrant Grassroots Transnationalism." *Global Networks* 6:1 (2006): 1-22.

Cannell, Fanella, ed. *The Anthropology of Christianity*. Durham: Duke University Press, 2006.

Carroll, Jackson W. *God's Potters: Pastoral Leadership and the Shaping of Congregations.* Grand Rapids: Eerdmans, 2006.

Casanova, José. "Religion, the New Millennium, and Globalization." *Sociology of Religion* 62:4 (2001): 415-41.

Castells, Manuel. *The Power of Identity.* Oxford: Blackwell, 1997.

César, Waldo. "From Babel to Pentecost: A Socio-Historical-Theological Study of the Growth of Pentecostalism." In *Between Babel and Pentecost: Transnational Pentecostalism in Africa and Latin America,* edited by André Corten and Ruth Marshall-Fratani, 22-40. Bloomington: University of Indiana Press, 2001.

Chamberlain, Mary, and Selma Leydesdorff. "Transnational Families: Memories and Narratives." *Global Networks* 4:3 (2004): 227-42.

Chandra, Nayan. *Bound Together: How Traders, Preachers, Adventurers, and Warriors Shaped Globalization.* New Haven: Yale University Press, 2007.

Chen, Carolyn. "From Filial Piety to Religious Piety: Evangelical Christianity Reconstructing Taiwanese Immigrant Families in the United States." *International Migration Review* 40:3 (2006): 573-602.

Chestnut, R. Andrew. *Competitive Spirits: Latin America's New Religious Economy.* Oxford: Oxford University Press, 2003.

Chidester, David. "Dreaming in the Contact Zone: Zulu Dreams, Visions, and Religion in Nineteenth-Century South Africa." *Journal of the American Academy of Religion* 76:1 (2008): 27-53.

Childs, Brevard S. "Speech-act Theory and Biblical Interpretation." *Scottish Journal of Theology* 58:4 (2005): 375-92.

Coakley, Sarah. "Why Three? Some Further Reflections on the Origins of the Doctrine of the Trinity." In *The Making and Remaking of Christian Doctrine: Essays in Honor of Maurice Wiles,* edited by Sarah Coakley and David A. Pailin, 29-56. Oxford: Clarendon Press, 1993.

―――. "God as Trinity: An Approach through Prayer." In *We Believe in God: A Report by the Doctrine Commission of the General Synod of the Church of England,* 104-21. Wilton, Conn.: Morehouse-Barlow, 1987.

Cohen, Emma. "What Is Spirit Possession? Defining, Comparing, and Explaining Two Possession Forms." *Ethnos* 73:1 (2008): 101-26.

Coleman, Simon. *The Globalisation of Charismatic Christianity: Spreading the Gospel of Prosperity.* Cambridge: Cambridge University Press, 2000.

Coleman, Simon, and Peter Collins. "The 'Plain' and the 'Positive': Ritual, Experience and Aesthetics in Quakerism and Charismatic Christianity." *Journal of Contemporary Religion* 15:3 (2000): 317-29.

Coles, Robert. *The Spiritual Life of Children.* Boston: Houghton Mifflin, 1990.

Collins, John N. "Ordained and Other Ministries: Making a Difference." *Ecclesiology* 3:1 (2006): 11-32.

Comaroff, Jean. "The Politics of Conviction: Faith on the Neo-liberal Frontier." *Social Analysis* 53:1 (2009): 17-38.

Comaroff, Jean, and John Comaroff. "Privatizing the Millennium: New Protestant Ethics and the Spirits of Capitalism in Africa, and Elsewhere." *Afrika Spectrum* 35 (2000): 293-312.

Sources

Conn, Harvie M. "The Missionary Task of Theology: A Love/Hate Relationship." *Westminster Theological Journal* 45 (1983): 1-21.
Copeland-Carson, Jacqueline. *Creating Africa in America: Translocal Identity in an Emerging World City.* Philadelphia: University of Pennsylvania Press, 2004.
Corten, André, and Ruth Marshall-Fratani, eds. *Between Babel and Pentecost: Transnational Pentecostalism in Africa and Latin America.* Bloomington: University of Indiana Press, 2001.
Costelo, Daniel. "Tarrying on the Lord: Affections, Virtues and Theological Ethics in Pentecostal Perspective." *Journal of Pentecostal Theology* 13:1 (2004): 31-56.
Coulter, Dale. "'Delivered by the Power of God': Toward a Pentecostal Understanding of Salvation." *International Journal of Systematic Theology* 10:4 (2008): 447-67.
Cox, Harvey. *Fire from Heaven: The Rise of Pentecostal Spirituality and the Reshaping of Religion in the Twenty-First Century.* Reading: Addison-Wesley, 1995.
Cox, James L. *A Guide to the Phenomenology of Religion: Key Figures, Formative Influences and Subsequent Debates.* London: Continuum, 2006.
———. "African Identities as the Projection of Western Alterity." In *Uniquely African? African Christian Identity from Cultural and Historical Perspectives,* edited by James L. Cox and Gerrie ter Haar, 25-37. Trenton: Africa World Press, 2003.
Crumbley, Deidre Helen. *Spirit, Structure, and Flesh: Gendered Experiences in African Instituted Churches among the Yoruba of Nigeria.* Madison: University of Wisconsin Press, 2008.
———. "'Power in the Blood': Menstrual Taboos and Women's Power in an African Instituted Church." In *Women and Religion in the African Diaspora: Knowledge, Power, and Performance,* edited by Ruth Marie Griffith and Barbara Dianne Savage, 81-97. Baltimore: The Johns Hopkins University Press, 2006.
———. "Patriarchies, Prophets, and Procreation: Sources of Gender Practices in Three African Churches." *Africa* 73:4 (2003): 587-88.
———. "Indigenous Institution Building in an Afro-Christian Movement: The Aladura as Case Study." Ph.D. thesis, Northeastern University, 1989.
Csordas, Thomas J. "Introduction: Modalities of Transnational Transcendence." *Anthropological Theory* 7:4 (2007): 259-72.
———. *Body/Meaning/Healing.* New York: Palgrave Macmillan, 2002.
———, ed. *Transnational Transcendence: Essays on Religion and Globalization* Berkeley: University of California Press, 2009.
Currid, Elizabeth. *The Warhol Economy: How Fashion, Art, and Music Drive New York City.* Princeton: Princeton University Press, 2007.
D'Alisera, JoAnn. *An Imagined Geography: Sierra Leonean Muslims in America.* Philadelphia: University of Pennsylvania Press, 2004.
Daneel, Marthinus L. "African Initiated Churches in South Africa." In *Christianity Reborn: The Global Expansion of Evangelicalism in the Twentieth Century,* edited by Donald M. Lewis, 181-218. Grand Rapids: Eerdmans, 2004.
———. *African Earthkeepers: Wholistic Interfaith Mission.* Maryknoll, N.Y.: Orbis, 2001.
———. *Quest for Belonging: Introduction to a Study of African Independent Churches.* Zimbabwe: Mambo Press, 1987.
Daswani, Girish. "Transformation and Migration among Members of a Pentecostal Church in Ghana and London." *Journal of Religion in Africa* 40:4 (2010): 442-74.

SOURCES

De Certeau, Michael. "Walking in the City." In *The Practice of Everyday Life*, translated by Steven Rendall, 91-110. Berkeley: University of California Press, 1984.
Deleuze, Gilles, and Felix Guattari. *A Thousand Plateaus: Capitalism and Schizophrenia.* Translated by Brian Massumi. Minneapolis: University of Minnesota Press, 1987.
DeParle, Jason. "Western Union Empire Moves Migrant Cash Home." *New York Times*, November 21, 2007, A-1, 20.
———. "A Good Provider Is One Who Leaves." *New York Times Magazine*, April 22, 2007.
Desai, Kiran. *The Inheritance of Loss.* London: Hamish Hamilton, 2006.
Devisch, René. "'Pillaging Jesus': Healing Churches and the Villagisation of Kinshasa." *Africa* 66:4 (1996): 555-86.
De Vries, Hent, ed. *Religion: Beyond a Concept.* New York: Fordham University Press, 2008.
De Witte, Marleen. "Spirit Media: Charismatics, Traditionalists, and Media Practices in Ghana." Amsterdam, 2008.
Dilger, Hansjörg. "Healing the Wounds of Modernity: Salvation, Community and Care in a Neo-Pentecostal Church in Dar Es Salaam, Tanzania." *Journal of Religion in Africa* 37:1 (2007): 59-83.
Dovlo, Elom. "African Culture and Emergent Church Forms in Ghana." *Exchange* 33:1 (2004): 28-53.
Duffy, Eamon. *Marking the Hours: English People and Their Prayers, 1240-1570.* New Haven: Yale University Press, 2006.
Dykstra, Craig. "Pastoral and Ecclesial Imagination: What Practical Theology Seeks to Nourish." In *For Life Abundant: Practical Theology, Theological Education, and Christian Ministry,* edited by Dorothy C. Bass and Craig Dykstra, 41-61. Grand Rapids: Eerdmans, 2008.
Eade, John, and David Garbin. "Reinterpreting the Relationship Between Centre and Periphery: Pilgrimage and Sacred Spatialisation Among Polish and Congolese Communities in Britain." *Mobilities* 2:3 (2007): 413-24.
Ebaugh, Helen Rose, and Janet Saltzman Chafetz, eds. *Religion Across Borders: Transnational Immigrant Networks.* Walnut Creek: Altamira Press, 2002.
Eck, Diana L. *A New Religious America: How a "Christian Country" Has Become the World's Most Religiously Diverse Nation.* San Francisco: HarperSanFrancisco, 2001.
Eire, Carlos M. N. *A Very Brief History of Eternity.* Princeton: Princeton University Press, 2010.
Eisenlohr, Patrick. "Technologies of the Spirit: Devotional Islam, Sound Reproduction and the Dialectics of Mediation and Immediacy in Mauritius." *Anthropological Theory* 9:3 (2009): 273-96.
Ellis, Stephen, and Gerrie ter Haar. *Worlds of Power: Religious Thought and Political Practice in Africa.* New York: Oxford University Press, 2004.
Elsner, Jas', and Ian Rutherford. Introduction to *Pilgrimage in Graeco-Roman and Early Christian Antiquity: Seeing the Gods,* edited by Jas' Elsner and Ian Rutherford, 12-30. Oxford: Oxford University Press, 2005.
Engberg-Pedersen, Troels. *Cosmology and Self in the Apostle Paul: The Material Spirit.* Oxford: Oxford University Press, 2010.
Engelke, Matthew. "Past Pentecostalism: Notes on Rupture, Realignment, and Everyday Life in Pentecostal and African Churches." *Africa: The Journal of the International African Institute* 80:2 (2010): 177-99.

Sources

———. "Reading and Time: Two Approaches to the Materiality of Scripture." *Ethnos* 74:2 (2009): 151-74.
———. *A Problem of Presence: Beyond Scripture in an African Church.* Berkeley: University of California Press, 2007.
———. "The Book, the Church and the 'Incomprehensible Paradox': Christianity in African History." *Journal of Southern African Studies* 29:1 (March 2003): 297-306.
Engelke, Matthew, and Joel Robbins, eds. "Global Christianity, Global Critique." *The South Atlantic Quarterly* 109:4 (2010).
Englund, Harri. "Ethnography after Globalism: Migration and Emplacement in Malawi." *American Ethnologist* 29:2 (2002): 261-86.
Englund, Harri, and James Leach. "Ethnography and the Meta-Narratives of Modernity." *Current Anthropology* 41:2 (2000): 225-39.
Ernste, Huib, Henk Van Houtum, and Annelies Zommers. "Trans-World: Debating the Place and Borders of Places in the Age of Transnationalism." *Tijdschrift voor Economische en Sociale Geografie* 100:5 (2009): 577-86.
Eves, Richard. "Engendering Gesture: Gender Performativity and Bodily Regimes from New Ireland." *The Asia Pacific Journal of Anthropology* 11:1 (2010): 1-16.
Farhadian, Charles E., ed. *Christian Worship Worldwide: Expanding Horizons, Deepening Practices.* Grand Rapids: Eerdmans, 2007.
Fiscal Policy Institute. "Working for a Better Life: A Profile of Immigrants in the New York State Economy." http://www.fiscalpolicy/immigration.html.
Fletcher, Richard. *The Barbarian Conversion: From Paganism to Christianity.* Berkeley: University of California Press, 1997.
Foley, Michael W., and Dean R. Hoge. *Religion and the New Immigrants: How Faith Communities Form Our Newest Citizens.* Oxford: Oxford University Press, 2007.
Foner, Nancy. *From Ellis Island to JFK: New York's Two Great Waves of Immigration.* New Haven: Yale University Press and New York: Russell Sage Foundation, 2000.
Ford, David F. *Christian Wisdom: Desiring God and Learning in Love.* Cambridge: Cambridge University Press, 2007.
———. *Theology: A Very Short Introduction.* Oxford: Oxford University Press, 1999.
Fowl, Stephen E. "Further Thoughts on Theological Interpretation." In *Reading Scripture with the Church: Toward a Hermeneutic for Theological Interpretation*, edited by A. K. M. Adam, Stephen E. Fowl, Kevin J. Vanhoozer, and Francis Watson, 125-30. Grand Rapids: Baker, 2006.
———. *Engaging Scripture: A Model for Theological Interpretation.* Malden: Blackwell, 1998.
Frederick, Marla F. *Between Sundays: Black Women and the Everyday Struggles of Faith.* Berkeley: University of California Press, 2003.
Freston, Paul. "Globalization, Southern Christianity, and Proselytism." *The Review of Faith and International Affairs* 7:1 (2009): 3.
———. *Evangelicals and Politics in Asia, Africa and Latin America.* Cambridge: Cambridge University Press, 2001.
———. "Globalisation, Religion and Evangelical Christianity: A Sociological Meditation from the Third World." Position Paper 151, Currents in World Christianity Project, 2001.
Friedmann, John, and Goetz Wolff. "World City Formation: An Agenda for Research and Action." *International Journal of Urban and Regional Research* 6 (1982): 309-44.

SOURCES

Froehle, Bryan T., and Mary L. Gautier. *Global Catholicism: Portrait of a World Church.* Maryknoll, N.Y.: Orbis Books, 2003.

Fulkerson, Mary McClintock. *Places of Redemption: Theology for a Worldly Church.* New York: Oxford University Press, 2007.

Fumanti, Mattia. "'Virtuous Citizenship': Ethnicity and Encapsulation among Akan-Speaking Ghanaian Methodists in London." *African Diaspora* 3:1 (2010): 13-42.

Gemignani, Regina. "Gender, Identity, and Power in African Immigrant Evangelical Churches." In *African Immigrant Religions in America,* edited by Regina Gemignani and Jacob K. Olupona, 133-57. New York: New York University Press, 2007.

Gerloff, Roswith. "'Africa as Laboratory of the World': The African Christian Diaspora in Europe as Challenge to Mission and Ecumenical Relations." In *Mission Is Crossing Frontiers: Essays in Honour of Bongani A. Mazibuko,* edited by Roswith Gerloff, 343-81. Pietermaritzburg: Cluster Publications, 2003.

Gifford, Paul. "The Bible in Africa: A Novel Usage in Africa's New Churches." *Bulletin of the School of Oriental and African Studies* 71:2 (2008): 203-19.

———. "The Nature and Effects of Mission Today: A Case Study from Kenya." *Social Sciences and Mission* 20 (2007): 117-47.

———. *Ghana's New Christianity: Pentecostalism in a Globalizing African Economy.* Bloomington: Indiana University Press, 2004.

———. Review of *The Bible in Africa: Transactions, Trajectories and Trends,* edited by Gerald O. West and Musa W. Dube. *Journal of Religion in Africa* 34:3 (2004): 397-401.

Glick Schiller, Nina. "Transnational Social Fields and Imperialism: Bringing a Theory of Power to Transnational Studies." *Anthropological Theory* 5:4 (2005): 439-61.

———. "Transmigrants and Nation-States: Something Old and Something New in the U.S. Immigrant Experience." In *The Handbook of International Migration: The American Experience,* edited by Josh DeWind, Charles Hirschman, and Philip Kasinitz, 96. New York: Russell Sage, 1999.

Glick Schiller, Nina, Ayse Caglar, and Thaddeus C. Guldbrandsen. "Beyond the Ethnic Lens: Locality, Globality, and Born-Again Incorporation." *American Ethnologist* 33:4 (2006): 612-33.

Gonzalez, David. "A Sliver of a Storefront, A Faith on the Rise." *New York Times,* January 14, 2007, A-1, 32-33.

Gornik, Mark R. "Andrew Walls and the Transformation of Christianity." *Catalyst* 31:3 (2005): 5-6.

Griffith, R. Marie. *Born Again Bodies: Flesh and Spirit in American Christianity.* Berkeley: University of California Press, 2004.

———. *God's Daughters: Evangelical Women and the Power of Submission.* Berkeley: University of California Press, 1997.

Groody, Daniel. "Theology in the Age of Migration." *National Catholic Reporter,* September 14, 2009.

Gyang-Duah, Charles. "The Scottish Mission Factor in the Development of the Presbyterian Church of Ghana: 1917-1957." Ph.D. thesis, University of Edinburgh, 1996.

Hackett, Rosalind I. J. "The New Virtual (Inter)Face of African Pentecostalism." *Society* 46:6 (2009): 496-503.

———. *Religion in Calabar: The Religious Life and History of a Nigerian Town.* Berlin: Mouton D. Gruyter, 1989.

Sources

Haight, Roger. *Christian Community in History.* Volume 3, *Ecclesial Existence.* New York: Continuum, 2008.

———. *Christian Community in History.* Volume 2, *Comparative Ecclesiology.* New York: Continuum, 2005.

———. *Christian Community in History.* Volume 1, *Historical Ecclesiology.* New York: Continuum, 2004.

Halter, Marilyn. "Africa: West." In *The New Americans: A Guide to Immigration Since 1965,* edited by Mary C. Waters and Reed Ueda, 283-94. Boston: Harvard University Press, 2007.

Hanciles, Jehu J. *Beyond Christendom: Globalization, African Migration, and the Transformation of the West.* Maryknoll, N.Y.: Orbis, 2008.

———. "God's Mission through Migration: African Initiatives in Globalizing Mission." In *Evangelical, Ecumenical, and Anabaptist Missiologies in Conversation: Essays in Honor of Wilbert R. Shenk,* edited by James R. Krabill, Walter Sawatsky, and Charles E. Van Engen, 58-66. Maryknoll, N.Y.: Orbis, 2006.

———. "Migration and Mission: Some Implications for the Twenty-first-century Church." *International Bulletin of Missionary Research* 27:4 (October 2003): 146-53.

Hancock, Mary, and Smriti Srinvas. "Spaces of Modernity: Religion and the Urban in Africa." *International Journal of Urban and Regional Research* 32:3 (2008): 617-30.

Hann, Chris. "The Anthropology of Christianity per se." *European Journal of Sociology* 48:3 (2007): 383-410.

Hansen, Thomas Blom, and Oskar Verkaaik. "Introduction: Urban Charisma On Everyday Mythologies in the City." *Critique of Anthropology* 29:1 (2009): 5-26.

Harnack, Adolf. *The Mission and Expansion of Christianity in the First Three Centuries.* Translated by James Moffatt. Gloucester: Peter Smith, 1972 [1908].

Harris, Hermione. *Yoruba in Diaspora: An African Church in London.* New York: Palgrave Macmillan, 2006.

———. "Continuity or Change? Aladura and Born Again Yoruba Christianity in London." In *Christianity and Social Change in Africa: Essays in Honor of J. D. Y. Peel,* edited by Toyin Falola, 307-34. Durham: Carolina Academic Press, 2005.

Harris, Leslie M. *In the Shadow of Slavery: African Americans in New York City, 1626-1863.* Chicago: University of Chicago Press, 2003.

Hastings, Adrian. *The Church in Africa 1450-1950.* Oxford: Oxford University Press, 1994.

———. *African Christianity.* New York: Seabury Press, 1976.

Harvey, David. *The Condition of Postmodernity.* Cambridge: Blackwell, 1990.

Harvey, Susan Ashbrook. *Scenting Salvation: Ancient Christianity and the Olfactory Imagination.* Berkeley: University of California Press, 2006.

Hauerwas, Stanley. "Beyond the Boundaries: The Church Is Mission." In *Walk Humbly with the Lord: Church and Mission Engaging Plurality,* edited by Viggo Mortensen and Andreas Osterlund Nielsen, 53-69. Grand Rapids: Eerdmans, 2010.

Healy, Nicholas M. "'By the Working of the Holy Spirit': The Crisis of Authority in the Christian Churches." *Anglican Theological Review* 88:1 (2006): 5-24.

———. "Practices and the New Ecclesiology: Misplaced Concreteness?" *International Journal of Systematic Theology* 5:3 (2003): 287-308.

———. *Church, World and the Christian Life: Practical-Prophetic Ecclesiology.* Cambridge: Cambridge University Press, 2000.

SOURCES

Heft, James L., ed. *Passing on the Faith: Transforming Traditions for the Next Generation of Jews, Christians, and Muslims.* New York: Fordham University Press, 2006.

Held, David, Anthony McGrew, David Goldblatt, and Jonathan Perraton. *Global Transformations: Politics, Economics and Culture.* Stanford: Stanford University Press, 1999.

Hirschkind, Charles. "Media, Mediation, Religion." *Social Anthropology* 19:1 (2011): 90-97.

Hoehler-Fatton, Cynthia. "Christianity: Independent and Charismatic Churches in Africa." In *Africana: The Encyclopedia of the African American Experience,* edited by Kwame Anthony Appiah and Henry Louis Gates Jr., 428-31. New York: Basic Civitas Books, 1999.

Hoerder, Dirk. *Cultures in Contact: World Migrations in the Second Millennium.* Durham: Duke University Press, 2002.

Hollingsworth, Andrea. "Spirit and Voice: Toward a Feminist Pentecostal Pneumatology." *Pneuma* 29 (2007): 189-213.

Hood, Clifton. *722 Miles: The Building of the Subways and How They Transformed New York.* Baltimore: The Johns Hopkins University Press, 2004.

Hoornaert, Eduardo. *The Memory of the Christian People.* Translated by Robert R. Barr. Maryknoll, N.Y.: Orbis, 1988.

Horton, Robin. *Patterns of Thought in Africa and the West: Essays on Magic, Religion and Science.* Cambridge: Cambridge University Press, 1993.

———. "African Conversion." *Africa* 41:2 (1971): 85-108.

Hunt, Stephen. "'A Church for All Nations': The Redeemed Christian Church of God." *Pneuma* 24:2 (2002): 185-204.

———. "'Neither Here nor There': The Construction of Identities and Boundary Maintenance of West African Pentecostals." *Sociology* 36:1 (2002): 147-69.

Hunt, Stephen, and Nicola Lightly. "The British Black Pentecostal 'Revival': Identity and Belief in the 'New' Nigerian Churches." *Ethnic and Racial Studies* 24:1 (2001): 104-24.

Hurtado, Larry W. *Lord Jesus Christ: Devotion to Jesus in Earliest Christianity.* Grand Rapids: Eerdmans, 2003.

———. "Religious Experience and Religious Innovation in the New Testament." *Journal of Religion* 80:2 (2000): 183-205.

Inge, John. *A Christian Theology of Place.* Aldershot: Ashgate, 2003.

Jackson, Kenneth T. "A Colony with a Conscience." *New York Times,* December 27, 2007, A-29.

Jackson, Kenneth T., and David S. Dunbar, eds. *Empire City: New York Through the Centuries.* New York: Columbia University Press, 2002.

Jacobs, Jane. *The Death and Life of Great American Cities.* New York: Vintage, 1992.

Jandt, Fred E. *An Introduction to Intercultural Communication: Identities in a Global Community.* 4th ed. Thousand Oaks: Sage, 2004.

Jeannerat, Caroline. "Of Lizards, Misfortune and Deliverance: Pentecostal Soteriology in the Life of a Migrant." *African Studies* 68:2 (2009): 251-71.

Jenkins, Philip. *The New Faces of Christianity: Believing the Bible in the Global South.* New York: Oxford University Press, 2006.

———. *The Next Christendom: The Coming of Global Christianity.* Oxford: Oxford University Press, 2002.

———. "The Next Christianity." *Atlantic Monthly* 290:3 (October 2002): 53-55, 58-62, 64-68.

Johnson, Luke Timothy. *Among the Gentiles: Greco-Roman Religion and Christianity.* New Haven: Yale University Press, 2009.
———. *The Writings of the New Testament: An Interpretation.* Revised Edition. Minneapolis: Fortress, 1999.
———. *Religious Experience in Earliest Christianity: A Missing Dimension in New Testament Studies.* Minneapolis: Fortress, 1998.
———. "Imagining the World Scripture Imagines." *Modern Theology* 14:2 (1998): 165-80.
Johnson, Paul Christopher. *Black Carib Religion and the Recovery of Africa.* Berkeley: University of California Press, 2007.
Johnson, Todd M. "The Global Demographics of the Pentecostal and Charismatic Renewal." *Society* 46:6 (2009): 479-83.
Jones, L. Gregory. "Job Description." *Christian Century,* January 10, 2006.
Jules-Rosette, Benetta. "African Religions: Modern Movements." In *The Encyclopedia of Religion,* Vol. 1, edited by Mircea Eliade, 82-89. New York: Macmillan, 1987.
———. *African Apostles: Ritual and Conversion in the Church of John Maranke.* Ithaca: Cornell University Press, 1975.
Kalu, Ogbu U. "A Discursive Interpretation of African Pentecostalism." *Fides et Historia* 41:1 (2009): 71-90.
———. *African Pentecostalism: An Introduction.* New York: Oxford University Press, 2008.
———. "Pentecostalism and Mission in Africa, 1970-2000." *Mission Studies* 24 (2007): 9-45.
———. "Preserving a Worldview: Pentecostalism in the African Maps of the Universe." *Pneuma* 24:2 (2002): 110-37.
———. "The Third Response: Pentecostalism and the Reconstruction of Christian Experience in Africa, 1970-1995." *Journal of African Christian Thought* 1:2 (1998): 3-16.
———, ed. *African Christianity: An African Story.* Trenton: Africa World Press, 2007.
Kalu, Wilhelmina J. "Soul Care in Nigeria: Constructing Pentecostal Models of Pastoral Care and Counseling." In *Religion, History, and Politics in Nigeria: Essays in Honor of Ogbu U. Kalu,* edited by Chima J. Korieh and G. Ugo Nwokeji, 202-15. Lanham: University Press of America, 2005.
Kärkkäinen, Veli-Matti, ed. *The Spirit in the World: Emerging Pentecostal Theologies in Global Contexts.* Grand Rapids: Eerdmans, 2009.
Kasinitz, Philip, John H. Mollenkopf, Mary C. Waters, and Jennifer Holdaway. *Inheriting the City: The Children of Immigrants Come of Age.* New York: Russell Sage Foundation and Cambridge: Harvard University Press, 2008.
Kasinitz, Philip, John H. Mollenkopf, and Mary C. Waters. "Worlds of the Second Generation." In *Becoming New Yorkers: Ethnographies of the Second Generation,* edited by Philip Kasinitz, John H. Mollenkopf, and Mary C. Waters, 1-19. New York: Russell Sage Foundation, 2004.
———. "Identity." In *Becoming New Yorkers: Ethnographies of the Second Generation,* edited by Philip Kasinitz, John H. Mollenkopf, and Mary C. Waters, 281-87. New York: Russell Sage Foundation, 2004.
Katongole, Emmanuel. *The Sacrifice of Africa: A Political Theology for Africa.* Grand Rapids: Eerdmans, 2011.
———. "A Tale of Many Stories." In *Shaping a Global Theological Mind,* edited by Darren C. Marks, 89-93. Aldershot: Ashgate, 2008.

———. Review of *Whose Religion Is Christianity? The Gospel beyond the West*, by Lamin Sanneh. *Pro Ecclesia* 15:1 (2006): 141-45.

———. *A Future for Africa: Critical Essays in Christian Social Imagination*. Scranton: Scranton University Press, 2005.

———. "The Tales of African Christianity: Singing a New Song in the Midst of Africa's Histories." Unpublished paper, 2005.

———. "Kannungu and the Movement for the Restoration of the Ten Commandments of God in Uganda: A Challenge for Christian Social Imagination." *Logos* 6:3 (2003): 108-43.

———. "A Different World Right Here, A World Being Gestated in the Deeds of the Everyday: The Church Within African Theological Imagination." *Missionalia* 30:2 (2002): 206-34.

———. "Prospects of Ecclesia in Africa in the Twenty-First Century." *Logos* 4:1 (2001): 178-95.

Keane, Webb. *Christian Moderns: Freedom and Fetish in the Mission Encounter*. Berkeley: University of California Press, 2007.

———. "Signs Are Not the Garb of Meaning: On the Social Analysis of Material Things." In *Materiality*, edited by Daniel Miller, 182-205. Durham: Duke University Press, 2005.

Keller, Eva. "Towards Complete Clarity: Bible Study among Seventh-day Adventists in Madagascar." *Ethnos* 69:1 (2004): 89-112.

Kelsey, David H. *Imagining Redemption*. Louisville: Westminster John Knox Press, 2005.

Kerridge, Roy. *The Storm Is Passing Over: A Look at Black Churches in Britain*. London: Thames and Hudson, 1995.

Khagram, Sanjeev, and Peggy Levitt, eds. *The Transnational Studies Reader: Intersections and Innovations*. New York: Routledge, 2008.

Kileyesus, Abbebe. "Cosmologies in Collision: Pentecostal Conversion and Christian Cults in Asmara." *African Studies Review* 49:1 (2006): 75-92.

Kim, Kirsteen. *The Holy Spirit in the World: A Global Conversation*. Maryknoll, N.Y.: Orbis, 2007.

Kim, Sebastian, and Kirsteen Kim. *Christianity as a World Religion*. London: Continuum, 2008.

Kirsch, Thomas G. *Spirits and Letters: Reading, Writing, and Charisma in African Christianity*. New York: Berghahn, 2008.

———. "Ways of Reading as Religious Power in Print Globalization." *American Ethnologist* 34:3 (2007): 509-20.

Klaits, Frederick. *Death in a Church of Life: Moral Passion during Botswana's Time of AIDS*. Berkeley: University of California Press, 2010.

Knibbe, Kim. "'We Did Not Come Here as Tenants, but as Landlords': Nigerian Pentecostals and the Power of Maps." *African Diaspora* 2:2 (2009): 133-58.

Knott, Kim. "From Locality to Location and Back Again: A Spatial Journey in the Study of Religion." *Religion* 39 (2009): 154-60.

Kollman, Paul. "Classifying African Christianities: Past, Present, and Future: Part One." *Journal of Religion in Africa* 40:1 (2010): 3-32.

———. "Classifying African Christianities, Part Two: The Anthropology of Christianity and Generations of African Christians." *Journal of Religion in Africa* 40:2 (2010): 118-48.

Sources

Komolafe, Sunday Babajide. "The Changing Face of Christianity: Revisiting African Christianity." *Missiology: An International Review* 32:3 (2004): 217-38.
Koning, Danielle. "Place, Space, and Authority: The Mission and Reversed Mission of the Ghanaian Seventh-Day Adventist Church in Amsterdam." *African Diaspora* 2:2 (2009): 203-26.
Krause, Kristine. "Transnational Therapy Networks among Ghanaians in London." *Journal of Ethnic and Migration Studies* 34:2 (2008): 235-41.
Lalami, Laila. "Native Speaker." *Boston Review*, September/October 2006, http://boston review.net/BR31.5/lalami.php.
Lang, Bernhard. *Sacred Games: A History of Christian Worship*. New Haven: Yale University Press, 1997.
Larbi, Emmanuel Kingsley. *Pentecostalism: The Eddies of Ghanaian Christianity*. Accra: CPCS, 2001.
Lauterbach, Karen. "Becoming a Pastor: Youth and Social Aspirations in Ghana." *Young: Nordic Journal of Youth Research* 18:3 (2010): 259-78.
Leonard, Karen I., Alex Stepick, Manuel A Vásquez, and Jennifer Holdaway, eds. *Immigrant Faiths: Transforming Religious Life in America*. Lanham: AltaMira, 2005.
Levitt, Peggy. "Roots and Routes: Understanding the Lives of the Second Generation Transnationally." *Journal of Ethnic and Migration Studies* 35:7 (2009): 1225-42.
———. *God Needs No Passport: Immigrants and the Changing American Religious Landscape*. New York: The New Press, 2007.
———. "Redefining the Boundaries of Belonging: The Institutional Character of Transnational Religious Life." *Sociology of Religion* 65:1 (2004): 1-18.
———. "Transnational Migration: Taking Stock and Future Directions." *Global Networks* 1:3 (2001): 195-216.
Levitt, Peggy, and B. Nadya Jaworsky. "Transnational Migration Studies: Past Developments and Future Trends." *Annual Review of Sociology* 33 (2007): 129-56.
Lewis, Donald M. *Christianity Reborn: The Global Expansion of Evangelicalism in the Twentieth Century*. Grand Rapids: Eerdmans, 2004.
Ley, David. "The Immigrant Church as an Urban Social Service Hub." *Urban Studies* 45:10 (2008): 2057-74.
Lieu, Judith M. *Christian Identity in the Jewish and Graeco-Roman World*. Oxford: Oxford University Press, 2004.
Liggett, Helen. *Urban Encounters*. Minneapolis: University of Minnesota Press, 2003.
Lindquist, Galina, and Simon Coleman. "Introduction: Against Belief." *Social Analysis* 52:1 (2008): 1-18.
Lobo, Arun Peter, and Joseph L. Salvo. *The Newest New Yorkers 2000: Immigrant New York in the New Millennium*. New York City: New York City Department of Planning, 2004.
Lobo, Arun Peter, Joseph L. Salvo, and Vicky Virgin. *The Newest New Yorkers 1990-1994: An Analysis of Immigration to NYC in the Early 1990s*. New York City: New York City Department of Planning, 1996.
Ma, Julia C. "Pentecostalism and Asian Mission." *Missiology* 35:1 (2007): 23-37.
Mackendrick, Karmen. *Word Made Skin: Figuring Language at the Surface of Flesh*. New York: Fordham University Press, 2004.
Maluleke, Tinyiko Sam. "Theological Interest in AICs and Other Grass-Root Communities

in South Africa: A Review of Methodologies." *Journal of Black Theology in South Africa* 10:1 (1996): 18-48.
Mannion, Gerard. "Constructive Comparative Ecclesiology: The Pioneering Work of Roger Haight." *Ecclesiology* 5 (2009): 161-91.
Marrs, Cliff. "Globalization: A Short Introduction to a New World Religion." *Political Theology* 4:1 (2001): 91-116.
Marsh, Charles. *God's Long Summer: Stories of Faith and Civil Rights*. Princeton: Princeton University Press, 1997.
Marshall, Ruth. *Political Spiritualities: The Pentecostal Revolution in Nigeria*. Chicago: University of Chicago Press, 2009.
Marshall-Fratani, Ruth. "Mediating the Global and Local in Nigerian Pentecostalism." *Journal of Religion in Africa* 28:3 (1998): 278-315.
———. "'God Is Not a Democrat': Pentecostalism and Democratisation in Nigeria." In *The Christian Churches and the Democratisation of Africa*, edited by Paul Gifford, 254-56. Leiden: Brill, 1995.
Martin, David. "Have Pentecostalism, Will Travel." *The Times Literary Supplement*, September 17, 2008.
———. *On Secularization: Towards a Revised General Theory*. Aldershot: Ashgate, 2005.
———. *Pentecostalism: The World Their Parish*. Oxford: Blackwell, 2002.
Mary, André. "Pilgrimage to Imeko (Nigeria): An African Church in the Time of the 'Global Village.'" *International Journal of Urban and Regional Research* 26:1 (March 2002): 106-20.
Maxwell, David. *African Gifts of the Spirit: Pentecostalism and the Rise of a Zimbabwean Transnational Religious Movement*. Oxford: James Currey, 2006.
———. "Post-Colonial Christianity in Africa." In *The Cambridge History of Christianity*. Vol. 9, *World Christianities c. 1914-2000*, edited by Hugh Mcleod, 401-21. Cambridge: Cambridge University Press, 2006.
Mazzucato, Valentina, and Mirjam Kabki. "Small Is Beautiful: The Micro-politics of Transnational Relationships Between Ghanaian Hometown Associations and Communities Back Home." *Global Networks* 9:2 (2009): 227-51.
Mbiti, John S. *Bible and Theology in African Christianity*. Nairobi: Oxford University Press, 1986.
McDannell, Colleen. *Picturing Faith: Photography and the Great Depression*. New Haven: Yale University Press, 2004.
———. *Material Christianity: Religion and Popular Culture in America*. New Haven: Yale University Press, 1995.
McDougall, Debra. "Rethinking Christianity and Anthropology: A Review Article." *Anthropological Forum* 19:2 (2009): 185-94.
McIntosh, Mark A. *Divine Teaching: An Introduction to Christian Theology*. Malden: Blackwell, 2008.
McIntyre, Alasdair. *After Virtue*. 2nd ed. Notre Dame: University of Notre Dame Press, 1984.
McLean, Janice A. "Living Their Faith: Identity and Mission among West Indian Immigrants in Pentecostal Churches in New York City and London." Ph.D. thesis, University of Edinburgh, 2009.
McLeod, Hugh, ed. *Cambridge History of Christianity*. Volume 9, *World Christianities c. 1914-2000*. Cambridge: Cambridge University Press, 2006.

Sources

McRoberts, Omar M. *Streets of Glory: Church and Community in a Black Urban Neighborhood*. Chicago: University of Chicago Press, 2003.
Meeks, Wayne. *The Origins of Christian Morality: The First Two Centuries*. New Haven: Yale University Press, 1993.
———. *The First Urban Christians: The Social World of the Apostle Paul*. New Haven: Yale University Press, 1983.
Meggitt, Justin. "Magic, Healing and Early Christianity: Consumption and Competition." In *The Meanings of Magic: From the Bible to Buffalo Bill*, edited by Amy Wygant, 89-114. New York: Berghahn Books, 2006.
———. "The First Churches: Religious Practice." In *The Biblical World*. Vol. 2, edited by John Barton, 157-72. London: Routledge, 2002.
Mercer, Claire, Ben Page, and Martin Evans. "Unsettling Connections: Development and African Hometown Association." *Global Networks* 9:2 (2009): 141-61.
Meyer, Birgit, ed. *Aesthetic Formations: Media, Religion, and the Senses*. New York: Palgrave Macmillan, 2009.
Meyer, Birgit. "Introduction: From Imagined Communities to Aesthetic Formations: Religious Mediations, Sensational Forms, and Styles of Binding." In *Aesthetic Formations: Media, Religion, and the Senses*, edited by Birgit Meyer, 1-28. New York: Palgrave Macmillan, 2009.
———. "Impossible Representations: Pentecostalism, Vision, and Video Technology in Ghana." In *Religion, Media and the Public Sphere*, edited by Birgit Meyer and Annelies Moors, 290-312. Bloomington: Indiana University Press, 2006.
———. "Christianity in Africa: From Independent to Pentecostal-Charismatic Churches." *Annual Review of Anthropology* 33 (2004): 447-74.
———. "'Make a Complete Break with the Past': Memory and Post-Colonial Modernity in Ghanaian Pentecostalist Discourse." *Journal of Religion in Africa* 28:3 (1998): 316-46.
———. "Commodities and the Power of Prayer: Pentecostalist Attitudes towards Consumption in Contemporary Ghana." *Development and Change* 29:4 (1988): 751-76.
Mirchandani, Kiran. "Practices of Global Capital: Gaps, Cracks and Ironies in Transnational Call Centres in India." *Global Networks: A Journal of Transnational Affairs* 4:4 (October 2004): 355-73.
Miles, Margaret R. *The Word Made Flesh: A History of Christian Thought*. Malden, Mass.: Blackwell, 2005.
Miller, Donald E., and Tetsunao Yamamori. *Global Pentecostalism: The New Face of Christian Social Engagement*. Berkeley: University of California Press, 2007.
Miller, Jon. *Missionary Zeal and Institutional Control: Organizational Contradictions in the Basel Mission on the Gold Coast, 1828-1917*. Grand Rapids: Eerdmans, 2003.
Mitchell, Margaret M. *Paul, the Corinthians and the Birth of Christian Hermeneutics*. Cambridge: Cambridge University Press, 2010.
Mohr, Adam. "'Their Journeys Were Not Without Demonic Confrontation': Healing and Migration in the Presbyterian Church of Ghana." Ph.D. thesis, University of Pennsylvania, 2008.
Moltmann, Jürgen. "Preface." In *The Spirit in the World: Emerging Pentecostal Theologies in Global Contexts*, edited by Veli-Matti Kärkkäinen, viii-xii. Grand Rapids: Eerdmans, 2009.
———. "Praying with Eyes Open." In *Loving God with Our Minds: The Pastor as Theologian*,

edited by Michael Welker and Cynthia A. Jarvis, 195-201. Grand Rapids: Eerdmans, 2004.

———. *Experiences in Theology: Ways and Forms of Christian Theology.* Translated by Margaret Kohl. Minneapolis: Fortress, 2000.

———. *The Source of Life: The Holy Spirit and the Theology of Life.* Translated by Margaret Kohl. Minneapolis: Fortress, 1997.

———. *The Spirit of Life: A Universal Affirmation.* Translated by Margaret Kohl. Minneapolis: Fortress, 1992.

Mooney, Margarita A. *Faith Makes Us Live: Surviving and Thriving in the Haitian Diaspora.* Berkeley: University of California Press, 2009.

Mukonyora, Isabel. "The Dramatisation of Life and Death by Johane Masowe." *Swedish Missiological Themes* 88:3 (2000): 409-30.

Mwaura, Philomena Njeri. "Integrity of Mission in the Light of the Gospel: Bearing Witness of the Spirit among Africa's Gospel Bearers." *Exchange* 35:2 (2006): 169-90.

———. "Unsung Bearers of Good News: AIC Women and the Transformation of Society in Africa." *Journal of African Christian Thought* 7:1 (2004): 38-44.

Narayanan, Vasudha. "Embodied Cosmologies: Sights of Piety, Sites of Power." *Journal of the American Academy of Religion* 71:3 (2003): 495-520.

Nasrallah, Laura. *An Ecstasy of Folly: Prophecy and Authority in Early Christianity.* Cambridge: Harvard Theological Studies, 2003.

Neyrey, Jerome H. *Give God the Glory: Ancient Prayer and Worship in Cultural Perspective.* Grand Rapids: Eerdmans, 2007.

Ngong, David Tonghou. "Salvation and Materialism in African Theology." *Studies in World Christianity* 15:1 (2009): 1-21.

———. "The Material in Salvific Discourse: A Study in Two Christian Perspectives." Ph.D. thesis, Baylor University, 2007.

Nienhuis, David R. *Not by Paul Alone: The Formation of the Catholic Epistle Collection and the Christian Canon.* Waco: Baylor University Press, 2007.

Noll, Mark A. *The New Shape of World Christianity: How American Experience Reflects Global Faith.* Downers Grove, Ill.: InterVarsity Press, 2009.

Nussbaum, Stan W. "African Initiated Churches." In *Dictionary of Mission Theology: Evangelical Foundations,* edited by John Corrie, 5-7. Downers Grove, Ill.: InterVarsity Press, 2007.

Nyende, Peter. "Institutional and Popular Interpretations of the Bible in Africa: Towards an Integration." *The Expository Times* 119:2 (2007): 59-66.

O'Collins, Gerald. *Jesus Our Redeemer: A Christian Approach to Salvation.* Oxford: Oxford University Press, 2007.

Ojo, Matthews A. *The End-Time Army: Charismatic Movements in Modern Nigeria.* Trenton: Africa World Press, 2006.

———. "African Charismatics." In *Encyclopedia of African and African-American Religion,* edited by Stephen Glazier, 2-6. New York: Routledge, 2001.

———. "Cherubim and Seraphim Movement." In *Encyclopedia of African and African-American Religion,* edited by Stephen Glazier, 82-84. New York: Routledge, 2001.

———. "Healing in Sub-Saharan Africa." In *Encyclopedia of African and African-American Religion,* edited by Stephen Glazier, 139-44. New York: Routledge, 2001.

———. "The Dynamics of Indigenous Charismatic Missionary Enterprises in West Africa." *Missionalia* 25:4 (December 1997): 537-61.

———. "The Charismatic Movement in Nigeria Today." *International Bulletin of Missionary Research* 19:3 (1995): 114-18.

Ojo, Tony. *Let Somebody Shout Hallelujah! The Life and Ministry of Pastor Enoch Adejare Adeboye*. Lagos: Honeycombs Cards and Prints, 2001.

Okoye Chukwuma, James. *Israel Among the Nations: A Mission Theology of the Old Testament*. Maryknoll, N.Y.: Orbis, 2006.

Okure, Teresa. "Africa: Globalization and the Loss of Cultural Identity." *Concilium* 5 (2001): 67-74.

———. "I Will Open My Mouth in Parables (Matt. 13:35): A Case for Gospel-Based Hermeneutics." *New Testament Studies* 46:3 (July 2000): 445-63.

Olupona, Jacob. "African Religion." In *Global Religions: An Introduction*, edited by Mark Juergensmeyer, 78-86. Oxford: Oxford University Press, 2003.

Olupona, Jacob, and Regina Gemignani, eds. *African Immigrant Religions in America*. New York: New York University Press, 2007.

Omenyo, Cephas N. "From the Fringes to the Centre: Pentecostalization of the Mainline Churches in Ghana." *Exchange* 34:1 (2005): 39-60.

———. *Pentecost outside Pentecostalism: A Study of the Development of Charismatic Renewal in the Mainline Churches in Ghana*. Zoetermeer: Uitgeverij Boekencentrum, 2002.

———. "Essential Aspects of African Ecclesiology: The Case of the African Independent Churches." *Pneuma* 22:2 (2000): 231-48.

Ong, Aihwa. *Flexible Citizenship: The Cultural Logics of Transnationality*. Durham: Duke University Press, 1999.

Onyinah, Opoku. "Pentecostalism and the African Diaspora: An Examination of the Missions Activities of the Church of Pentecost." *Pneuma* 26:2 (Fall 2004): 216-41.

Orobator, Agbonkhianmeghe E. *Theology Brewed in an African Pot*. Maryknoll, N.Y.: Orbis, 2008.

Orsi, Robert A. *Between Heaven and Earth: The Religious Worlds People Make and the Scholars Who Study Them*. Princeton: Princeton University Press, 2005.

———. "Is the Study of Lived Religion Irrelevant to the World We Live In?" *Journal for the Scientific Study of Religion* 42:2 (2003): 169-74.

Ositelu, Rufus Okikiolaolu Olubiyi. *African Instituted Churches: Diversities, Growth, Gifts, Spirituality and Ecumenical Understanding of African Initiated Churches*. Münster: LIT Verlag, 2002.

Padwick, Timothy John. "Spirit, Desire and the World: Roho Churches of Western Kenya in the Era of Globalization." Ph.D. thesis, University of Birmingham, 2003.

Page, Max. *The Creative Destruction of New York: 1900-1940*. Chicago: University of Chicago Press, 1999.

Park, Joon-Sik. "'As You Go': John Howard Yoder as Mission Theologian." *Mennonite Quarterly Review* 78:3 (2004): 363-83.

Parrinder, Geoffrey. *Religion in an African City*. London: Oxford University Press, 1953.

Peel, J. D. Y. "Postsocialism, Postcolonialism, Pentecostalism." In *Conversion after Socialism: Disruptions, Modernisms and Technologies of Faith in the Former Soviet Union*, edited by Mathijs Pelkmans, 183-99. New York: Berghahn Books, 2009.

SOURCES

———. "Comment" on "Continuity Thinking and Christian Culture." *Current Anthropology* 48:1 (2007): 26-27.

———. *Aladura: A Religious Movement among the Yoruba*. London: Oxford University Press, 1968.

Pelkmans, Mathijs. "'Culture' as a Tool and an Obstacle: Missionary Encounters in Post-Soviet Kyrgyzstan." *Journal of the Royal Anthropological Institute* 13:4 (2007): 881-99.

Peterson, Derek R. Review of *African Christianity: An African Story*, edited by Ogbu U. Kalu. *Journal of Ecclesiastical History* 57:1 (2006): 87-89.

Pew Forum on Religion and Public Life. "Spirit and Power: A 10-Country Survey of Pentecostals." October 2006.

Pfeiffer, James. "Commodity *Fetichismo*, The Holy Spirit, and the Turn to Pentecostal and African Independent Churches in Central Mozambique." *Culture, Medicine and Psychiatry* 29 (2005): 255-83.

Phan, Peter C. "A New Christianity, But What Kind?" *Mission Studies* 22:1 (2005): 59-83.

Phiri, Isaac, and Joe Maxwell. "Gospel Riches." *Christianity Today*, July 2007.

Pitchers, A. L. "Facing the Reality of the Ethiopian Encounter." In *Study of Religion in Southern Africa*, edited by Johannes A. Smith and P. Pratap Kumar, 191-203. Leiden: Brill, 2005.

Pobee, John S., and Gabriel Ositelu II. *African Initiatives in Christianity: The Growth, Gifts and Diversities of Indigenous African Churches — A Challenge to the Ecumenical Movement*. Geneva: WCC Publications, 1998.

Poon, Michael N. C. "Patristic Theology." In *Global Dictionary of Theology*, ed. William R. Dyrness and Veli-Matti Kärkkäinen. Downers Grove, Ill.: IVP Academic, 2008, 628-37.

Porterfield, Amanda. *Healing in the History of Christianity*. Oxford: Oxford University Press, 2005.

Portes, Alejandro, and Rubén G. Rumbaut. *Legacies: The Story of the Immigrant Second Generation*. Berkeley: University of California Press and New York: Russell Sage Foundation, 2001.

Prakash, Gyan, and Kevin M. Kruse, eds. *The Spaces of the Modern City: Imaginaries, Politics, and Everyday Life*. Princeton: Princeton University Press, 2008.

Prempeh, Samuel. "The Basel Mission and Their Successors in the Gold Coast and Togoland, 1914-1926: A Study in Protestant Missions and the First World War." Ph.D. thesis, University of Edinburgh, 1977.

Probst, Peter. "The Letter and the Spirit: Literacy and Religious Authority in the History of the Aladura Movement in Western Nigeria." *Africa* 59:4 (1989): 478-95.

Putt, B. Keith. "'Too Deep for Words': The Conspiracy of a Divine 'Soliloquy.'" In *The Phenomenology of Prayer*, edited by Bruce Ellis Benson and Norman Wirzba, 142-53. New York: Fordham University Press, 2005.

Pype, Katrien. "Dancing for God or the Devil: Pentecostal Discourse on Popular Dance in Kinshasa." *Journal of Religion in Africa* 36:3-4 (2006): 296-318.

Rabelo, Miriam C. M., Sueli Ribeiro Mota, and Cláudio Roberto Almeida. "Cultivating the Senses and Giving in to the Sacred: Notes on the Body and Experience among Pentecostal Women in Salvador, Brazil." *Journal of Contemporary Religion* 24:1 (January 2009): 1-18.

Sources

Rainbow, Paul, and George E. Marcus with James D. Faubion and Tobias Rees. *Designs for an Anthropology of the Contemporary.* Durham: Duke University Press, 2008.
Ray, Benjamin C. "Aladura Christianity: A Yoruba Religion." *Journal of Religion in Africa* 23:3 (1993): 266-91.
Renne, Elisha P. "Consecrated Garments and Spaces in the Cherubim and Seraphim Church Diaspora." *Material Religion* 5:1 (2009): 70-87.
———. "'Let Your Garments Always Be White . . .': Expressions of Past and Present in Yoruba Religious Textiles." In *Christianity and Social Change in Africa: Essays in Honor of J. D. Y. Peel*, edited by Toyin Falola, 139-63. Durham: Carolina Academic Press, 2005.
Ribeiro, Gustavo Lins. "Non-Hegemonic Globalizations: Alternative Transnational Processes and Agents." *Anthropological Theory* 9:3 (2009): 297-329.
Rice, Andrew. "Mission from Africa." *The New York Times Magazine*, April 12, 2009, 30-37, 54, 57, 58.
Robbins, Joel. "Pentecostal Networks and the Spirit of Globalization: On the Social Productivity of Ritual Forms." *Social Analysis* 53:1 (2009): 55-66.
———. "Continuity Thinking and the Problem of Christian Culture: Belief, Time, and the Anthropology of Christianity." *Current Anthropology* 48:1 (2007): 5-38.
———. "Anthropology and Theology: An Awkward Relationship?" *Anthropological Quarterly* 79:2 (2006): 285-92.
———. "The Globalization of Pentecostal and Charismatic Christianity." *Annual Review of Anthropology* 33 (2004): 117-43.
Robert, Dana L. *Christian Mission: How Christianity Became a World Religion.* Malden: Wiley-Blackwell, 2009.
———. "Encounter with Christ: Luke as Mission Historian for the Twenty-first Century." In *Evangelical, Ecumenical and Anabaptist Missiologies in Conversation: Essays in Honor of Wilbert R. Shenk*, edited by James R. Krabill, Walter Sawatsky, and Charles E. Van Engen, 19-27. Maryknoll, N.Y.: Orbis, 2006.
———. "Shifting Southward: Global Christianity since 1945." *International Bulletin of Missionary Research* 24 (April 2000): 50-58.
Robert, Dana L., and M. L. Daneel. "Worship among Apostles and Zionists in Southern Africa." In *Christian Worship Worldwide: Expanding Horizons, Deepening Practices*, edited by Charles E. Farhadian, 43-70. Grand Rapids: Eerdmans, 2007.
Roberts, Sam. "More Africans Enter U.S. than in Days of Slavery." *New York Times*, February 21, 2005, A-1, B-4.
Robinson, Jennifer. *Ordinary Cities: Between Modernity and Development.* London: Routledge, 2006.
———. "Global and World Cities: A View from Off the Map." *International Journal of Urban and Regional Research* 26:3 (2002): 531-54.
Rosen, Rae D., Susan Wieler, and Joseph Pereira. "New York City Immigrants: The 1990s Wave." *Current Issues in Economics and Finance* 11:6 (June 2005), available at SSRN: http://ssrn.com/abstract=760926.
Rowe, C. Kavin. *World Upside Down: Reading Acts in the Graeco-Roman Age.* New York: Oxford University Press, 2009.
Said, Edward. *Reflections on Exile and Other Themes.* Cambridge: Harvard University Press, 2000.

Saint-Blancat, Chantal. "Islam in Diaspora: Reterritorialization and Extraterritoriality." *International Journal of Urban and Regional Research* 26:1 (2002): 138-51.

Samers, Michael. "Immigration and the Global City Hypothesis: Towards an Alternative Research Agenda." *International Journal of Urban and Regional Research* 26:2 (2002): 389-402.

Sanjek, Roger. "Keeping Ethnography Alive in an Urbanizing World." *Human Organization* 59:3 (2000): 280-88.

———. *The Future of Us All: Race and Neighborhood Politics in New York City.* Ithaca: Cornell University Press, 1998.

Sanneh, Lamin. *Disciples of All Nations: Pillars of World Christianity.* New York: Oxford University Press, 2008.

———. *Whose Religion Is Christianity? The Gospel beyond the West.* Grand Rapids: Eerdmans, 2003.

———. *Abolitionists Abroad: American Blacks and the Making of Modern West Africa.* Cambridge: Harvard University Press, 1999.

———. *Translating the Message: The Missionary Impact on Culture.* Revised and expanded edition. Maryknoll, N.Y.: Orbis, 2009.

Sanneh, Lamin, and Joel Carpenter, eds. *The Changing Face of Christianity: Africa, the West, and the World.* Oxford: Oxford University Press, 2005.

Sarró, Ramon, and Ruy Llera Blanes. "Prophetic Diasporas: Moving Religion across the Lusophone Atlantic." *African Diaspora* 2 (2009): 52-72.

Sassen, Saskia. "The Many Scales of the Global: Implications for Theory and for Politics." In *The Postcolonial and the Global,* edited by Revathi Krishnaswamy and John C. Hawley, 82-93. Minneapolis: University of Minnesota Press, 2008.

———, ed. *Deciphering the Global: Its Scales, Spaces, and Subjects.* New York: Routledge, 2007.

———. *Territory, Authority, Rights: From Medieval to Global Assemblages.* Princeton: Princeton University Press, 2006.

———. "Regulating Immigration in a Global Age: A New Policy Landscape." *Parallax* 11:1 (2005): 35-45.

———. "Introduction: Locating Cities on Global Circuits." In *Global Networks, Linked Cities,* edited by Saskia Sassen, 1-36. New York: Routledge, 2002.

———, ed. *Global Networks, Linked Cities.* New York: Routledge, 2002.

———. "Global Cities and Diasporic Networks: Microsites in Global Civil Society." In *Global Civil Society 2002,* edited by Marlies Glasius, Mary Kaldor, and Helmut Anheier, 217-38. Oxford: Oxford University Press, 2002.

———. *The Global City: New York, London, Tokyo.* 2nd ed. Princeton: Princeton University Press, 2001.

———. *Globalization and Its Discontents: Essays on the New Mobility of People and Money.* New York: The New Press, 1998.

Scharen, Christian Batalden. "'Judicious Narratives,' or Ethnography as Ecclesiology." *Scottish Journal of Theology* 58:2 (2005): 125-42.

Schwartz, Regina Mara. *Sacramental Poetics at the Dawn of Secularism: When God Left the World.* Stanford: Stanford University Press, 2008.

Scott, A. O. "Stories from a World in Motion." *New York Times,* March 16, 2008, AR-1, 16.

Scott, Michael W. "'I Was Like Abraham': Notes on the Anthropology of Christianity from the Solomon Islands." *Ethnos* 70:1 (March 2005): 101-25.
Searle, Alison. "'The Role of Mission' in *Things Fall Apart* and *Nervous Condition*." *Literature and Theology* 21:1 (2007): 49-65.
Shandy, Dianna J. "Nuer Christians in America." *Journal of Refugee Studies* 15:2 (2002): 213-21.
Shank, David A. "What Western Christians Can Learn from African-Initiated Churches." In *Mission from the Margins: Selected Writings from the Life and Ministry of David A. Shank*, edited by James R. Krabill, 219-30. Elkhart: Institute for Mennonite Studies, 2010.
Shaw, Teresa M. *The Burden of the Flesh: Fasting and Sexuality in Early Christianity*. Minneapolis: Fortress Press, 1998.
Sheldrake, Philip. "Placing the Sacred: Transcendence and the City." *Literature and Theology* 21:3 (2007): 243-58.
Shenk, Wilbert R. "New Wineskins for New Wine: Toward a Post-Christendom Ecclesiology." *International Bulletin of Missionary Research* 29:2 (2005): 73-79.
———. "Recasting Theology of Mission: Impulses from the Non-Western World." *International Bulletin of Missionary Research* 25:3 (2001): 98-107.
Shoaps, Robin A. "'Pray Earnestly': The Textual Construction of Personal Involvement in Pentecostal Prayer and Song." *Journal of Linguistic Anthropology* 12:1 (2002): 34-71.
Shorto, Russell. *The Island at the Center of the World: The Epic Story of Dutch Manhattan and the Forgotten Colony that Shaped America*. New York: Doubleday, 2004.
Simone, Abdou Maliq. *For the City Yet to Come: Changing African Life in Four Cities*. Durham: Duke University Press, 2004.
Smith, Christian, and Melinda Lundquist Denton. *Soul Searching: The Religious and Spiritual Lives of American Teenagers*. New York: Oxford University Press, 2005.
Smith, James K. A. *Thinking in Tongues: Pentecostal Contributions to Christian Philosophy*. Grand Rapids: Eerdmans, 2010.
———. *Desiring the Kingdom: Worship, Worldview, and Cultural Formation*. Grand Rapids: Baker, 2009.
———. "Philosophy of Religion Takes Practice: Liturgy as Source and Method in Philosophy of Religion." In *Contemporary Practice and Method in the Philosophy of Religion*. eds. David Cheetham and Rolfe King (London: Continuum, 2008), 133-47.
———. "Teaching a Calvinist to Dance." *Christianity Today*, May 2008, pp. 42-43.
Smith, Michael Peter. *Transnational Urbanism: Locating Globalization*. Malden: Blackwell, 2001.
Smith, Neil. *The Endgame of Globalization*. New York: Routledge, 2005.
Smith, Noel. *The Presbyterian Church of Ghana, 1835-1960: A Younger Church in a Changing Society*. Accra: Ghana Universities Press, 1966.
Smith-Christopher, Daniel L. *A Biblical Theology of Exile*. Minneapolis: Fortress Press, 2002.
Soothill, Jane E. *Gender, Social Change and Spiritual Power: Charismatic Christianity in Ghana*. Leiden: Brill, 2007.
Spencer, Sarah Busse. "Becoming Global? Evangelism and Transnational Practices in Russian Society." In *Deciphering the Global: Its Scales, Spaces and Subjects*, edited by Saskia Sassen, 79-96. New York: Routledge, 2007.

SOURCES

Stark, Rodney. *The Rise of Christianity: A Sociologist Reconsiders Christianity.* Princeton: Princeton University Press, 1996.

Stevens, W. David. "Spreading the Word: Religious Beliefs and the Evolution of Immigrant Congregations." *Sociology of Religion* 65:2 (2004): 121-38.

———. "'Taking the World': Evangelism and Assimilation among Ghanaian Pentecostals in Chicago." Ph.D. thesis, Northwestern University, 2003.

Stinton, Diane B. "Jesus-Immanuel, Image of the Invisible God: Aspects of Popular Christology in Sub-Saharan Africa." *Journal of Reformed Theology* 1 (2007): 6-40.

———. *Jesus of Africa: Voices of Contemporary African Christology.* Maryknoll, N.Y.: Orbis, 2004.

Stoller, Paul. *Money Has No Smell: The Africanization of New York.* Chicago: University of Chicago Press, 2001.

———. *Stranger in the Village of the Sick: A Memoir of Cancer, Sorcery, and Healing.* Boston: Beacon Press, 2004.

———. *Sensuous Scholarship.* Philadelphia: University of Pennsylvania Press, 1997.

Sugirtharajah, R. S. *The Bible and the Third World: Precolonial, Colonial and Postcolonial Encounters.* Cambridge University Press, 2001.

Sundkler, Bengt. *The Christian Ministry in Africa.* Uppsala: Swedish Institute of Missionary Research, 1960.

———. *Bantu Prophets in South Africa.* London: Lutterworth Press, 1948.

Sundkler, Bengt, and Christopher Steed. *A History of the Church in Africa.* Cambridge: Cambridge University Press, 2000.

Sutton, Matthew Avery. *Aimee Semple McPherson and the Resurrection of Christian America.* Cambridge: Harvard University Press, 2007.

Taves, Ann. *Religious Experience Reconsidered: A Building-block Approach to the Study of Religion and Other Special Things.* Princeton: Princeton University Press, 2009.

Taylor, Charles. *A Secular Age.* The Belknap Press of Harvard University Press, 2007.

Taylor, Mark C. *After God.* Chicago: University of Chicago Press, 2007.

———. *Confidence Games: Money and Markets in a World without Redemption.* Chicago: University of Chicago Press, 2004.

———. *The Moment of Complexity: Emerging Network Culture.* Chicago: University of Chicago Press, 2001.

Taylor, Peter J. *World City Network: A Global Urban Analysis.* London: Routledge, 2004.

Ter Haar, Gerrie. *How God Became African: African Spirituality and Western Thought.* Philadelphia: University of Pennsylvania Press, 2009.

———. "A Wondrous God: Miracles in Contemporary Africa." *African Affairs* 102 (2003): 409-28.

———. *Halfway to Paradise: African Christians in Europe.* Cardiff: Cardiff Academic Press, 1998.

———. "Strangers in the Promised Land: African Christians in Europe." *Exchange* 24:1 (1995): 1-33.

Thiselton, Anthony C. *The Hermeneutics of Doctrine.* Grand Rapids: Eerdmans, 2007.

———. *The First Epistle to the Corinthians: A Commentary on the Greek Text.* Grand Rapids: Eerdmans, 2000.

Thomas, Linda Elaine. *Under the Canopy: Ritual Process and Spiritual Resilience in South Africa.* Columbia: University of South Carolina Press, 1999.

Sources

Thompson, T. Jack. *Capturing the Image: African Missionary Photography as Enslavement and Liberation.* New Haven: Yale Divinity School Library, 2007.
———. "A Place to Feel at Home." *Studies in World Christianity* 10:2 (2004): 155-59.
———. "African Independent Churches in Britain: An Introductory Survey." In *New Religions and the New Europe,* edited by Robert Towler, 224-31. Aarhus: Aarhus University Press, 1995.
Tiénou, Tite. "Evangelical Theology in African Contexts." In *The Cambridge Companion to Evangelical Theology,* edited by Timothy Larsen and Daniel J. Treier, 213-24. Cambridge: Cambridge University Press, 2007.
Torrance, Thomas F. *The Ground and Grammar of Theology.* Belfast: Christian Journals, 1980.
Tsing, Anna Lowenhaupt. *Friction: An Ethnography of Global Connection.* Princeton: Princeton University Press, 2005.
Turner, Harold W. *African Independent Church.* Vol. 1: *History of an African Independent Church.* Oxford: Clarendon Press, 1967.
———. *African Independent Church.* Vol. 2: *The Life and Faith of the Church of the Lord (Aladura).* Oxford: Clarendon Press, 1967.
———. "Problems in the Study of African Independent Churches." *Numen* 13:1 (1966): 26-42.
———. *Profile Through Preaching: A Study of the Sermon Texts Used in a West African Independent Church.* London: Edinburgh House Press, 1965.
Turner, Victor, and Edith L. B. Turner. *Image and Pilgrimage in Christian Culture.* New York: Columbia University Press, 1978.
Tweed, Thomas A. *Crossing and Dwelling: A Theory of Religion.* Cambridge: Harvard University Press, 2006.
Ukah, Asonzeh Franklin-Kennedy. *A New Paradigm of Pentecostal Power: A Study of the Redeemed Christian Church of God in Nigeria.* Trenton: Africa World Press, 2008.
———. "Mobilities, Migration and Multiplication: The Expansion of the Religious Field of the Redeemed Christian Church of God, Nigeria." In *Religion in the Context of African Migration,* edited by Afe Adogame and Cordula Weissköppel, 317-41. Bayreuth: Eckhard Breitinger, 2005.
———. "'Those Who Trade with God Never Lose': The Economics of Pentecostal Activism in Nigeria." In *Christianity and Social Change in Africa: Essays in Honor of J. D. Y. Peel,* edited by Toyin Falola, 253-74. Durham: Carolina Academic Press, 2005.
———. "The Redeemed Christian Church of God (RCCG), Nigeria: Local Identities and Global Processes in African Pentecostalism." Ph.D. thesis, Bayreuth, 2003.
Van der Horst, Pieter W. "Silent Prayer in Antiquity." *Numen* 41 (1994): 1-25.
Van der Meulen, Marten. "The Continuing Importance of the Local: African Churches and the Search for Worship Space in Amsterdam." *African Diaspora* 2 (2009): 159-81.
Van der Toorn, Karel, Bob Becking, and Pieter W. van der Horst, eds. *Dictionary of Deities and Demons in the Bible.* Leiden: Brill and Grand Rapids: Eerdmans, 1999.
Van Dijk, Rijk. "From Camp to Encompassment: Discourses of Trans-subjectivity in the Ghanaian Pentecostal Diaspora." *Journal of Religion in Africa* 27:2 (1997): 135-59.
Vanhoozer, Kevin J. *The Drama of Doctrine: A Canonical-Linguistic Approach to Christian Theology.* Louisville: Westminster John Knox, 2005.

Vásquez, Manuel A. *More Than Belief: A Materialist Theory of Religion*. Oxford: Oxford University Press, 2011.

———. "The Limits of the Hydrodynamics of Religion." *Journal of the American Academy of Religion* 77:2 (2009): 434-45.

———. "The Global Portability of Pneumatic Christianity: Comparing African and Latin American Pentecostalisms." Unpublished paper 2009.

———. "Studying Religion in Motion: A Networks Approach." *Method and Theory in the Study of Religion* 20:2 (2008): 151-84.

———. "Historicizing and Materializing the Study of Religion: The Contribution of Migration Studies." In *Immigrant Faiths: Transforming Religious Life in America*, edited by Karen I. Leonard, Alex Stepick, Manuel A Vásquez, and Jennifer Holdaway, 219-42. Lanham: AltaMira, 2005.

———. "Tracking Global Evangelical Christianity." *Journal of the American Academy of Religion* 71:1 (2003): 157-73.

———. *Religion Rematerialized: Embodiment, Practice and Emplacement*. Oxford University Press, forthcoming.

Vásquez, Manuel A., and Marie Friedmann Marquardt. *Globalizing the Sacred: Religion Across the Americas*. New Brunswick: Rutgers University Press, 2003.

Velho, Octávio. "Missionization in the Post-Colonial World: A View from Brazil and Elsewhere." *Anthropological Theory* 7:3 (2007): 273-93.

Vergara, Camilo José. *How the Other Worships*. New Brunswick: Rutgers University Press, 2005.

———. *Subway Memories*. New York: The Monacelli Press, 2004.

Vertovec, Steven. "Cheap Calls: The Social Glue of Migrant Transnationalism." *Global Networks* 4:2 (2004): 219-24.

Volf, Miroslav. "When Gospel and Culture Intersect: Notes on the Nature of Christian Difference." In *Pentecostalism in Context: Essays in Honor of William W. Menzies*, ed. Wonsuk Ma and Robert P. Menzies, 223-36. Sheffield: Sheffield Academic Press, 1997.

———. "Materiality of Salvation: An Investigation in the Soteriologies of Liberation and Pentecostal Theologies." *Journal of Ecumenical Studies* 26:3 (1989): 447-67.

Volf, Miroslav, and Dorothy C. Bass, eds. *Practicing Theology: Beliefs and Practices in Christian Life*. Grand Rapids: Eerdmans, 2002.

Wacquant, Loïc. *Body and Soul: Notebooks of an Apprentice Boxer*. New York: Oxford University Press, 2004.

Währisch-Oblau, Claudia. *The Missionary Self-Perception of Pentecostal/Charismatic Church Leaders from the Global South in Europe*. Leiden: Brill, 2009.

Wakin, Daniel. "In New York, Gospel Resounds in African Tongues." *New York Times*, April 18, 2004, A-1, 32.

Walls, Andrew F. "World Christianity and the Early Church." In *A New Day: Essays on World Christianity in Honor of Lamin Sanneh*, edited by Akintunde E. Akinade, 17-30. New York: Peter Lang, 2010,

———. "Migration and Evangelization: The Gospel and Movement of Peoples in Modern Times." *The Covenant Quarterly* 63:1 (2005): 3-28.

———. "Inculturation." In *Encyclopedia of Protestantism*. Vol. 2, edited by Hans J. Hillerbrand, 932-35. New York: Routledge, 2004.

———. "Converts or Proselytes? The Crisis over Conversion in the Early Church." *International Bulletin of Mission* 28:1 (January 2004): 2-6.
———. "Mission and Migration: The Diaspora Factor in Christian History." *Journal of African Christian Thought* 5:2 (December 2002): 3-11.
———. *The Cross-cultural Process in Christian History: Studies in the Transmission and Appropriation of Faith*. Maryknoll, N.Y.: Orbis, 2002.
———. *The Missionary Movement in Christian History: Studies in the Transmission of Faith*. Maryknoll, N.Y.: Orbis, 1996.
Ward, Graham. *Cities of God*. London: Routledge, 2000.
Warikoo, Natasha. "Cosmopolitan Ethnicity: Second-Generation Indo-Caribbean Identities." In *Becoming New Yorkers: Ethnographies of the Second Generation*, edited by Philip Kasinitz, John H. Mollenkopf, and Mary C. Waters, 361-91. New York: Russell Sage Foundation, 2004.
Warner, R. Stephen, and Judith W. Wittner, eds. *Gatherings in Diaspora: Religious Communities and the New Immigration*. Philadelphia: Temple University Press, 1998.
Waters, Joanna L. "Transnational Family Strategies and Education in the Contemporary Chinese Diaspora." *Global Networks* 5:4 (2005): 359-77.
Weber, Max. *The Protestant Ethic and the Spirit of Capitalism*. London: Routledge, 2002 [1930].
Welbourn, F. B., and B. A. Ogot. *A Place to Feel at Home: A Study of Two Independent Churches in Western Kenya*. London: Oxford University Press, 1966.
West, Gerald O., and Musa Dube, eds. *The Bible in Africa: Transactions, Trajectories and Trends*. Boston: Brill, 2001.
Westerlund, David. *African Indigenous Religions and Disease Causation: From Spiritual Beings to Living Human Beings*. Leiden: Brill, 2006.
———, ed. *Global Pentecostalism: Encounters with Other Religious Traditions*. London: I. B. Tauris, 2009.
Wijsen, Frans, and Robert Schreiter, eds. *Global Christianity: Contested Claims*. Amsterdam: Rodopi, 2007.
Wikie, A. W. "An Attempt to Conserve the Work of the Basel Mission to the Gold Coast." *International Review of Mission* (1920): 86-94.
Wilkerson, Isabel. *The Warmth of Other Suns: The Epic Story of America's Great Migration*. New York: Random House, 2010.
Williams, Ritva H. *Stewards, Prophets, Keepers of the Word: Leadership in the Early Church*. Peabody: Hendrickson, 2006.
Williams, Rowan. *On Christian Theology*. Oxford: Blackwell, 2000.
———. "On Making Moral Decisions." *Anglican Theological Review* 81:1 (1999): 295-308.
Wolterstorff, Nicholas. "Historicizing the Belief-forming Self." In *Knowledge and Reality: Essays in Honor of Alvin Plantinga* edited by Thomas M. Crisp, Matthew Davidson, and David Vander Laan, 111-35. Dordrecht: Springer, 2006.
———. *Divine Discourse: Philosophical Reflections on the Claim that God Speaks*. Cambridge: Cambridge University Press, 1995.
Wright, N. T. *Simply Christian: Why Christianity Makes Sense*. SanFrancisco: HarperSanFrancisco, 2006.
Wuthnow, Robert. *Boundless Faith: The Global Outreach of American Churches*. Berkeley: University of California Press, 2009.

SOURCES

Yoder, John Howard. "On Not Being Ashamed of the Gospel: Particularity, Pluralism, and Validation." *Faith and Philosophy* 9:3 (1992): 285-300.
———. "On Christian Unity: The Way from Below." *Pro Ecclesia* 9:2 (2000): 165-83.
———. *For the Nations: Essays Public and Evangelical*. Grand Rapids: Eerdmans, 1997.
———. *As You Go: The Old Mission in a New Day*. Scottdale: Herald Press, 1961.
Yong, Amos. *The Spirit Poured Out on All Flesh: Pentecostalism and the Possibility of Global Theology*. Grand Rapids: Baker Academic, 2005.
Yorks, Lyle, and Elizabeth Kasl. "Toward a Theory and Practice for Whole-Person Learning: Reconceptualizing Experience and the Role of Affect." *Adult Education Quarterly* 52:3 (2002): 176-92.
Zukin, Sharon. *Naked City: The Death and Life of Authentic Urban Places*. New York: Oxford University Press, 2010.

PERSONAL COMMUNICATION

Nimi Wariboko, E-mail Correspondence, June 1, 2007.
Nimi Wariboko, E-mail Correspondence, July 29, 2004.
Nimi Wariboko, E-mail Correspondence to Zone 18, November 6, 2006.
Correspondence from Rev. C. B. Ahwireng to Rev. Moses Biney, April 13, 2005.
Correspondence from Cathedral Headquarters in Monrovia to Marie Cooper, December 26, 1995.

PRINTED CHURCH MATERIALS

Church of the Lord (Aladura) Worldwide

The Church of the Lord (Aladura) Worldwide Calendar 2006–My Year of Divine Satisfaction.
The Church of the Lord (Aladura) Worldwide Calendar 2007–My Year of Divine Favour.
Sunday School Bible Study Guide 2001 For Youth and Adults.
Church Man's Caledar 1992.
Church Man's Calendar 2004.
The Church of the Lord (Aladura) Worldwide English Hymn Book — 1993 enlarged edition.
The Church of the Lord Aladura House of Prayers Membership Booklet.
The Cross-Bearers and Rules of the Cross by the Late, Most Rev. Apostle S. O. Oduwole.
Divine Revelations for the Year 2006 from Holy Mount of Tabieorar.
Divine Revelation for the Year 2005 from Holy Mount of Tabieorar.
Divine Revelations from the Holy Mount Tabborrar 1973.
40th Year of Sweet Remembrance of Late Pro. General Dr. Josiah Olunowo Ositelu 2006.
The Handbook of Liturgy.
Financial Regulations of the Church of the Lord (Aladura) Worldwide for the Millennium, 2001.
Tabieorar @ 70, Theme: Divine Favour Programme 2006.
Tabieorar 2007 Divine Revelations Booklet.

Sources

Presbyterian Church of Ghana

Almanac, 2007.
Manual of Order, revised edition, 2004.
Twifo Asafo Asore Dwom Nhoma (hymnal), 2000.
Okristoni (The Christian) Pictorial Journal of Ghana.
Presbyterian Church of Ghana, Constitution, 2000.
Presbyterian Church, U.S.A Tenth Anniversary Celebration, 1995.
Presbyterian Church of Ghana in New York, "Welfare By-Laws," 2007.
The Presbyterian Church of Ghana Almanac (Calendar), 2006.

Redeemed Christian Church of God

Baptism Manual.
Global Vision, 2004.
House Fellowship Manual, 2000/2001.
Junior Church Manual, 2002/2003.
Marriage Counseling Manual.
Order of Church Service.
Redemption Bugle, 2004.
Redemption Light, 2001.
Search the Scriptures, 2006/2007.
Success Stories (New York City), 2002.
Sunday School Manual, 2001/2002.
Sunday School Manual, 2002/2003.
Sunday School Manual, 2003/2004.
Sunday School Manual, 2004/2005.
Workers-In-Training Manual.
Workers Training Manual, North America, 2003.

NEWSPAPERS

African Abroad USA
Light of the World
New York Times
West African News

CHURCH WEB SITES

The Apostolic Church
http://the apostolicchurch.org

CANA Convocation
http://canaconvocation.org/

Celestial Church of Christ
http://www.celestialchurch.com/

SOURCES

Cherubim and Seraphim Movement, USA
http://csmovementchurchusa.org/

Church of the Lord (Aladura)
http://www.aladura.info/

Church of Pentecost, USA
http://www.pentecostusa.org/

Christ Apostolic Church (Agbala-Itura)
http://www.cacvocny.org/home.aspx

Emmanuel Gospel Center
http://ewcny.org/

Ethiopian Orthodox Church Tewahedo Church of our Savior
http://www.angelfire.com/ny2/medhanealem/

International Central Gospel Church
http://www.centralgospel.com/

International Central Gospel Church, New York
http://www.icgcny.org/

Lighthouse Chapel
http://www.lighthousechapel.org/

Lillies International
http://www.liliesinternational.org/

Presbyterian Church of Ghana
http://www.pc-ghana.org/

Redeemed Christian Church of God
http://www.rccg.org/

Redeemed Christian Church of God, North America
http://www.rccgna.org/

Redeemed Christian Church of God International Chapel, Brooklyn
http://rccgbrooklyn.org/

Winners' Chapel, USA
http://www.winnerschapelusa.org/home/index.php

Acknowledgments

This project has a long history, and has truly been an experience of learning in community.

At the Presbyterian Church of Ghana in New York, the Church of the Lord (Aladura), and the Redeemed Christian Church of God International Chapel, Brooklyn, I met not just partners in my research, but people who became friends. For their openness in allowing me to tell their stories, for encouragement, for patience in answering questions, for prayers, and ultimately trust, I am profoundly grateful. What I could not imagine became more than I could have hoped for.

While I cannot here recognize everyone who answered a question, offered me assistance, or shared a story, in particular I want to acknowledge a number of individuals in each church without whom I could not have completed this project.

At the Presbyterian Church of Ghana I must thank the elders of the church for allowing me to write about their congregation. The Rev. Yaw Asiedu always had his office door open to me. Moses Biney was an important conversation partner early in this project. Amma Amponsah was a wonderful friend whose regular contact means so much. I was fortunate enough to often cross paths with Rex Agyemang, and thank him particularly for the ways he shared his world and ministry with me. Alfred Kissiedo and Diana Owusu were always and especially helpful. Samuel Asare was kind of enough to walk me through much of the healing ministry that he brings from Ghana. Elder Angelina Akiwumi was most understanding, and helped me a great deal. I am also indebted to Kwasi Agyare and the Bible Study and Prayer Group. And of course, thanks to my fellow "Kwame's and Amma's."

It was a brief meeting with Primate Rufus Ositelu of the Church of the Lord (Aladura) in Germany that led to my first contact with Mother Cooper and the church in the Bronx. Mother Cooper spent many hours sharing with me her personal story and life in the Church of the Lord (Aladura). My immense gratitude is also extended to Minister Joy, Evangelist Sarah, Evangelist Eleanor, David Grigsby, David Rquarm, Edwin Flowers, Brother Clarence, and of course Alana.

To this day, I do not know who at the church answered my first telephone call in the quest for directions, but I was welcomed from that moment forward at the Redeemed Christian Church of God International Chapel, Brooklyn. My profound thanks go most certainly to Nimi and Wapaemi Wariboko. During our frequent conversations, in person and by telephone and e-mail, Pastor Nimi helped me to think in new ways about theology and faith. He is a pastor and a professor! Thank you also to Segun and Bola Oyesanya, Sister West, Sister Catherine, James and Egbefun Adieze, Matilda Oyeyemi, Emmanuel and Omo Obogbaimhe, and Justin Emineke for encouraging me on my way and teaching me so much. Pastor Adebisi Oyesile answered many questions, and opened his life to me as a mentor. I remember Pastor Dolapo Osinfade, who died unexpectedly on December 1, 2010. Although she served all too briefly, her legacy continues through the church she led and people she touched.

The first steps in this work and my overall study of world Christianity began in 2000 with Andrew Walls at Princeton Theological Seminary. Without his influence, without his openness to a stranger from New York City, this project would not exist. Indeed, it is safe to say that Professor Walls has caused to me look afresh at religion and Christianity as a whole, and profoundly influenced not just my vocational calling. For over ten years, Professor Walls has not only provided direction and encouragement in my research, but also shaped a way of thinking and doing theological education. I remember Doreen Walls for her spirit of welcome. I thank God for their influence on my life, and on City Seminary.

Eventually I made my way to the Centre for the Study of Christianity in the Non-Western World Christianity (now the Centre for the Study of World Christianity) at New College, the University of Edinburgh. This was the ideal setting for what became the focus of my doctoral work. A better supervisor than Dr. T. Jack Thompson I could not imagine. His interest in and support of my project were obvious from the start, and I always left my meetings with him thankful for his insights and direction. Without his guidance and friendship, this project would not have been possible. I am grateful profoundly for Jack's example as teacher and scholar, and he has

Acknowledgments

influenced perhaps more than he knows. She may not remember, but Phyllis Thompson taught me how to dance in Scotland.

I would like to acknowledge the late director of the Centre, David Kerr, for accepting me into the program, Elizabeth Koepping for her welcome, James Cox for his early insights, and Margaret Acton for invaluable research help at the Centre. I want to thank fellow students Geomon George, Lazarus Phiri, and Martin Lunde for adding to the joy of my experience while at the Centre. My thesis examiners, Dr. Afe Adogame and Dr. Gerrie ter Haar, provided a most engaging and memorable "conversation" around my work. Their comments and questions sharpened my thinking, and I thank them for the attention they gave my work.

While in Edinburgh, we found ourselves welcomed and cared for in a community of faith called St. John's Episcopal Church. To Bishop Peter and Dee Price for suggesting we first visit and of course much more, our family is in their debt. Leslie Hodgson first opened the door for us, and Peter and Sheelagh Brand helped us in ways we will never forget. That we gained John and Clare Armes as friends is reason enough to have lived in Edinburgh. They generously made a home for me whenever needed. I will never forget the celebration they provided for me following my viva.

On Orchard Brae, "Leslie and the girls" were wonderful neighbors to our family. Roy and Liz Robertson added to our rich Edinburgh experience. Thank you, Roy, for helping me dress properly for graduation. Ewan Kelly and his family provided a meal for us that made us feel most welcome in the city. To Nora and Mattyi and their family, thanks for being part of our time in Edinburgh and now Budapest.

At City Seminary of New York, I would like to thank the Board of Directors for allowing me to pursue this project. I am especially and always thankful for the gift of Manuel Ortiz and Susan Baker. They walked with me on this and other areas of God's calling to the city, sharing their lives and visions.

Maria Liu Wong, the Dean of City Seminary of New York, has had to live with this project in our office. When the last days of this work came, and that was on more than one occasion, she applied her immense skills, graciousness, and time to the final production. Thank you, Maria, for all of your help and support, and your vision and work on behalf of the seminary. And Tony, Joshua, and Josiah for sharing as well! Janice McLean is not only a wonderful colleague and friend, but helped me get this out the door. Her work on the index and many a last minute decision was a wonderful gift. And to Miriam Ruiz, thank you for jumping into everything with joy, faith, and commitment that we all celebrate. Thank you also, Laura Speiller, Jonathan Roque and Adebisi Oyesile, for the ways you have helped me along, and shaped our learning community.

To all the students who are part of the City Seminary community, I thank you for what you are continually teaching me. A "thumbs up" to my fellow pilgrims of "Cohort 1" who have been part of this from the beginning — Alan Farrell, Maria Liu Wong, Philip Santos, Eric Yuen, Debbie Temple, Laura Speiller, Ryan Myers, Hansen Law, Roger, Carol Staubi, Tony Wong Alan, Tak Hunag, Tony Shaw, and Tony Rose. Our early learning community grew, and I thank Yolanda Solomon, Adrienne Croskey, Sonja Chen, Ben Dodd, Biju George, Vivian Grubb, Alex Haiken, Neil Holzapfel, Donald Kim, James Kim, Olivia Koentjoro, Sung Lee, Dominic Lewis, Derrick Miu, Peter Ong, Hiroko Otani, Adebisi Oyseile, Mavis Pan, Gloria Paoli, Jonathan Roque, Brian Stanton, Latonja Serling, and Oghogho West-Erhaber for sharing the first years.

Bethia Liu designed the wonderful map and helped bring the photographs to production. I'm so grateful for the many ways and times she helped bring this all together. Carrie Myers read through and commented on numerous early drafts of my work and in the process of asking questions made me a clearer writer.

In his usual generous way, Charles Marsh continues to open many doors for me, not least of which was an invitation to participate in the Virginia Writers Seminar, a program of the Project on Lived Theology at the University of Virginia made possible by the generosity of the Lilly Endowment. The insights and encouragement of the group of now friends — Carlos Eire, Patricia Hampl, Susan Holman, Alan Jacobs, Charles Marsh, and Charles Matthewes — were always timely. A grant from the Virginia Writers Seminar carried this work forward at a crucial time. Once more, I extend my gratitude to the Lilly Endowment for a unique opportunity, and to John Wimmer and Craig Dykstra for their encouragement.

No one knows the field of globalization and religion better than Manuel Vásquez. It was therefore a unique opportunity to obtain his incisive feedback at numerous points during my project. I am thankful for the many ways Manuel's scholarship has influenced the way I understand religion in a global world, but even more for his friendship and his model of collegiality.

For additional research help, I would also like to especially thank Grace Mullen, Karla Grafton, and Emily Sirinides. Kenneth Jackson made room for me in his course on New York City history. Roswith Gerloff in-

Acknowledgments

vited me to a conference in Germany that proved very important. Thank you, Deidre Crumbley, for urging me to meet the Primate, and Kwabena Asamoah-Gyadu and Matthews Ojo, for sharing their insights with me. Pastor Daniel Diakanwa, Pastor Mulugeta Abate, and Dominic Nunu helped me with some of my earliest questions in New York. The late Ogbu Kalu was most encouraging in my earliest conference presentations, and he is greatly missed.

Mother Cooper, Rev. Asiedu, and Pastor Wariboko each read through my material and provided encouraging feedback. I especially thank Pastor Wariboko not only for his detailed comments, but also a new series of questions. Chuck Matthewes graciously read through the material and provided many helpful suggestions. Laura Hudson skillfully read through an early draft when I needed it most.

For various opportunities to present some of the earliest ideas in this book to larger groups, I offer my appreciation to Charles Marsh, Jacob Olupona, J. Kwabena Asamoah-Gyadu, Chris Scharen, Dwight Baker, and Jon Bonk.

Along the way I have enjoyed the friendship, encouragement, spiritual direction, support, and theological vision from many people — whether they know it or not — among them John Algera, Nina Anderson, Ray Bakke, Antoine Bennett, Matt Brown, Bill Burrows, Jerry Callaghan, Bruce and Marjorie Calvert, David Denisch, Sister Grace, Ken Haran, Elder and Minister Amelia Harris, Tim Keller, Anne-Maria Kool, Skip Masback, Reg McLelland, Ike Newman, Chris Scharen, LaVerne Stokes, Miroslav Volf, Brian Walsh, and Nicholas Wolterstorff. To Mariano Rivera and Patricia Lee Smith, thanks for helping to make New York what it is. The music of Bruce Cockburn remains very much part of the journey.

An early meeting with Fr. Emmanuel Katongole proved to be important in many ways, not least for his friendship. I am greatly humbled by how he has helped me take account of my pilgrimage. More than once during this project I thought, "What would Harvie think?" Blessed be the memory of Harvie Conn. Long ago at Covenant College, John M. L. Young had me read my first book on African Christianity, and it reminds me once again of the formative influence of Covenant College. As usual, Steve Fowl played many roles in my thinking, and I'm grateful for his friendship and guidance.

Allan Tibbels and I talked about this book and so much else for years, conversations I deeply miss. In memory and in the light of the radiance of God, thank you, Allan, for a life-changing friendship. Nice jacket, by the way. Thank you, Susan, for staying on the journey. More will be said, but for

ACKNOWLEDGMENTS

now, blessings on you, Susan, Jenny, and Jessica. As with so much in my life, Sandtown stands behind this study, and I hope this offers something that might be of service. To New Song Community Church in Harlem and especially my co-worker in the ministry, Jeff White, thank you.

To the wonderful team at Eerdmans, especially Jon Pott, Linda Bieze, David Bratt, and Michael Thomson, I offer my gratitude. To Sam Eerdmans, thank you.

My Hungarian in-laws, Adjoran and Ildiko Aszalos, are wonderful in so many ways, not least in the expertise with which they are grandparents. Attila Aszalos is the best of uncles for the boys, and we hope for his move to New York City. Baba Visnitz made a sojourn to Edinburgh so I could travel. Zoli and Kata Aszalos represent our community and family of friends in Budapest.

That I have such a family as Rita, Peter and Daniel gives me reason to testify. When this project via Edinburgh became a possibility, in her typical spirit of global adventure Rita said, "Go for it!" Needless to say, I am grateful she said yes. So as always, this and everything is shared with Rita, whose love and commitment to serving Christ, our world, and our family is a daily witness to me.

The joy and laughter, the challenge and growth of our life as a family, is a gift of ceaseless wonder. Peter and Daniel have, in their own ways, not only been a part of and supported me in this work, but also proven to be signs of the Spirit who gives life in abundance. Their rugby practice in the hallway each morning reminds me of the connection to Scotland we share as a family. If nothing else, the African churches of New York City have taught me how to pray for my sons and what matters in theology. So this book also belongs to Peter and Daniel.

This book is also dedicated to my parents, Raymond and Sally Gornik. They set me on a journey of faith and provided me with everything and more a son could ever hope for. I know Susan and Karen join me in giving thanks to God for our parents, and I give thanks to God for my sisters, and Thomas and Bo. Shortly before he died, there was a moment while walking in Central Park with my father that I mentioned this project would eventually take place and be dedicated to him and my mother. This work is a small token of my thankfulness for my parents.

To everyone listed here, and others I may have unintentionally neglected to mention or in the background, thank you for sharing in this journey. My hope is that this study may be a small way of seeking God's peace for the city.

Index

African Christianity, 3-5, 8-10, 13-17, 19, 21, 23-27, 87-89, 257-59, 262-64; and global city, 43-48; and globalization, 116-22; and pastor, 51-64; and scripture, 160-65; gifts offered by, 268-75; typology, 22, 28-40
African Churches in New York City, 19, 21-22, typology of, 24-37. *See also* Church of the Lord Aladura-Bronx, Presbyterian Church of Ghana in New York; Redeemed Christian Church of God-Chapel of Hope, Redeemed Christian Church of God-International Chapel
African Independent Churches (AIC), 28-30
Agymeng, Rex, 246, 248, 281. *See also* Presbyterian Church of Ghana in New York
Asamoah-Gyadu, J. Kwabena, 10, 32, 66, 84, 172, 179, 201, 270, 275
Asiedu, Rev. Yaw, 54-56, 64-65, 80, 82-83, 85, 96-97, 176, 233-34, 243-45. *See also* Presbyterian Church of Ghana in New York

Bronx, 3, 19, 26, 30, 33-34, 37, 59, 91, 97, 101, 103, 105, 186, 276, 282
Brooklyn, 4, 21, 26, 30, 33, 34, 64, 80-81, 83-84, 112, 114-16, 180, 191, 195-98

Catholic Church, 22, 26-27, 121
Church of the Lord Aladura-Bronx, 3, 4, 78, 83, 99-107, 280; global vision of, 185-86; healing, 204; liturgy, 99-100; mission, 194-95; prayer, 129-31, 137-39, 158-59; preaching, 176-77; and scripture, 165-71; second generation, 250; and Tabborrar, 235-42. *See also* Cooper, Mother Marie; Church of the Lord Aladura; Turner, Harold
Church of the Lord Aladura, 3, 30, 39, 100-104; global vision of, 183-84; and scripture, 173. *See also* Cooper, Mother Marie; Church of the Lord Aladura-Bronx
Cooper, Mother Marie, 3, 4, 56-61, 64-65, 103-4, 137-39, 147, 148; and James E. Cooper Foundational Academy and Smiling Face Orphanage, 211-12. *See also* Church of the Lord Aladura-Bronx

Dreams, 29-30, 58, 60, 64-65, 71, 73, 102, 136, 144, 269, 289

Ethiopian Orthodox Church, 24-26

Fasting, 83, 102, 116, 127. *See also* prayer
Fowl, Stephen, 163-64, 168, 297
Francophone Churches, 35-36

Ghana, Accra, 8, 47, 91, 97, 260, 278

Hanciles, Jehu, 12, 42, 209
Healing, 76-80; and mission, 201-6

Jenkins, Philip, 162, 214-15, 265

Kalu, Ogbu U., 19, 31, 33, 182, 230, 270
Katongole, Emmanuel, 5, 15, 215, 264-68, 294

347

INDEX

Lay leadership, 83-86
Liberia, Monrovia, 3, 8, 47, 57-8, 105, 138, 211-13, 282
Liturgy, importance of, 87-89; in Church of the Lord Aladura, 89-91; in Presbyterian Church of Ghana, 99-100; in Redeemed Christian Church of God, 107-9

Manhattan, 17-18, 26, 33, 41, 42, 261
Migration missions, 206-10. *See also* Mission
Mission, and Africa, 210-13; and healing, 201-6; as church planting, 195-200; as intercession, 194-95; as member care, 191-93. *See also* Migration missions; Worship service as mission enterprise

New York City, 3-4, 8; Africans in, 40-42; as global city, 43-48, 259-61; and church liturgy, 89-100
Nigeria, Lagos, 8, 35, 44, 47, 222, 224, 230, 260-61, 281

Obama, Barack, 247, 283-84

Pastor, 51-64; as agent of healing, 70-71, 74-80; as cultural intermediary, 70-71, 81-83; as institution builder, 70-71, 80-81; as spiritual director, 70-74
Pentecostalism, 6, 31-35; and material world, 150-59; and tongues, 141
Pilgrimage, 219-42, 263, 286
Prayer, 78-80, 127-29; and church communities, 129-36; and fasting, 144, 146-50; and material world, 150-59; in the Spirit, 143-46; night vigil, 136-43
Preaching, 176-78
Presbyterian Church of Ghana in New York, 4, 76-78, 80, 91-99, 281-82; and Bible, 165-69, 172; global vision of, 183-85; and healing, 204; liturgy, 89-91; prayer, 133-36, 142-43; second generation, 243, 245-50; 175th anniversary, 232-35. *See also* Agymeng, Rex; Asiedu, Rev. Yaw
Presbyterian Church of Ghana, and African Charismatic Movement, 93-94; influence of European missionaries on, 92-93; member care, 191-93; scripture identity, 175

Queens, 4, 21, 26, 37, 42

Redeemed Christian Church of God–Chapel of Hope, 196-200
Redeemed Christian Church of God–International Chapel, 4, 83-85, 107-16, and Bible, 165-68, 172-75; church planting, 195-200; and healing, 203-4; liturgy, 107-9; prayer, 132-33, 139-42; preaching, 177-78; second generation, 251-55. *See also* Wariboko, Pastor Nimi
Redeemed Christian Church of God, 109-11; global vision of, 188-200; Holy Ghost service, 222-32; North America, 18, 222-32; and scripture, 173-75

Salvation, 65-70
Sanneh, Lamin, 6, 291
Sassen, Saskia, 8, 43, 45, 128, 259, 262
Scripture, and identity, 171-75; and power, 178-80; reading in community, 168-71; world imagined by, 165-68
Senegal in America, 18
Staten Island, 21, 36-37
Stoller, Paul, 12, 82, 296

Turner, Harold, 28, 102-3, 175, 177, 185-86, 241-42, 299-301

Vásquez, Manuel A., 9, 118-21, 293, 295, 301

Walls, Andrew, 3, 5, 7, 25, 28, 89, 151, 181, 259, 265-67, 272, 291, 292, 297-98
Wariboko, Pastor Nimi, 61-65, 139-42, 257-58, 279-81. *See also* Redeemed Christian Church of God-International Chapel
Worship service as mission enterprise, 200. *See also* Mission

www.ingramcontent.com/pod-product-compliance
Lightning Source LLC
Chambersburg PA
CBHW021134230426
43667CB00005B/112